Brother's Keeper

*The United States, Race, and Empire in the
British Caribbean, 1937–1962*

JASON C. PARKER

OXFORD
UNIVERSITY PRESS
2008

OXFORD

UNIVERSITY PRESS

Oxford University Press, Inc., publishes works that further
Oxford University's objective of excellence
in research, scholarship, and education.

Oxford New York
Auckland Cape Town Dar es Salaam Hong Kong Karachi
Kuala Lumpur Madrid Melbourne Mexico City Nairobi
New Delhi Shanghai Taipei Toronto

With offices in
Argentina Austria Brazil Chile Czech Republic France Greece
Guatemala Hungary Italy Japan Poland Portugal Singapore
South Korea Switzerland Thailand Turkey Ukraine Vietnam

Published by Oxford University Press, Inc.
198 Madison Avenue, New York, New York 10016

www.oup.com

Oxford is a registered trademark of Oxford University Press

Library of Congress Cataloging-in-Publication Data
Parker, Jason C.
Brother's keeper : the United States, race, and empire in the British
Caribbean, 1937–1962 / Jason C. Parker.
p. cm.
Includes bibliographical references and index.
ISBN 978-0-19-533201-8; 978-0-19-533202-5 (pbk.)
1. Decolonization—West Indies, British. 2. West Indies, British—History
—20th century. 3. West Indies, British—Race relations. 4. West Indies,
British—Foreign relations—United States. 5. United States—Foreign
relations—West Indies, British. I. Title.
F2133.P37 2008
325'.309729—dc22   2007031905

Acknowledgment is made for permission to reprint portions of
" 'Capital of the Caribbean': The African American-West Indian
'Harlem Nexus' and the Transnational Drive for Black Freedom,"
The Journal of African American History, Volume 89, A
(Spring 2004), pp. 98–117.

1 3 5 7 9 8 6 4 2

Printed in the United States of America
on acid-free paper

To my parents,
Bruce and Sharon Parker

Preface and Acknowledgments

This is a short history of a small place. But it forms a chapter of a much bigger story, indeed one of the biggest. I began the present investigation as a student of the Cold War, in hopes of shedding new light on a development usually overlooked in the Caribbean theater of that war: the decolonization of the British West Indies. In the course of researching and writing this study, and of wrestling with the deep, complex relationship between the Cold War and decolonization, I came to see the full importance of the latter. The dismantling of European empires and the end of white supremacy are signal events not only of the last century but of the last millennium. In the historical blink of an eye, they undid imperial institutions that dated back to Columbus and overturned practices of statecraft that dated back to Ramses. Empire as a way of life, to borrow William Appleman Williams's phrase, has not necessarily disappeared. But the practice of acquisitive territorial expansionism of the type that defined "state" power throughout history has vanished, as near completely as piracy or slavery. Yet, babies born on "independence day" in the nations that emerged from the European empires are only now reaching middle-age. Thorough, disciplined historical examination of this enormous and very recent subject has thus only begun.

The timing of this development is excellent indeed. In recent years, the historical profession has endorsed what is called the "transnational" or "international" approach to researching and writing history. This historiographical turn—perhaps better termed a revolution—has invigorated a number of subfields and subjects of study, but none more so than decolonization. The transnational or international approach privileges movements, processes, and peoples over borders and the nation-state; decolonization presents the historical moment when those movements, processes, and peoples etched borders and constituted nation-states. These acts of creation, moreover, are increasingly understood as multilateral ones. Actors "on the ground" could shape the process rather than just suffer it at the hands of the imperial and Cold War centers of power. Central to this conclusion, and to the transnational turn, is the employment of a multinational archival base. Far from tracking conversations between clerks about the dynamics of decolonization as seen from Washington or London, the use of archives in several countries allows the reconstruction of those dynamics from varied angles and in their full complexity. This study attempts just that, drawing on twenty-two archives in seven countries to tell its tale.

Appropriately for such a venture, this book could not exist without support, inspiration, and collaboration from all over the map. I remain humbly grateful for research funding that made my multiarchival odyssey possible. I am especially thankful for the time freed up by fellowships from the University of Florida College of Liberal Arts, the Harry S. Truman Library Institute, and West Virginia University's Eberly College of Arts and Sciences. Equally, I am indebted to many institutions for their generosity in funding my archival research: the Truman Library Institute, the Franklin and Eleanor Roosevelt Institute, the John F. Kennedy Library Foundation, the Society for Historians of American Foreign Relations, the University of Florida History Department, and the History Department, Eberly College, and Faculty Senate of West Virginia University.

As every scholar knows, however, funding is not the only kind of essential support. From the lofty to the mundane—from intellection, debate, critique, and companionship to the loan of a roof, couch, or car—support of all kinds is indispensable to the production of a book like this one. On the American side, I am especially indebted to the extended Kumin family, both for morale boosts back home and for shelter on the research-road: Elaine and Hillel, Michael, and Sheila Smallberg Cohen and family. I would also like to thank Charlotte Owen for entrusting her house to me during the crucial home-stretch of the dissertation stage. The number of such couch- and guestroom-debts that I owe feels almost too high to count, most of all in Washington, DC; there, I heartily thank Meredith Hindley, Adam Howard, Jim Siekmeier and Catherine Tall, D'arcy Brissman, and Alan McPherson. Their hospitality kept me solvent, and their company kept me sane. The same is true of several individuals in the Caribbean, with the added difference that they kept me "found" in unfamiliar and beguiling places. Jason and Vidya Seejattan Forrester, and Sherman Baksh in Port-of-Spain; and in Jamaica, Matthew Smith, Nicole Plummer, Remi Lawrence, and especially the extended family of Lesley Miller—Curl and Courtney Bramwell, and "Aunt" Claudette and "Uncle" Junior King—all have my unending thanks for their kindness.

Regarding kindnesses of a different kind, I must thank everyone whose insights and commentary have shaped my thinking, and thereby shaped this manuscript over the course of its long life. Some of those individuals pulled double duty, offering not only the hospitality noted above but also a close reading of the document at various stages; I especially thank Meredith, Jim, Alan, and Matthew in this regard. Others have been there since the very beginning of the project at the University of Florida. To my dissertation advisor Bob McMahon, I am especially grateful; without his unfailing support and unfailingly sage advice, I could never have undertaken and succeeded in this project. I cannot quite shake the habit of calling him Fearless Leader, though a better nickname would be the Anti-Barkley, for a better role model could not be found, and my gratitude knows no end. In Gainesville, I also benefited beyond measure from my "other advisor," David Colburn, who deserves singular thanks. His contributions on my committee, and my time working for him at the Reubin Askew Institute on Politics and Society, taught me invaluable things. I was also honored to be part of a stimulating cohort of graduate students in diplomatic (and diplomatic-ish) history—Adam, Mark Hove, James Thompson, Steve Hach, and Steve Ortiz—whose feedback on this study made it stronger, and made grad school more fun. Partly thanks to their encouragement and critiques, portions of this text have been previously published in the *International History Review,* the *Journal of African American History*, and the Berghahn Books volume *Anti-Americanism in Latin America and the Caribbean*; I would like to acknowledge and thank the editors of all three for permission to republish here.

Beyond the Gator Nation, I must thank those friends and colleagues whose comments on this project over the years have done so much to strengthen it. Ken Osgood, Andy Johns, Kathryn Statler, and Brian Etheridge deserve special gratitude on this front. Co-panelists and commenters over the course of this project are similarly due my deepest thanks. The insights and suggestions of Carol Anderson, Todd Bennett, Tim Borstelmann, Frank Costigliola, Mary Dudziak, Eric Duke, Mark Gilderhus, Michael Krenn, Fred Logevall, Kyle Longley, Darlene Rivas, Eric Roorda, Tom Schoonover, Jeff Taffet, Bill Walker, and Tom Zeiler pointed me to overlooked sources, helped to solve interpretive dilemmas, and added much conceptual breadth to the work. For the wind they put in my sails, I am deeply grateful. I must also express my profoundest thanks to my editor Susan Ferber, with whom it is an unqualified pleasure to work, and my gratitude as well to the anonymous readers whose suggestions did so much to improve the manuscript. Any and all flaws that remain are entirely my own.

I have also been most fortunate to undertake revisions of this project in some outstanding scholarly settings since leaving Gainesville. My colleagues at West Virginia University, especially Liz and Ken Fones-Wolf, Katherine Aaslestad, Matt Vester, and Steve Zdatny, were all one could ask for. Along with the original "Rookie Professors" outside my department—Lara Farina, Hala Nassar, Dilia Lopez-Gydosh, Mike Smith, and Lesley Miller—they not only made Morgantown feel like home, but sharpened my understanding of nationalism, the Caribbean, and "imperial eyes." I am now writing from outside Appalachia, in the midst of unpacking and settling into a new scholarly community in College Station, which I am thrilled to be joining. Indeed, I owe thanks for the dividends that have already started coming in, as new colleagues and neighbors Terry Anderson, Jeff Engel, and Andy Kirkendall have offered valuable feedback on and support for this project.

I would be remiss not to mention two other communities I've been lucky to be a part of while working on this manuscript. After Morgantown, I was able to spend a year in residence at the Mershon Center for International Security Studies at the Ohio State University. Mershon Director Rick Hermann performs an invaluable service to the scholarly profession by fostering an intellectual community of the highest caliber, including both permanent and visiting expertise. It is an ideal place to work on international topics. Although I was there to work on a different project than this one, it was a joy to do the final "wrap-up" work on the latter in Columbus. I would also like to credit the National History Center's International Seminar on Decolonization with strengthening the present study. I took part in the seminar to work on a project—a comparative study of postwar federations—that builds on this one. But the seminar proved to be as useful for refining the first manuscript as for developing the future one. I am particularly indebted to seminar leaders William Roger Louis, Marilyn Young, and Dane Kennedy, and especially to Pillarisetti Sudhir and Miriam Hauss for last-minute "production" help; and also to participants Dan Branch, Lucy Chester, Yasmin Khan, Adrian Howkins, and Chantalle Verna for their encouragement, insights, and sharp-eyed readings.

Historians could hardly produce a page were it not for archivists willing to share their mastery of primary-source collections. I profited greatly from the good works of such teams at the Roosevelt, Truman, Eisenhower, and Kennedy Libraries; the U.S., U.K., and Canadian National Archives; the Library of Congress; the Schomburg Center for Research in Black Culture; the Moorland-Spingarn Research Center; the Main Library Special Collections of the University of the West Indies in both Jamaica and Trinidad; the National Library of Jamaica; the Jamaica Archives at Spanish Town; and the Barbados Department of Archives. I would also like to single out for thanks, for service above and beyond the call of normal archivist duty: Ken Heger, Dennis Bilger, Tom Branigar, David Haight, Clifford Muse, Ida Jones, Glenroy Taitt, Kathleen Helenese-Paul, David Williams, and Ingrid Cumberbatch. Finally, I would like to express my profound gratitude to the Manley family, for permission to access the Norman Manley Papers, allowing this story to be told in its fullest and proper dimensions.

Speaking of family, I must conclude with the deepest thanks of all to my own. My parents, to whom this book is dedicated, set for me the example of curiosity, persistence, reflection, and wisdom—a template that proved essential to this scholarly endeavor, and to life more broadly beyond it. My brother Josh and my uncle Tom, along with aunts, uncles, and cousins too many to list, never ceased to offer both encouragement and perspective, even as they all undoubtedly wondered what the heck I was working on that could possibly take all this time. My children Océane and Logan are also due thanks.

They arrived at roughly the same time I began working on this book, and their lives intertwine with it in ways I find hard to explain. I can only hope that someday they will understand why papa wasn't always able to play with them—and how grateful he was when he could. Such play with such children is the richest respite one could hope for. Finally, my words fall short in trying to express my loving gratitude to Pascale, who started me on this Antillean journey, lo these many years ago. *Merci sans fin, mon amour*; your love, support, patience, and smile made this book, and make so much else, possible.

Contents

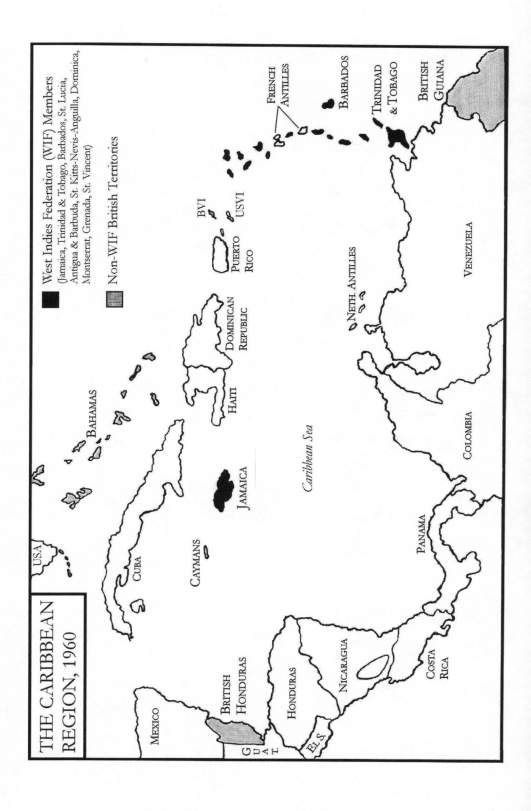

THE CARIBBEAN
REGION, 1960

West Indies Federation (WIF) Members
(Jamaica, Trinidad & Tobago, Barbados, St. Lucia,
Antigua & Barbuda, St. Kitts-Nevis-Anguilla, Dominica,
Montserrat, Grenada, St. Vincent)

Non-WIF British Territories

FRENCH ANTILLES

BARBADOS

TRINIDAD & TOBAGO

BRITISH GUIANA

BVI

USVI

PUERTO RICO

NETH. ANTILLES

VENEZUELA

DOMINICAN REPUBLIC

HAITI

BAHAMAS

Caribbean Sea

COLOMBIA

JAMAICA

CUBA

CAYMANS

USA

PANAMA

COSTA RICA

NICARAGUA

HONDURAS

BRITISH HONDURAS

EL. S.

GUAT

MEXICO

Brother's Keeper

Introduction

The Caribbean area is a perfect case study for a number of things. If one wants to study the end products of imperialism, this is the perfect region. If one wants to know the effect on . . . depressed areas, this is the place to look. If one wants to study the difficulties of establishing a democratic political system, the Caribbean area will show one. Few areas are better subjects for study.

Norman Manley

When Norman Manley—one of the earliest champions of West Indian nationalism and future chief minister and "National Hero" of Jamaica— spoke these words in 1954, his beloved island and the rest of the European-ruled Caribbean were undergoing a historic transformation that underscored his point.[1] The Caribbean was far from the only part of the imperial world to win its freedom after World War II. The great wave of "Third World" nationalism and colonial independence, which saw dozens of countries join the atlas in one generation, swept virtually the entire globe and was a central feature of the postwar era. In some places, the transition produced violence and tragedy; in others, stagnation; in still others, progress. All shared the challenges inherent in building new, unified, and viable nations from a welter of ethnocultural traditions, economic dilemmas, and imperial detritus. Yet the Caribbean, as Manley indicated, was unique within this larger pattern. He might have added that the area showcased the challenges of winning independence in the shadow of a superpower, establishing a new country from old and diverse constituent parts, and the limits of racial-cultural ties, during a period of revolution, change, and hot and cold wars.

Indeed, the story of British West Indian independence represented the confluence of two historic streams, of sufficiently differing lengths to raise questions about the post–World War II era as a whole. In one respect, the decolonization of the British Caribbean was terribly late in coming. After all, most of its immediate neighbors had been independent for a century and a half, having won their freedom in the age of New World revolution.[2] From another angle, however, the West Indies were not historically "late" but rather right on time, gaining independence in step with the rest of the postwar Third World.[3] This makes the British Caribbean a special and provocative case. They were virtually the only European-ruled colonies to have a shoreline seat for the two great waves of independence from Europe to occur in the modern era. This allows for close examination of a vital issue of global history—nationalist Third World decolonization—and for exploration of this issue as it related to the Cold War that dominated world affairs for four decades. If the Caribbean transition did not give the world the drama of a Cuba or the violence of a Congo, it could—as Manley suggests—in other ways bridge the two and illuminate the deeper dynamics of the postwar historical moment. It thus offers a chance to address a central puzzle of twentieth-century foreign-relations and international-history scholarship: what, exactly and fully, was the relationship between Third World decolonization and the Cold War?

That question is more complex than it first appears. Scholars have exhaustively investigated the dramatic collisions between decolonization and the Cold War.[4] But the volume of that scholarship, and the gripping stories that it tells, can give those episodes a false representativeness. The literature covers flashpoints like Vietnam or Algeria in voluminous detail and impressive analytic depth. Odd Arne Westad's outstanding book, for example, makes a powerful argument for the way in which the Cold War took quasi-demonic possession of such local conflicts amid imperial retreat and disfigured them beyond recognition. But most of the literature does not adequately integrate those "flashpoint" stories—manifestly worst-case scenarios of violence, crisis, and tragedy—into a holistic narrative that captures the postwar story in its broadest meaning. Indeed, intense scholarly attention to these individual episodes of Cold War history reinforces the notion that they were primarily and precisely that: Cold War stories.

While such study conveys a rich, deep, and in one sense inarguably true understanding of these crises, it carries the risk of repeating Washington's most fundamental postwar error: seeing the world through what Matthew Connelly calls "Cold War lenses."[5] Such lenses there certainly were, and not without reason. Cold War dynamics could and did drastically warp the shape of decolonization in "hot spots" like those named above. But those dynamics and those episodes were not the full story. Decolonization may have flowered during the first two decades of the superpower conflict, but it had been germinating for more than two decades before that. Activists, intellectuals, reformers, and common folk in varied corners of the imperialized nonwhite world had begun agitating to redraw the map long before containment was a gleam in George Kennan's eye. Some were driven by an energized sense of racial identity or destiny. Others were motivated by outrage at labor and social conditions under colonial rule, or by visions of an independent nation-state or pan-national entity. Whatever the impetus, these actors had been working by fits and starts against the colonial regime for years by the time the Cold War metastasized its way into their struggles. Framing decolonization thusly as a broader historical process that touched more than just its obvious crisis flashpoints—that also touched the West Indies and similar "cold spots," as it were—invites a reconception of the ways in which it intertwined with the Cold War that it predated.

One such "cold spot" was the Caribbean, pointing us back to Manley's 1954 statement—which is just as true today but not in exactly the way he meant. "Few areas are better for study" today than the British Caribbean, in large part because that region is only now beginning to *receive* sufficient study. Despite their position on the strategic, political, and racial map of World War II and the Cold War, the West Indies are largely absent from the literature on international affairs of that period. By accidents of history and geography, the West Indies found themselves on the doorstep of a hegemonic superpower, during a Cold War that saw two worlds collide and a third explode. Nonetheless, the story of their progress to independence within this overarching context remains obscure. With few recent exceptions, the West Indies have been more or less invisible in scholarship on the Cold War, decolonization, diplomacy and race, and U.S. relations with Britain, with the Americas, and with the Third World.[6]

This invisibility is perhaps understandable. Well before the shadow of the "American Century" fell upon the West Indies, the colonies had become backwaters in the historical current. Even today, popular acquaintance with the islands is mostly confined to reggae, postcards, cruise-ship ports of call, and the rest of what might be called the touristic imagination. But beyond the sun and sand lies a pained and tragic history. From Columbus forward, the islands were the playthings of European empires. Slavery and sugar—the colonies' mutually cultivating curses—brought riches to white planters and brought agony to enslaved Africans. Emancipation in 1834 ended some of the agony but little of the poverty that marked the black majority's daily life. It also led to the importation of East Indian labor to some colonies, notably Trinidad and Guiana. Over time these populations—small white and large Indian minorities, and black pluralities or majorities—settled into an uneasy political economy of industrial sugar production and peasant agriculture. "Uneasy," moreover, translated to unrepresentative; fearing uprisings by their impoverished masses, most colonies were governed from London rather than risk more than a token local role in rule. By the turn of the twentieth century, the European dream of El Dorado was long dead and most European interest in the New World along with it. The West Indies were largely forgotten, left to produce more misery than they could consume locally. Especially compared to the "scramble for Africa" then in full flush, by 1898 these were yesterday's empires, invisible to distant landlords and the nearby rising hegemon alike.

However, if this invisibility—at the time in world affairs, and since then in the historical literature—is understandable, it is also unfortunate. As throwbacks to the Monroe Doctrine's "grandfather clause" pledging noninterference with western-hemisphere areas still under European colonial rule, the West Indies do not fit the usual templates of inter-American relations. Yet thanks to their location, they pose much the same strategic dilemma as their neighbors. As New World trophies of empire, the Caribbean colonies seem to have little to do with the liberation of Africa and Asia. Yet they won independence in step with the rest of the Third World and produced some of the premier intellectuals of race consciousness and decolonization, among them Sylvester Williams, C. L. R. James, Eric Williams, and George Padmore. As backwater scenes of relative calm, the Caribbean colonies never saw the Cold War turn hot. Yet they had at least as much potential as Cuba to do just that, and had improbably much to do with more distant places that did. Finally, as isolated nodes of the African diaspora, the West Indies seem more witness than participant in the historic struggle for black freedom. Yet the islands' ties to the black mainland gave them a higher profile in that struggle, and in U.S. diplomatic calculations, than much of distant Africa had.

While it is true that the colonies never presented the sustained, high-stakes conflict of other Cold War theaters, their symbolic and strategic importance nevertheless invites close inspection. During the decades-long course of their decolonization, the West Indies found their region pressed frequently into larger global dramas. In the longer view, during the *centuries*-long course of their engagement with their Yankee neighbor, the West Indies often found themselves in treacherous regional crosscurrents. Even before the Spanish-American War, U.S. actors had cast an intermittently covetous eye on their circum-Caribbean neighbors, but rarely followed through except in such free-lance personae as the filibusterers of the 1850s. Once Washington officially became a Caribbean landlord in 1898, its imperialist, interventionist, and acquisitive behavior over the next few decades put American boots on the ground at one point or another in most territories around the littoral. The European-ruled colonies were on the whole exceptions in this "American Lake." If hegemony belonged to the United States, sovereignty still belonged to Europe. Yet even an Old World flag, as Washington's 1917 purchase of the Danish Virgin Islands showed, was no guarantee against American incursion.

West Indians usually experienced such incursions differently than did their neighbors. In contrast to the occupations that brought the Marines to Hispaniola, West Indians did not see the American military arrive on their own shores. They did, however, find themselves leaving those shores to follow in train of the "imperialism-lite" that accompanied the spread of U.S.-owned railroads and plantations around the Spanish-speaking parts of the archipelago and isthmus. The largest such endeavor, the construction of the Panama Canal, brought thousands of laborers from the islands—and to a Jim Crow regime transplanted to the tropics. This experience with both white supremacy and the Yankee dollar left no doubt in West Indian minds as to the mix of opportunity and menace that the mainland represented. If the history of U.S. interventionism had not directly landed in their islands, that history was nonetheless known throughout them. Equally well known was the fact that this history, for West Indians, was not the whole American story. In the early twentieth century, tens of thousands migrated north, settling in urban "islands" such as Harlem. The impact of this migration was deep and subtle.[7] It laid the groundwork for new connections, reconnections, and mutual influence between island-born and mainland-born progeny of the African diaspora. These connections, though sited on the mainland, were as important for their "lateral" aspect between islands. Jamaicans, Barbadians ("Bajans"), and Puerto Ricans found themselves neighbors on the streets of New York, in immediate and dialogic ways not much available in their often isolated home islands. This discovery sparked all manner of discussion. Thanks to the mainland crossroads in urban black America, expatriates delved into what it meant to be "West Indian"—and what, in turn, it might mean to one day be politically independently so—to be part of a diaspora whose members were no longer quite so estranged.

In ways that presaged the West Indies' place in U.S. foreign affairs, this amounted to a kind of spontaneously generated "diasporan Good Neighbor Policy" to accompany the Roosevelt administration's official initiative of that name. It meant that despite the lack of a physical presence in the European West Indies, the U.S. profile there was well known and many-faceted. That profile included certain features unique to the West Indies, most of all the diasporan connection. But it shared other features of the familiar imperialist-interventionist and white-supremacist story of Washington's inter-American relations, and indeed of American foreign policy beyond the region. In World War II, for example, the West Indian colonies were the southern frontlines of the Battle of the Atlantic. During the early Cold War, the colonies saw the passing of the "imperial" baton from British to U.S. hands. They were in subsequent years a *sine qua non* of Truman's defense buildup and complicated the creation of the "Inter-American System" of postwar hemispheric security cooperation. After Truman, the West Indies were important factors in the Eisenhower administration's anticommunist covert operations and were a flashpoint of 1950s anti-Americanism. Finally, they were a pillar of Washington's anti-Castro strategy as well as a showcase for U.S.–Third World diplomacy. Integrating the decolonization of the West Indies—and American, African-American, British, and Caribbean contributions to that long process—into the narrative of the Cold War thus yields both a diplomatic history of policy and strategy, and an international history of power, race, and empire.

This study explores the key questions regarding the relations of the Anglo-American-Caribbean triangle. How did the mainland—both the U.S. government and black America—address the Caribbean transition to self-government? How did Washington's perceptions of that transition change with the evolving dynamics of depression, world war, and Cold War, in a region long labeled the "American Lake"? What accounts for the difference in U.S. relations with the West Indies, generally more constructive than destructive, compared with neighboring Latin America? In what ways did the United States seek to balance its interests in the British metropole and Caribbean colonies as those two parties negotiated decolonization? The reverse applies as well. How, and how successfully, did the declining British metropole and rising West Indian nationalists use the American presence to further their own ends? How did the hegemon's proximity, and the consequent island–mainland ties linking Caribbean expatriates and African-Americans, shape relations? Finally, what can these transnational racial ties, and the geopolitical parameters within which they worked, tell us about the West Indies' place in the Third World transition to independence and about the importance of that transition to the Cold War?

The answers emerge in the tracing of several themes, in the islands of Jamaica and Trinidad, across a loose chronological framework. The two islands were the largest and politically most important of the West Indies in American, British, and many Caribbean eyes.[8] This importance owed not only to the two islands' relative size and wealth but also to their unique qualities: Jamaica's ties to black America and its role in black consciousness worldwide, and Trinidad's importance in U.S. defense plans. Both islands played both roles to a degree; Jamaica was a potential "frontline" garrison for the West after the Castro revolution, and Trinidad sent many of its sons and daughters to Harlem. But Jamaica sent the larger number abroad, and more importantly that number included Marcus Garvey, Claude McKay, and in a later generation Bob Marley. Its role as the birthplace of Rastafarianism, affirming an African connection even before the Italo-Ethiopian War that so fired the diasporan imagination, further cements its place as a locus of black consciousness in the hemisphere and world. For its part, Trinidad's location astride both the coastal oilfields and the eastern approaches to the Panama Canal ensured its centrality to hemispheric security as seen from Washington. The chronological framework of this study is loose in that it uses a combination of U.S. and Caribbean events—mainly presidencies and social unrest— as its reference points, but privileges none as an exclusive determinant of relations. This is meant to underscore the point that neither the American, West Indian, nor British side was fully in control. Each was by turns both actor and reactor. The initiative shifted across time, with all three sides taking turns driving relations between them.

Although the U.S.–British–West Indian relationship was a three-sided one, the more or less bilateral relations between the mainland and islands receive special attention in this study. Those relations were equal parts complex, unique, and revealing. They proceeded unevenly and along several tracks at once and rarely followed the more predictable give-and-take that characterized dealings between the colonies and the British metropole. U.S.–West Indian relations during decolonization pose an interpretive challenge because of the strategic, racial, cultural, historical, and symbolic matrix in which they evolved. The strategic context of war and Cold War fed both American action and West Indian suspicion. But if the U.S. record of Caribbean intervention, and of the racial and cultural regimes that accompanied it from back home, were well known around the region, West Indians were nonetheless not blind to the advantages of the American connection, whether through Washington or Harlem, and sought to use it when possible to advance the nationalist cause against the British.

The interpretive challenge lies in the fact that the colonies were indeed important to Washington, but much more so at some moments than others and rarely in the same way twice. This suggests that U.S.–West Indian relationship is best conceived of as a uniquely "protean partnership" in the hemisphere. Positing such a partnership sheds light on the basic American approaches to both that particular region of the globe and to the racial and anticolonial currents roiling through others. In this framework, the islands were always the junior, at times an invisible, often an unenthusiastic partner—but always an important one to Washington's Cold War strategy in the inter-American arena and even, to a degree, in the global arena beyond. If the islands were only of intermittent—but intermittently intense—importance to Washington, this left much initiative in the hands of West Indian and British actors, and gave mainland–island ties during decolonization their "protean" shape. The themes that animate its story fall into two broad categories: Cold War geopolitics and race-culture matters in diplomacy.

The dominant theme in the first category is the American search for national security. U.S. pursuit of bases, strategic materials, and sympathetic local leaders during World War II and the Cold War was not limited to the Caribbean. As Melvyn Leffler and others have shown, the post-1945 American search for national security was entirely global in scale and sought to secure preponderant military power and a favorable economic order as the means to protect American prosperity.[9] U.S. relations with the West Indies fit this template, but with two important twists. First, that template took its prototypical shape in the West Indies. The islands provided a kind of local testing ground for Washington's global Cold War national security strategy.[10] Second, that strategy rested on a fundamental distinction between core and periphery. Finite American resources, according to the doctrine, should be used foremost to pursue national interests in the core. However, in the British Caribbean, unlike most of the imperial world, the United States confronted an area that was both core *and* periphery: core in geostrategic and symbolic terms, but peripheral in population and economic importance. If the Caribbean provided an early version of the national-security formula, it did so despite a basic definitional uncertainty, which could have grave consequences in places like Korea. Although the West Indies avoided such an outcome, the colonies' ambiguous status posed conceptual challenges to policy-makers. However, in the event, it did not prevent the national-security factor from trumping all others with which it came into conflict. Even when the United States deferred responsibility for events on the West Indian ground to Britain—as it did most of the time—this deferral was predicated on the understanding that British actions would ultimately serve American national security. The pursuit of that goal goes far in explaining the course of U.S. relations with the postwar Caribbean.

Moreover, the pursuit of national-security assets in U.S.–West Indian relations connects that diplomacy to two broader, and older, patterns. One involves the historic American preoccupation with internal stability and foreign incursion into the western hemisphere. After all, instability and incursion had, for a century before the Cold War, been used to invoke the Monroe Doctrine and justify U.S. intervention in the circum-Caribbean. No such intervention occurred in Jamaica or Trinidad because Washington was able to achieve U.S. objectives without it. British and West Indian stewardship of the decolonization process in Jamaica and Trinidad only rarely clashed with U.S. designs for the region as a whole. When it did, as in the 1957 Chaguaramas controversy, the stakes rose enormously. In that crisis, two distinct but interrelated American national-security needs—a military anchor in the southern Caribbean and a West Indian regime friendly to the United States— were pitted against each other. The eventual solution protected not only immediate Cold War security needs but also the long-standing American goal of a stable Caribbean. In the latter sense, Jamaican and Trinidadian progress stood in welcome contrast to turmoil elsewhere in the region, above all in Cuba. That contrast was much on the minds of American, British, and West Indian actors, who conducted their mutual relations with a sharp eye for developments in the neighborhood. Indeed, although most accounts of inter-American relations focus on crises and interventions in the Spanish-speaking areas, it must not be forgotten that U.S. actions in those areas pro-ceeded with an eye to the larger regional context. That context included areas, and actors, vital to understanding how such "crisis" relations unfolded. Washington's policy response to Castro did not hinge on the West Indies— but it enveloped them in such ways that the U.S.–Cuba story is incomplete if they are left out of it.

The second broader pattern into which the pursuit of national security fits relations is that of Anglo-American "collaboration" in empire. American policy, by turns, pushed for an end to the British empire, upheld it as a pillar of stability, and replaced it when London could not keep that pillar standing. The result in many parts of the world looks like not so much the end of Brit-ish imperialism as the passing of the imperial baton to the United States. In the latter half of the century, Washington confirmed this transition by incor-porating what remained of British-imperial sovereignty into its own expanded, albeit informal, empire.[11]

American relations with the decolonizing West Indies suggest at least a partial exception to the pattern. In the long view, it is true that the formerly British West Indies looked much the same in 1900 as they did upon formal independence in 1962, or for that matter in 2000: mostly impoverished islands with some form of dependence on the outside world, nestled behind an Anglo-American military shield. But this picture is incomplete. For one thing, the shield is now much more American than British, the opposite of a century ago. For another, American "support" of the British empire in the West Indies was predicated on that empire reforming its way to extinction. U.S. accommodation to, or "collaboration" with, the British empire was condi-tional on British reform of its colonial regime. Moreover, to the extent London designed those reforms to practice the "imperialism of decolonization"— the continuation of influence, of access to markets and resources, and of the advantages of a global role without quite so many of the costs—that effort in the Caribbean rated at best a partial success. The sheer proximity of the mainland meant that the United States, with only intermittent forethought or active pursuit in doing so, eclipsed Britain in the region in strategic, geo-graphic, demographic, and economic terms. Although Washington bolstered the crown in its imperial outposts there and farther afield at key postwar moments, there was never a question of reverting to "empire" in the old-line, Cecil Rhodes sense of the term. Collaboration, then, did not mean continuation; American empire in the 1960 Caribbean was a different animal from British empire in the 1930 West Indies. Whether this shift from formal British to "informal" American empire amounted to substantive change on the ground is debatable. Certainly most Jamaicans and Trinidadians, who in 1962 danced as the Union Jack was lowered for good, believed that it did.

This included the leaders of the long trek to independence, who represented and encouraged the nationalist ferment of their fellow West Indians in admirable fashion, and whose initiative did much to give decolonization its internally often-contentious but ultimately peaceful shape. The importance of the leadership on all sides comes through the story quite clearly. On the U.S. and British sides, battles between diplomats, military men, and colonial officials determined day-to-day moves toward decolonization. At times of crisis, these moves received high-level attention, which was on the whole constructive, even if it often fell short of fulfilling West Indians' highest hopes. Varying levels of U.S. presidential interest, and the shift in British governments, did much to give relations their final shape. As for the major West Indian leaders, their caliber was virtually unmatched in the colonial world. Norman Manley and Alexander Bustamante in Jamaica, and Eric Williams in Trinidad, and intellectuals such as George Padmore and C. L. R. James, provided almost an embarrassment of leadership riches, and all out of proportion to their islands' small populations at that.[12] While several of these individuals and their colleagues were at times too close to radical agendas for American comfort, most of them—and almost all of the major nationalists who ascended to office—shared an anticommunism strong enough to reassure Washington that none of them would become a West Indian Castro. Moreover, their resourcefulness enabled them to play American and British interests off each other and helped to smooth the path to independence.[13]

In doing so, they represented not only the popular agency of their fellow islanders in pursuit of an envisioned national destiny but also followed their fellows who had decamped for points north. The contributions of these actors to decolonization deserve extra emphasis here. In a very real sense, though one overshadowed by the Cold War, they worked to make their own fates. In the islands during the 1930s, their unrest began the decolonization process. In the 1940s, their savvy and agitation capitalized on their ties forged on the black mainland, ties binding the expatriate communities and African-American sympathizers in urban America, to move the process along. Cooperative activism along diasporan lines introduces the second category of themes comprising the protean partnership: race-culture matters in diplomacy. The unpredictable, multivalent influence of these matters on foreign relations, as noted, has received serious scholarly consideration.[14] Most of this work focuses on race, and especially on Jim Crow, as a liability in America's global reputation. This was unquestionably the case in U.S.–West Indian relations. Yet those relations reveal another facet of race: the influence, and limits, of transnational black solidarity in the twin crusades against imperial rule and white supremacy. Solidarity within the hemispheric black "community" waxed and waned according to external events and to the ultimately different, specific objectives of blacks in island and mainland. The potential of race-based activism to influence relations was greater than is usually perceived. However, and perhaps paradoxically, the potential of this solidarity to overcome parochial intra-"ethnic" priorities was less.

The influence of race-based activism on U.S.–West Indian relations was perhaps most fully pronounced during the Roosevelt years. Top lieutenants in the administration had ties to African-American leaders, themselves in touch with expatriates in New York City. Migration decades earlier had created an influential West Indian community in Harlem; not for nothing was New York known as the "capital of the Caribbean." This "Harlem Nexus" became a site of transnational cooperation—of what might be called diasporan diplomacy—in the broad cause of black freedom.[15] Thanks to ties between black New York and the Roosevelt administration, West Indians and African-American sympathizers were able to exert influence not only on U.S. policy but also on internal West Indian developments. True, the policy influence was indirect at best. It was not thanks to any Roosevelt appointees of Caribbean origin, since none existed. However, the lack of black officials did not preclude Roosevelt's appointment of individuals such as Charles Taussig who were familiar with, and sympathetic to, the agenda of many Caribbean intellectuals regarding the regional crisis. Complementing this back-channel access to official power, moreover, were islanders' connections to expatriate and African-American communities. The activism made manifest in these transnational connections produced entities which would today qualify as nongovernmental organizations. In an interesting parallel—and sometime companion—to the transnational "civil rights" dynamics recently explored by Jonathan Rosenberg, these groups wielded a crucial influence on developments inside the colonies, including moral and financial support for the first Jamaican nationalist party to contest that island's first-ever popular election in 1944.[16]

However, the subsequent experience of the West Indies Federation (WIF) suggests that race-based solidarity also had its limits. These were reached in the attempt to transform that solidarity from, as it were, a transnational into a "national" phenomenon. The story of the WIF in both its hemispheric and Third World contexts is a fascinating political tragedy that bridges the geopolitics and race-culture-diplomacy themes of this study. In part this owes to the way in which the federation's failure continues to haunt visions of pan-Caribbean cooperation and identity.[17] As a historical matter, this fascination also stems from the fact that the WIF was not alone. It was one of a half-dozen British empire unions constructed as vehicles either for decolonization or post-colonial pan-nationalism. Nor was the impulse to federate confined to the British empire, as the latter's European counterparts, and indeed Western Europe itself, undertook to construct pan- or supra-national entities in the postwar era. Almost all of these experiments in federation—which have faded from many scholarly maps—ended as unsuccessfully as did the WIF. But few did so as relatively peacefully and in spite of as many apparent advantages as the WIF enjoyed.

In part, too, the fascination grows from the way in which federation projects like the WIF married together such wildly disparate visions of decolonization. Among these were "realist" metropolitan or hegemonic attempts to preserve stability and prevent communist gains. This was the main reason why London sought to create such a union and why Washington gave the enterprise its blessing. Also among these visions were the "romantic" pan-nationalist solidarities of blood, race, region, or culture, currents that historically had run deeply through—though at times against—West Indian society, culture, and identity. Yet it is these which lead us back, in the case of the federation, to the limits of race-based solidarity. The Caribbean had produced intellectuals and movements utterly central to the advance of transnational black consciousness, in spite of their position within what Nikhil Pal Singh calls "the long history in which black global dreams have foundered on the shoals of America's racial dilemma."[18] As noted, island leaders and mainland sympathizers had worked together to sway policy and politics alike in both places. Yet when given the opportunity to establish a bona fide political entity that could make that consciousness concrete, West Indians democratically declined—an event that underlines again their agency in shaping the process of their own decolonization. Exploring the paradox of a historical fount of black-diasporan consciousness choosing insularity over community, and the sustained and evolving impact of this decision on the Anglo-American-Caribbean triangle, is a major focus of this book.

It is important to note that this apparent paradox was not confined to transnational black activism, as this suggests another theme in the race-culture-diplomacy category in this study: the limits of cooperation, and the extent of manipulation, by all parties of each other in Anglo-American-Caribbean relations. The difficulties encountered during the construction of the West Indies Federation, and its collapse before its fourth birthday, provide a ready example—but far from the only one. Neither the British nor the Americans were above exploiting colonial divisions for advantage. Nor did the metropole and hegemon hesitate to manipulate one another when it served a larger purpose. David Reynolds has called the 1930s Anglo-American relationship "competitive co-operation," and the label is apt for its West Indian incarnation during the decades that followed as well. The successful exploitation of American interests by British, of British by American, and of both by Jamaican and Trinidadian leaders, suggests an addendum: "mutual manipulation" as a prominent feature of relations.

This assessment of the U.S.–British–West Indian experience points us back to that central puzzle: the broad relationship between the Cold War and Third World decolonization. It bears repeating that the question is thornier than it first appears. Most Third World nationalist movements, after all, originated during the first half of the century, even if they culminated only in the second. As Thomas Borstelmann points out, the dominant issue in the Third World of the 1940s was not the superpower conflict but Western colonialism.[19] Yet the two are bound up together, by chronology if by nothing else. That chronology furnishes our historical and historiographical map, and facilitates understanding of the

Cold War–decolonization connection. In the West Indies, this map reveals the link between the islands and the Korean War—namely, that the bauxite mined in the former was indispensable to the U.S. war effort in the latter. Washington's pursuit of the mineral reverberated through subsequent internal colonial developments and through U.S. relations with both Britain and the West Indies. Other examples—the nationalists' struggle with communists in their ranks or the islands' role in helping the United States meet the Castro challenge—show a similarly demonstrable, "organic" connection between the Cold War and the process of decolonization in the British Caribbean.

Connections of this sort cannot by themselves tell the whole story, but tracing them across the Atlantic and the Caribbean alike does allow this study to offer one solution to that puzzle: the Cold War had sequential and contradictory influences on the decolonization process, an early phase of repression that stifled it, followed by a later phase of liberation that nourished it. In the West Indies, this meant that the Cold War first slowed and then quickened a historical process already underway. The process had been launched by colonial activists years before the superpower conflict. That conflict accelerated it by forging the "protean partnership" between mainland and island, which enabled a larger American regional role that the declining British metropole and the decolonizing West Indies could, in turn, exploit. To borrow a theatrical metaphor, the Cold War brought some new characters, props, and dialogue to the stage. But these joined a drama already well into its second act. More importantly, the drama was not scripted by omnipotent playwrights in Washington, London, or Moscow but coauthored by the actors—the "partners"—themselves.

It is this partnership to which the book's title alludes. Cain's question, as it is usually interpreted, is not a perfect fit for any of the several bilateral and multilateral relations at work in this story; no grievous crime is being obscured by its asking. Yet on further reflection the question, taken at rhetorical face value, fits well enough. As a general and a historical matter, it suggests the hegemon's dilemma: how powerful states can interact with weak states in ways that best protect the interests of both parties or at least that minimize the harm to each. Applied to the historical episode at hand, it hints at the changes in the Anglo-American alliance over the course of the twentieth century, as the younger brother became the richer, stronger guardian of the older. It sketches too the issues that animated and haunted the collapse of the British empire, as the metropole and the colonies recast the regime's responsibilities leading up to the nationalist transition. Finally, it evokes the promise and limits of transnational solidarity across the African diaspora in the age of black consciousness and nationalist revolt. The fundamental matter of how to weigh moral, historical, and other responsibility may be a filial one in Cain's story. But it is one never entirely absent from the shared life of nations and peoples, and one certainly present during the Third World's epochal transition of the last century.

The decolonization of Jamaica and Trinidad brought into existence the first new nations in the hemisphere in more than fifty years. As such, they were the Americas' representatives of the global "race revolution" against imperial rule and white supremacy in the postwar era.[20] In contrast to many areas, where such transitions left blood on the ground and smoke in the air, Jamaica and Trinidad cut a peaceful path to independence. This had been far from a sure thing. Riots, unrest, and war had started the process in the late 1930s; the last-minute collapse of the federation, amid the chaos spreading across the Caribbean in the early 1960s, might have ended it badly. That this did not occur came as an enormous relief to all parties. If independence proved no panacea for Jamaican and Trinidadian problems, deft navigation of the process leading to it nonetheless enabled those islands, the metropole, and the hegemon alike to get much of what they claimed to want out of it. The contrast with newly emerging Third World nations elsewhere is striking. The diplomacy of U.S.–British–West Indian relations amid world war and Cold War deserve consideration in that larger context. The story is not strictly an "east–west" problem of war, power, and empire, but also a "north–south" phenomenon of race, nation, and freedom, with ramifications all around the compass—and one whose relatively peaceful, relatively successful outcome was far from inevitable.

1

The West Indian Watershed

In 1928, the United States Navy drew up war plans for an imagined conflict with Great Britain. Such an improbable conflict was, in Winston Churchill's words, "not unthinkable." A war, though regrettable from so many standpoints, would in the Navy's view at least present the United States with the strategic opportunity to bolster American security by taking over the West Indies.[1] Nor were the islands purely a strategic prize. Since the 1920s, some Americans had called for Britain to hand over its western hemisphere possessions as payment for World War I debts. Once the Great Depression left the transatlantic economy bedridden, such arrears seemed intolerable—and all the more so given that the offending party ruled an empire upon which most Americans looked with bemused disdain. Hard-liners said the West Indies should simply be annexed. American businesses could exploit their riches, and surpluses in the U.S. population could settle their lands. The territories, so the argument went, would surely benefit from American influence, as Haiti had recently done.

However, the story of U.S.–British–West Indian relations in the years before and during World War II goes beyond such questions of strategy or profit. Trends below the geopolitical radar would have an important impact as well. As part of the wave of Gilded Age immigration to the United States, for example, inhabitants of the British Caribbean came northward in a steady flow. By 1940, U.S. residents of West Indian derivation numbered nearly 100,000. The majority gravitated to New York City, where one-quarter of the population that brought forth the Harlem Renaissance was of West Indian stock.[2] West Indians, most famously Marcus Garvey, stoked black consciousness and helped to set the agenda for black America. Their ties to African-American activists would enable

16

them to exert an influence, via sympathetic members of the Roosevelt administration, on U.S. policy toward a British Caribbean in flux.

In their home islands, a related consciousness exploded in the late 1930s. With the onset of the Depression, the West Indies fell into dire circumstances. The economic squeeze produced social tensions, proto-nationalism, and labor violence all across the Caribbean, sparking what historian Cary Fraser labels the "crisis of colonial rule" in the region.[3] The labor riots were rooted in anger over working conditions, but owed more generally to the harshness of daily life in the islands. The unrest drew attention to the shortcomings of British stewardship and incurred soul-searching on both sides of the Atlantic. The riots did not engender an immediate, revolutionary change in the colonies, but all parties knew that *some* change would have to come. Moreover, thanks to the northward exodus noted above, the rioters' actions had an audience in the cultural capital of the United States. Their agency on the ground at home thus reverberated in the American atmosphere near-abroad, as war approached inexorably across the Atlantic.

Backlit by these strategic, racial, and sociopolitical trends, the Caribbean from 1937 to 1945 presents a fascinating topography, in which the 1941 establishment of U.S. bases in the West Indies stands as a watershed. The year before, when Roosevelt and Churchill initiated the trade of bases for warships, commentary focused on the usual geopolitical suspects: waning British power, waxing American hegemony, and the Nazi menace. All of these were and are important in assessing the Bases-for-Destroyers Deal, its precursors, and its effects, but they miss much of the story. Anglo-American-Caribbean affairs from 1937 to 1945 witnessed the confluence of Allied geopolitics, hemispheric racial trends, and colonial turmoil, and these affairs belong as much within the story of the wartime Grand Alliance as within that of the interwar "Good Neighbor" period, with which they share features of U.S. activity elsewhere in the hemisphere. The buildup of crises from 1937 to 1941 in U.S.–British–West Indian relations pointed toward a transition rife with uncertainty.

Tropical Depression, Tropical Storms: 1937–1939

By the late 1930s, the British colonies had been a technical rebuke to the Monroe Doctrine for over a hundred years. The Doctrine had averred that areas of the western hemisphere then newly independent of Spain and Portugal—and more broadly, of Europe—would remain so. It also, however, included a "grandfather clause." The clause promised noninterference with those areas, such as the British colonies, still ruled from Europe as of 1823. It might thus be said that the British colonies rebutted the intent of the Doctrine, even as they testified to the implicit Anglo-American *entente* upholding it. American attention to the circum-Caribbean historically focused on the Spanish-speaking areas, in part because European sovereignty in the remaining pockets could better resist Yankee inroads, whether carved by gunboat or dollar diplomacy. Moreover, British assent in American regional hegemony was a major reason that the United States had mostly avoided pursuit of its own, potentially conflicting objectives in the European West Indies. The two powers' interests there, in short, largely overlapped well into the 1930s.

As that decade neared its end, though—and as British power faltered—the calculus of strategic interdependence changed. London's Ambassador to the United States, Lord Lothian, cabled home in 1939 to say as much and to find a silver lining in Europe's gathering storm clouds. If Munich showed that "[the United States] can depend on the British fleet no longer and if [Washington thus] decides to provide...an American Atlantic fleet with new bases...to the Gulf of Mexico, Munich may well be...the event which transformed the Unspoken Alliance." Munich *did* effect such a transformation to some extent. The handoff of security responsibility began taking shape in military minds in 1938.[4] Roosevelt's 1937 "quarantine" speech included a "Western Hemisphere Neutrality Zone." In June, he secretly asked London for bases in three Caribbean colonies. London acceded, presaging, as David Reynolds notes, the 1940 destroyers–bases deal.[5] British observers of the U.S. fleet reported that "[its] operations [were] of special interest as involving the whole area of the West Indies which, whether in American or Allied possession, [are] the natural strategic screen of the...Panama Canal."[6] The British applauded the May appointment of Admiral William Leahy as Governor of Puerto Rico, the first naval officer to hold that post. Not only did it signify the strategic importance of the Caribbean but the choice of the "staunch Anglophile" Leahy indicated a U.S. grasp of the shared burdens of ruling the region.[7] These included defense of sea-lanes as well as maintaining order within the islands, the latter being arguably more important prior to the outbreak of hostilities.

Beyond Allied geopolitics in the Caribbean, the late 1930s also touched the region in two other important ways. First, these years were a transformative moment in the history of the African diaspora. The 1935 Italian invasion of Ethiopia had galvanized blacks the world over; African-Americans who were generations removed from the ancestral continent followed the crisis closely.[8] Colonial officials saw its effects on the ground. During the Jamaica riots, British Secretary of State MacDonald reported to the Cabinet on "a good deal of racial feeling between coloured and white people, which had been stimulated by events in Abyssinia and had now become serious."[9] As in Jamaica, historian Harvey Neptune writes that Trinidad too saw a series of "Hands Off Abyssinia" rallies as well as a range of smaller, day-to-day markers of the changed, charged atmosphere: beards grown in honor of Emperor Haile Selassie I, calypsos praising Ethiopia and denouncing Mussolini, secondary-school debating societies devoting their meetings to the invasion. Neptune notes that on the ground in Trinidad, "Ethiopianness operated as a challenge to Britishness."[10] Further afield, the episode was key to what historian Penny Von Eschen calls the "making of the politics of the African diaspora." Its legacies included the politicization of Britain's League of Coloured Peoples, and the 1937 establishment of both the International African Service Bureau in London and of the ICAA—the precursor of the Council on African Affairs—in New York.[11]

Blacks in the hemisphere sustained an impassioned interest in the global dimensions of racial and colonial oppression. White-supremacist imperial rule came under searing attack by black voices in the United States, including by many West Indians. Indeed, those of Caribbean origins figure so prominently in black radicalism that it is impossible to envision it without them; Garvey is far from the only example. The scholar Winston James has analyzed this cohort's role:

> The Caribbean presence in radical[ism] in the U.S. was remarkable in...three important respects. First, it was out of proportion to the group's numerical weight within the black population. Second, Caribbeans founded and led not only black nationalist [groups] like the UNIA, but also important political currents on the revolutionary socialist left. Third, the migrants also provided some of the most distinguished black intellectuals at the time.[12]

Some of these individuals arrived as radicals; others were radicalized by their mainland experience. In either case, the parallel "Great Migration" that brought West Indians alongside African-Americans in the urban North guaranteed that black activism would encompass anticolonialism. When it did, the West Indian presence gave the Caribbean an immediacy that other areas of the colonial world lacked. Sympathy for the peoples of Asia and Africa was palpable and genuine in black anticolonial discourse. Yet that sympathy was also present regarding the West Indies, with the added difference that West Indians themselves were standing on Harlem street corners—and organizing mass meetings, and offering "History Classes" to the public, among other activities—to proclaim it.[13]

It is significant, for example, that the first group to fuse nascent Jamaican nationalism with a demand for self-government opened a branch in New York before it opened one in Kingston. The Reverend Ethelred Brown founded the Jamaica Progressive League (JPL) on September 1, 1936. The JPL made good use of the political space furnished by black New York, organizing frequent mass meetings in Harlem. These opened with the tellingly named "Exiles' Hymn," sung as an invocation: "Full well we know, our country, that we can serve you best / by claiming for you freedom beneath the Empire's crest / a Nation among nations, proud in your liberty! Jamaica, glorious homeland, we swear that this shall be."[14] The expatriates' commitment and activism thus provided a kind of foundation-stone for the West Indian nationalism that would eventually supplant the colonial regime, once war and decolonization unraveled the latter. Both the philosophical origins and the envisioned end point of their movement are of interest—as is the role of the New York crucible in the genesis of each. As the program for a January 1937 JPL-organized mass meeting in Harlem affirmed:

> Declaration: Firmly believing that any people that has seen its generations come and go on the same soil for centuries is, in fact, a nation, the JPL pledges itself to work for the attainment of self-government for Jamaica, so that the country may take its rightful place as a member of the British Commonwealth of Nations.[15]

The following year a JPL chapter was organized in Jamaica, one in frank emulation of the New York branch that was, in the words of its founding resolution, "working fearlessly and conscientiously for the national... advancement of Jamaica."[16] An early president of the JPL, W. Adolphe Roberts, was a U.S. citizen of Jamaican heritage and an early advocate of Jamaican self-government who embodied the New York–Caribbean connection. The JPL was one of a dozen New York "Progressive Leagues" founded by expatriates to push for colonial self-determination for their homelands. In terms of the broader anticolonial movement, these activists supported self-rule for Africa as well, but for obvious reasons the West Indies were closer to their hearts. The proliferation of such Leagues illustrates the importance of New York City as what Ken Post calls a "stimulating atmosphere" for anticolonial ferment and as a cross-pollinating seedbed of racial and political consciousness.[17]

This West Indian presence ensured that when the islands exploded, Harlem shook. This—the pinnacle of five years of violent labor unrest—was the second important way in which 1937 shaped subsequent Anglo-American-Caribbean relations. For decades, crushing poverty and labor conditions had made of the West Indies, in the words of one prominent Jamaican, a "powder house [with] a lot of lighted candles around."[18] Labor activism had lit some of these, despite its uneven spread throughout the region; in the 1930s, new elements combined to light yet more. The decline in world prices for West Indian commodities meant that the Depression was the deep bottom of a long slide. Sugar had historically brought many misfortunes—slavery, poverty, monoculture, and disease among them—to the Caribbean. The problems that accompanied the crop's production were among the biggest obstacles to Caribbean progress. Other commodities, such as cocoa and bananas, presented a similar quandary, albeit on a smaller scale.[19] A colonial economy thus stunted all aspects of island life even absent the Great Depression. That event managed to make an unbearable situation almost unbelievably worse.

Below such macrostructural dynamics, other factors—psychological, cultural, and racial—further contributed to the volatility of 1930s West Indian society. Islanders returning home from vanished jobs abroad weighed their privations on a scale of higher expectations; as one British businessman in Jamaica put it, "the emergence of the 'vociferous element' was to be blamed on migrants returned from the USA, where they 'had acted as bell boys and had made bigger money and had also learnt to be race conscious.' "[20] As in black America, the Ethiopian conflict fired racial consciousness and fused the felt connections between African-American and U.S.-resident West Indians. This also fed movements stressing unity and struggle, epitomized by the rise of Rastafarianism. Indeed, events in Ethiopia had made that sect look prophetic, given their lionization of Selassie even before the Italian invasion, and their calls for black consciousness and a return to Africa testified to the breadth of diasporan imaginings in the decade.[21] In addition, labor victories in the core inspired resistance in the periphery. The 1930s success of American unions caught the attention of West Indian labor leaders, who sought the ties and techniques of their mainland brethren.[22] All of these, particularly in a context of world economic crisis, threatened social combustion.

Spark began touching powder in mid-decade. Beginning in 1934, social unrest, often rooted in labor strikes but drawing on much broader and deeper dissatisfactions, became an annual event. By 1939, disturbances had struck almost every colony in the British Caribbean, leaving each one in a state of tension at best and emergency at worst.[23] Two explosions are of particular interest. The first occurred in Trinidad in 1937; the second, in Jamaica the following year. Because they involved the most populous and prosperous of the West Indies, these disturbances together form a watershed of modern Caribbean and indeed modern imperial history. The dramatic story of the riots has been well told elsewhere. By way of quick sketch, it is worth noting here that what began as strikes in certain sectors spread quickly through many others. In Trinidad, the island's largest oil company paid its shareholders a 35% dividend in the same year that it lowered workers' wages by roughly the same figure.[24] In June 1937, borrowing the "sit-in" tactic from American autoworkers, oilworkers in the town of Fyzabad protested this and related injustices. When the police tried to arrest their leader, the fiery Grenadian Tubal Uriah "Buzz" Butler, violence erupted and quickly spread throughout the whole island. Butler, a powerful speaker, gave voice to the urgency of the crisis and the agency of his fellows: "The hour has come to show your might and power and get things for yourselves. Our brutal taskmasters have proudly and cruelly turned down our prayers [and] challenged us to prove our right to life and happiness!"[25] In a melee that night at Fyzabad, policeman Charlie King was burned alive, the most gruesome of the fifteen fatalities that the unrest produced in the following days.[26] In Jamaica, the disturbances began in the eastern cane fields, leapt over to sugar lands in the west, and soon spread to the Kingston docks. The tumult brought people to the streets and society to a stop. As Alexander Bustamante later remarked, "in May 1938, Jamaica was on the march. Not even dogs were left in their homes."[27]

Moreover, this unrest coincided with intellectuals' promotion of greater self-government and reform. The turmoil also brought the heretofore suppressed racial dimensions of colonial society to the fore. After the first series of riots in Barbados in 1935, the U.S. consul foresaw "the gradual submergence of the white man as an economic, political, and social factor, in a tide of color."[28] In a 1936 Garveyite newsletter, a columnist argued that "the whites today is [*sic*] now fully aware of the mistake of their ancestors but are now powerless. The Blacks are not so powerless, for they are in the majority...Arise Jamaicans from your slumber and let your slogan be, 'Jamaica for the Jamaicans.'"[29] A mixture of concession and intimidation served to restore order. However, the political, and psychological, landscape would never be the same.[30]

Three legacies of the unrest shaped subsequent U.S.–British–West Indian affairs. First, the riots refined the practice and vision of island politics. They showed the strength of the labor movement, which became a launch pad for most of the major leaders of the following decades. These adhered to the British Labour pattern, and they thereby helped to stabilize island politics—albeit unevenly, according to authorities. Butler of Trinidad, for example, who led the black oilworkers' union, was seen as a messianic race demagogue. A charismatic ex-soldier and itinerant preacher given to rhetorical flights often as riveting as they were baffling, his place on the frontlines of Trinidad's labor struggles made him the most popular, and populist, island figure. Jamaica's Bustamante was seen in much the same way, though less messianic than opportunistic. A labor mediator rather than a laborer himself, Bustamante seized the 1938 moment to create an umbrella union in his own name and thus make himself the "creole" leader of the laboring black masses. Like Butler, Bustamante brought an outsized personality, an intuitive sense of the crowd, and a zeal for political power and political theater to a cause long inchoate but now taking shape. Norman Manley, by contrast, won praise for his calming influence. Without him, officials averred, the strife would have been worse.[31] As a veteran of His Majesty's army in World War I, and as a light-skinned lawyer representing black strikers, he struck a balance between being a "company man" and an agent of the masses. His ability to articulate Jamaicans' grievances even while keeping them from spiraling into further destruction won him a global profile among nationalists in the British empire and great admiration in the Colonial Office. Prominent Labourite Stafford Cripps, for example, thought Manley the West Indies' Nehru and put the two men in touch.[32] Butler, Bustamante, and Manley would remain influential for years, and their reputations grew in the directions they had taken during the unrest. Moreover, the riots, by casting light on the failings of British administration, invited questions about the future. The episode thus altered the regional agenda; native, expatriate, and metropolitan voices now all called for change, including greater eventual self-government.

Even after the riots, few voices called for that objective in the immediate future. But the power of the few was not lost on American observers. Concurrent disturbances in Puerto Rico and the Virgin Islands underscored the volatility in the region. Worse still, expatriates provided links to mainland radicals. The U.S. consul reported from Trinidad that "the [riots] clearly indicate that a...few radicals, can completely paralyze...the colony at any time."[33] After the Jamaica riots, the embassy in London received hints that the Comintern was funneling money "for the purpose of exploiting the labor disputes" to West Indian agitators via New York.[34] State Department analysts had no proof of such a pipeline, but found that "communist-affiliated organizations," such as the National Negro Congress (NNC) and Max Yergan's ICAA, were sending money to help the strikers. Paul Robeson mentioned the riots to the *Daily Worker*, lamenting "those fellows that are being shot down in Jamaica today."[35] Yergan was reported to have founded an "American–West Indian Defense Committee," and U.S. officials identified other expatriates of radical persuasion, many of whom appeared in subsequent FBI reports.

Even among the most radical, however, few saw self-government as a panacea. Most regarded it as an adjunct to the real issue—the dismal quality of colonial life—new attention to which was the second important legacy of the riots. In response to the unrest, the crown appointed the West India Royal Commission (the so-called Moyne Commission), to investigate matters. The Moyne Commission's findings, including disease, malnutrition, and illegitimacy that recalled fifteenth-century London, leapt off the page. Typhoid, yaws, and tropical diseases were rampant; in one Jamaican parish, 74 percent of the tested population was found to be infected with hookworm. The rate of infant mortality in some islands neared a horrifying 300 per 1,000 live births. Literacy, while higher than in much of the empire, barely broke 50 percent, and it was estimated that a third of the population had never seen the inside of a school. The shocking news was not entirely new. Earlier, smaller-scale investigations such as that of the Rockefeller Hookworm Commission in Jamaica estimated an average housing density of five persons per one-room home, and the unrest had led to contemporary mainstream reporting on the pittance wages and grueling conditions of labor in the colonies. But the Moyne findings showed the British government just how piercingly bad things were. So damning was the Moyne report that publication was withheld for six years, for fear of handing Goebbels a propaganda windfall.[36]

The government released a summary of its recommendations in 1940. These proposed massive expenditures aimed at relieving the perpetual socio-economic disaster in which West Indians lived. This departed from previous policy in that it avowed a positive British duty to improve the islands' welfare. The Moyne Commission urged increasing sugar subsidies in order to avoid economic meltdown, alternatives to sugar for future development, health and education initiatives, and some limited political reforms. The recommendations envisioned London-led efforts at welfare and development within a context of "improved" imperial rule, with only minor concessions to self-government and future independence. However, the unrest helped to push even hard-liners toward reform, not least because the Caribbean riots seemed a canary in the imperial coal mine; as Thomas Holt puts it, "there was [much British] concern that events in the West Indies prefigured the future of the entire colonial empire."[37]

London was growing more aware as well of American eyes over its shoulder:

> The USA is...inclined to judge British colonial administration by [its] specimens...adjacent to the American continent...One sees signs of a growing [American] interest in the administration of these territories [in the US press]. The W[est] Indies are, to some considerable extent, the British show-window for the USA.[38]

This post-riot impulse to reform harmonized with later American designs, with one important conceptual difference. The Moyne Commission distinguished between political and economic reform, and leaned toward the latter. In the Moyne view, economic diversification was a riskier bet than sugar, and in any case any such reorganization and welfare efforts stood apart from political change. Imperial tutelage, that is, would continue with minor modifications.

The Americans, once the Bases Deal allowed them to inject an opinion, dis-agreed. Economic and political change had to go hand in hand, and both in the direction of greater self-determination. On this point, the U.S. government con-curred with black voices on the mainland. The British position—sweeping enough, compared to centuries of inertia—looked feeble in the charged atmo-sphere of the late 1930s.

Notwithstanding philosophical differences, a post-unrest Anglo-American harmony of interests foreshadowed later cooperation. This was the third leg-acy of the riots as regards diplomacy. Above all, these interests focused on security, especially as British power—and the ability to project it in the Carib-bean—grew more tenuous. The riots terrified the white minorities and absen-tees who held stakes there: "It is most essential that White Troops be stationed there for years," because of "the ever present possibility of a racial clash."[39] As those "whose lot is cast in this island [we] the oil, sugar, and other industrial companies feel that, if... troops cannot be stationed in the colony, it is essen-tial that... a naval or aeroplane base should be established in Trinidad, with as little delay as possible." In August, the British Commander in the region agreed. He underlined the need to bolster the "inadequate" police force there, "if necessary by provision of military forces from the UK or elsewhere."[40]

Indeed, even before the riots, authorities were concerned about security. Opinion in the critical government, oil, and military sectors had come to feel keenly the island's vulnerability to attack and its importance in case of war in Europe:

> Trinidad is the greatest petroleum-producing center of the Empire, and one of the easiest to defend in case of war... The primary objective of the British Gov-ernment [is] to provide a strong air, military, and naval base on a direct route from England to Australia via the Panama Canal as a substitute for the present Mediterranean route likely to be untenable during any future European war. The whole British navy could be easily protected, provisioned, and refueled from local supply of petroleum in Trinidad.[41]

When the *Trinidad Guardian* asked British oil magnate John Cadman if London would construct such a facility, he replied, "And why not? Trini-dad possesses natural advantages which make it admirably suited to the establishment of [an] air and naval base."[42] The need to protect the oil industry, which monthly pumped 1.25 million barrels crucial to any Brit-ish war effort, drove officials to bolster island security. The riots showed that at least as large a threat loomed from internal sources.[43] Hence, the need to project power in the Caribbean grew more urgent still, even as, at precisely that late-1930s moment, the metropole was less and less able to do so.

Post-riot sentiment elsewhere in the West Indies no doubt mirrored that of Trinidad. The riots thus helped, quite unintentionally, to prepare island opinion for the American arrival two years later. Having seen that internal unrest was a threat, at least some members of the most reactionary, pro-imperial class in the region—white elites—approached the conclusion that any protection was better than none. Whatever else a Yankee incursion would portend, it promised a security that the metropole was becoming unable to provide. To be sure, this would be offset by fears that the U.S. presence would upset island labor relations. But as the smoke cleared, the prospect of white military protection—"from the U.K. or elsewhere"—became more appealing to elites on the island. Beyond security questions and beyond the elites, there is reason to believe that this appeal reached the masses as well. Writers such as Alfred Mendes in his novel *Black Fauns* captured the ambivalence many West Indians felt about the mainland. But the ambivalence ebbed as the possibility of a greater American presence grew more real. As the Trinidadian publication *People* noted in 1936, America's reputation in the islands, though forever fraught, had never been better.[44] Familiarity with American oil company personnel, with the currents of Harlem and Hollywood, and with the power of the U.S. dollar left ordinary Trinidadians equivocal, even enthusiastic about the still-theoretical prospect of a Yankee incursion. These attitudes were arguably mercenary or tactical—for greater economic opportunity or against the British colonial regime—but no less real for it. These currents, in tandem with the riots' impact on colonial politics and reform, would shape Anglo-American-Caribbean relations once the war brought the United States more fully into the picture.

Two other points regarding the American role bear consideration. Both foreshadow the complicated Anglo-American matrix of security, economy, and decolonization that would emerge soon after the war began. First, the post-riots drive to bolster security raised questions not only of defense responsibility but also of economic privilege. The 1938 effort to establish a Trinidadian airport at Piarco—where Washington, after the Bases Deal, would build one of its two major air facilities on the island—prompted maneuvering by British, Dutch, and American airlines. Each hoped for concessions, or better still a monopoly. The U.S. consul reported, alas, that "the Public Works director has stated unofficially that non-British lines will receive little consideration."[45] So too with U.S. oil companies, who pressed the State Department for help in getting a foothold in post-riot drilling; the crown staved them off and kept most control in the hands of imperial producers. The important point, however, is less this economic competition than the nascent security cooperation, i.e. the overlapping Anglo-American interest in enforcing stability. At given points, economic and security interests become difficult to distinguish; the State Department and Pan Am, for example, could use each other to blaze inroads into the British possessions. But to the extent that economy and security can be distinguished, the latter predominated in Anglo-American moves in the post-riots West Indies.

The second point also speaks to the allies' verisimilitude in the prewar and war years. Anticolonialism, as voiced by white and black Americans, tends to eclipse the prewar status quo: the United States and Britain faced each other as imperial peers. U.S. possessions from Puerto Rico to Alaska to the Philippines did not have the long history of Britain's holdings, but they did have roughly the same status of colonial wards. However, during the war and as part of its legacy, Americans forsook this conception of empire for another. That they did so owes partly to their experience with the British West Indies, because that region was held up as a model, and leading American anticolonialists cut their teeth on it. Washington looked at the Caribbean in 1937 and saw the empires that were and might have been; it looked again a few years later and saw the empires that should no longer be. The war, when it came, changed everything.

Between Metropole and Hegemon: Subs and Coca-Cola, 1940–1941

In the West Indies, as elsewhere on the imperial map, World War II superimposed a global conflict upon a local one long simmering. There were, in effect, two wars going on in the Caribbean, and the new American presence influenced them both. The first could be seen in the plumes of smoke that followed submarine attacks, in the empty pantries of the islands, and in the frenetic construction of U.S. military bases. The second was subtler. It took place in the hearts of the combatants, themselves often not even physically present in the islands during the war. The British war against the Nazis, by prompting the United States to broaden its regional role, helped to drive the islands' war against the British.

Events in Europe carried in their train any prospective changes in Britain's Caribbean. The Moyne report was nearing completion when the war erupted. A summary of its embarrassing findings—or at least those few the British government allowed to be published—subsequently guided a major reform in colonial administration. Heeding the Moyne recommendations, the Colonial Development and Welfare Act (CDWA) of 1940 appropriated over five million pounds annually for education, health, and welfare projects. Given that Britain was at the time strapped for cash, the Act was as much symbolic as substantive.[46] The CDWA, however, represented two things: British acknowledgment that their stewardship had been wanting and an implicit determination that it should both continue and improve. The American Embassy in London saw the wisdom of "this Colonial New Deal...What might in peace-time have been a major political scandal of colonial maladministration [becomes] a useful wartime counterfoil to enemy propaganda...against the alleged evils of British imperialism."[47]

Shortly after the Act was announced, German victories pushed the future of the Caribbean colonies even further into flux. The fall of Holland and France in the spring of 1940 raised the threat of their Caribbean possessions serving as enemy bases. Roosevelt perceived a "significant threat" to the hemisphere. Among observers of Caribbean affairs, especially expatriates in North America, these events sparked rumors of a pre-emptive U.S. takeover of certain islands, starting with the French.[48] The prospect of such a takeover did not frighten everybody, according to an American visitor: "it seems evident that the masses of Jamaicans would welcome...a transfer of the island to American ownership, as they believe that their economic situation, which is very serious, would be improved thereby. This view is not held by the English residents, whom I find, on the whole, the most anti-American group in the West Indies."[49]

West Indians on the mainland were more ambivalent about the United States, but they recognized the hegemon's potential utility to their cause. Once the war reached the English Channel, the weakness of the metropoles and the southward expansion of the U.S. defense perimeter gave them an opening. Activists led by émigrés Wilfred A. Domingo, Richard B. Moore, and H. P. Osborne responded by organizing the West Indies National Emergency Committee in New York. WINEC attempted to use the security crisis to lobby for American support of West Indian rights and interests, including self-government. The strategic moment had come; as Domingo put it, "we should try to win our autonomy by winning the sympathy of Latin America and [then] playing those countries against the US."[50]

Although fears of U.S. advance into European possessions turned out to be overstated, apprehension about the colonies was not limited to black and West Indian New York. Indeed, in a suggestive exception to pre–Pearl Harbor isolationism, a large majority of U.S. public opinion supported defense of the hemisphere against the Nazis. In July 1940, FDR's secretary of state Cordell Hull and his Latin American counterparts met to outline such a defense. The result of their meeting, the Havana Declaration, affirmed a right to defend foreign-owned territories against Axis encroachment. In the context of U.S.–Latin American relations, this unity was the dividend of the Good Neighbor Policy, and the economic ties under its aegis. As Hull put it, "the political lineup followed the economic lineup," and the hemispheric perimeter was drawn.[51]

In the narrower matter of who was to decide the fate of the Caribbean possessions, however, the Havana Declaration demonstrated that it would not be their inhabitants. Domingo, Moore, and their fellow activists were determined to correct the rebuke. WINEC was renamed the West Indies National Council (WINC), as part of the founders' efforts to broaden and strengthen West Indian claims.[52] As Domingo put it to Roberts, he had sought all types in recruiting for the larger organization: "liberals, reactionaries, Communists, pro-Allies, etc. It was my intention to give the movement a truly national character, feeling sure that we could agree on the one important point that come what may we, the people affected, should have a voice in determining our future."[53] This was most necessary, Roberts concurred in his reply, and urgently so: "The real crisis is almost upon us. Jamaicans—and West Indians generally—will be infatuated dupes if they fail to realize that the British Empire is going to fall, and that if self-government is not claimed now it may be impossible to get it for another generation."[54] WINC sent a delegate, Hope Stevens, to Havana to press for Caribbean self-government. Stevens had no official standing at the meeting. He was, however, allowed to distribute pamphlets calling for Caribbean self-determination. Moore later claimed that if not for WINC's presence at Havana, the United States would have " 'put it all over' [Latin] American delegates with the idea of taking the

West Indies and treating the natives like sheep."[55] Domingo credited WINC's "Declaration of Rights of the Caribbean Peoples" with influencing the final Havana document, which "constitute[s] a substantial political gain for the colored race in the Western world.... This fact and its logical consequence, the possibility of creating new black nations in the Caribbean, should be of the highest significance to American Negroes."[56]

For other advocates of Caribbean independence, however, the Havana Declaration had two sharp edges. The idea of a concert of American powers "protecting" the islands rankled. Speaking for WINC, Moore declared in his "Reply to Cordell Hull" that "this Committee must firmly oppose any plan whereby the [American] Republics, at the behest of the United States, shall act as custodians, receivers, and bailiffs for European Empires."[57] An expanded American-Caribbean empire was only a slightly lesser fear than Axis attack. Indeed, given what West Indians knew as the twin sins of U.S. circum-Caribbean interventionism and its odious racial regime, such an outcome was not only more likely but perhaps equally dreaded. Interventionism had, after all, only been renounced seven years earlier; prior to the Good Neighbor Policy, there had been hardly a given year of the twentieth century in which American forces were not in-country somewhere around the Caribbean littoral. This history was as well known to West Indians as the ongoing reign of Jim Crow, especially those who had themselves suffered that regime while laboring to build the Panama Canal or to pick United Fruit bananas in Guatemala.[58] As Manley put it, "America is still a long way from a solution of the problem created by racial minorities, especially Negroes. No amount of white-washing can hide this glaring truth."[59]

However, Manley and other activists in both New York and Jamaica gave the Declaration their blessing and gave WINC due credit for making the document worthy of it. Domingo noted to Manley that Havana "provides the islands, especially Jamaica, with a basis for making demands" for greater self-rule. As for race, Domingo pointed out to Howard University history professor Rayford Logan the Declaration's fuller dimensions on the subject: "Mr. Hull was obliged, through our activity, to concede to black West Indians rights which up to now the Negroes of his State, Tennessee, have not gained."[60] In retrospect, Moore's claim about the U.S. agenda at Havana and about Stevens's influence on it overestimated his colleague's mission and misread ultimate U.S. designs. But it nonetheless showed West Indian determination to play a role in the devolution of authority in the Caribbean. Caribbean reformers knew that the greater U.S. presence could work against as well as for them. They were heartened to find the latter current surprisingly strong; Roberts, "pulling wires" to land post-Havana meetings with State Department officials, found them "all... impressed—indeed surprised—at the soundness of Jamaica's claim to recognition."[61] From well before the Nazi blitz, and especially after Havana, the expatriate activists recognized the changing balance of power. They were determined to play it to advantage: "in foreign relations," Roberts argued, "Jamaica's chief concern is, and always must be, the United States"—as both potential ally and potential threat.[62]

Manley focused on the latter, citing the Havana document as license for a U.S. presence that could become a takeover if Britain became too weak or preoccupied in Europe. He and his People's National Party (PNP) used the new circumstance to call for a nationalist movement capable of resisting the imposition of U.S. rule should it come.[63] The post-Blitz Havana Declaration, as an implicit acknowledgment of imperial weakness, provided a platform on which to raise the question of Caribbean freedom before the world. In addition, Havana offered activists a potential weapon against the British. The Declaration could be the thin wedge of a greater American presence that could help to displace an empire without replacing it.

WINC, while hardly a commanding influence on U.S. policy and Caribbean affairs, was but one of a dozen groups in New York carrying a torch for West Indian freedom. Their ties back home ran deeper than just emotional attachment. Their activities paralleled those of key colonial groups, in some cases sharing personnel. This was especially true of the JPL. The JPL midwifed Manley's PNP and acted as its mainland branch office. The League was also in some ways the parent of the more radical WINC; Domingo had served as JPL vice president before founding WINC in 1940. These and the other expatriate groups used the forums of black New York to promote West Indian independence.

However, the principal parties of Jamaica, to take that island as an example, varied in their expatriate ties. The PNP, and Bustamante's Jamaica Labour Party (JLP), defied easy ideological categorization. The latter party had greater numerical support at home, drawn mostly from the working masses and poorer, darker-skinned Jamaicans. It had its roots in the "umbrella" labor conglomerate Bustamante headed, the Bustamante Industrial Trades Union (BITU), whose member groups had played key roles in the 1938 unrest. Bustamante's leadership during that chaotic time had catapulted him to the top of the political scene. The BITU, and the JLP which spun off from it in 1943, did not attach any real political philosophy to its intensely localized, worker's rights agenda, and the larger-than-life personality who championed it. The PNP, by contrast, had a more cogent program, culled from Fabian socialism and strengthened by continuing internal debate. The PNP also had a more international profile. The New York JPL had raised funds and voices for the group, and Sir Stafford Cripps was present to bless the party's birth in September 1938. This international dimension owed to the cosmopolitan connections of its lighter-skinned leadership and its educated, middle-class base. The PNP also made nationalism central to its mission, which the Bustamante organization did not. Race was an issue for both parties, as each drew distinctions between itself and the white minority. However, class and charisma were more salient, as workers cheered Bustamante's fiery calls for change. Manley's socialist appeals drew more favor with educated Jamaicans. The labor conflicts of the 1930s, in short, inspired the formation of both the JLP and the PNP as the vessels of labor and the Left, respectively. The parties' different appeals to the working class—and to the West Indian diaspora—continued to define them.

It oversimplifies their differences to say that the JLP spoke to labor while the PNP tried to speak for it, but this distinction helps to explain the early history of both groups. A conflict between them was hardly preordained; indeed, early on, they were allies, as Manley and the PNP sought to weld the programmatic Left to Bustamante's organized labor. The alliance would descend into conflict during the war, although at the time of Havana, partnership carried the day. Their alliance notwithstanding, the PNP tended to have more success winning the sympathies and cash of mainland groups such as the JPL. The mainland contacts of the Bustamante side might have been more numerous—perhaps the majority of northward migrants were working-class West Indians of the type at the core of Bustamante's base—but were also more tenuous. PNP voters, more middle class and better educated, upon arriving in New York could draw upon a network of politically active countrymen and -women. It was this higher mainland profile that abetted their creation of the JPL and their cultivation of ties with their African-American counterparts.

Among other consequences, this meant that Harlem conversations about the struggle for black freedom often had a West Indian accent. This transnational dimension is a not uncommon feature—indeed, it was arguably a prerequisite—of twentieth-century black-consciousness movements. Just as, for example, the Antillean writer Aimé Césaire had to leave Martinique for metropolitan France before discovering *négritude*, British Caribbeans found their American sojourn a transformative experience. It transformed them, in a sense, from Bajans or Jamaicans or Grenadians into West Indians; the irony of displacement and relocation, James writes, was that "the most pan-Caribbean of Caribbean peoples are to be found in the Caribbean diaspora—not in the Caribbean itself."[64] Like their contemporary Afro-French counterparts in Paris, interwar West Indians landed in a broadly white milieu—but, importantly, one that encompassed a jelling cohort of African-Americans in the urban northeast. Activists there, particularly the NAACP and the NNC, had been paying attention to West Indian developments from well before Havana. Even without the expatriate presence, African-American organizations in New York would have rallied for West Indian freedom, as they did for African. In the wake of the Ethiopian crisis and Caribbean labor unrest, anti-imperialism had become central to African-American thinking on diplomacy. The Havana Declaration focused this impulse on the West Indies.

In the weeks after Havana, the situation in Europe grew yet more dire. British appeals for American aid took on added urgency as the Nazis approached English shores. In comparison, English-ruled shores in the western hemisphere were a lesser concern. British officials debated a spontaneous offer of bases to Washington, though the Colonial Office protested that this "would be the first step to U.S. domination in the Caribbean."[65] At the end of July, Churchill renewed his June request to Roosevelt for assistance, emphasizing the desperate need to reinforce the Royal Navy. To this end he asked Roosevelt for warships. While Roosevelt was eager to grant his wish, he was hampered by domestic political constraints.

The maneuvering that grew from this mix of British desperation, American hesitation, and colonial turmoil ended with the action that would fix American hegemony in the Caribbean. Facing re-election, Roosevelt had to tack carefully amid political and geopolitical squalls: anti-British and isolationist sentiment, the need to prevent both British collapse and Nazi aggression in the Atlantic, and the deteriorating situation in the Pacific. The president was convinced of the need to bolster Britain and prepare for war; he sought to do as much as possible, but had to do so largely behind the scenes. On August 1, a faction of the Committee to Defend America by Aiding the Allies recommended exchanging the requested warships for two concessions. The first was a British guarantee that the Fleet would under no circumstances be surrendered; the second, British base concessions in the western hemisphere. The next day, Roosevelt floated the idea to his Cabinet. After a month of haggling with Churchill and the Republicans over the terms and presentation of the exchange, the deal was closed.

The Bases-for-Destroyers Deal took the form of an exchange of notes between the British and American governments on September 2, 1940. As a solution to political and military problems in that crisis summer, the Deal was a stroke of genius. British trading of Atlantic base areas for antiquated American destroyers exchanged defense responsibilities London could not meet for war matériel Washington could not use. It also signaled British endorsement of the Havana Declaration, essentially inviting the United States to enforce it.[66] Like that document, the Deal took little account of opinion in the affected territories. Once again, West Indians' future had been decided over their heads. Roosevelt proclaimed "the most important...reinforcement of our national defense...since the Louisiana Purchase," while Churchill, though aware that Britain had gotten the short end of the deal, took comfort in the warships and more importantly in the ways in which the Caribbean abetted the "mix[ing] up together" of Anglo-American affairs.

Beyond its uncertain and potentially immense implications for American involvement in the European war, however, the Deal held even greater mystery in its hemispheric context. For one thing, the dust had hardly settled on the labor unrest; the region was in a state of flux. Compounding the uncertainty was the fact that trade contacts were few, as imperial preferences discouraged American business. Finally, although West Indians had added their voices to the diasporan dialogue, none had posts in Washington or the mainstream press from which they might publicly sway the Roosevelt administration. On its face, the Deal reflected the naked logic of American hegemony. In truth, it took place in a virtual intelligence vacuum, as the U.S. government knew little about the situation on the West Indian ground.[67]

To remedy this deficit, a member of FDR's "Brain Trust" long familiar with the Caribbean suggested a fact-finding tour. Charles W. Taussig, friend of Franklin and Eleanor Roosevelt, wrote to the President and Hull regarding the need for this mission.[68] Before joining the New Deal as director of the National Youth Administration, Taussig had served as president of the American Molasses Company, which had given him better knowledge of the Caribbean than almost any white American of his time. In fact, he had met with Roosevelt in early 1937 to warn him of the ongoing crisis in the region. At that time, he and fellow New Dealer—and future Puerto Rico Governor—Rexford Tugwell had just returned from a Caribbean tour in the wake of unrest in the British and American possessions. The trip convinced them of the serious regional crisis, as Taussig conveyed to the president; he and Tugwell reflected later that "our premonition of trouble to come" planted the seed of what would become, five years later, the Anglo-American Caribbean Commission (AACC).[69] In addition, as a New York City Democrat, Taussig had a keen awareness of the West Indian diaspora embedded in black America.

Taussig's knowledge of the islands partially compensated for the dearth of on-site intelligence. But what Taussig knew demanded that more be learned. He feared that "well-organized seditious activities, such as might originate in Europe," might shake British ability to maintain order—especially now that the Bases Deal obliged the United States to share security liabilities. If widespread unrest re-erupted and prompted U.S. intervention, "there would be consequent unfavorable repercussions in South America."[70] Moreover, any use of force to put down uprisings would be "unsound" if the social conditions that sparked them were not addressed. Taussig thus urged, in effect, an American Moyne Commission whose findings could be used to open joint discussions on improving conditions across the Caribbean.

This early suggestion of what would later become the AACC overshot the immediate objective—a better sense of the diplomatic dynamics in the post-riots, post-Deal region—but the idea of a mission found takers. Roosevelt forwarded Taussig's memo to the Navy brass with his endorsement. Undersecretary of State Sumner Welles and Hull agreed. The War and Navy Departments, Welles wrote, wanted to join the mission in order to reconnoiter base locations. Taussig's history, reputation, and contacts, Welles added, would mean the trip would attract minimal British suspicion while bridging a gap in U.S. intelligence.[71] Roosevelt approved the trip the day after receiving Welles's memo. A month later, he named Taussig head of an ad hoc commission to study the West Indies, with officers from the Army and Navy on board as well. Their itinerary included all of the British islands except Bermuda, and Puerto Rico and the Virgin Islands as well. Time and personnel constraints prevented the undertaking of Taussig's desired study of social and economic problems. The focus instead was on those features of the colonies that touched on American security interests.[72]

These, it bears mention, were very real. In the fall of 1940, British defeat remained a possibility, and one that would provoke American occupation of the islands. Taussig knew, however, that security interests were not the only ones in play. Also important were the racial and political dimensions that overlapped in Harlem, the "capital of the Caribbean." Before leaving, Taussig consulted with individuals conversant with the West Indian situation, including members of the black intelligentsia in New York, Washington, and Atlanta.[73] Taussig's efforts would pay dividends on his tour and would come to alter the scope of American policy.

Among those with whom Taussig consulted was Walter White, executive secretary of the National Association for the Advancement of Colored People. White was among the best-known African-Americans of the time. As the public face of the NAACP, he commanded attention throughout white and black America, as well as the larger African diaspora outside the United States.[74] White and his organization, though measured in their criticism of Roosevelt's foreign policy during the 1930s, had nonetheless taken clear and well-known stands on issues of race and colonialism. In consulting White and others, Taussig showed an awareness of the political and cultural contours of America's Caribbean situation. He also came to grasp that he personified the coincidence of U.S. policy and African-American–West Indian political interests. Such was the reputation of Taussig and his African-American "character witnesses" that some West Indians were shocked, upon meeting Taussig, to discover that he was white.

In his writings and appearances after the Bases Deal, White emphasized the heightened importance of the West Indies and race to American diplomacy, noting especially the damage done to America's reputation by its racial practices.[75] But White did not restrict himself to this message, nor to public efforts alone. When Taussig left for the islands, he carried a second document as important as his letter of appointment from FDR: a letter of introduction from White. The letter, intended for native leaders, praised Taussig's feel for the Caribbean and its people "irrespective of race or color…I urge you to talk frankly and freely with him."[76] This, White knew, "would permit [Taussig] to talk with some Negro leaders in the British Caribbean islands more frankly than if he were just another white American coming down there."[77]

Having his bona fides endorsed over White's signature opened doors for Taussig that he would otherwise have found closed as the head of an all-white team. For example, Jamaica's Manley was reputed to be suspicious of whites, whether British or American. Taussig might have come off as just another imperialist. That he did not owed to White's willingness to vouch for him. Taussig's consequent contacts with Manley and other West Indians allowed him to penetrate the official British line. This, in turn, would generate a more aggressive U.S. policy regarding reform in the British Caribbean.

The mission met with West Indians ranging from London-appointed officials to urban labor leaders to rural folk. All painted the dire poverty of the region, giving Taussig ammunition for his larger project of a joint commission. More urgent for the American mission, though, were the political, racial, and labor dynamics affecting the construction and future of the bases. All three matters were interlinked, indeed inseparable. The fact that these issues had an audience in the United States complicated the matter and lent weight to the words of figures, like Manley, who boasted minor celebrity abroad. In Jamaica and Trinidad, Taussig noted, labor leaders' contacts in the United States and Europe created "transmission belts" that might be used to coordinate subversive action against still-vulnerable U.S. installations.[78]

Even before the first brick was laid on the new bases, all parties realized that the political dynamics of the situation had become trilateral. Previous hands between island and crown leaders now dealt in a third player, the U.S. government. A fourth element—the black diaspora in Britain and the United States—acted as a wild card. Taussig reported that before the Bases Deal became public, prescient rumor had held that the United States would acquire bases in the British Caribbean. At that time, "West Indian negro leaders vigorously opposed the idea. Now that it is an accomplished fact, they have changed their policy." The leader of the CIO-affiliated Workers' Union in Trinidad, Adrian Rienzi, told Taussig that Trinidadians welcomed the Americans, in the hopes that it would lead to U.S. takeover of the islands and subsequently to their independence.

Taussig perceived the same sentiment in other colonies as well, although it did not strike him as spontaneous. Rather, it seemed a "well-discussed and studied policy [directed at] breaking the ties with the British Empire.... They feel that it would be easier to acquire their ultimate freedom from the United States."[79] Indeed, as Taussig wrote Welles,

> The general attitude...toward the U.S. is...so friendly in fact that under certain circumstances it could prove embarrassing. For instance: the important negro labor leaders in Trinidad told us that they felt that [West Indians] would be better off under the U.S. flag than under the British. In the event of any serious disturbances...it would not be surprising to see a substantial movement on the part of West Indian masses for the U.S. to annex [the colonies].[80]

To what extent this was simple flattery is unclear. Certainly, island leaders took this stance at least in part to gain leverage against the British. Yet their rationale went beyond a perceived shared principle of anticolonialism. They held a practical asset as well, which Taussig noted: "even a casual investigation [shows] that there is definite campaign in the West Indies for federation and self-government [whose] headquarters [are] in New York City."[81]

The Caribbean freedom movements and African-Americans animating this campaign shared the conviction that reform had to entail racial progress as well as political change. The imminent insertion of the Americans into the delicate and complex racial situation in the islands made this a concrete concern. A regime like that of the U.S. South, even if limited to the vicinity of the bases, would upset existing social arrangements and stain the American reputation. Such fears cooled enthusiasm for the arrival of the Yanks. Taussig noted that Rienzi and others voiced apprehension at the racial implications of the U.S. presence and expressed the hope that the worst could be avoided. The racial tightrope stretched highest over the labor situation in the islands where bases would be built. The disturbances of the late 1930s left open the threat of further disruption. American base construction seemed certain to unsettle pay scales, working conditions, and race relations in the wartime West Indies.

The promise of higher wages mixed with anxiety over Jim Crow in West Indian minds. Taussig emphasized the centrality of good labor relations not only to the completion of the bases but also to the future relationship "between the U.S. and the governments and peoples of the British West Indies."[82] To this end, he urged that base labor policy be drawn up in consultation with West Indian leaders. That policy, Taussig wrote, should include a uniform, elevated wage scale. The issue was important even absent the Americans; as Post notes, "[the war gave] impetus to the labour movement and its struggle for better conditions and higher wages."[83] At precisely that moment arrived the U.S. military, which could pay such wages. Thus, the U.S. presence would exacerbate a dynamic already in place. In addition, Taussig wrote that the policy should be carried out by American officials specially chosen for their racial sensitivity.

The American bases, then, were to host a West Indian variation on the Good Neighbor Policy.[84] Taussig's talks with a cross-section of islanders led him to recommend a reformist anticolonial stance to Roosevelt. In this plan, the United States would tacitly acknowledge its racial faults, redress them in the construction and conduct of its military presence, and cooperate with the British while competing with them for West Indians' allegiance. This last point was to be pursued by public efforts, including the creation of a joint commission, at raising the islands' standard of living. This, pointedly, incorporated Taussig's concern that Caribbean problems be treated regionally— that is, not only in British but American and other possessions as well.

British records disclose an awareness of the likely purpose of the Taussig mission. A tone of resistance, especially in the Colonial Office, leavened by resignation characterizes correspondence in its wake. "'[CO] feel strongly that these visits will produce a most unsettling effect on the islanders,'" although as Post notes, "if anything, the unsettling effect was on the British officials."[85] However, that effect was by no means universal. American and British officials shared concerns about the trinity of political, labor, and racial dynamics in the colonies. On the British side, reaction split between those who sought to assuage those concerns and those who sought to amplify them. In the latter category, one of the West Indian governors expressed his displeasure over a radio gaffe. He told Taussig acidly that he had heard an American announcer report on Roosevelt's December tour of the new "American *possessions* in the Caribbean [emphasis added]." Lord Lloyd of the Colonial Office ranted to the Cabinet that the United States was "bent on supplanting the British in the Caribbean....Privately, [he] was even more intemperate. 'These people are gangsters.'"[86]

Accentuating the positive, the governor of Jamaica reported that Taussig was "most anxious to fall in with [our] views and very open to receive advice...I stressed the need of great care avoiding colour and racial friction, [which he] appreciated."[87] Trinidad Governor Hubert Young reported that the island's Legislative Council accepted the need for allied cooperation and even welcomed some aspects of the Bases Deal. However, while Young concurred about the importance of the Deal "to U.S.–British relations [in] the coming century," he also urged inclusion of a Trinidadian voice.[88] This was an undetected omen; he warned against concluding a long-term agreement without the participation of the politically awakened colony, and he correctly foresaw future difficulty in the American choice of Chaguaramas as the site of its main facilities in Trinidad. Given the atmosphere of crisis,

however, these concerns were shunted aside. The coming American presence was certain; its ultimate impact was, as yet, not. In both islands, fears
of instability cohabited with hopes of gain. The "Panama precedent"—especially
the racist mistreatment and unjust wages received by West Indian laborers
on the Canal—lived on in the Caribbean grapevine.[89] Rumors in Jamaica
about base-work wages exerted a "disquieting effect" on the labor situation.
Trinidadian sacrifices for the Bases Deal, argued Governor Young, should be
reciprocated. As things stood, U.S. facilities would occupy thousands of acres
at sites spread throughout the island, the largest of which would block Trinidadians' access to their "recognized holiday area" at the beaches on the
Chaguaramas peninsula.[90] Young warned that uncertainty as to whether
they would be allowed to use the beaches, or the roads, rails, and other
infrastructure the bases would bring, risked engendering deep enmity among
the islanders.

Other British and colonial opinion took a skeptical, even hostile shape.
Part realism, part delusion, these views formed part of the larger Anglo-
American conflict over the future of Western empires. Impolitic Americans
stoked British suspicions. In Trinidad, where disputes over the size of the
leased areas rose to shouting volume, Young bemoaned the newcomers'
attitude: "Colonel Knox [said in the press] that 'the British West Indian possessions are going to be ours someday anyway by willing consent; and
I would not attempt to drive a hard bargain while Britain is fighting for her
life.'" Young was rightly nettled, given Trinidad's importance in the evolving
scheme. He wrote that "One [American] remarked...that it was commonly
said in [U.S.] military circles in that Trinidad represented forty out of the
fifty destroyers that had been handed over"—and this importance attached
not to defense of the empire but as a jumping-off point for [U.S.] operations
in the South Atlantic.[91]

The empire per se was not always the point of British pique; often, its
subjects were. The colonial secretary wrote after the Taussig mission to
describe "a fear [among] West Indians that...the bases will affect British
sovereignty [and] their cherished British nationality."[92] Islanders "are yet
most apprehensive of the [U.S.] arrival. This is due partly to a deep-seated
loyalty and attachment to British traditions, and not less to the fear that
American treatment of the Negro and coloured population will follow the
lines notorious in the [U.S.] South." Other writers seconded these concerns,
albeit usually without acknowledging the racial regime of the colonial status
quo.[93] Throughout the war and after, the British referred to American racial
problems in order to parry diplomatic moves against the empire. This was
seen as a way to disarm U.S. initiatives, whether these were expansionist
or just naive. American counterattacks on the comparatively fluid racism of
the colonial regime were rare. A fascinating double standard runs through
intra- and intergovernmental conversation on the subject: the British attack
American race relations on racial-justice grounds, while British-colonial
inequalities are blasted in the racially nonspecific language of self-determination.
On both sides, a certain pragmatism prevented race-based charges from

becoming paramount—perhaps reflecting an unspoken *entente* that both countries, as predominantly white nations ruling nonwhite peoples at home and abroad, must handle the issue with greatest care.

In any case, while the above British sentiments echoed Caribbean ambivalence regarding the racial implications of the Bases Deal, they were more than a bit off the mark concerning islanders' "deep-seated loyalty" considering the views of the latter on the usefulness of the United States as a tool against British rule. Post-Taussig British commentary underscored the significance of the cross-section of islanders with whom the mission met. This suggests the importance—and not only to the administration but to colonial reformers as well—of the mission's contacts in New York, which permitted a peek behind the colonial curtain and closed much of the intelligence gap.[94] This shaped Roosevelt's decision to conduct a policy conscious of its importance to West Indian independence, provided that it was also sufficiently racially sensitive to prove American good faith in both black New York—increasingly important to Democratic political calculations on the eve of Roosevelt's second re-election bid—and the Caribbean.

Taussig devised a plan to keep base construction going physically smoothly in the islands and politically smoothly at home. Supervisors were chosen for their ability to work with West Indian "negroes, who have an entirely different social and political status than in the U.S."[95] As for the personnel to be stationed at the bases, friction would be avoided by a pact with the colonial government: if servicemen broke local laws, they would fall under military jurisdiction, so as to avoid their cases being decided by black police or judges.[96] These and similar gestures smoothed the American military's inroads into the West Indies, albeit at the cost of allowing certain manifestations of Jim Crow, such as the jurisdiction question, into the islands. Given, however, that these were—by design— the extent of that regime and not a foretaste of its future expansion there, their result was to help keep an uneasy if unjust peace in the environs of the new U.S. facilities. The Taussig arrangements were, in a sense, an inoculation: they injected a racist double standard into criminal jurisdiction in hopes of preventing deeper, less curable race tensions over time.[97] As such, they offered what African-Americans and West Indians saw as a test case of American intentions that the United States could—however barely—pass.

Roosevelt was unusually sensitive to the ways in which U.S. actions would be watched. This owed partly to his New York roots and partly to his experience with the Haitian occupation, which as assistant secretary of the Navy, he had overseen. As president, he had ended it. Taussig wrote Welles that he had not suggested to the president that the race issue be defused from on high, but Roosevelt had "very definite ideas on this" gleaned from the Haiti experience— ideas in harmony with Taussig's recommendations—and had decided to preempt any problems by an order to the military. On March 19, Roosevelt instructed his Navy and War secretaries that U.S. representatives must be sensitive to local racial customs: "in acquiring bases, the U.S. faces...situations which many Americans refer to as the 'color line'.... Officers on duty in these [islands] must conform with the practice [there]."[98]

White, speaking on principle as well as for his West Indian compatriots, also made this point to Hull.[99] Everyone knew that America's racial reputation would precede it. Unlike the earlier episode in Haiti, however, the West Indies had a vocal community inside the United States. As Roberts wrote Edna Manley in early 1941, "I addressed the JPL in Harlem yesterday.... The group is very much alive and ready for positive action whenever that becomes practicable."[100] Moreover, both ends of the Harlem–Kingston axis were determined to keep that community energized. Domingo wrote Manley from New York that "out of self-interest West Indians need to keep close contacts with friends in this country, and Americans of color are our logical friends [especially since] considerable help and publicity can be had from organizations like the NAACP."[101]

Race was not paramount in determining post-Deal relations, but neither could it be ignored in imperial and diplomatic calculations. These, in early 1941, took place amid changed power realities. London's worst fantasies about American designs were not entirely groundless; Governor Tugwell wrote Interior Secretary Harold Ickes that the United States should immediately set up a "Caribbean Protectorate" over the European possessions before the metropoles' imminent fall made the Caribbean "not our third or fourth but our *first* line of defense."[102] The new context was inescapable, no matter how distasteful to the sentinels of George VI's empire. British power, dying by a thousand cuts since 1914, was at a deep ebb. American assertion in the Caribbean was in London's interest, and wiser British heads knew it.

Those fighting for West Indian independence saw the same prospect, but in a different light. In the British journal *Survey Graphic*, Roberts noted that between Havana and the Bases Deal, American dominion over the Caribbean was complete. Britain "no longer needed a military policy" for the region.[103] This, he feared, gave Britain an escape hatch. The expensive Moyne Commission reforms might well be jettisoned if British disengagement from the region continued in earnest. Moreover, this left open the door to U.S. annexation, a possibility that many West Indians suspected was already in progress. As late as July 1942, expatriates held a meeting in Harlem on the topic of "Will United States Take Over the West Indies?"[104]

Roberts suspected otherwise. Showing a keen grasp of American racial dynamics and of Good Neighbor rhetoric, he argued that Washington would not annex the islands because of U.S. reluctance to add to its black population. In addition, the "more articulate colonies" would keep pressing the issue of self-determination. This would test the Good Neighbor renunciation of intervention and the sincerity of U.S. Pan-Americanism as well. Roberts predicted American sovereignty over the smaller islands, and autonomy for Jamaica, Trinidad, and British Guiana. Where the Colonial Office saw the U.S. presence as an infringement of British rights, Roberts saw London using the Americans to shirk British responsibilities.[105]

Uncertainty over those "responsibilities"—what they were, who held them—was endemic in the Caribbean of the late 1930s and early 1940s. Labor turmoil had thrown the social and political future of the West Indies

into question. Before an answer could be found, war in Europe had introduced two new variables. One was the newly committed—and weakened—
imperial metropole. The other was the newly involved hegemon, seemingly
intent on more than just consolidation of its hemispheric power. In addition,
the wild card of the post-Ethiopia African diaspora, particularly the West
Indian population now well astir in black-activist America, ensured that race
would play a part in any new calculations. The U.S. presence, in short,
changed the strategic, political, and racial equation, in ways profound but
uncertain for the different agendas in play. The next few months, and four
years of war, would render them more concrete.

2

A More American Lake

The September 1940 exchange of notes formalizing the Bases Deal offers a convenient, and conventional, turning point in U.S.–British–West Indian relations. But it was an abstract one; the document itself changed little on the ground. A series of smaller developments aggregated in the middle months of 1941 to form a more concrete watershed. Some of these markers were physical and visible, such as the building of the bases. Others were less public, or mostly psychological: the pursuit of other strategic assets, the attempts to improve material life in the islands and to adjust their political status, and the transnational racial dynamics that coursed through all of the above. All, however, revealed the impact of the U.S. presence on the calculations of all parties—the United States, Britain, West Indians, and African-Americans—and consummated the changes hinted at in the prewar turbulence. This consummation, in turn, would shape the postwar drive to decolonization.

Three interlocking factors dominated America's Caribbean policy from 1941 through the death of Roosevelt. These might be called the "three R's" of his administration's Caribbean relations. The first—realism, or military-strategic concerns—encompassed bases, the submarine menace, the quest to develop and control vital regional resources such as oil and bauxite, and the securing of American hemispheric hegemony. The second, reformism, entailed the energetic but ultimately incomplete American-championed drive to remake the region socially, politically, and economically. Third was race. This factor was the most amorphous and most volatile, inseparable from the first two. The ensemble of the three shaped U.S. policy and wartime Anglo-American-Caribbean relations.

The war years revealed undercurrents in those relations that would come to deeply influence the islands' pursuit of nationalist independence and national identity, and would indeed reverberate through the broader decolonization process elsewhere. Washington's and London's tug-of-war over Jamaican bauxite, for example, presaged how strategic raw materials could cause the allies' postwar visions of both the international economy and national security to clash. That clash, in turn, could alter internal colonial dynamics, as West Indian nationalists staked their own claim in such disputes and thus affirmed that the Anglo-American concert would not alone shape the islands' future. In another consequence, U.S. reformism in the islands helped to nurture the idea of a regional federation, an idea then in its embryonic stage in British and West Indian minds. As a result, the West Indies would soon adopt an iteration of the federation model, of which a half-dozen would be built as vehicles for decolonization elsewhere in the British empire.

However, in other respects, the currents flowing through wartime U.S.–British–West Indian relations were peculiar to the region. U.S. intervention in the Caribbean littoral, for example, had historically far outpaced that in any other theater. Beyond this, the fact that both Britain and the United States were Caribbean landlords led them and their subjects into what might be called the game of "competitive colonialism." Each used its respective territories to point out the faults in, and exert pressure on, the other. The colonial subjects themselves were active players in this imperial one-upsmanship, recognizing the leverage it offered, and they were able to take advantage of island–mainland race networks to practice "diaspora diplomacy." No other area of the world had the unique combination of neighboring American and British colonies, with the latter's expatriate presence embedded in the former's mainland minority, and a joint vehicle—the Anglo-American Caribbean Commission (AACC)—for colonial reform. The impact of this combination would extend beyond the war years, influencing the U.S. vision of national security, the British conception of alliance and stewardship, and the diasporan imagination of progress, independence, and "national" solidarity.

Pot and Kettle on the AACC: Race, Reform, Anticolonialism, and the Puerto Rico Problem

As base negotiations and construction provided background noise, debate over Taussig's proposed commission highlighted developments in the spring of 1941. Between the March 27 Leased Bases Agreement and the August 14 Atlantic Charter, American focus on the Caribbean intensified. Negotiation of the U.S. leases affronted colonial officers, who fulminated about the arrogance of the Yanks. A joint commission seemed to them little more than the formalization of American authority in the West Indies. Jamaicans agreed; after the announcement of the commission the next year, one writer concluded that "the economic future of Jamaica [and] the West Indies, Self Government or no Self Government, is linked to the United States....The existence of the [AACC] more than suggests that."[1] The Colonial Office's determination to stonewall the AACC in its zygotic stage reflected a desire to protect imperial prerogative. It also exasperated Washington and the Foreign Office. Just when Lend-Lease brought the Atlantic alliance one step closer to fruition, the Colonial Office threatened to march it two steps back.

Taussig's rationale for a commission, which the president had adopted, held that political was inseparable from economic reform, and that Caribbean problems were not flag-specific but regional. Pooling resources would reduce overlap and costs. In meetings with Roosevelt and Welles, Lord Halifax—who supported the American initiative—correctly surmised two forces behind it, as subsequent Anglo-American conversations would demonstrate. The first was the president's set of "quite large ideas": eventual inclusion of the other colonial landlords, regional economic union, and "betterment of the natives."[2] This corresponded with the British vision, to a certain extent. A meeting between Taussig and Sir Frank Stockdale, Chairman of the British Fund for Development and Welfare, revealed the contours—and limits—of collaboration.[3] Setting aside for the moment the hypothetical possibility of French and Dutch participation, the meeting identified areas for joint attention. Taussig named several, including agriculture, land reform, and nutrition. This suggests the influence of the Americans' original "large ideas" laboratory: the New Deal decade at home. The domestic experiences of Roosevelt's Caribbeanists shaped their approaches to the region, as well as their view of Britain. Tugwell put it well to Ickes: "The Democratic Revolution must be agreed to by Britain—*as it has not been yet*....This war can only be won as a by-product of carrying the New Deal to the world."[4] The British had wondered with good reason about the strategic dimensions of American expansion; talk of reform was seen as window dressing. Yet it is important not to overlook the continuity of approach to social problems: Roosevelt's New Dealers, faced with such problems away from the mainland, brought with them mainland answers.

Stockdale demurred. The British agreed in the abstract that these issues needed progress, but London had not yet endorsed the principle of collaboration. Until it did, talks were toothless. Stockdale added that his own authority did not extend to policymaking. This was technically true of Taussig as well, a status belied by his zeal. American resolve thus contrasted with British reserve at this initial meeting, a pattern that recurred throughout the commission's early years.

Britain had its own, far smaller version of the second source that Halifax detected: the diasporan nexus in Harlem. New York West Indians, though, had an organizational advantage over their London cousins, in that they could join forces with homegrown groups. Welles spelled out the domestic ramifications to Halifax: "conditions in the West Indies are likely to become difficult [in case of war], and the Negro population in New York are likely to become troublesome in that event."[5] War had brought a strategic threat to the hemisphere, to be met by the bases; but the bases were also an opening through which to address the economic crisis of the area, either by goading the British into reforms or by finding the means by which the United States could introduce them. American efforts at reform were meant not only for the islands' welfare but were also directed at the islands' sons and daughters watching from New York, who increasingly voted Democratic.

These efforts thus stood, during the tensest months of 1941, at the intersection of American national-security needs and the transnational-racial axis connecting the colonies to the mainland. Welles was not exaggerating the ability of that axis to stoke unrest. When, for example, Governor Richards greeted Domingo's arrival in Jamaica by arresting him, on grounds that his activities would "undermine the public safety," a pro-Domingo rally in Harlem drew more than three hundred participants on short notice.[6] NAACP head Walter White lobbied U.S. officials on behalf of Domingo, who had come at Manley's invitation. The detention of Domingo, Bustamante, and other figures on similarly dubious grounds during the first half of the war primarily reflected internal colonial politics.[7] Yet all parties now understood that actions could not be confined to a given island. The dynamics of Caribbean affairs had changed. British authorities now confronted colonies that had the Americans' ear, thanks to the latter's presence in the islands and thanks to Harlem. Moreover, this community now had a link to FDR's zealous Caribbeanists on the nascent AACC through which future pressure could be applied. Where that pressure might lead was unclear, but Jamaicans such as Manley saw it as decisive: "America will decide our future status [at which time] 'self-government' will mean independence."[8]

White and his Caribbean compatriots kept the focus on race and reform in their contacts with Taussig, Welles, and Roosevelt. The Atlantic Charter, black representation on the AACC, and black American base labor animated their 1941 correspondence.[9] This pressure, along with reports from the islands as base construction continued that fall, kept the labor and racial aspects of the U.S. presence at the forefront of Roosevelt's concerns about the region. These overlapped with the thorny issue of criminal jurisdiction, as he and Taussig had foreseen and feared. Military police at Trinidad proved unable to oversee the troops, which left open the door for "coloured" native police and courts to arrest and judge Americans, while civilian base-workers fell under U.S. military jurisdiction, tempting friction. Roosevelt feared a "big flare-up" in these matters before construction ended.[10] Taussig had not abandoned the commission, reporting that he was being urged to pursue it by sympathetic voices in the islands: "Nothing much will be achieved unless pressure is kept up from your end."[11] The establishment of the State Department's Caribbean Office in October was a sign the pressure would continue—and could be a conveyor of the pressure that White, and black New York, were exerting on the administration.

The attack on Pearl Harbor intensified these dynamics and made progress urgent on both tracks of American policy in the Caribbean: short-term military construction and long-term socioeconomic reconstruction. The former, especially, was now paramount. Varied problems beset base construction. In most islands, "resentment and annoyance" were mounting, principally for race-related reasons, as "the delicate question of the color line [was] present." The clashes over jurisdiction—themselves the product of a number of violent, race-tinged incidents between U.S. servicemen and islanders—soured day-to-day relations on the West Indian ground, even if many incidents were kept out of the island press.[12] Nonetheless, neither these nor the heightened world crisis altered American plans for the AACC. On the contrary, from the American point of view, that entity was now indispensable. The war caused critical food and supply shortages in a region rich in neither in the best of times. Welles suggested to Halifax that the commission, though conceived as an advisory body, could facilitate supply distribution. For the Americans, this was a logical, crisis extension of the AACC's planned agenda. For the British, this reinforced suspicions about U.S. designs, as the Americans blithely sent the commission into relief work.[13] For West Indians, the immediate threat was starvation; the more symbolic threat was the AACC's failure to include an island voice. All parties, in short, hoped for something from the commission beyond what they would be likely to get. But given the dynamics of the Atlantic alliance, the expansion of American influence in the region, and the British need to persuade colonials to stick with the empire, the logic of collaboration grew irresistible.

However, American pressure could backfire. The Colonial Office and Churchill pointed out repeatedly that Washington too was an imperial landlord. In early discussion of the AACC, the Colonial Office saw it as a Trojan horse and demanded a counterbalance. "If there is to be [this] infiltration in our possessions...shouldn't it include [Puerto Rico]?" The Americans agreed, even though this left them vulnerable, a fact not lost on British officials: "the Puerto Rico situation is so embarrassing politically that [Washington] can...be blackmailed."[14] The AACC provided a forum for such blackmail, in the form of one-upsmanship between rival colonialisms. In arguing for publication of the Moyne report, for example, one British official remarked that "the Puerto Rico reports published by the Americans show equally bad, or worse, conditions there. [Publication will] leave a real credit balance on our side [as] we have been tending to fall behind the Americans in public attention to West Indian problems."[15]

This clash of colonialisms thus had the salutary effect of raising imperial self-consciousness on both sides of the Atlantic—and of raising the stakes of reform by including the issue of political change. Roosevelt's specialists knew this and lobbied for reform in Puerto Rico as proof of U.S. resolve, urging an elective governorship there as a statement to the world:

> Such a move...would clearly show that the United States has no ambitions to be a colonial Power, and desires only to establish the freedom and well-being of peoples.... [This] is submitted as a suggestion, indeed more for its general than for its local effect. All subject peoples in the world ought to be stirred by its implications.[16]

While other factors also contributed to changes in Puerto Rican status, the world's attention to the comparative American and British treatment of their respective colonies played a key role. Taussig and Tugwell recognized that world opinion had come to view such treatment as an acid test of U.S. and British intentions for the organization of the postwar world.

Such attention did not always strike against the British empire. U.S. officials of an anti-British and anticolonial persuasion, such as Senator Robert Taft, were chastened by a wartime visit to America's imperial outpost, where the alleged misgovernment of Tugwell offered a target to critics of the New Deal. Yet their trip had an unexpected impact. To the hail-Britannia sentries of empire, it seemed quite a boon. "[Puerto Rico] has caused [Taft] doubts...as to whether the U.S. are as fully entitled to preach on colonial matters...Taft [was] very much perturbed at this quantitatively small but qualitatively large beam in the American eye." Roosevelt was found to share this pique with his critics: he had "that righteous and defensive attitude which the US maintains in its adventure in imperialism, [asserting] that wages [and literacy were better] in Puerto Rico...than in any other island of the Caribbean."[17] As an empirical matter, Roosevelt was right. As later confirmed in the still-unpublished Moyne report, in the British Caribbean, life expectancy, unemployment, infant mortality, and most other indices of societal well-being fared worse than in Puerto Rico. Neither was the vacation paradise of more recent imagination—and the very relative superiority of the American colony underscored the Americans' case for urgent and collective action on this largely shared state of affairs.

The announcement of the AACC in March 1942 sought to channel these tensions constructively—or at least to hide them behind an ostensibly unified push for reform. Yet the invocation of American and British responsibility for island conditions brought up uncomfortable realities of power. Roosevelt had been urged from early on to state a disclaimer regarding U.S. intentions, which he ultimately did: "the United States does not seek sovereignty over the...colonies where the bases are located."[18] Although the AACC claimed to bring the allies together as equals, the absence of a comparable British disclaimer spoke volumes. True, London had not gained bases in Puerto Rico, so without the possibility of British encroachment, no disclaimer was technically necessary. Still, the commission joined allies who were not exactly equals.

The urgent need for that power became evident in the first half of 1942. Threats mounted in kind and degree. Submarine attacks were commonplace; up to fifteen U-boats were operating in the area by mid-year. Indeed, what is conventionally known as the Battle of the Atlantic could easily add the phrase "and of the Caribbean" to its title. Smoke plumes from sinking ships could regularly be seen from Caribbean beaches. Historian Fitzroy Baptiste notes that "in 1942–1943 a 150-mile strip around Trinidad suffered the greatest concentration of shipping losses experienced anywhere during World War II."[19] The plumes, of course, signaled different things to islanders than to the Americans. For the latter, every ship sunk was an Axis boot mark on the Monroe Doctrine. For the former, the sinkings meant a diet more meager with each ship lost. On shore, the Nazi menace often had a human face; consulate records track U.S.- and foreign-born Bundists plotting sabotage. The French islands were thought to be seedbeds of subversion, and officials watched for signs the Nazis were using *les Antilles* to refuel their submarines.[20] The U.S. bases seemed particularly vulnerable both to naval attack and internal subversion.

As U.S. servicemen took up their stations, the AACC began deliberations— and, to the irritation of the British, action. The food and supply situation in the islands had grown desperate. Inadequate storage and export agriculture left most islands, American included, with less than thirty days' food supply. The AACC met for the first time that spring. Prodded by Taussig, the commission agreed that supply officers from both countries should meet post-haste to organize emergency supply routes. This addressed the immediate problem, although complete resolution would await victory in the Battle of the Atlantic in spring 1943.

Yet, as the British had feared, Taussig and his colleagues saw the commission's relief work as a door to larger initiatives. Taussig wrote Welles that to meet basic needs, the colonies should at once convert one-third of sugar lands to food production. Since they "are not likely to adequately curtail their sugar crop" on their own, the United States, he argued, should use the War Shipping Administration to compel it.[21] Welles, perhaps playing the good cop, forwarded Taussig's letter to Halifax. It confirmed what Taussig's British counterpart, Stockdale, suspected: the latter's report on the AACC's first meeting expressed "alarm at...U.S. enthusiasm" for broad social reforms.[22] The October 1942 Washington visit of Colonial Undersecretary Sir George Gater proved that Stockdale's alarm had been well-founded, erasing any British doubt that Taussig's zeal had Roosevelt's approval.[23] The U.S. troops and bases were the most obvious example of the new American presence in the British Caribbean. But behind the scenes, at the diplomatic negotiating table, it was the AACC that loomed large. The commission embodied the New Deal reformism that Washington sought to export to the Caribbean—a dynamic just as palpable if not as visible as the U.S. military presence.

Both felt the powerful gravity of the third "R" of Roosevelt's Caribbean relations: race. The war raised racial issues on a global stage, recasting relations within and among countries, colors, and peoples.[24] But the Caribbean bases revealed race's particular gravity in U.S.–West Indian affairs. Base construction employed nonwhite labor and brought soldiers into contact with locals. Construction, to everyone's relief, went more or less smoothly. This was in part thanks to the suppression of news of those individual islander– mainlander conflicts that ended in violence, and in spite of PNP efforts to exploit the Yankee presence—including its racial overtones—in the party's increasingly vocal push for self-government. These maneuvers, combined with the worsening submarine and supply crisis, and with the intensified JLP–PNP conflict that followed Bustamante's February release from detention, created an atmosphere of crisis in Jamaica that lasted throughout 1942.[25]

In this atmosphere, American racial liabilities loomed large. The contentious matter of legal jurisdiction, for example, came to a head several times. On one occasion, a melee between U.S. civilians and Jamaican constables led to the arrest of some Americans, sparking retaliation. The U.S. base commander wrote the consul that "prompt prosecution of the guilty Americans [is] essential to curb...a serious race problem." The consul agreed, advising Washington that "the color question is becoming more acute in Kingston, and that agitators are becoming more active."[26] The U.S. Chief of Naval Operations in Jamaica voiced his anxieties to Washington:

> The natives are unruly, very anti-government, and anti-American...Violence and bloodshed [is] feared. The blacks [say] they will try to overthrow the government [and] do away with all the whites...US nationals are not contributing factors to this [but since they] represent a form of power any one of them could easily become a victim...Very serious trouble is definitely brewing [in] Jamaica.[27]

The writer suspected Axis or communist agents, believed to be at work in Trinidad as well: "Race propaganda...has [circulated] that this is a war of races in which the negro or the indian [will] derive no benefit from a victory of the United Nations...while he might expect to derive substantial benefits from a Japanese victory."[28] Axis agents were likely at work in the islands, although they constituted a minor feature of a stormy political scene. Wiser Americans knew that West Indians needed no prodding to be suspicious of the United States' true racial colors. Supervision at the bases could not prevent all incidents. No platitudes could erase West Indian knowledge of the mainland racial regime. In time of crisis, race could become the spark in this volatile social and psychological mix. When Taussig reported to the president that the important thing was not how many incidents there had been but rather how few—few enough that progress toward U.S. objectives had proceeded as planned, and that island leaders felt that these were "just incidents" and not an expression of policy—he was arguing determinedly for a glass half-full.[29]

Race, of course, was not the only element in play at ground level in the islands. Much of the time, it was not even the chief factor shaping colonial politics. However, it was inescapable in U.S.–West Indian relations. In part this owed to Jim Crow but also to something else: the success of West Indians in the United States and their cooperation with African-Americans. As Eric Williams put it, "the people of the Caribbean are vitally aware of American Negroes [and] are keenly interested in the NAACP....All over the Caribbean you hear the same refrain: 'We need some organization like the NAACP here.'"[30] These ties, though, created tensions of their own. Although united on the need to end imperial rule, native-born and West Indian blacks in America splintered along ideological and even island lines. African-Americans such as Walter White served as conduits for West Indian pressure on the Roosevelt administration, magnifying that pressure by adding NAACP support to it. But African-Americans and West Indians often had different ideas about how, precisely, the push for West Indian freedom should proceed.

The AACC highlighted this divide. Taussig secured the appointment of two persons of color to the Caribbean Advisory Committee to the U.S. section of the

AACC, Martin Travieso of Puerto Rico and William Hastie of Howard Law School. Roosevelt had named Hastie federal judge in the Virgin Islands in 1937, in reply to British appointment of West Indians to the colonial bench. As an African-American with Caribbean experience, Hastie was an obvious choice. Although the request for a black presence on the AACC proper had not been met, the NAACP—with whom Hastie had a long affiliation, serving both on the organization's Board of Directors and on its Committee on Administration—was satisfied.

This was decidedly not the case for West Indians in the United States. Reaction to the appointment was sufficiently inflamed to bridge ideological chasms in the community. Prominent Trinidadian expatriate Dr. Charles Petioni, a charter member of WINC, had sought to stop what he saw as his organization's slide to communism by breaking away to form an anticommunist rival, the American West Indian Association (AWIA). The Hastie appointment fused the two factions in common cause, and jointly they submitted a list of West Indian candidates to take the place of Hastie.[31] That Hastie was black, knew the Caribbean, and enjoyed indirect access to the president was insufficient. True representation attached not broadly to race but narrowly to birth. The expatriates failed to change Taussig's mind; Hastie remained, and indeed would be appointed to the AACC proper after the war. His posting to the Advisory Committee suggests the limits of race as an influence on U.S.–Caribbean affairs. Taussig no doubt congratulated himself for bringing non-Anglo-Americans on board. White did not protest the naming of an African-American over a West Indian; a nonwhite had been included, and an influential one at that, considering Hastie's status within the NAACP. Petioni and the New York Caribbeans were left with half of their request for a black islander fulfilled.

This turn of events surely came as a relief to London; given earlier American actions, the British had reason to wonder how far the United States would go to mollify Harlem. The British understood the racial dynamic facing the Roosevelt administration and the greater import it carried in America than Britain. At times, they sought to exploit it; Jim Crow was, after all, an easy way to score points off the "land of the free," even when British officials compared their colonial racial record with that in the United States:

> The relations of white [with black] Americans have been far from happy and although ours have not been marked by any very constructive solicitude for the physical welfare of the coloured peoples of the West Indies, they have been conducted with less in the way of offensive [racial] discrimination and less restriction of liberty than has been the case in large areas of the U.S.[32]

While the British did not always distinguish African-American from West Indian expatriate influences when it came to racial matters, they did perceive that the colonial battle was joined on a number of fronts: against the U.S. government, against West Indian activists, and against their black American allies.

In British eyes, the first of these fronts was by far the most important. A spirited debate between the Colonial and Foreign Offices in 1942 centered on the need to check American anticolonialism. The Colonial Office chafed at the American tendency to "intervene" in island affairs, via the AACC and an ambiguous military jurisdiction. These impugned crown authority, whose "exclusive business" the islands were.[33] The Foreign Office balked. This attitude, they felt, risked endangering allied relations by feeding U.S. doubts. A Foreign Office analyst argued for cooperation: "we have to get along with the Americans; the future of the colonial empire largely depends on our doing so."[34] The Colonial Office also denied the reasonable premise that cooperation might bring regional gains. Both offices agreed that the immediate problem was one of public relations, specifically the need to win over prominent, skeptical Americans such as Wendell Willkie.

Moreover, the United States, through unilateral action in its own colonies and on the AACC, could always one-up the British. The promise of an elective governorship for Puerto Rico that summer was a recent such trump, attracting praise in the British press.[35] The British knew also that in addition to pressure from Harlem, Washington faced growing anticolonial sentiment among the public throughout 1942. The Churchill government thus sought to engage the United States in ways that would blunt American thrusts at reform, project the good faith of British efforts at the same, equalize the standings in U.S. and world opinion, and maintain London's freedom to maneuver within the Indies. The British looked for ways to achieve their objectives, particularly around Gater's invitation to Taussig to visit London that autumn. The naming of Oliver Stanley as colonial secretary was one such way. Although Stanley's urbanity led many to false assumptions about his flexibility on colonial questions, he in fact took a hard-line on preserving the empire. Welles was not taken in. He warned Taussig that Stanley was "'the most narrow, bigoted, reactionary Tory,' that he had met." Welles saw the appointment as a sign of Churchill's determination "to dominate postwar planning...along reactionary lines."[36]

Taussig's talks with Stanley and Churchill seemed to bear this out. These reproduced in miniature the larger philosophical divide within the AACC: British insistence on dictating social and economic improvements, and on the separation of these from political reform; American response that the three were inseparable and must be addressed accordingly. Taussig pressed the British to act on the Moyne recommendations and to spend more money on colonial welfare, as first steps toward a more sweeping reform of the colonial regime. He argued that such change was vital, as was the need for it to be dictated from London, since the more reactionary island governments would likely refuse to enact points agreed upon by the allied conference.[37]

The colonial secretary parried Taussig's efforts. He urged proceeding gently, given certain of the "reactionary" colonies' constitutional arrangements, and for fear of provoking secession of any of the British West Indian territories in time of war. He acknowledged U.S. concerns and admitted anxiety over Jamaica, "the most dangerous situation in the West Indies," in part due to the Jamaican presence in New York. Indeed, Jamaica was second only to India in damaging Anglo-American relations. As the Labourite founder of the Fabian Colonial Bureau Arthur Creech-Jones reported of the Stanley–Taussig talks, "it seems to be the view of the Americans that we are not moving fast enough...in the West Indies, and the views of [FDR] are emphatic...Clearly he wants to see an [extended] franchise and more self-government....The way in which [Richards and Jamaica] feeds our critics in America [is] astonishing."[38] Stanley also acknowledged the legitimacy of American concern and of allied cooperation. This point echoed Taussig's conversation with Churchill, for whom cooperation served the larger goal of intertwining British with American interests. Otherwise, Churchill gave even less ground than Stanley—perhaps unsurprising, given that a month earlier, the prime minister had famously said that he did not intend "to preside over the liquidation of the British Empire." He spoke of plans to "take care of our colonies" after the war, but within the context of a stout defense of the empire and a continued refusal to apply the Atlantic Charter outside of Europe.[39]

The London conference also revealed a more inviting landscape than the United States had previously perceived. Contact with a variety of officials brought to light a diversity of views that offset Colonial Office intransigence, belying the stolid face of imperial resistance and helping to generate agreement on key points. To Taussig's surprise, London agreed to reforms even broader than those endorsed by the Moyne Commission on such important issues as economic reorganization and political reform. The underlying consensus was that they should be addressed on a regional basis, thus endorsing the American vision of the AACC. Political reform was to take the form of a new constitution for Jamaica and the recall of Governor Richards. The Taussig visit also produced agreement on a series of AACC-sponsored "Caribbean Conferences." The conferences would include colonial representatives, would eventually administer some of the regional services discussed at the London meeting, and would midwife a regional federation, "which is, or should be," the Colonial Office averred, "the objective of our longterm policy."[40] The London meeting thus brought British and American views into closer alignment than Taussig had thought possible. Churchill's bluster notwithstanding, the prospects for cooperation seemed greater, and the complications fewer, than had previously been the case.[41]

The same could not be said when it came to race and colonialism in American policy, where the complications seemed to multiply. A British investigation of American anticolonialism, launched after the London meeting, found that the two sides of the north Atlantic had more in common than most Americans admitted: the "obvious analogy" of a fundamentally racist and largely shared white man's burden in both U.S. and British colonial holdings.[42] But both U.S. and British colonial subjects themselves disagreed. Challenging the obvious analogy, they discerned differences that could be put to better tactical use against their respective landlords. West Indians rallied in particular to Puerto Rico in pressing for change, arguing that the island manifested the "superior" brand of American colonialism. As a sympathetic British editorial put it, "with the American example before them popular reform movements in Jamaica [and] Trinidad will become even more active and the British response will be a test of British sincerity."[43] Part of that response came with the March 1943 announcement of the new Jamaican constitution, to take effect the following year. Activists such as Domingo had made explicit the influence of the American island's example, having argued for years that the revised charter "must make provision for adult suffrage. The Americans gave it to the Puerto Ricans who were more illiterate than Jamaicans are today."[44] If Puerto Rico had become a spark for reform efforts, though, it also brought to light lingering issues of race, region, and colonialism.

Following Roosevelt's directive to avoid racial conflict, some of the garrisons, such as that stationed at Trinidad, included African-American units. Even if it helped to keep Jim Crow out of U.S.–island relations, this strategy created other local misgivings. Colonial authorities doubted the black soldiers' military competence in case of attack; Trinidadian men saw them as rivals for the affections of local women.[45] By 1943, the British were appealing to Washington to remove the black troops. Washington replied that they would be replaced with Puerto Rican units that fall. This made the British even more nervous. Puerto Rican troops, they feared, would prompt West Indians to ask why nonwhite U.S. Caribbeans were defending islands whose own nonwhite natives were discouraged from local service. Why, in short, could American but not British colonials defend British colonies? Nor could complex racial and regional aspects be ignored. To U.S. policy-makers, Puerto Rican soldiers were neither black nor white but were brethren to West Indians by virtue of geography. Puerto Rican troops would personify both the progressiveness of U.S. policy and the regional unity of the Caribbean. The British did not want the troops for the same reason. Puerto Ricans had a complicated relationship with race; as one observer noted, "[they] think of themselves as white Latins and not as colored colonials."[46] They and West Indians felt much more the racial, linguistic, and cultural differences between them than any kinship based on a shared latitude.

British correspondence makes this plain. The governor told London that "Puerto Ricans would not get on well with the local population [in part because] they...think themselves white. True they were better than American coloured troops, but only because of the very low standard of the latter."[47] Nor were such views limited to Trinidad. U.S. officials solicited British reaction to the idea of Puerto Rican troops in Jamaica, in hopes of deploying them there. That reaction was blunt: "[it would be] a public calamity [raising] every sort of political, social, and racial problem." The British noted the hypocrisy of the U.S. position: "in Puerto Rico itself there is no proposal to replace white troops, despite the new proposal to give [the island] independence."[48] The issue simmered throughout 1943. Washington and London finally agreed to limit Puerto Rican troops to select colonies, with deployments to be agreed upon in advance. British fears turned out to be baseless; in 1945, Halifax noted that despite "CO [fears], the troops got on perfectly well with the local inhabitants."[49] The dispute was an instructive microcosm of the AACC's crosscurrents of race and "competitive colonialism." These coursed through both the commission's long-term agenda and its short-term addressing of the region's security crisis, the latter coming to a conclusion in early 1943.

Moments of Truth? The AACC, the End of the Security Crisis, and the Jamaican Election

By the summer of 1943, Caribbean uncertainties multiplied even as the regional security crisis waned. Military successes had neutralized the submarine threat, and the AACC's management of food and supply distribution prevented wartime deprivations from deteriorating into worse. The replacement of Richards by Sir John Huggins, followed by the release of Domingo and other "subversives," won U.S. approval and went a long way toward calming the political currents in Jamaica—although the new governor did not universally impress, as Tugwell put it: "His mind is one big cliché of orthodox opinion."[50] However, success in staving off dangers such as the supply crisis dampened reformist urgency. In part this dampening also owed to a growing confluence of American and British views on the future of the empire, as Washington began looking to London as an anchor of postwar stability. The channeling of anticolonial zeal into the AACC bureaucracy, and the turned tides of war, further contributed to the change; accommodation of the colonial regime, not activism against it, seemed to take root. As Tugwell dejectedly put it, "Perhaps I was wrong. Colonialism may not be over" after all.[51]

However, the drop in reform activity can be overstated. To a considerable extent, change had been institutionalized during the window of opportunity early in the war. This had been a daunting task; "sovereignty in the [Caribbean] was spread out under fifteen flags. In Washington alone [a dozen] agencies [had] jurisdictional responsibilities."[52] Now, however, both the United States in Puerto Rico and Britain in Jamaica had committed to change. This progress in itself diverted anti-imperial energies. "As Jamaica prepares for its first election under universal suffrage," wrote analyst Paul Blanshard, "[one result] is the temporary subordination of imperialism vs. Self government as an issue in local politics."[53] The AACC, although advisory and slowed by a lack of British enthusiasm now that the security crisis had passed, had a solid reputation and an open-ended mandate. It was also sufficiently visible to be cited as a model of postwar allied cooperation and organization at the Casablanca conference.[54] Even as options such as a customs union were discarded, the idea of cooperation had found an institutional home. The West Indian Conference, set for the following year, promised to bring at least some native representation to the table. If Washington, London, and some West Indian actors scaled down calls for reform, it was because change was no longer being forced at the point of a U-boat gun or of a stevedore's hook, but rather that of a commissioner's gavel.

To the extent that the United States retained its anticolonial vigor, it did so thanks to Taussig and Roosevelt—and to black activists on the mainland who kept up the fight. Taussig pressed for further Puerto Rican reform in light of the Jamaican constitutional revision; the two islands were by now unquestionably pawns in a game of competitive colonialism. Taussig's tenacity stood out. Even though, as Roosevelt remarked in June 1943, "[the British are] impossible [and] we are getting nowhere with [them] on Colonial postwar policy, [he] expressed pleasure with the progress being made in the Caribbean and remarked that [Taussig] seemed to be the only official making any progress with the British in the postwar Colonial field."[55]

Taussig also continued efforts to involve blacks on the mainland in commission work. In addition to Harlem, a second nucleus of activism emerged at Howard University.[56] In addition to Hastie, there were several faculty members with roots or experience in the Caribbean: Rayford Logan, Ralph Bunche, and Eric Williams, AACC researcher and future first prime minister of Trinidad and Tobago. Taussig enlisted Logan to convene a Howard Advisory Committee to the AACC, whose assignments included advising the Office of War Information on a series of radio programs. Theirs was a delicate task. Committee members were wary of being maneuvered into endorsing American racial practices, but shared the conviction that the United States could provide a better model than British colonialism and even induce the latter's eventual eviction.[57]

A mid-1943 Howard conference on the Caribbean brought diasporan conflicts over Britain's eventual eviction from the islands to the fore, pointing to the limits of transnational solidarity.[58] But if African-American and West Indian activists and intellectuals differed on the specifics of decolonization, they found easy agreement on key overarching issues. One of these was the need to keep Jim Crow out of the islands. Another was the expectation that the hemispheric black diaspora would have even closer relations as a result of the war and continue working together for an end to empire. West Indians felt that these transnational black ties held a particular importance: they provided space in which nationalism could continue to mature. At the Howard conference, Petioni stated that "the movement for [West Indian] independence would have to find its leadership among colored British West Indians in the US." He thereby articulated what many along the Kingston–Harlem axis already believed: differences aside, diasporan cooperation was crucial to colonial independence.[59]

This cooperation was not equally balanced, however; West Indians needed African-Americans' sympathy more than African-Americans needed theirs. The contacts and resources of Harlem were seen as vital to success in the islands, as was black American support. In Norman Manley's words to a mainland audience, "the inspiration that we have received from our brethren in this great democracy has been of invaluable aid in our struggle for self-determination." Nor was it only nonwhite Americans who inspired; Manley went on to proclaim that "we in Jamaica [and] the whole empire of coloured peoples…may draw strength in our movement from what is happening in the rest of the world."[60] However, unlike the broader Third World, the black mainland supplied the West Indies with both moral and financial support. West Indians reciprocated in what ways they could. Showing their interest in the transnational connection—and their determination that such ties could advance the cause of self-rule—Afro-Trinidadian residents of one area of Port of Spain renamed their neighborhood "Harlem" in tribute to the diasporan currents coursing through the American metropolis.[61]

Washington took note. The 1943 wave of race riots in Detroit and other mainland cities prompted the government to pay closer attention to racial links abroad, for fear that "outside" connections might be fomenting the trouble. This included an expatriate community excited that the Jamaican constitution might spur further reform. The new constitution was, in Blanshard's words, "the most important step toward democracy in the whole history of the West Indies." Moreover, Caribbean observers gave the United States credit for the reforms; "it is generally known here," reported Blanshard, "that President Roosevelt stands for more democracy in the West Indies."[62] Expatriates, islanders, and their allies kept up efforts to leverage this American support: "It is reasonable to assume that the increasing interest of [the U.S.] government and of individual American citizens in the welfare of the West Indies has...stimulated the citizens of British Caribbean possessions to petition for greater degrees of self-goverment."[63]

The "stimulation," though, carried a cost. The year 1943 saw U.S. authorities further scrutinize those groups, both African-American and expatriate, involved with West Indian affairs.[64] American surveillance identified two 1944 rallying points for these activities. The first was the AACC's inaugural West Indian Conference, held in March in Barbados. The conference revealed more about the geopolitical than the racial contours of the Anglo-American-Caribbean situation, as it contrasted competing U.S. and British colonial reforms. The Colonial Office, moreover, continued to view the AACC at Barbados as elsewhere as "a cover for the extension of US influence in the West Indies."[65] They missed, or ignored, the fact that American proposals more often than not were in tune with those of African diasporan activists—partly a consequence of their transnational connections, and of their contacts with officials such as Taussig.

The U.S. report on the conference contained three pleasant surprises. One—the shadow of Jim Crow notwithstanding—was the popularity of the United States, which "West Indians [saw] as a moral force for improving Caribbean conditions."[66] Also surprising were the divisions among West Indians. Any observable solidarity seemed more anti-British than pro-Caribbean. The U.S. delegation, which included Hastie and several Puerto Ricans, displayed much greater unity. The Puerto Ricans in some respects held greater symbolic value than did Hastie. Hastie was black, but the Puerto Ricans were islanders and were treated as apparent equals by the U.S. delegation, with no restrictions of speech or selection, unlike the British side, whose colonial delegates were chaperoned at every point.

The third surprise was precisely this hoped-for contrast between the two powers. The U.S. colonials had the desired effect; they embodied the contrast between British and American ideas of island "representation." This frustrated British officials' hope that the conference would teach the Americans how difficult colonial administration was, and thus temper their anti-colonialism. The U.S. Embassy in London reported that "the impact...of the Puerto Rican[s would] be felt for a long time, both as to the West Indian people in general, and as to the men in control, in particular....Reaction to all Puerto Rican delegates was excellent [out of] great respect for Puerto Rico as a more advanced dependency than British ones."[67] Even adjusting for the note of self-congratulation, there was little doubt that West Indians and Puerto Ricans regarded the competing colonialisms with interest.

The British counterpoint to Puerto Rican progress was the new Jamaican constitution, set to take effect in late 1944. The charter would be the first in West Indian history to grant universal suffrage, expanding the electorate tenfold overnight. As a result, the election spurred intense fighting between Manley's PNP and Bustamante's JLP. The prize was no longer the mere title of "native leader," worthy of consultation by the crown, but elected office in a government moving—albeit slowly—toward independence.

The JLP had the numerical advantage, given the charismatic Bustamante's appeal to rural and urban-labor voters. Manley, however, had an asset to counter this, thanks to his contacts among expatriates and African-American sympathizers on the mainland. Beginning in 1943, Manley's party met "our critical need" for funds this way, raising about one thousand dollars a year through Harlem.[68] As important as the money was the forum Harlem offered. At times Manley came to the United States to make appearances, usually accompanied by prominent African-Americans. At others, his allies used the New York press to lobby a world audience, as well as the expatriate community; as Walter McFarlane of the Kingston JPL put it, "[the New York] League is the most efficient body through which the...West Indian element can be reached in the U.S., and [it is] expected to play a distinctive part in this big game." This outlet was crucial because of the restrictions colonial authorities could place on protest. Moral and monetary support from the black mainland bolstered Manley's chances in Jamaica's first election under the new constitution.[69] In the end, though, these funds were not enough; the PNP was crushed, and Manley himself failed to win a seat. The JLP beat the PNP two to one, a result that, as George Padmore acknowledged in a letter to C. L. R. James, confirmed Bustamante as a "national hero."[70]

The U.S. consul noted that much of the campaign was "based on the color question, [on] 'Jamaica for the Jamaicans.'" The PNP defeat was attributed to its "avowal of socialism."[71] Bustamante biographer George Eaton noted the "deep-seated fears...that a victory for the independence party would mean 'brown-man' (middle-class) government and continuing enslavement of the masses."[72] A key dimension of the election, however, reached beyond Jamaica, as the contest confirmed that transnational black ties were strong, varied, and anchored in New York. New surveillance suggested their implications for U.S. foreign policy. In late 1943, intelligence in the West Indies and New York began to provide a fuller picture of these diasporan links.[73]

The intelligence indicated that race activism was rising. The irony was rich. London, Washington, and the West Indies had all feared that U.S. bases would provoke racial strife in the islands, but island–base relations were "generally excellent." Aside from bar fights and *faux pas*, such as the U.S.O. help-wanted ad seeking a "white female," interactions were peaceful if not always friendly.[74] Where the bases had sparked racial activism was back on the mainland. Washington launched a series of public-relations maneuvers aimed at calming tensions, including the First Lady's 1944 tour of the islands, the killing of a House bill for their annexation, and an expansion of the farm-labor program that brought West Indians to the United States.[75]

These gestures did not satisfy diasporan calls for change. Moreover, such calls came increasingly from the Left. Activists, for example, continued to attach great importance to the absence of a West Indian on the AACC. H. P. Osborne of WINC reiterated the call in *Congress Vue*, an NNC publication whose editorial board read like a who's who of the black Left. The article caught the attention of the FBI, which was monitoring WINC and the NNC. This vigilance also netted word of a WINC fundraiser for the PNP in New York attended by black American and West Indian communists.[76] Further informants' reports suggested that Caribbean radicals were strengthening their contacts with sympathetic American institutions and individuals, including American labor organizations and Congressman "Adam Clayton Powell...who is reported to consort with communists, [and is regarded] as a friend of West Indians."[77]

Reports from Blanshard and Henry Field, an "anthropologist" connected with the Office of Strategic Services, filled out this picture. These indicated that there were more activists and organizations than authorities had realized, and that many such that were already known had moved to the Left. The JPL, for example, by 1944 had been abandoned by moderates, who believed that "all of the officers of the League were either Communist or fellow travelers." Moreover, moderate expatriates were not counter-organizing as before. The AWIA, originally formed to combat communist influence in WINC, had been infiltrated and rendered inactive.[78]

Washington tracked this leftward drift with some concern. The most comprehensive analysis of diasporan ties came in a top-secret December 1944 report by Field, recapping the actions of WINC and other expatriate groups since 1939. Field reassured the administration, however, of the limits of both transnational solidarity and race-based communist appeals:

> In general, it cannot be said that the native organizations of West Indians in Harlem exercise any great influence in the Caribbean. Nor can it be said that [they] are fundamentally communist. Communist influence is appearing rapidly throughout the colonial world, particularly the Negro world, but this increase...does not seem to be the result of any large-scale missionary effort by Negro Communists in the Caribbean or in New York.[79]

Field's conclusion was correct as far as it went: Harlem West Indians were at least two degrees removed from power in the islands themselves. In addition, many groups were island-specific, and their efforts thus diffuse. But his analysis overlooks the real import of their U.S. presence. Thanks to ties with African-American groups, they raised money and attention from Americans like White and Taussig. Moreover, "no great influence" is a judgment call. New York sent the PNP the better part of its campaign funds in the first real election in Jamaican history, no small point regardless of the party's loss. In addition, Field's conclusion regarding communism was perhaps reassuring to Washington. Although a potential long-term threat, colonial communism seemed little affected by New York-based activism—and the triumph of Bustamante suggested that communism had not taken firm root on the British Caribbean ground. Indeed, events in Jamaica and Trinidad—notably the formation of the West Indian National Party in the latter, indicating greater black self-assertion against East Indians—suggested that racial tensions might become the bigger threat to stability.[80]

The Battle for Bauxite, the Colonial Question, and the Jamaican Aftershocks

Although it drew little interest from activists, the struggle for Jamaican bauxite figured centrally in allied discussions of the region's future in the latter part of the war. Four tons of bauxite, first refined into two tons of alumina and then smelted, produce one ton of aluminum. After steel, aluminum was the most important metal in war production, especially of air and naval matériel—and the United States had not had consistent, secure access to it even in peacetime. The president wrote before Pearl Harbor that the ongoing "shortage [is] a serious problem for defense program," one which had not been solved by December 7.[81] In part, the problem owed to the monopoly held by the Aluminum Corporation of America (Alcoa). The government's two-pronged solution was to launch an antimonopoly lawsuit against Alcoa and to sign contracts with the competing Reynolds Metals Company. In part, the shortage was also due to a lack of steady access to high-grade bauxite ore. Domestic U.S. deposits were of poor quality; higher grade Guianese ores met most Anglo-American needs. Even prior to wartime, unpredictability in Guianese mine-production schedules and steep price fluctuations impeded steady U.S. supplies of bauxite. The regional supremacy of the U-boat wolf packs in the first years of World War II meant that even this supply would diminish to an undependable trickle.

The December 1942 discovery of bauxite in Jamaica promised to ease these difficulties. If the new deposits could be opened to another American company, the cartel might be broken. Upon learning of the new sites, Reynolds Vice President Walter Rice wrote the State Department for help in getting access. State complied, directing the consulate and the ambassador in London to investigate that possibility. Resistance came from three quarters, the last an unexpected one: the Colonial Office; the Canadian and Dutch companies, especially Alcan, who dominated Guianese bauxite extraction and who feared losing their monopoly; and the Aluminum Committee of the allies' Combined Raw Materials Board, whose British and Canadian members twice outvoted Washington in the latter's pursuit of Jamaican bauxite.

This dismayed Reynolds and the Hull State Department, who saw Jamaican bauxite as a test of economic principle, in addition to being a specific security concern. American plans for the postwar economy were taking shape, and the tenet of equal access was at their core. In September the Aluminum Committee reiterated its stance against Reynolds, on the grounds that the proposed development was no longer a wartime necessity. Sufficient production could be had from existing imperial operations. The British had won a third round. Hull and State did not entirely give up the fight, but elected not to spend more diplomatic capital on a losing battle.

In 1944, Reynolds' fortunes appeared to turn, and turn back again. Previously, the Jamaican government had held that bauxite was state property. Kingston now changed this line. Rice immediately flew to Jamaica, where officials agreed, in the interest of economic development, to "arrangements... for obtaining concessions [for Reynolds]." Private and crown lands were to be made eligible for sale to the company, opening the way for Reynolds to compete with Alcan. Kingston, alas, did not have the last word. In July, Foreign Minister Anthony Eden laid out to Ambassador Winant the metropole's take.[82] Eden held out the prospect of nationalization or private British/Canadian monopoly on the Jamaican deposits. Imperial privileges, that is, would not be surrendered; the guarantees to Reynolds were conditional ones.

Learning of this, Rice returned to Jamaica. He told the governor of his company's plans to do more than just dig, promising agricultural operations on leased lands and patronage of local businesses. The governor was sold. He supported the company's efforts to gain access, but noted that the final decision would come from London. With Kingston on board, Rice returned to Washington, where by the end of the year he won a reiteration of State's "vigorous support" for Reynolds' pursuit of Jamaican bauxite.

The timing was crucial, to Washington and Reynolds alike. The former intended to win a larger share of world aluminum production, both as a national security issue and as a victory for free-trade principles. The latter held options, expiring in 1945, on lands containing millions of tons of ore. In a letter to State, Rice painted a dire scenario. The British could stifle the U.S. aluminum industry "for a hundred years" by cornering world production. London held the Damoclean sword—nationalization—over Reynolds' leases. On the other hand, commonwealth rivals, notably Alcan, were buying up all the Jamaican deposits they could find but doing little to develop them, obviously intending to block Reynolds. "[Our] exclusion from Jamaica," Rice continued, "would mean that this strategic reserve would be kept for the British Empire," with serious consequences for U.S. security, not to mention for Rice's company. The State Department and Roosevelt agreed with Reynolds. The administration knew that Guiana sources under imperial control were ultimately unsure.[83] Alcoa and Reynolds were feverishly pursuing technical breakthroughs in the refining process. Successful, these could render not only the Guianas' ores undesirable but Jamaica's as well, and free the U.S. from dependence on imported bauxite. Still, with no guarantee of such a breakthrough, the State Department continued to focus on Reynolds' Jamaica project, the best prospect for sustaining American aluminum production.

The British, however, held fast, and the conflict stalemated around the time of FDR's death. Reynolds was able to renew its options, but London continued to put up roadblocks. The State Department again conceded the unlikelihood of victory and ceased pursuit in the face of continued imperial resistance. The British prevented Reynolds' development of Jamaican bauxite for five more years. At that point, the British search for a cure for the recurring sterling crises, the Truman defense buildup, and the Korean War presented an unanswerable argument for incursion. In short order Reynolds would become one of the island's largest employers, and Jamaica would become the leading supplier of bauxite to the United States. In 1945, however, that outcome still lay in the future and was still far from guaranteed.

From one standpoint, the bauxite battle reveals the "contradictions of monopoly capitalism" and the dictates of imperial economics, as one empire used the pretext of war to penetrate another.[84] In this view, collusion between U.S. corporate interests and the State Department is charged with superseding the AACC and the CDWO. Similar collusion on behalf of winning Caribbean routes for Pan American Airways, for one British observer at the time, provided further evidence of real U.S. intentions: "we are not fighting [the] tyranny of…central Europe in order to submit after the war to any thralldom by Pan-American airways."[85] This U.S. "power play" subordinated socioeconomic reform to a postwar order from which the United States would principally benefit.

While a sound interpretation, weaknesses appear upon closer inspection. The contention that business interests governed wartime U.S. actions in the West Indies is hampered by the absence of any corporate effort to take over what were already the islands' biggest industries. Sugar, for example, figures in AACC projects aimed at economic diversification—but as an obstacle to progress rather than an object of takeover. Control of the islands' historically most profitable sector—agricultural commodities—appears virtually nowhere as a goal of U.S. activity, despite the fact that Taussig, as a former sugar executive, might have been expected to pursue it. If business and profit motivated U.S. diplomacy, one would expect to find some indication that Taussig's efforts sought to produce advantages in them for his industry. Although sugar, oranges, bananas, and rum constituted 80 percent of Jamaica's foreign trade, American discussion of them mainly characterizes them as hindrances to development rather than opportunities for expansion. Other "penetrations" predated the war. U.S.-style advertising, cinema, and radio—much of it brought by returning immigrants and more popular than British versions—register in official correspondence as neither considerations nor goals of U.S. policy.[86]

The exceptions were aviation and bauxite. Washington took an active interest in both, with some success. American efforts led to greater access to Caribbean markets for U.S. airlines, especially Pan Am, and metal companies, especially Reynolds. Yet these were not strictly or even primarily commercial ventures. They are better understood as being central to the national-security strategy that would guide U.S. Cold War policy, of which access to key raw materials was a hallmark. The pursuit of these *particular* assets—as opposed to the Caribbean's more traditional products—suggests that their strategic aspects outweighed their financial ones.

Nor was the American attempt to secure these security-commercial footholds at odds with projects for reform. As noted, the AACC's calls for socioeconomic change quieted somewhat after 1943. So too did those of the British government, for whom such passions had burned less brightly. This, however, does not necessarily signal a sellout to U.S. business, or the death of reform in an Anglo-American commercial crossfire. Early in the war, the AACC identified two handmaidens of the region's oppressive monocultural economy. One was inadequate inter-island transport, which deepened each colony's isolation. Another was the nondiversified, preindustrial economy that held sway everywhere except Trinidad, whose oilfields saved it from the other islands' bitter, sugar fate. Expanded transport capacity and investment in bauxite were seen as ways to alleviate these chronic problems. True, these rationales ranked below security concerns, and arguably lower than the profit motive, in compelling Washington to pursue American business access to Caribbean air routes and bauxite. Nonetheless, such pursuit should not be seen as the strangulation of reform or of development efforts by corporate interests. It was, rather, a convergence of all three.

British resistance stood on the same grounds. Cynical references to Yankee greed gave way to the realization that the allies' interests in Jamaican bauxite were two sides of the security coin, with the British side labeled "imperial" and the American side "national." London grasped the import of this nominally commercial dispute for the postwar era, even before Winant put the question to Eden as a test case of the "equal access" principle. Some officials had in mind the nationalization of the new resources. This would accomplish two things: first, it could "assure orderly development" of, by, and for the colony itself. Second, it would shore up Jamaica's local and Britain's global postwar position: "the end of the war will find us alone of the victor[s] largely stripped of our foreign assets. We should therefore think twice before we [share imperial] reserves of natural wealth."[87] In any event, the battle went beyond bauxite: "the facts 1) that Jamaica lies in the American hemisphere, 2) that the [U.S.] may run out of their own supplies of bauxite fairly soon, combine to give this question volcanic possibilities."[88]

Regarding Jamaican bauxite, the tactical answer for Britain lay in Canada; this appears to have gone far in persuading the State Department to abandon the fight. The success of this parry owed at least partly to a reappearance of the Puerto Rico problem. In 1943, the Canadian Metals Controller wrote the U.S. War Production Board to use America's colony against it: "[Reynolds'] position is the same as [Alcan's] would be if the latter asked for ... equal terms in discoveries which Reynolds had made in Puerto Rico."[89] Only the most legalistic, hairsplitting, and unconvincing of answers to this point could be made, and Reynolds turned its attention elsewhere, as did

Washington. Preferring not to fight a two-front diplomatic war against the Commonwealth, the Roosevelt administration pursued its battle against the Alcoa monopoly within its borders instead of the imperial one outside them. But beyond Jamaican bauxite, the broader question of the "equal access" principle did not vanish, and indeed would be at the center of Anglo-American disputes elsewhere as Axis defeat drew nearer.

Choosing its battles, both literal and figurative, became even more crucial to Roosevelt's foreign policy in early 1945. Yalta and the drive to Japan drew American attention away from the Caribbean and other peripheries. Yalta pulled in its train the dispensation of the postwar world, including the colonial question. In policy terms, the result was ironic: as the colonial question rose to global prominence, the fate of particular colonies blurred. To a degree, the West Indies avoided this fate; reference to the AACC as a model marked Anglo-American clashes over mandates versus trusteeship.[90] Still, in American diplomacy, the region largely met the same fate as the rest of the colonial world: the concrete status of a given colony went temporarily behind the curtain while the abstract matter of colonialism took the stage.

Military endgame, Roosevelt's declining health, and British determination to control the pace of colonial change all complicated the plot. All three affected U.S.–British–West Indian relations, but the last held perhaps the greatest importance, and produced inertia in U.S.–Caribbean affairs in early 1945. Conversations between Roosevelt and Stanley showed the intent of the British kettle to refute the American pot: "the president [said], 'I do not want to be unkind or rude to the British but in 1841 . . . you did not acquire [Hong Kong] by purchase.' Stanley's instant rejoinder was, 'Let me see, Mr. President, that was about the time of the Mexican War.' "[91] Nor did the British neglect to use the sharper arrows in their quiver. Soon-to-be Colonial Secretary Creech-Jones asked Taussig about the State Department's new Office on Dependent Areas. "[He] inquired whether [it] would deal with the American dependencies . . . and whether it would concern itself with the problems of the 'fifteen million dependent peoples in the U.S. proper' [meaning], they explained, the American Negro."[92] At a February meeting in London, Creech-Jones reiterated the point: "Americans . . . are apt to forget that they have an empire of their own [and] even today the colored population of the United States lives under conditions which British opinion finds hard to reconcile with American condemnations of British rule in the colonies."[93] Citing African-Americans' plight blurred the line separating racial and colonial problems, and underscored the extent to which the two powers shared them. A colonial representative at the meeting dissected the matter: "[A] West African . . . was interested to hear . . . that two English-speaking nations could not agree on what was meant by self-government. With him, English was only an acquired language but even so he . . . knew what [it] meant." The British hardening—and American softening—of resolve on colonial issues went beyond the Caribbean. However, since the region was a laboratory for the area-commission model and for competing definitions of "self-government," the West Indies found themselves the front lines.

As the American-inspired, British-directed change took root under the new regime in Jamaica, the mood was, in Blanshard's words, "a season of uneasy suspense."[94] If the West Indies were a test case of colonial reform for the world, Jamaica was the test case for the region. Parties from London to Port of Spain played wait-and-see as Bustamante's party assumed power. His election had come as a shock to West Indian and foreign observers. The first few months of his tenure revealed key features of "transitional" colonialism— above all its gradual, collaborative, and decidedly nonrevolutionary nature, and the importance of capable "native" leadership—with accompanying implications for U.S. policy as the West Indies moved gradually toward self-rule.

First, the Jamaican constitution had scored more points for the United States than for Britain in the game of competing colonialisms. Blanshard noted that the document gave Jamaicans less power than Puerto Ricans had; despite the fanfare over universal suffrage, "the essential planning of governmental activities . . . will continue in the same hands as today." The difference was that Bustamante could be expected to frustrate that planning when so inclined. The limited gains of the new constitution, for U.S. observers— not to mention for Jamaicans—were disappointing, further evidence of British ability to resist American pressure and to steer reforms toward crown interests. There was, though, a silver lining: in the "image wars" over colonialism, the United States was ahead and could continue leading by example in its own colonies.

Second, race and class dominated the newly expanded sociopolitical arena. The white oligarchy and, more recently, "coloured" white-collar workers previously comprised the polity. Universal suffrage had created a different—much blacker and much poorer—electorate. As Blanshard put it, "there [was] not a district in the island where a British white man could have won." Even in defeat, Manley saw in this a reason for hope. He wrote Blanshard that suffrage "is wiping out the old rancorous color conscious factors that have in the past been a disabling factor in local life."[95] While coloured–black tensions may have subsided, they were too ingrained in colonial life to disappear. But for the moment, the election confirmed that a fault line now split the class continuum that had joined whites and coloureds, the latter group now joined instead to the black masses of whom it was often disdainful.[96]

Indeed, the election had greatly complicated the issue of class. The two major parties had their roots in labor agitation. Both claimed to represent the working class. But in practice, the election pitted labor versus the Left. The coloured-middle-class PNP ran on a platform of coy socialism; the JLP, on a slapdash raft of labor reforms. Bustamante's charismatic demagoguery had carried the latter to victory. Blanshard reported a British characterization of "his tactics [as] 'a mixture of the Sermon on the Mount and John L. Lewis.'" Still, "he cannot be dismissed as a bad joke because he represents genuine class power. He is unquestionably the most powerful labor leader in the British Caribbean today."[97]

Bustamante's victory, however, was also welcomed by the mostly white "'businessmen's party," the Jamaica Democratic Party, which despite much publicity won not a single seat. As its poor fortunes came to light midway through election day, JDP adherents began voting JLP, and took solace: "the upper class was distinctly relieved that...Bustamante won." This was the result Governor Richards had hoped for, as Blanshard recorded: "Richards [said] he feared Manley more than Bustamante and that he released Bustamante...in order to cancel the growing influence of Manley. So...the ascendancy of Bustamante is a triumph of Machiavellian colonial policy." Manley's "socialist ideas" seemed a greater threat than Bustamante's "eccentric dictatorship." Hence the scene: the ideological left had lost its erstwhile base to a nonideological labor strongman, who for all his unpredictability had the support of the moneyed class, which believed it could control him. Moreover, illustrating the double helix of race and class in the new Jamaican polis, "some [whites] have been frank enough to [say] that they welcome Bustamante because they think he will make 'nigger government' ridiculous."[98]

The implications of the Jamaican election for U.S. policy were not immediately clear. The PNP had consciously sought to stoke Jamaican nationalism and desire for self-government. They lost badly. Bustamante had blasted their cause as "'the road back to slavery,'" an escape hatch for Britain to leave the island bereft and bankrupt. The fact that islanders had endorsed the latter position no doubt gave pause to Americans such as Taussig. Why, after all, should American anticolonial passions burn hot when colonials themselves, given a chance, had opted for deliberation and gradualism? Moreover, Bustamante's labor victory was, in Blanshard's analysis, simultaneously "a serious setback for democracy in the Caribbean" and the triumph of a "quite genuine[ly]" pro-American leader. Perhaps John L. Lewis was a less apposite comparison than FDR's "son-of-a-bitch" Trujillo next door. At any rate, if his campaign was any guide, he would be unlikely to press urgently for self-government; American interests thus seemed best served by waiting to see where the mercurial Bustamante would finally come down.

Yet the Jamaican result ultimately sounded as a contrapuntal note of caution in a swelling chorus for change. In the broader Caribbean, FDR's analysts Blanshard and Field reported that "very few demand complete independence, for they recognize that [it] might bring starvation, but they do demand the [most] self-government possible....Even the promises and grants of substantial constitutional reform in Puerto Rico [and] Jamaica...have only whetted the appetite for more democracy. Revolt against the imperial system is evident everywhere."[99] As Manley's PNP colleague Frank Hill put it: "We are a newly-awakened people whose political consciousness is tempered with caution. Self government means freedom to be independent; it means being able to hold up our heads with dignity...in the assurance that our freedom is not an economic sham."[100] It bears emphasizing that the Jamaican election results notwithstanding, the writings of Hill, Manley, and others at the forefront of West Indian proto-nationalism and reform were not merely the preoccupations of the educated. They reflected popular sentiments, above all West Indians' growing determination to shape their own fate. If its precise shape was as yet uncertain, the actions of West Indians since the late 1930s—from the stevedores' strikes, to Bustamante's exhortations, to Manley's penstrokes—had kept the political possibilities churning. As for the U.S. role in that churn, according to Blanshard and Field, the "intelligentsia are consistently anti-Britain, anti-imperialist, and frequently anti-American because of race discrimination in the U.S." Despite generally smooth relations between West Indians and U.S. personnel in the islands, intimacy had bred its share of contempt:

> One [Trinidadian] said recently: "when the Americans first came, they were welcomed, and most of us would have preferred American to British rule. Today, after years of contact with American racial attitudes among the troops, we would prefer the rule of almost any other nation to that of the United States."[101]

American intelligence thus found West Indians' desire for independence strong but inchoate, and their wariness of the United States just as strong. This, Taussig knew, had the potential to disrupt U.S. strategic interests in the Caribbean, given that "[the military] contemplated...a substantial force in the area after the war [which] would be greater than at any time during [it]."[102] Given this landscape, the Jamaican example urged caution: constitutional reform was contagious and required careful handling by all Caribbean powers; the days of white rule were numbered; radical leftism was defeated but not dead; the nationalist impulse was potent but diffuse.

The West Indies' War Winds Down?
Calm, Confusion, and Anticlimax

In light of such uncertainties, added to growing British resistance to American meddling and to preoccupation with the military finale, it is not surprising that U.S. policy toward the West Indies went adrift. For the half-year between the Jamaican election and the April 1945 United Nations conference in San Francisco, too many questions loomed and too much attention was required elsewhere. Even one so committed as Taussig questioned what could be achieved while the settlement of broader issues was pending. As he told Roosevelt before the January 1945 meeting with Stanley, "the affairs of the West Indies were less urgent than the question of mandates and trusteeship."[103]

Taussig could take some solace in the burst of anticolonial passion early in the war that had set some reforms in motion and had created mechanisms for further change. The potency of this apparatus was uncertain, according to many officials at the time and to observers in years since. Yet there is a difference between potency and potential, and the AACC possessed at least the latter. The commission had always been advisory in nature, as agreed upon by both the British and, reluctantly, the Americans. While it can be argued that by 1945 the Americans had fully resigned themselves to an "advisory" role for the AACC, the commission's very existence kept open the possibility of other roles as well, including that of regional arbiter.

A March 1945 conversation revealed the meaning of "advisory" to Taussig, Welles, and Nelson Rockefeller at that time. Rockefeller reported that at the just-completed Inter-American Conference at Chapultepec, Mexico, some Latin American countries had probed the possibility of annexing the Caribbean colonies. He and Taussig agreed that this was unacceptable— and something the AACC could prevent. Short of achieving an unfeasibly quick independence, the colonies had to be "integrated into the general hemispheric organization and...this might be done through the commission." Nor were the Americans alone in envisioning an "advisory" body as a wedge for other opportunities. The colonies' foreign policy was still controlled by the metropole, but Rockefeller and the State Department were wary of letting Caribbean republics onto the commission, fearing the establishment of "a Caribbean block [*sic*] which would be a menace to the solidarity of the Pan American System."[104] Whatever its deficiencies as an engine of reform, the AACC by its mere existence had become a geopolitical factor and a potential vehicle for Caribbean and American interests alike.

Those interests ostensibly included regional economic progress, although by 1945 that prospect seemed to Washington to be as distant as ever. The AACC had by then spent three years researching Caribbean prospects. At a roundtable on colonial policy in January, the subject turned to Puerto Rico. One veteran of that island's affairs observed that "one of the principle economic answers for Puerto Rico was diversification" —just as it had been twenty-four years earlier when he had himself researched the matter—"and we are still talking about the same thing."[105] American officials may have been pessimistic, but they were also well informed and chastened. They had come to share the frustrated resignation felt by most who study the Caribbean economy. The AACC had indeed failed to achieve the economic reconstruction of the region and was unlikely to achieve it anytime soon. But the ground had undoubtedly shifted, and the institutional presence of the commission amid the coming postwar flux widened the realm of reform possibilities.

One such possibility extended the logic of the AACC and married it to the nationalism that the war years had stoked. The decade of crisis between 1935 and 1945 gave new life to an idea—federation—that had swirled in the pipe-smoke of the Colonial Office for a century. Eden favored it, and Taussig agreed, arguing that a regional union should be the ultimate goal and offspring of the joint commission. In addition to this top-down support, the vision had gained traction along the Harlem–Caribbean axis. In September, Manley began organizing informal discussions in the islands and among "the West Indian communities...in America [about] the question of West Indian Federation, [in which] there is a great and growing interest." These plans would come to fruition, among other places, two years later when the NAACP hosted a New York City conference on the subject. Not everyone was persuaded; Rayford Logan had warned that the federation would face "tremendous difficulties."[106] But everyone was interested, which gave the idea momentum. Thanks to the AACC—which provided a template for cooperation and the stimulus of competing colonialisms—and to churning Caribbean nationalism, less than a year after the war Tugwell could write that a federation "seems inevitable."[107]

Cultivation of the federation idea was one way in which wartime U.S.–British–West Indian relations portended the postwar era. Another was the "trial run" of a prototype of the Cold War national security doctrine—the pursuit of a "preponderance of power" assembled from such assets as bases, transit rights, and strategic raw materials—that would be applied on a larger scale after 1945, as American strategic interests came to cover the globe instead of just the hemisphere. Yet the area retained the feature that made it, even while serving as a model for the broader decolonization process, nonetheless unique within that process: the transnational diasporan energies that had helped put political and socioeconomic reform atop the regional agenda. It is entirely possible, though ultimately unknowable, that absent such energies Washington and London would have moved in various ways toward reform of the colonial order. But the remarkable extent of those energies—launching the process in the late 1930s, undergirding a reformist equilibrium during the war, and pushing unity and federation as the long-term solution afterward—should not be overlooked. They belied West Indians' ostensible powerlessness over their fates. Even augmented by the "three R's" of the Roosevelt's Caribbean relations, they were not sufficient to overturn an entrenched regime during the war. They did, however, help to guarantee that that regime would never be the same. By reshuffling the Caribbean deck in favor of American hegemony, the war years bequeathed the cards for change for anyone—colonial activists, African-American sympathizers, British and American diplomats—who elected to play them after the lull of early 1945. What lessons the Truman administration, or for that matter African-American and West Indian activists, would take from the war and apply to its aftermath remained to be seen.

3

A Chill in the Tropics

The drift that beset U.S.–Caribbean relations following the Jamaican election and the death of Roosevelt lasted for years. Optimists might have been forgiven for hoping the new administration would renew the push for reform, either by invoking the region's "prototype" status in national-security strategy and Third World relations or at least by bureaucratic default. After all, in an abrupt transition of power amid crisis, an incoming leader often defers to the holdovers from the previous administration. If this meant greater latitude for the likes of Taussig, there would have been good reason for hope. In the event, during the brief twilight between world war and Cold War, the Caribbean mostly vanished from Washington's policy radar. Europe and Asia held higher priority in a global struggle with communism, one which for many Americans had the dark feel of apocalypse. The Old World thus eclipsed the Caribbean—a region Washington felt it could more or less take for granted—in its potential hour of change. Deferral to Britain in its territories complemented American regional dominance without incurring additional American burdens.

Still, in an ironic twist, even as the Caribbean region was overshadowed, the Truman administration applied the basic tenets of the national-security "prototype" to the wider postwar world. Washington followed a script written for its original sphere of influence, adapting it after 1945 for a communist rather than imperialist threat on a global rather than hemispheric stage. The consequences within the overshadowed region unfolded unpredictably, in only slightly less "protean" fashion than during the war. This was due to the Caribbean's unique position astride Anglo-American, inter-American, African-diasporan, and Third World relations. That position defied the distinction between core and peripheral interests on which the national-security doctrine depended.[1] It was a distinction Truman's team increasingly failed to make, most grievously in areas such as Korea and Vietnam. This produced an erratic policy that did little to prevent—and in some cases fostered—turmoil in decolonizing areas well after Truman's tenure. Yet, in hindsight, the conflation of core and periphery is understandable given the right circumstances. In the oldest corner of the overseas British empire, the United States faced just such a scenario. Washington welcomed in principle the prospect of imperial withdrawal from the Caribbean, but looked warily on the instability that decolonization might bring and which communists might exploit. This could compromise the security of what had been called the "American Lake" since long before the Cold War. In the West Indies, the United States confronted the decolonization of territories that were both core *and* periphery: core in geostrategic and symbolic terms, but peripheral in population and economic importance.

This ambiguous status pulled U.S. Caribbean policy under Truman in several directions at once. In some ways, the region became little more than an ungainly appendage of the British–American alliance.[2] At certain points after 1945, U.S. policy toward the West Indies was for all practical purposes simply inert. Washington repeatedly deferred to the British there; any trace of the wartime reformism appeared gone. What claim the region still exercised owed to its "core" properties: geography, strategy, and symbolism, the latter term here intended to mean the two principal ways in which the United States used the Caribbean to prove its bona fides to the watching Cold War world. In the first instance, it demonstrated that the United States would not abandon its postwar defense responsibilities but would instead protect its sphere of influence; and second, that the United States would use its Caribbean policy to prove its racial and anticolonial sincerity, its worthiness as an ally, and its sponsorship of reform for colonial peoples who stayed in the Western camp. Relative to Cold War crises over the likes of Berlin, this slow march toward a decolonized Caribbean seemed to hold lower stakes. But as part of those global tensions—and the need, because of them, to maintain the "special relationship"—Caribbean developments had suggestive implications for the United States, Britain, and the peoples of the West Indies.

Geographic, strategic, and symbolic concerns battled for supremacy in Truman-era U.S.–British–West Indian relations. Even though these "core" properties were often outshined by the region's "peripheral" status, they were nonetheless instrumental in shaping what policy did emerge. The matter of strategic assets—bases and resources—rose in importance once the Korean War began. Symbolic concerns centered on issues of transnational reach, especially race, colonialism, and the elusive specter of communism. All overlapped in unexpected ways. The continuing "diaspora diplomacy," for example, although somewhat more attenuated than during the previous decade, set the West Indies apart from its hemispheric neighbors and its global Third World brethren. The colonies' anomalous status in the New World complicated inter-American geopolitics. At the same time, the West Indies' progress toward federation joined the area to other decolonizing regions far afield, some of which, such as South Asia, were defying the repressive "freeze" of the early Cold War by achieving self-rule. The geostrategic and symbolic concerns at work in the islands thus shed instructive light beyond the islands themselves on the interplay between the superpower conflict and the awakening Third World.

Examination of these issues shows that the surface calm in postwar U.S.–British–West Indian relations is deceptive. While there were neither the explosions of riot and war nor the anticlimax of formal independence, all of these aspects of relations underwent change; none here found resolution. Like the middle miles of a long-distance run, the Truman years lack both the starting burst and the finish-line sprint. The period nonetheless influenced the subsequent course of decolonization—that is, to continue the metaphor, influenced how the marathon later ended. Anticolonialism, race, anticommunism, nationalism, and geostrategy all mark a period of quiet flux. The major developments of the period, including moves toward federation, entrenchment of Anglo-American and inter-American anticommunism, and the U.S. pursuit of bauxite, illustrate how relations during the Truman years disappointed reformers dreaming of better, heartened Cold Warriors fearing worse, and reassured those on island and mainland who saw the world seem to grow more dangerous by the day.

Horse Latitudes: Stilled Winds of Change, 1945–1946

The Caribbean colonies may well have been the very last thing on Harry Truman's mind when he was sworn in as president. The war there had in effect been over for two years, while the war in Europe and Asia was reaching endgame and commanded his full attention. Thorny, higher-stakes questions—the deteriorating Grand Alliance, defeating Japan, and looming postwar chaos— were more pressing. Regarding the Caribbean, this inattention had a broader meaning than just a reorientation toward the nascent Cold War. Roosevelt had been a powerful anticolonial voice, despite late-war capitulations in places like Indochina. This led to setbacks on the colonial question, among the gravest of which occurred after FDR's death, at the United Nations conference. The delegation there included Taussig, who found little support for his vision of a progressive policy of colonial independence, a vision he hoped would receive the multilateral imprimatur of the U.N. Charter. The opposition of Britain and France, and the acquiescence of the Truman administration, ended his battle.[3] However, as the West Indies would demonstrate, the American surrender can be overstated. While the United States did retreat from its 1942 high tide of anticolonial sentiment, postwar collaboration did not mean renunciation of reform. Rather, collaboration entailed a *modification* of the colonial regime. The U.S. retreat did help to sustain the British empire for a while, but the continued American presence assured that that empire would not be the same as before. At the moment in 1945, though, the uncertainty was palpable. FDR had improved inter-American relations and had paid special attention to the West Indies. Truman, by contrast, was an unknown quantity. He was no fan of colonialism, but he lacked Roosevelt's active interest in addressing the issue. As a result, the drift that had set into U.S.–Caribbean policy following the Jamaican election continued.

Roosevelt's leading Caribbeanist had not given up the fight. Taussig conceded, as he had told Roosevelt in 1945, that Caribbean issues were hard to settle while larger questions regarding U.S. policy and colonialism in general were pending. But he thought the glass half-full. He felt that the Atlantic allies shared the goal of "progressive development of dependent peoples toward self-government," though they interpreted that goal somewhat differently; the United States advocated independence when colonial peoples were "worthy of it and ready for it," whereas "the British expect[ed] colonial areas to attain self-government within the framework of Commonwealth."[4] Closer to his heart, he continued: "The U.S.' acute interest in the Caribbean should not be allowed to relax into indifference. [We] should not interfere with internal political structures but should indicate [our] interest in the maintenance of peace and security . . . and [should help] bring about a greater degree of education, social welfare, and economic stability."

Taussig, unfortunately, had much less clout under his new boss; even though he remained chair of the U.S. Section of the AACC, he now lacked the leverage to make his vision a reality.[5] In part this owed to the dilution of American influence on the commission following its 1946 expansion, when it became the Caribbean Commission to reflect the addition of France and the Netherlands. In part, too, this was the fault of the presidential transition. But it owed at least as much to the fact that American interests had evolved with the war's end, and the United States now faced a dilemma that would haunt its diplomacy across the Third World: balancing Wilson with Machiavelli, weighing the rhetoric of self-rule against the reality of instability. A State Department discussion in late 1945 captured this nicely. Ralph Bunche, who served on the AACC, recognized the Caribbean as a test of the Atlantic powers' "treatment of colonial peoples" and reiterated the AACC's role as a model for other areas. State analyst Abe Fortas teased out the main problem: "a fundamental question was whether [we] seek the goodwill of the various peoples in the Caribbean islands or the goodwill of the governments which control their respective colonies. To do the latter would perhaps tend toward stability in the area."[6]

Those present, meeting as an ad hoc committee to prepare for the second West Indian Conference, accepted this formulation. Another way of phrasing the dilemma would have pitted socioeconomic reform, which made governments uneasy, against strategic interests, which benefited "peoples" only at long remove. In some ways this was a false choice. Taussig, for one, argued that reform served both stability and strategy. He drew on the lessons of the 1930s to contend that one demanded the other; the Caribbean was vulnerable to both internal and external threat. The committee, though, now deferred to the latter and allowed the initiative to pass from U.S. hands. They did conclude that the United States should keep supporting the Commission and its idea of a federation, which would be at least an implicit step toward self-rule.

As significant as these points were reiterations of others long unpronounced: affirmation of the Havana Declaration of 1940 and of Roosevelt's

1941 statement that America "seek[s] no sovereignty" in the West Indies. These encapsulated U.S. security priorities for the Caribbean, as part of a global military infrastructure then taking shape. The Havana reiteration exchanged the Nazi threat for a vaguer communist one and underscored the U.S. commitment to keeping hemispheric territories from falling under foreign sway. The "sovereignty" reaffirmation was meant as much for the British as for West Indians. Together these two American positions, in the context of efforts to solidify inter-American defense plans, went some distance toward "the overriding strategic goal," which "was to have 'a stable, secure, and friendly flank to the South, not confused by enemy penetration—political, economic, or military.' "[7]

Washington thus folded the British colonies into its hemispheric security arrangements and continued its retreat from West Indian reform. The retreat, however, was not the whole picture; Washington had made less a change of strategy than a change of tactics. Advocates despaired of finding a rapid end to the colonial regime, but no one seems to have believed the system was entering a permanent, old-line resurgence. Some change, at least, was already in progress. The ad hoc committee noted that the United States could "point with pride" to reforms in the U.S. possessions, which had pressured the British to follow suit, as with the constitutional changes in Puerto Rico and Jamaica.[8] This brand of "competitive colonialism" had an advantage: reform could be pushed unilaterally. Joint-power reform via the Caribbean Commission always carried the risk of backfiring and was necessarily more complicated, given its place in the complex matrix of Anglo-American economic and security concerns.

Truman gave an insight into the balancing act in his message to the 1946 West Indian Conference for which Taussig and his team had been preparing. Truman's message, delivered by Taussig to the conference, reaffirmed U.S. support for "any suitable plan" for cooperation and union among the non-self-governing Caribbean territories. However, this came at the close of a message whose main thrust was that there was no hurry. Truman outlined U.S. policy toward the West Indies as support for Chapter XI of the U.N. Charter, "to the end that the progressive development of the peoples of the region in political, economic, educational, and social matters shall be ensured," and that this was the responsibility of the metropolitan government, moving at its chosen pace.[9]

Outside the halls of government, Caribbean reform remained a live issue. It continued to course through the worldwide dialogue on black freedom, a dialogue at that moment evolving into a Cold War version estranged from its earlier black internationalism.[10] However, its outlines, including the nature and objectives of transnational black allegiances, remained in place. Manley's 1944 defeat, for example, did not cost him his allies on the black mainland. On the contrary, he came to the United States roughly once a year to raise funds and publicity, and kept up correspondence with expatriates and sympathizers. One luncheon during a 1945 trip attracted Pearl Buck, Wendell Willkie, and an honor roll of black and white activists.[11] A New York event during a follow-up trip was sponsored by the NAACP. Walter White's letter to members lauded Manley as "one of the most distinguished world figures of our time.... Of all the figures I have met, none impressed me more favorably than he." Manley's message hit home; one attendee at the luncheon, Mabel Staupers of the National Black Nurses Association, wrote White afterward to thank him for the invitation, commenting on the parallels between the Caribbean regime and the "feudalism" of the U.S. South.[12]

The luncheon, also co-sponsored by the NAACP, attracted the notice of the FBI. The FBI tracked Manley's visit not because his message was extravagantly subversive; it was not. Rather, the African-diasporan nexus merited surveillance because it harbored suspected communists and fellow travelers, including Manley himself.[13] However, while communism in the Caribbean, as elsewhere, threatened to spur U.S. reaction, its menace was muted in the West Indies. For one thing, Manley was known to be mindful of the need for U.S. support. For another, Britain was responsible for checking communism on the colonial ground. The most the United States could do was to keep tabs on West Indians' potential communist links to the mainland, as the FBI did with the Manley visit, and to consult with London on its anticommunist efforts.

Racial and, to a lesser degree, ideological ties thus characterized unofficial U.S.–Caribbean relations in the first two years after the war; security concerns and deferral to the British shaped official ones. At frequent intervals either of these official or unofficial dimensions of relations would break the surface, and then submerge again just as a quickly. When the National Council of Negro Women launched an "International Nights" lecture series in January 1946, its inaugural event focused on the West Indies, partly in recognition of the many Caribbean students at nearby Howard University.[14] Down Georgia Avenue and up the scales of power, the War Department reiterated the importance of a military presence in the Caribbean, and this only a short while after U.S. intelligence found that Britain was having trouble keeping order in her empire "in the face of ever-increasing agitation for self-government and independence."[15] However, at no point did these factors converge into a crisis à la Greece and Turkey, and the region remained more or less a Cold War backwater.

However, race, reform, security, and the minuet of British reassertion and U.S. deferral did begin to coalesce around one issue in the mid-1940s. The idea of a regional federation had long floated about the Colonial Office. At its most basic, a West Indian union held out the prospect of administrative efficiency and economic viability. Most of the colonies, beholden to sugar, could not easily be made self-sufficient, let alone industrially modern. A federation could permit, among other things, a common market and economies of scale. Although it had never been seriously pursued, the strife of the 1930s and the war dusted off the federal idea for reconsideration. Much of federation's new support came from the labor movement and from intellectuals. For the former, a transnational identity was a natural outgrowth of class solidarity; for the latter, of cosmopolitan education abroad. As Eric Williams put it, "federalism was indicated not only by economic considerations but by every dictate of common sense.... The Caribbean, like the whole world, will federate or collapse."[16]

The genius of the federal idea was that it could offer something to everyone. In so doing, it defused many of the tensions that accompanied decolonization. For the Colonial Office, it was a way to control the pace of the process, and for the broader British government, it was a way to navigate a smooth transition to independence that would nonetheless preserve British influence in strategic regions. Viewed cynically, federation both as process and as objective offered cover to colonial officials who sought delay. As the U.S. consul at Trinidad put it, "the Colonial Government hopes to delay more active agitation for increased local participation in...government by directing the thoughts and energies of the local population towards the eventual Federation."[17] But any cynicism was offset by the Labour government's genuine commitment to exploring the idea, and local leaders' reactions ranged from curious to enthusiastic. Colonial Secretary Creech-Jones in 1946 began to prepare the ground, calling the 1947 conference at Montego Bay at which the federal idea was fleshed out. The conference called for the establishment of the Standing Closer Association Committee (SCAC), made up of colonial and metropolitan representatives and charged with studying ways to make a federation work. For Whitehall, federation rebutted critics as a creative step towards self-government. Washington supported federation as a vehicle for decolonization, not least because it offered a promising model for other such areas. From the early 1940s, Taussig had repeatedly voiced his support. For him, federation extended the logic behind the AACC: that regional cooperation could smooth the imperial transition and offer real political and economic benefits to colonial peoples.[18]

Taussig, in contrast to some of his British counterparts who hedged on the point, had always envisioned federation as a virtually irrevocable step toward self-government. In this, he was in agreement with West Indian nationalists. Most of them felt that federation offered, at a minimum, a halfway house on the path to independence and economic progress.[19] To that end, in 1946, the Jamaican and Trinidadian legislatures endorsed establishment of a federation. The idea also harmonized with calls for black solidarity. A federation could be an expression of "pan-African" unity. If it did not actually incorporate Africa, it was still a way to show the world that the diaspora shared an identity and an agenda worthy of the political means to pursue them.

Not everyone was on board. Bustamante resisted proposals to federate, not least because Manley had championed them from Kingston to New York. Bustamante blasted London for seeking to shirk its duties, saying he wanted no part of a "federation of paupers." This reflected the view of many Jamaicans; the island, due to its size, wealth, and location, was the odd man out in most federal schemes. A constitutional federal balance is difficult to achieve in the best of circumstances; doing so within the matrix of the Cold War, the Colonial Office, and American hegemony was still more so.[20] Jamaicans were right to wonder how their interests could be served in a distended system. Nor was it clear that union would necessarily shorten their road to

self-government. For some, the federal idea in its early stages was a diver-
sion *away* from greater self-rule, not a means to it. By 1950, for example,
Manley had lost support from some JPL members (including some of his
rivals) who thought his pro-federation position called into question the sincerity of his *Jamaican* nationalism.[21] Other residents of the Caribbean, such
as the East Indians who made up more than 40 percent of Trinidad's population and a bare majority of British Guiana's, had mixed emotions. A federation that protected their rights as a religiously and racially distinct minority
would be welcome; one that obeyed a regional black majority, given the rise
of "race feeling," would be less so.

These concerns reflected the broader currents in the colonies after the
war. Both islands experienced labor unrest between 1946 and 1948, which
recalled the riots of the 1930s even if they did not match them in scale. The
unrest had its roots in the refusal by employees around the U.S. bases and
the Trinidadian oilfields to return to the land. Economic times, for once,
were relatively good. Oil grew Trinidad's economy, and bauxite would soon
do the same for Jamaica, while world demand for the islands' agricultural
produce was rising.[22] But these paper gains mostly failed to benefit workers,
and in any case, those who had flocked to the bases, oilfields, and cities now
found farm wages unappealing. Unemployment had begun to swell.

Socialist and nationalist movements sought to capitalize on the discontent, complicating progress toward federation and self-rule. In Jamaica,
Bustamante's demagoguery and the leftist tint of the rival PNP led to union–
party clashes that drew blood. In Trinidad, universal suffrage in the 1946
elections saw similar competition, with the added effect of raising black–
Indian antipathy. In both islands, street-level popular action complemented
the deliberations of party leaders and crown officials. One result was "the
supersession of anti-colonial agitation by intra-class electoral competition."[23]
A two-party political culture in Jamaica, and a multi-faction two-race clash
in Trinidad, were taking root—and overshadowing anticolonial sentiment.
Crown officials, and to a lesser extent their American counterparts, posited
federation as a means to channel nationalism and check radicalism before
either one turned dangerous.

In the two years after the war, the federal idea was still passing from the
conceptual to the embryonic stage, and for both proponents and opponents,
the devil would be in the details. This is not to suggest that there was conceptual clarity. Did federation represent progress or only the illusion of it?
Could federation end up working *against* the interests of peoples and territories within it? Was federation even feasible? These questions in some ways
added to the idea's appeal because concerned parties—West Indians, British
and U.S. officials, African-Americans—could see in it almost any promising
if vague solution they wished. Federation provided common ground where
race, reform, British reassertion, and American interests converged. It was a
locus of U.S.–British–West Indian relations in the early postwar, in part
because there was so little concerted activity of any kind. The era then dawning, though, had the potential to change that.

Passing—and Passing Back?—the Baton: Relations under the Truman Doctrine, 1947–1950

Colonial leaders surely wondered what Churchill's "iron curtain" speech meant for them. An Anglo-American focus on Europe might free up political space around the periphery, as appeared to be taking place in South Asia. On the other hand, the need for a unified front might also create pressure to tighten up the allied flanks away from the core, dampening American anti-colonialism as in Indochina. Then there were the wild cards: the parlous financial situation of Britain and France which left them at America's mercy, although the latter could hardly afford to see them fail; the "rising wind" of race consciousness among African-American and colonial peoples; and always the specter of communism, manifest as demagogue, soldier, guerilla, or saboteur, stalking the hungry and downtrodden. For American and British leaders, the crisis year of 1946 confirmed that the world was splitting into hostile camps. For empires and their discontents, the immediate postwar was the calm before the Cold.

Events in early 1947 furnished some clarity. The British empire began to show its cracks in the Mediterranean. U.S.–Soviet tension was sufficient to make this a problem, in American eyes, and the brewing crisis combined with apprehension about Soviet intentions to prompt the Truman Doctrine. Truman announced the Doctrine in March 1947 in an appeal to Congress for aid to Greece and Turkey, and more generally for efforts to contain communism. The Doctrine pledged support for "subjugated peoples fighting for their freedom." This clause, on its face, seemed to have rich potential for colonial nationalists. It was, however, limited in its scope, since it meant subjugation by communism rather than by empire. Indeed, the example of Greece and Turkey showed the limits of the rhetoric. The fight against "subjugation" in practice meant the replacement of British by American power where necessary and the bolstering of the British empire by the United States elsewhere.

The Truman administration had not turned its back on the Third World; it was committed to what Leffler calls the "orderly decolonization" of a diverse geographical area united only by "the dilemma it posed for the foreign policy of the United States."[24] But the Soviet threat seemed grave enough to give higher priority to the Atlantic alliance, and the national-security doctrine made the British empire indispensable. This did not mean U.S. accession to European empires in perpetuity. An underlying premise of American diplomacy, which many in London conceded, held that the "age of empire" was nearing its end. The British Ambassador said as much in a speech in Philadelphia.[25] The conflict had evolved from U.S. anticolonialism versus British imperialism—a clash of first principles—into a debate about the course of decolonization—a dialogue of splittable differences. British reassertion was more about the process than about the ends.[26] Unfortunately, for those who wished to push that process along, U.S. acceptance of that reassertion in the name of Cold War unity meant that the alliance came first.[27]

If the Truman Doctrine thus inaugurated a new-old era in Anglo-American relations, the Caribbean retained a unique place in it. As part of the U.S. sphere of influence, the Caribbean and Latin America would be among the first regions of the world to see the Doctrine in action. Historian Roger Trask writes that the twin acts of the 1947 Rio Pact on Inter-American Defense and the 1948 founding of the Organization of American States (OAS) at Bogotá, Colombia, which united the hemisphere in a common defensive and ideological alliance, were models "for a host of later Cold War collective defense treaties and regional organizations. They were among the earliest examples of [Truman's] implementation of the containment policy."[28]

The West Indies complicated these arrangements on two fronts. The Policy Planning Staff in 1947 deemed the colonies a potential security threat. Although the Soviet military was unlikely to be able to reach them anytime soon, they were vulnerable to subversion or sabotage. Even more troubling, their colonial status placed them under the U.N. Charter instead of inter-American arrangements. Thus, although Trinidad was party to the Rio Pact, legal priority went to the United Nations because the island was not sovereign. This meant that if the colony—seven miles from Rio signee Venezuela—should come to pose a threat, any "necessary" U.S. intervention would incur opprobrium. U.S. policy had to forestall this scenario and to satisfy its neighbors "that we had no selfish imperialistic ambitions" even while "[heading] off demands from the Chicago Tribune school that we should demand the colonies outright."[29]

In addition, the British possessions aroused imperialistic ambitions in their neighbors. The colonies' very existence chiseled away at the inter-American unity—ostensibly anticommunist and anticolonial—pursued in the Rio and OAS accords. The colonies especially complicated the latter. At first glance, the OAS had nothing in particular to do with any area still ruled by Europe, whether in the western hemisphere or not. The organization had been created to serve both the U.S. interest in a forum that would collectively shield Washington's sphere of influence, and the Latin American governments' interest in a shield against the United States. To that end the OAS affirmed anti-interventionism, and its cousin anticolonialism, as two of its bedrock principles. This had the added virtue of constructing anticolonialism as common grounds for solidarity among the twenty member nations, harking back to the great age of the American, Haitian, and Latin American revolutions a century and a half before. However, it ensured that Europe's lingering western-hemisphere colonies would offend both the principle and practice of inter-American diplomacy. The offense that colonies posed to anticolonial principle was obvious enough. Less obvious, but increasingly clear, was that U.S. assent in the continued existence of the colonies invited Latin American powers to make claims on them. The diverse territories they coveted, such as the Falklands/Malvinas, British Honduras, and Dutch Antilles, pointed to a problem noted by the State Department: a basic "conflict of interest between the Inter-American System and the continued existence of colonies in the western hemisphere."[30]

U.S. negotiators at the OAS conference in Bogotá confirmed that the colonies pitted the Atlantic alliance against the inter-American system. Guatemala, for example, sought resolution language declaring "colonial possessions to be a danger to the peace and security."[31] This was more than a bit cynical; Guatemala had designs on British Honduras, and indeed came close to making annexation a part of its constitution. But cynical or not, this stance showed the British holdings to be a weak hemispheric link in more ways than one. They manifested both a physical and philosophical inconsistency in the newly reaffirmed inter-American bloc. They presented a similar sticking point in the Anglo-American alliance should U.S. anticolonialism rise anew in response to British imperial reassertion. Finally, as always, they constituted a potential security threat, albeit more from communist subversion than direct Soviet attack.

The final shape of American policy indicates that the last of these threats was seen as the most grave. Inter-American tension could be lived with, especially given the U.S. belief that Latin American anticolonialism was window dressing. (Third World observers could be forgiven for thinking the same about the United States.) Anglo-American tension was more troubling, and the United States conceded the West Indian field to British reassertion given an unspoken understanding of three points of agreement. First, reassertion entailed progress toward colonial improvement and self-government. Second, U.S. base needs would be unaffected by the deferral to London.[32] Third, British efforts had to aid regional stability and contain communism. The Truman Doctrine thus dispensed with the West Indian dilemma by a qualified bow to British sovereignty, predicated on, among other things, the latter's anticommunist vigilance.

This was more complicated than it first appeared. On the one hand, anticommunism was the raison d'être of the Cold War western alliance. Moreover, British officials had wide latitude in policing colonial thought. Censorship, arrest, and deportation were powerful tools for the task, and London was using them; a May 1948 order required West Indian governors to file monthly reports on communist activity. On the other hand, British politics did not treat the Left with the same paranoia that American politics did. This is not to suggest British lassitude when it came to colonial communism. As Jamaican scholar Trevor Munroe writes, "an element of paranoia led London to see real or potential Soviet communists behind every nationalist outbreak."[33] But British and American versions of "vigilance" in the West Indies might differ enough to leave gaps through which subversives could slip.

The task of bridging those gaps was simplified by leaders like Bustamante and Manley, who channeled volatile politics into a reasonably stable rivalry. Bustamante was anticommunist, which brought him electoral success; Manley consorted with "reds" but stopped short of publicly doctrinaire positions.[34] Bustamante laid out his position and blasted his rivals, in no uncertain terms. He told the *Gleaner* that "we want no socialism. I hate communism. I do not believe any one of the socialists who have been elected means any good to this country."[35]

Officials feared that communism lurked in the Jamaican shadows, but was more or less contained by the PNP–JLP equilibrium. The PNP, however, housed a Marxist cohort that might muddy the waters, especially as labor unrest spread after 1947.[36] In Trinidad, Albert Gomes and the "old guard" shied away from communism, balancing figures like John Rojas who were seen as fellow travelers. Small-scale marches and rallies constituted the bulk of communist activity. These did have troubling ties to the Caribbean Labour Congress (CLC), which linked them to Manley and to mainland-based black leftists such as Bindley Cyrus.[37] However, at least until about 1950, the communist threat on the ground in the West Indies seemed small and in check.

Trends elsewhere, though, prompted concern that the threat might grow. The paradox of the Truman Doctrine regarding the Third World—support for "subjugated peoples" but alliance with imperial subjugators—gave Moscow an opening. The U.S. retreat from anticolonialism invited Stalin to steal that particular thunder, and fuse it with the idea that only communism meant true liberation. An Intelligence Review dated one day after Truman's address to Congress acknowledged precisely that danger, even extending to the U.S. "empire" in Latin America, but especially elsewhere in the Third World given the resonance there of the neutralism preached by Indian Premier Jawaharlal Nehru, which Washington feared would create the nucleus of a bloc vulnerable to Soviet entreaties.[38]

A basic part of the dilemma lay in the conflicting time horizons of U.S. diplomacy. As a State Department paper concluded in December 1947, in the short term, the U.S.–Soviet clash required strong affiliation with the teetering imperial masters. In the long term, "U.S. policy toward dependent areas is sympathetic to the national aspirations of non-self-governing peoples." Between these points in time lay the communists' opportunity, and the West's risk:

> Since political advancement of dependent peoples is inevitable....the U.S. should be sure that [supporting] European colonial policies may not in the long-run alienate non-self-governing peoples to such an extent that US prestige will be damaged irreparably [and the United States] find itself supported only by a group of politically precarious European governments.[39]

If communists could tie the Truman Doctrine to old-line imperialism and sustain a propaganda offensive to make colonial liberation and communism more or less synonymous, this would give them an early Cold War victory. It would drive a wedge between the allies, as the United States tried to finesse its concurrent support for imperial masters and colonial subjects.

Officials feared that this could occur even in areas of advanced collaboration, such as the Caribbean. The Caribbean Commission had caught Soviet interest when it added the remaining two European Caribbean powers to its ranks. The British feared that Soviet propaganda in the area might prove effective and lead Washington to take a "radical new line on colonial policy...which might wreck U.S.–British cooperation on the [Commission]."[40] Dean Acheson tried to put a positive spin on allied partnership in the region. He reiterated that the Commission was a model for other decolonizing areas and an appropriate response to the "standing danger" of instability. The United States was leading by example in Puerto Rico, and the British were following suit. This take was not wholly without merit. The American areas had the best socioeconomic indices in the region, and the British, despite some intransigence, were progressive enough. But this rosy spin suggested the delicacy of balancing enemies, friends, and hoped-for friends in the Caribbean.

Race, even more than anticolonialism or anticommunism, was a wild card in these calculations. Indeed, race threaded through the other two in ways that at times made it difficult to separate them. A CIA report in 1948 concluded that race was a potentially devastating Soviet weapon, capable not only of splitting the West over treatment of "dependent peoples"—African-Americans for the United States, colonial subjects for Europe—but also of turning such peoples against the West.[41] Nor was the race–communism nexus a figment of the imperial imagination. A founder of the PNP's communist cell in Jamaica, Richard Hart, reflected on the sequential fusion of race, leftism, and nationalism: "Garvey's 'Black is Beautiful' was the sort of foundation stone on which everything developed. And when the PNP came along with the idea that we could rule ourselves, although we were black, this was a sort of eye-opener, a revelation to many people."[42]

African-Americans and West Indians in the United States had long raised the anticolonial banner. Many, though by no means all, also leaned left in searching for solutions to the colonial and white-supremacy world dilemma. Although the United States had left the lion's share of responsibility for West Indies anticommunist surveillance to the British, this nexus of race and communism reached the black mainland, incurring American vigilance. Moreover, the ascent of race at home guaranteed continued mutual interest of black Americans and West Indians in independence. The cause of black freedom created a point of transnational contact between the domestic and foreign spheres, even if that cause became attenuated in the early Cold War.

African-American–West Indian ties, however, reveal the limits of that attenuation. As historian Penny Von Eschen shows, the McCarthyite clampdown foreclosed radical visions of black solidarity and transnational race-based activism. African-American organizations like the NAACP distanced themselves from more radical bodies like the Council on African Affairs (CAA). Even one-time militants like CAA founder Max Yergan voiced support for the Truman Doctrine. Many black leaders in the United States abjured pan-African anticolonialism, instead joining white liberals to argue that it was racial injustice at home—not empires abroad—that impeded U.S. foreign policy. In a sense, anticolonialism's loss became antiracism's gain.

The pattern held true for the West Indies—up to a point. After the war, and in spite of Manley's electoral loss, the NAACP–PNP bond remained strong. Walter White hosted the 1947 New York meeting of Manley and other leaders to discuss federation, showing the idea's appeal even to those allegedly now less passionate about transnational black solidarity. Indeed, Harlem's interest in the Montego Bay conference was quite pronounced and produced essential funding for its support.[43] Initiatives like this burnished the NAACP's appeal. West Indians in Panama wrote asking for formal affiliation with the group. Another proposed a Jamaican branch office: "thousands of colored people in Jamaica [are] ready to line up behind the NAACP for the international progress of the colored race."[44] Individual Jamaicans wrote letters praising the group, requesting help getting settled on the mainland. A poignant letter from a Trinidadian expressed pride "to hear of the progress the coloured people are achieving in America."[45]

Manley kept in contact with Harlem, which returned the favor. Even African-Americans who were pulling to the NAACP's left followed the Caribbean situation; Adam Clayton Powell and Paul Robeson, for instance, visited Jamaica in 1948.[46] Nor were these the only notables of the black Left to keep the "Harlem Nexus" alive. CLC members Cyrus and Augustine Austin met Manley at the Montego Bay conclave, where they proclaimed their support and offered to raise money for any actions advancing the federation idea including the New York conference. Manley counted such mainland support as utterly crucial to the early stages of the federation project. A 1949 trip to New York netted Manley more money for the PNP as well as meetings with Robeson, A. Phillip Randolph, and Marian Anderson, the last of whom agreed to come to Jamaica to perform on Manley's behalf.[47]

However, although Manley, Cyrus, and others drew inspiration from left political visions, these may have undermined race unity as much as they reinforced it. For many West Indian and African-American actors, the essential dyad was race and *nationalism*, not race and socialism or communism. One American observer, after a Caribbean tour, wrote that he was "impressed by the determination of the blacks to achieve 'independence' [but] by 'independence' I mean getting rid of people who aren't black....In the West Indies it is not a question of democracy versus red fascism. It is a question of black against white."[48]

Developments in Harlem, however, suggested the limits of this dynamic, as broad-brush ethnic solidarity foundered on ideology. In 1942, a faction of WINC had split off to form the AWIA in reply to what it saw as a "communist takeover" of the parent body. AWIA, still active, now found an ally in the United Caribbean American Council (UCAC) of New York, formed late in the decade for the same reason. UCAC was not anti-Left but anticommunist; the group raised funds for the CLC, but boycotted meetings at which Robeson spoke. They vowed to withhold contributions unless communists were excluded from organization activities.[49] The controversy extended beyond the grassroots. In the spring of 1947, the JPL notified the PNP—its own organizational offspring—that it would discontinue their affiliation because of "a [PNP] faction...declaring itself to be communistic [that] has created confusion and apprehension in the minds of our people."

The ideological split among West Indians, and among their African-American allies, may help to explain the Truman administration's willingness to defer to the British in the containment of colonial communism: West Indian communism was at least partly self-contained. However, it was not clear that this would suffice to defuse the race issue, which by the late 1940s had two faces. The first centered on prospective race unity across the diaspora. The second involved the United States' racial image, which could become a rallying point for the first. The repression of African-Americans belied the image of the "land of the free," an image vital to waging the Cold War. Proving U.S. worthiness as a friend to Caribbean peoples required attention to that image, to the end of showing that the hegemon could be an anticommunist bulwark while also making positive racial progress.

This led relations into the realm of symbolism. As during the war, Puerto Rico offered an opportunity for the United States to "lead by example." Truman articulated this claim during a 1948 visit to the island: "I rejoice that here in Puerto Rico we have a true tolerance, where races and creeds and personal views are forgotten in a common citizenship."[50] Real reform in the island's governance was still four years down the road, but the rhetorical trope of Caribbean multicultural equality was too good to pass up in 1948. In the same vein, American racial good faith vis-à-vis the Caribbean took the form of nominations, including Truman's first major black appointment. After the segregationist James Byrnes was named Secretary of State, some blacks speculated that Bunche might be sent to Liberia, Haiti, or Madagascar on the "black circuit" of foreign postings. Instead, Bunche was appointed in late 1945 to the AACC. This won the president accolades from the black press, although many, including White, complained that Bunche was out of touch with other black leaders. It brought praise too from ordinary African-Americans, one of whom wrote Bunche to say "it does my heart good to see that you will be serving *us* and the rest of your country."[51]

A few months later, Truman made another such choice. Hastie, former federal judge in the Virgin Islands and Dean of Howard Law School, was an obvious choice when the Virgin Islands' governorship came open in 1946. The post carried a joint appointment to the AACC. However, Hastie's race and ties to groups like the NNC made him suspect in the eyes of senators voting on his confirmation.[52] Truman took the risk and named him. Opponents tagged Hastie a "dangerous radical," but no real resistance emerged. Once again the black and island press praised Truman. The gesture even threatened a new round of colonialist one-upsmanship; when Manley received an honorary doctorate of law from Howard in 1946, Jamaicans called for him to be appointed governor of Jamaica, "[like] Judge Hastie in the Virgin Islands."[53]

These gestures, however, did not bleach out the stain of American racial practices. In the context of U.S.–West Indian relations, these and other such gestures, including the desegregation of the military, took on special significance. This was equally true in U.S. relations with most of the nonwhite world. Activists pointed out the harm done to the American image by lynchings in the South and by segregation in Washington.[54] The CIA concluded that the West was much more damaged by its race reputation than were its "Eastern" adversaries.[55] More so than most Third World peoples, West Indians had firsthand experience of American racism. Truman's State Department took this familiarity seriously and moved to bolster the U.S. image in the islands while monitoring West Indian racial activism. Consular officers attested to race's salience in the region: "[American] racial discrimination ... is well known and [our] information program should be directed toward showing what is being done to improve the situation."[56]

The race solidarity that resentment of Jim Crow might engender could also furnish, U.S. officials feared, a communist "Trojan horse" even in those colonies with weaker ties to the mainland. But the ramifications of race did not extend exclusively to the United States. In Trinidad, the race problem did connect to racial-*cum*-colonial revolt in a distant place, yet the problem turned neither on links to Harlem nor on Jim Crow. Rather, tensions flared between blacks and East Indians, the latter of whom followed India's progress to independence with great interest. Trinidad had been given a new constitution in 1946 as a follow-up to the Jamaican experiment. As in the latter, the document grew the electorate tenfold, challenging the political system to accommodate the consequent energies. One of these was the invigoration, real and imagined, of island communists. Officials feared that rising black–Indian tensions would coincide with, if not abet, "red" subversives. The U.S. consul in 1947 noted with equanimity that no evidence linked rising labor and racial strife to Communist subversion, although the colonial government feared that this was occurring.[57]

By 1949, however, London concurred with the latter, and reopened the wartime Regional Intelligence Office in Port of Spain, indicating "a renewal of interest in what appear to be increasing subversive activities." The British informed the U.S. military that they "expected active communism to take place somewhere in the West Indies, but [were] not aware as to where it would break out, and [were] very much concerned [about it]."[58] The United States also took the threat seriously by the turn of the decade. When West Indian communists, such as Jamaica's Ken Hill, were feared to be inciting racial and class tensions, the consul agreed with a U.S. businessman who felt that communism "could easily take root."[59]

The most important of West Indian political developments, after universal suffrage, was the continuing, uneven progress toward federation. Race solidarity, self-government, regional stability—all were wrapped up in the federal dream. That dream had its flaws. Bustamante's government, to Washington's relief, was proving to be stable and friendly. As Bustamante put it, "I am publicly and privately pro-American in every way."[60] Regarding federation, though, his government was still skeptical. Most worrisome, federation might not necessarily offer an anticommunist bulwark. The United States wondered if the British were not being "taken in" by leaders such as Manley, who were suspected of supporting federation only as a means to eventual leftist takeover.[61] This was not enough to derail American support for a federal union. But it did make Washington sensitive to the shortcomings of its policy of deferral to the crown.

American accommodation of British reassertion in the Caribbean was predicated on the latter achieving two main things: (1) "progressive" colonial administration leading eventually to self-government; and (2) containment of racial and radical movements under British jurisdiction. "Passive" surveillance of these movements satisfied American responsibility for these pockets of British sovereignty within U.S. hegemony. Such accommodation did not, however, extend to strategic matters. On these, Washington meant to have its way, massaging the alliance in ways that would bolster U.S. power and, secondarily if at all, benefit the West Indies and their landlord. Race, anticolonialism, and communism added color to the picture of U.S.–British–West Indian relations under Truman, but national-security concerns drew the lines.

These concerns split roughly into economic and military ones, although it was often hard to distinguish between the two. The United States had neither the financial nor military means to replace the British in all corners of the globe. London's rickety finances, which had seemed to stabilize after the American loan of December 1945, collapsed when sterling convertibility took effect in July 1947 and grew acute again in 1949. These fell into the economic category of national-security concerns, while U.S. contemplation of its base requirements fell into the military one. The pursuit of strategic materials blurred the line between the two. These were more a part of the basic national-security calculation—access to assets crucial to projecting power—than of a concerted economic offensive.

In contrast to Latin America, where American influence had largely displaced British, the West Indies remained imperial redoubts when it came to trade. This mercantilist policy was aimed at shoring up the metropole at the expense of colonial development, and as such it deepened the gap between London and the West Indies, further feeding colonial nationalism.[62] The schism turned island minds northward once again. The mainland was the obvious source for the capital needed for development. Furthermore, U.S. national-security needs created exceptions to British mercantilism in the West Indies. These exceptions took the form of transport infrastructure and raw materials. Negotiations over both became the most prominent feature of the Truman administration's West Indies policy.

Anglo-American tensions over military responsibility for the colonies had long roiled, despite a basic strategic unity between the two powers. Both parties shared an interest in stability, which they perceived to be threatened as much by internal unrest as by external attack. After the war, Washington, aware of its ally's limitations, sought to consolidate its military umbrella. Many of the bases leased in 1941 were now unnecessary, and the United States began returning these. Trinidad, though, remained a pillar of hemispheric-defense plans. Both there and in Jamaica, American facilities caused low-level static even before the Truman Doctrine took effect.[63] These spats did not take the exact shape of the later Chaguaramas controversy—the clashes were confined to the colonial government and the State Department, rather than between a nationalist popular movement and the U.S. military—but they hinted at its contours.

The distribution of power was never in question. State warned that the War Department would be "only too glad to 'get tough'" with Trinidad, even if it meant poisoning relations and holding up the "whole [program] of turning over surplus buildings [and] land."[64] The U.S. consul saw things differently. He detected a gap between the Colonial Office and its appointees, on one hand, and Trinidadians, on the other. The latter "harbor little resentment of the U.S." and were conscious of the economic benefits the bases provided.[65] But they resented that the British had granted the bases without having consulted them. The presence of the bases, in this view, was not the problem; the principle of ignoring island desires was. The consul granted that crown and island shared some resentment of the United States, based on the impression that "[our] officials feel free to disregard local wishes." On the whole, though, colonial feeling was more anti-Britain than anti-American. In the 1950s, nationalist leadership in some islands would reverse and intensify that dynamic, but as yet this clash rose only to the level of minor friction.

In any case, even if there had been greater anti-American unrest in the colonies, there was no chance the United States would pull out of *all* its West Indian holdings. The CIA assured Truman that the Atlantic powers' control of their colonial areas was "reasonably secure" even with only token forces present.[66] The joint chiefs were less sure. Their 1949 assessment affirmed that the Caribbean was "of primary strategic importance to the U.S. [but that] Soviet capabilities in the area were definitely limited" at the moment.[67] Much the greater threat lay in local communists' intrigues and sabotage, to which the region and its forces were highly vulnerable. Surveillance of subversives and mobile garrisons would address the threat in part. Minimizing American exposure while maximizing its Caribbean reach would do the rest. This meant "trading away" nonessential bases to guarantee retention of key ones such as Trinidad.[68]

As the CIA and joint chiefs indicated, however, the Caribbean was a special kind of military frontier. Its distance from the enemy meant that it was not a frontline like the East German border, even if the Antillean perimeter did guard the American underbelly. Its security importance, though, lay equally in its potential for the projection of power—in its role not only as a great wall but also as a springboard and an arsenal as well. Aside from the naval use of Trinidad as a rallying point, the island also lay astride the "belt of bases" that facilitated military transport worldwide and was thus indispensable to the national-security doctrine. The CIA named Trinidad as a key stop in the Caribbean–South Atlantic sector of this global network.[69]

Of still greater importance to the national-security doctrine was the West Indies' place in the global network of strategic materials, especially oil and bauxite. Trinidad was a key producer and protector of oil in the Americas. As late as 1950, it was the leading crude producer in the British empire, and it guarded the oilfields stretching westward from its shores, which figured prominently in Western plans for both war and peace.[70] Although it would soon be eclipsed by the Middle East, Trinidad was thought to have the richest deposits in the empire. Moreover, Mideast oil would not fully eclipse Trinidad's importance, since the latter would be more secure in case of European or Arab–Israeli war.[71] Planners stipulated this security but did not take it for granted. If the short-term Soviet military threat to the island was small, wargamers nonetheless anticipated submarine attack and sabotage if hostilities should occur even as soon as two years hence. In addition, the threat to Trinidad not only endangered oil production and regional defense. The island was also a key transshipment point for a crucial raw material, bauxite, en route from one of its primary sources in the Guianas to North American aluminum plants.[72]

The vulnerability of this supply line, combined with the Truman defense buildup, the Korean War, the recurring sterling crisis, and the confirmation of large ore deposits in Jamaica, led Washington to renew its pursuit of bauxite in that island. Shortfalls in American aluminum output had bedeviled weapons production throughout the late war.[73] Nor had the outlook brightened after hostilities ended, as bauxite deposits within the United States were small and of poor quality. Wartime miracles of aircraft production could not be duplicated—as the postwar superpower's global responsibilities might demand at any moment—unless an ore supply could be assured. U.S. policymakers showed acute awareness of this circumstance. Indeed, the empire's successful wartime blocking of Reynolds did little to dissuade that company— or the U.S. government—beyond the short term. Reynolds' project in Jamaica, Hull had written to Stimson, was part of the "national defense of the U.S."[74] Rejection followed, but Foggy Bottom kept the issue alive, taking it up with the new Labour government just before the war's end, to no avail. The end of hostilities removed the urgency of war production and added some clarity to the conflict over imperial resources. The Colonial Office avowed that the crown wished only to secure what was best for Jamaica— which in practice meant that Reynolds', and Washington's, quest would remain frustrated in the immediate postwar years.

However, two events in 1947 changed the equation. The Truman Doctrine that winter lent urgency to the question of American war-making capacity. Then the sterling crisis that summer—in which London's declaration of pound-sterling convertibility set off a stampede out of that currency and into the dollar—showed the utter dependence of Britain's recovery on the U.S. economy, and thus forced the crown to reconsider American access to imperial resources and markets. Another, longer-standing concern—the need for West Indian development—also came to bear, though it carried less weight. Together these factors energized U.S. pursuit of Jamaican bauxite, finally resulting in a much different outcome.

Even before the Korean War, the current had begun to run against imperial protectionism and given additional impetus to Reynolds' project. The sterling crises in 1947 and 1949 made it critical to find sources of dollar exchange for colonies and metropole alike. On the American side, the Truman administration—fearing the recurrence of strategic-materials shortages should war break out—was formulating plans to stockpile such assets. U.S. diplomats conveyed to British officials the unanimity of American agencies, who "considered the project highly desirable."[75] Among these were the President's Materials Policy Commission (PMPC), the National Strategic Resources Board, the Strategic Materials Department, and the Economic Cooperation Administration (ECA). It was this last which helped to broker the final arrangement. The ECA loaned eleven million dollars to the British government, to be repaid by deposit of Jamaican-derived aluminum into American stockpiles.[76] For their part, Manley and Bustamante shelved their

rivalry and agreed upon the desirability of this massive American investment. The island legislature and appointed governor seconded their position. This sentiment "trickled up," and even the Colonial Office grudgingly
supported the project by 1949.[77]

A second one-two punch, in 1950, decisively recast the bauxite question and U.S.–British–West Indian relations in general. In the autumn of
1949, a pair of Cold War crises—Soviet acquisition of the atomic bomb and
the communist triumph in China—had prompted the Truman administration to rethink a containment doctrine that seemed, all of a sudden, to be
faltering. The fruit of this process was a new American strategic blueprint,
NSC-68, which outlined an aggressive response to the now fully global, and
soon fully atomic, communist threat. Two months after Truman approved
NSC-68, the outbreak of the Korean War seemed to confirm its dire analysis. This sequence of events altered the diplomatic calculus not only between
the United States, its imperial allies, and its East-bloc enemies, but also
reshuffled relations between those entities and the Third World—including
the West Indies.

Peripheral, but Not the Periphery: U.S.–Caribbean Affairs in the Shadow of Korea

War in Korea emerged as if on cue to confirm NSC-68's argument that the communist threat was fully a global one—including in those decolonizing quarters of
the globe, which the Korean peninsula technically was. The United States now
faced the possibility that nationalism and communism could violently collide,
rendering transitions of governance explosive. The West Indian transition, already
underway, albeit slow and tentative, presented little apparent risk. Given the colonies' location, however, *any* risk was too much. Washington devoted most of its
attention after 1950 to Korea and to European recovery, but continued to moni-
tor West Indian developments, and in the case of bauxite, to direct them. Extraction of this ore was the greatest concern of U.S.–West Indian diplomacy during the
war, precisely because aluminum was indispensable to fighting it. This was accompanied by a resurgent fear and surveillance of colonial communism and race-
based activism, and the need to ensure a smooth transition between an "improved"
British colonialism and a still inchoate regime of self-government.

The convergence of factors favoring the Reynolds project now added a final,
decisive one. Military aircraft requirements for Korea were comparable to those
of World War II.[78] NSC-68, moreover, meant that those requirements were
more or less permanent. The creation of this air force demanded that Jamaican
production be brought quickly on-line. Efforts to do so were sped up, although
even a year into the war the PMPC weighed the need for another ECA loan to
stimulate greater Jamaican output.[79] This proved unnecessary; production rose
in stunning fashion. The buildup pushed U.S. bauxite consumption up to seven
million tons per year—nearly double the amount of the total known deposits on
the mainland—and midway through the Korean War, Jamaica was furnishing
the majority of it.[80]

Even so, the NSC and the PMPC worried that this "general easing" of the situation would be short-lived. The "four scarce metals"—aluminum, copper, nickel, and tin—commanded the attention of Truman and Churchill at a January 1952 meeting.[81] The two leaders assured adequate supplies through an exchange of key commodities: imperial and commonwealth bauxite and aluminum to the United States, and American steel to Britain. At the end of the meeting, Churchill declared the arrangement "a great advance" vital to both America's and Britain's Cold War needs. By Eisenhower's inauguration, Jamaica was pouring 500,000 tons of aluminum into U.S. stockpiles annually, and thousands of pounds sterling in royalties into colonial coffers, monies utterly crucial to balancing Jamaica's sterling–dollar exchange. Moreover, what the Korean War bestowed, peace did not take away. After the armistice, Jamaica's annual contribution to U.S. aluminum stocks would double to one million tons.[82]

However, the American pursuit of national-security assets in the West Indies, while a strategic success, carried with it menacing consequences. The bauxite operations brought a huge influx of dollars and jobs to Jamaica, even larger than that brought by the 1940s construction of U.S. bases. An expansion of Trinidadian oil facilities around the same time, although with less U.S. involvement, similarly stirred the waters there. The resulting flux in labor relations invigorated the colonial Left. West Indian communism, though partly self-contained, had not disappeared, and there were signs that it was growing more active.[83] Its proponents also continued to fuse racial activism with political radicalism, and capitalized on rising race consciousness both within the colonies and against the United States. The latter's suppression of radicalism within its own borders renewed attention to the race–communism nexus as a foreign policy problem in the Caribbean.

The bauxite expansion and its repercussions gave labor organizations greater standing in island affairs. Unlike the United States, where the Taft-Hartley Act had forced unions to expel communists, West Indian unions had not disavowed the far Left. Nor, for that matter, had Manley's PNP, which shared some of its leadership with the more radical labor groups. Manley's lieutenant Frank Hill took advantage of the bauxite influx to win gains for labor and the Left's agenda. The Colonial Office reported that the three mining companies had failed to act together on wages for the construction and extraction phases of operations. Hill played them off each other, and thus secured higher wages than Jamaica had ever known.[84]

It was not only their negotiating success that brought West Indian communists to the fore. Ties to international subversion and transnational racial movements pushed this process along. Links between the islands, as well as to the British Communist Party and unions abroad, had concerned officials for some time. There was no formal Communist Party in either Jamaica or Trinidad. But the governor in Kingston reported to Whitehall that "evidence of growing Communist sympathies...continues to appear," and authorities kept tabs on a "number of persons who are substantially more than 'fellow travelers,'" such as Wills Isaacs, the "four H's" (who formed the core of Jamaica's main communist cell: Frank Hill, Ken Hill, Arthur Henry, and Richard Hart), and even Manley himself in Jamaica, and the unpredictable Butler and Rojas in Trinidad.[85] Events in mid-1950 convinced the governor that "signs of contact with Communist influences abroad are increasing." He allowed that "it is folly to think that there is a Soviet-inspired and -financed Communist movement. Yet the pattern is a hideous one, we can easily be choked in its tangles, and it is as necessary to beware as though the direction were straight from Moscow."[86]

As ominous as the "red" foreign ties were the black ones. Officials were unsettled by the sharp rise—fomented by communists and lamented by civic leaders—in racial tension.[87] The phenomenon was not strictly local, as all parties recognized. In 1951, for example, the issue of South Africa raised questions of racial, national, and imperial identity in the West Indies. The PNP championed resolutions protesting disfranchisement of, and expressing solidarity with, blacks and Indians in South Africa, and asking that Jamaica ban imports from that country. Nor was this the only area to galvanize such race feeling. "The Mau Mau troubles," reported the Colonial Office, "have attracted a good deal of attention in Trinidad," even inspiring a short-lived imitator called the Make Move Association. Although little more than symbolic, these acts suggested that increasingly powerful ties—prompting the PNP to support black South Africans, or Indo-Trinidadians to celebrate Indian independence—connected the corners of the empire along racial and ethnic lines.[88]

These, of course, also connected the islands to the United States. Washington during the early Cold War responded to race and Left radicalism by targeting its proponents, infamously revoking the passports of Robeson and DuBois rather than risk their sowing anti-Americanism abroad.[89] Even in the West Indies, unique in the Third World for their American ties, the visits of "a man like Robeson can do a great deal of harm to both Britain and the U.S.," as one American official put it.[90] The apparent rise in communist strength in the area raised the risk still higher and called for a counter-campaign. If nonwhites in distant parts of the world—egged on by Soviet propaganda—could develop a feeling of solidarity with African-Americans, how much more easily might that feeling develop among blacks in the western hemisphere, some of whom were already living as neighbors in the northern United States?

Yet neither the counter-campaign nor the repression of radicals black or white achieved much success. The propaganda could do little to stanch the international bad blood that flowed from Jim Crow, even without the agitation of Robeson or DuBois. Over time, awareness of this fact penetrated the highest levels of the Truman administration, although this in itself did not suffice to prompt more than symbolic change.[91] As for the repression, the African-American–West Indian bond suggests that transnational racial ties that obeyed certain limits were able to weather it. The left-leaning New York JPL, for example, invited White to a reception honoring Manley in 1951.[92] Officials suspected Manley of being a communist, but nonetheless did not bar him entry to the United States at that or any other time. Nor was he prevented from making appearances, such as a speech at Howard University and a JPL-sponsored rally at Harlem's Abyssinian Baptist Church during his 1951 tour.[93] Manley, perhaps guessing that his Howard audience included the FBI, praised Gandhian nonviolence and the American record in Puerto Rico, and announced that he knew no "card-carrying communists."[94] While disingenuous, his statement signaled a willingness to cut ties with those farther left than he, something Walter White had done when he pushed to expel communists from the NAACP. In an eerie parallel to the mainland witch-hunts, the issue of communism in the islands came to a head in 1952, and leftist leaders there took a page from White's playbook.

Communist activity had been on the rise for almost a year up to that spring.[95] In March, Manley responded by directing a purge of communists from his PNP. Several anticommunist members had already left to form a rival party on the grounds that the PNP leadership harbored communists. This, combined with upcoming elections, prompted Manley to act. He led a "quasi-judicial inquiry" that concluded the PNP was indeed "tainted by Communism," a conclusion seconded in a vote of party delegates. That vote led to the expulsion of the "four H's," four of Manley's longtime associates, and the island's most vocal communists. Some viewed the act as house-cleaning; others as window dressing; still others as a "grave moral weakening" that revealed Manley not as a noble patriot but as a dull opportunist. In the event, the gamble did not pay off. The Colonial Office reported "a distinct swing of public opinion in favour of the JLP. The PNP has lost ground with the purge of fellow-traveling elements." It was not clear, however, whether this was because of or in spite of the purge.[96] In Trinidad, much the same pattern unfolded. There, Butler used the visit of communist Janet Jagan of British Guiana to stave off his own rival on the Left, labor organizer Rojas. At party meetings during her visit, Rojas and others who attempted to praise communism were shouted down.[97] Around the same time, one of the expelled Jamaicans was denied entry to Trinidad, with Butler's blessing.

The events of 1952–53 chastened the West Indian Left but did not kill it.[98] Although the immediate public reaction in Jamaica to Manley's move was mixed, one effect was greater room to maneuver for the PNP. This was especially important as discussion continued of regional federation, which Manley was determined to shape. At a conference in Barbados just a few months after the purge, he gave "speeches of an anti-imperialistic nature" and reaffirmed that:

> A West Indian Federation must come about through the adoption of socialism throughout the West Indies, and that until socialist principles had been generally accepted, it would be better to go slowly towards Federation, if [doing otherwise] meant a Federation dominated by chambers of commerce.[99]

In a sense, Manley had sacrificed communism to protect socialism. By pruning the branches that stretched beyond the bounds of colonial politics, he had won a measure of stability for the leftist trunk that remained. He and his party went on to win the next general election in 1955. Nor was the episode wholly unrepresentative, given the pattern among West Indians beginning well before the Cold War, of intra-community tensions over communist infiltration. At any rate, Manley's action could easily be seen as simply a tactical retreat.

Given that federation lay on the horizon, this was arguably wise. Doing less would have raised eyebrows in Washington, not to mention in Whitehall, which had responsibility for mapping the way to federation. Even with the Jamaican purge and "self-containment" of West Indian communism, the specter had not necessarily been exorcized to American satisfaction. As Manley indicated at Barbados, federation might be a vehicle for what the Americans saw as an unacceptably leftist regime. Certainly Manley had telegraphed his ambitions, including his intention to play a major role in shaping and leading a federated region. Acheson asked the U.S. consul to remain vigilant, since events suggested that racial unrest, communist agitation, and federation might converge into a threat to U.S. interests. Still, federation remained the best way to channel West Indian political energies of all types—communist, socialist, nationalist, and Bustamante-style "boss unionist"—by offering a federal structure that could preserve stability and check leftist advance, and in any case the British were already moving ahead with it.[100]

This is not to say that the United States had changed its stance on federation as the West Indian future. Washington was wary, slightly more so than before, of the possibility that it was a Trojan horse. Nevertheless, in the view of the Truman administration, it was the best option for a number of reasons. Principal among these was that federation could be the capstone of reform of Britain's colonial regime, embodying "progressive" decolonization: welfare and development aid, stable political institutions, regional cohesion, and eventual self-government. The United States could claim some credit for urging this process on by rhetoric—and, so it said, by example. West Indians did express admiration for the American colonial experiment in Puerto Rico. As St. Lucian economist Arthur Lewis summed up his advice to his fellow West Indians: "Study what has been done in Puerto Rico and go, thou, and do likewise!"[101]

However, Lewis's example is telling. The deep ambiguity of that island's status—made deeper during the Truman years—pointed to the larger problem the United States faced in the West Indies and in the Third World at large. Few now questioned the European metropoles' positive duty to improve colonial welfare, but that duty had to maneuver between a hoped-for ideal of self-determination for all and a reality of instability for most. The Korean War, though it did not involve a transition from European rule, showed the potential stakes of *any* transition in a bipolar world. The violence in post-independence South Asia gave pause to all who had looked to that area as a model for decolonization. Anticommunist stability became the highest American priority in the colonial world.

The federal solution was the most palatable for the West Indies, because, as a State Department publication of March 1952 put it, "[the United States] affirms the right and capacity of all peoples to work toward self-government or independence, but we recognize that all are not equally ready to shoulder these responsibilities." The middle way lay in progressive colonial policies that would allow the United States to support both its imperial allies and the colonial audience in good conscience.[102] In short, the dynamics of anticolonialism—and to a lesser extent of race—in the international arena were evolving. Creative, "progressive," and above all noncommunist solutions like Operation Bootstrap or a West Indian federation could elicit agreement from metropole, hegemon, and much of the engaged colonial polity alike.

The Middle of the Marathon: Bases, Bauxite, Bolsheviks, and the Races to Union

U.S.–British–West Indian relations during the Truman years thus formed part of the larger policy dilemmas of the early Cold War: strengthening the anti-Soviet alliance, recharging the world economy, seeking stability in the First and Third Worlds, and building a worldwide military arsenal. U.S. relations in the Caribbean, however, were ultimately but a small part of these dilemmas. All of the major themes of postwar American diplomacy make an appearance there: the twitching fear of communism on the march; squaring the anticolonial circle within the Western alliance; tracking and tempering the rise in race activism; creating "a preponderance of power." None of these, however, can be said to have consistently dominated relations with the West Indies under Truman. The last—bases, bauxite, and oil—make the strongest claim, but even this must be placed in the general pattern of inertia.

The pattern is understandable, given the Truman administration's preoccupations elsewhere. When the West Indies did rise to high-level attention, such as for bauxite, it was largely as a function of events elsewhere, such as the Korean War. Even dramatic episodes such as the communist purges were dutifully reported to Washington, where they were of some comfort to area specialists but rarely rose to the level of presidential concern. This, perhaps paradoxically, renders Anglo-American-Caribbean relations quite suggestive about the real contours of power and principle in the early Cold War. American "disengagement and imperial reassertion" might be better thought of as cooperative American deferral to a changing British empire. The Truman administration was content to leave anticommunism in the West Indies to the British, provided they kept things well in hand. Washington felt it could take the Caribbean for granted once this and certain other hurdles—colonial reform, suppression of race radicalism—were cleared. Truman's team then kept its eye on the national-security ball elsewhere.

Ideological concerns about colonialism and communism usually led Truman's team to defer to British and West Indian action, while strategic concerns led to the substantive actions, and racial concerns to the symbolic ones, that his tenure did produce. By the end of Truman's presidency, the Policy Planning Staff surmised that all of these concerns were merging:

> The rebellion of Burma against Britain [for example] is therefore essentially the same kind of thing as the rebellion of the factory worker against the power and privileges of the factory owner, or of the American Negro against white supremacy....It is a manifestation of class war.[103]

This matrix of strategic, ideological, and racial factors places U.S.–British–West Indian relations during Truman's tenure into helpful comparison with his predecessor's. Some continuities emerge. American consolidation of its military and strategic interests, under the rubric of a national-security strategy, and the persistence of transnational networks practicing "diaspora diplomacy," fall into this category. Yet more numerous were the changes forced by the Cold War and the quickening of decolonization. Most prominent among these were the questions that the Cold War raised for U.S. policy toward European empires—including its consequences for raw-materials development, inter-American diplomacy, and a united anticommunist front—and the answers starting to take shape, above all in the form of a federation model capable of navigating the way to decolonization. If the early Cold War was marked by the general repression of racial, colonial, and ideological challenge, these years nonetheless laid some of the groundwork for change over the next decade. Ultimately, if the Truman administration in the West Indies, where core and peripheral interests intersected, did not fulfill the Roosevelt promise, at least neither did it precipitate the disaster that so often followed U.S. policy into the decolonizing Third World. Whether this particular run of luck would continue under Eisenhower, Dulles, and the "New Look" was anybody's guess.

4

Building a Bulwark

On the 1952 campaign trail, Dwight Eisenhower promised to change American foreign policy on the hottest fronts of the Cold War. Stalemate in Korea and charges of "losing" China peppered the presidential contest and brought into focus the evolving nature of the communist threat. Yet it was unclear in what ways the new president would remake U.S. policy in theaters away from the Eurasian front lines, and little of his campaign rhetoric attended to the most important of contemporary currents: the explosive nationalism among Third World peoples. Policy-makers in the early postwar had fared little better in their grasp of this nationalism, owing to their view that checking the spread of communism was the paramount challenge they faced. The incoming administration, though it differed on the means appropriate to the task, shared the conviction that the anticommunist mission was the highest priority for American policy.

This mission undergirded the Eisenhower administration's relations with the West Indies. In most respects, the new administration continued the basic approach of its predecessor, but this was by no means the whole picture. Anglo-American-Caribbean affairs in this period were not only a function of the anticommunist crusade. They also transpired within several overlapping subcontexts: Washington's pursuit of strategic assets abroad, especially bases and raw materials; U.S.–European relations as the territorial empires were dismantled; U.S.–Third World relations as the resulting states emerged; inter-American relations, of which the West Indies were a geostrategically vital part; and the continuing rise of race as a broad foreign policy concern.

Another context, transnational race relations, also continued to form part of the U.S.–West Indian relationship, albeit to a lesser degree. "Diaspora diplomacy" was less visible under the new Republican administration than it had been under its two Democratic predecessors. As a consequence, race was less a factor in American calculations regarding the West Indies than it had been. The Harlem nexus of active, mutual African-American–West Indian support still existed, but in somewhat attenuated form. By this time it was quite clear that African-Americans and West Indians, though mutually sympathetic, were ultimately fighting different enemies. Alike in the white-supremacy abstract, John Bull and Jim Crow were different in key ways and attacking them required different tactics.

The paradox lay in the fact that this relative decline in mutual cooperation occurred amid an undeniable rise in world awareness of the racial-colonial problem, and an unstoppable gain in momentum toward its resolution. Historian Tim Borstelmann calls this the *Brown*-Bandung-Montgomery watershed in global race relations; to this could be added the Suez Crisis, Ghanaian independence, and the Little Rock Crisis.[1] Regional evidence of the mid-1950s momentum could be found in the progress toward the West Indies Federation. Yet what was perhaps the most promising of the half-dozen unions designed to negotiate the decolonization process also demarcated the extent of transnational race solidarity, the dangers of the transition to nationhood in the thick of the Cold War, and the limits of Washington's ability to grasp and manage both.

For the first six years of Eisenhower's tenure, the United States deferred to London in the Caribbean colonies while lending support to British anticommunist efforts there and working to aggressively combat communism in neighbors like Guatemala. The colonies complicated inter-American relations during the Eisenhower years, as they had under Truman. However, to the new administration's relief, the West Indies demonstrated that they could be more asset than liability in the anticommunist struggle. London proved willing to intervene, and leading colonies showed a strong internal anticommunist streak— developments Washington heartily welcomed. Moreover, in contrast to its record elsewhere in the decolonizing world, Eisenhower's team not only grasped West Indian nationalism but actively supported it—on the condition that it be channeled through an embryonic federation. However, U.S. pursuit of national-security assets would override this position, even when, on the eve of the federation's birth, it brought the United States into direct conflict with its new neighbor. This conflict built upon lesser skirmishes to break the continuity with the Truman administration's approach. Shortly after this conflict brought the United States to the center of the West Indian stage, developments elsewhere in Latin America and the Third World would culminate in an important milestone in Cold War American relations with all three.

New Look over London's Shoulder: 1953–1954

The "New Look" Eisenhower promised in foreign policy included what historian Stephen Rabe calls "a coherent, consistent strategy for Latin America," one focused on anticommunism, free trade, and a pro-West stance.[2] Among the initiatives embedded in the new approach were several that bore on the West Indies, including setting a new tone regarding communism and colonialism. The two issues intertwined, as officials feared that the fading of the latter invited the former. Addressing them held uncertain implications for U.S.–Caribbean affairs.

American specialists had taken great satisfaction early in 1952 when Manley purged a communist cell from his People's National Party. The actions had put Jamaica, and by extension the West Indies, into good U.S. graces; here, communism seemed self-contained. However, it soon became clear that the expelled Jamaicans had not ceased their activism, finding their way to neighboring areas and continuing to organize, publish pseudonymously, and seek funds from sympathizers abroad. In addition, in a report prepared for the incoming administration, Jamaican population growth and economic stagnation foretold "a troubled future" with "much potential for chaos." The arrival on the island of a "competent communist" West Indian organizer—Ferdinand Smith of the PNP-affiliated National Maritime Union, himself freshly deported from the mainland under the McCarran Act—suggested that radical forces meant to capitalize on the unstable situation.[3]

Alarmed, the State Department ordered the Kingston consulate to expand its intelligence-gathering, fearing that Jamaican communists were "being welded into a single striking force." Some U.S. officials concluded that the activities of the bitterly anti-American Smith required an accelerated aid program to the area: "we must run very hard to keep in our present position." In Trinidad, communist activity had fallen since the previous autumn, but the governor reported in April that communist literature had started pouring into the island.[4]

These developments were not seen as presenting an immediate threat to U.S. interests, of which the most vital were regional security and bauxite extraction. Chief Minister Bustamante, for example, assured officials that Jamaica would never nationalize bauxite mining, and North American and British companies responded with further mineral surveys on the island. Soon after, bauxite production was pronounced militarily as well as politically safe.[5] But, beyond the short term, little was certain. British and American observers kept a close watch on Smith, Hart, Rojas, and other active "reds," even after the first two men left Jamaica in the summer of 1952. If these individuals were to peel away labor from its factional ties to Bustamante's and Manley's parties, the result might be a communist foothold in the Caribbean.[6]

In May 1953, just four months into the new administration, those fears became reality at the far end of the West Indies. In British Guiana, the People's Progressive Party (PPP) of Cheddi Jagan won the first genuinely popular election in the colony's history. This brought to power a leader who veered much too close to communism for American and British comfort. The PPP had risen to power on the charisma of Jagan, a Howard University-educated dentist of East Indian descent. Unlike Manley, who struck observers as center-socialist with an occasional lunge leftward—and who was in any case in the opposition—Jagan struck observers as left-communist with an occasional lunge to the center. His agenda prescribed workers' rights, land reform, and other items guaranteed to make London and Washington see Red. The PPP also moved to revise the constitution. Jagan swore to use "peaceful means," but labor violence "intensified the atmosphere of crisis." The governor reported that "the situation was beyond redemption." He asked Churchill to intervene; the PPP was, he reported with considerable hyperbole, " 'trying to use the machinery of democracy to destroy democracy'....Intelligence services warned 'bloodshed would break out' and there was 'a plot to burn down the capital.' "[7]

Jagan's rise was feared to have ramifications all around the littoral. British Guiana, one diplomat predicted, would become the regional center of communist expansionism.[8] The Eisenhower administration surely wondered whether its policy of deferral to Britain in the West Indies would suffice to contain communism. In particular, the United States feared that its national-security assets were becoming more vulnerable. The ripple effects of a radical regime in British Guiana could not be predicted. Even the arrival of British troops in the colony in October, to suspend its constitution and end PPP rule, did little to assuage U.S. fears that the proverbial genie was out of the bottle.

Three weeks before Jagan's victory, the British War Office had given assurances that bauxite facilities in Jamaica were secure. Operations were peaking and none too soon. The Eisenhower administration ranked bauxite the third most important raw material.[9] Mining in Jamaica, transshipment at Trinidad, and extraction of Guianese ores—the latter now facing an uncertain future under the PPP—were the key links in the chain. The matter was urgent enough that NSC discussions concluded that smelting should occur at existing Canadian plants, despite the risk of depending on production outside U.S. borders. Even this did not solve the problem. Eisenhower noted that in peacetime the country still faced a shortage.[10]

The Caribbean was key to meeting this need—and this created cause for concern. In the months after Jagan's victory, reported Consul-General John Hamlin, "communist activity in Jamaica passed the formative stage." November saw Smith and Hart back in Kingston, "probably presag[ing] a step-up in communist activities in Jamaica and the Caribbean to offset the setback in British Guiana." "[Their] presence," Hamlin warned, "shows that [this] part of the world...has been singled out for concentrated attack." This called for "appropriate counter-measures" in cooperation with British authorities.[11] The perceived danger was both physical and ideological. On the first count, in both Jamaica and Trinidad, bauxite and oil facilities were deemed vulnerable to sabotage by "energetic and resourceful...subversive elements." On the second, developments in the political sphere—abetted by the opening in Port of Spain of a United States Information Agency (USIA) office—could help to neutralize this possibility.[12]

In late 1953 Bustamante began calling for a ban on communism in Jamaica. Casting the PPP and Jagan as bêtes noires, Bustamante asserted that the PNP meant to lead Jamaica down the British Guiana path. British and Canadian officials on-site concurred: "Events in British Guiana have had a salutary effect on the Jamaican political situation and there has been an increase in the general determination to prevent the growth and spread of communist influence in Jamaica."[13] In Trinidad, Bustamante's counterpart Butler came to a similar conclusion: "Better Whitehall rule than Kremlin rule." During the following month and into 1954, Bustamante pressed the governor to outlaw communism. He pointed out that despite the PNP purge, radicals such as Smith and Hart were more active than ever. Hamlin agreed with Bustamante that there "[was] evidence of increasing activity...by Communists in Jamaica....Rather than let the situation get out of hand [it] appears desirable to outlaw communism outright."[14]

Since Jagan had proven that the West Indies were not safe from the communist contagion, Bustamante argued, drastic steps must be taken. Although Bustamante did not get the formal ban he wanted, the governor cut off contact with communist-leaning labor and expanded strikebreaking operations, achieving the desired result.[15] Ever the opportunist, Bustamante had an ulterior motive; his anticommunism was sincere, but it was also politically expedient. Disarming "red" unions, and blasting allies and foes alike for being soft on communism, damaged his rivals. A Colonial Office discussion showed keen awareness of the situation. Whitehall's challenge was to neutralize island communism while protecting legitimate left-political organizations and withholding from Bustamante the tools to destroy his opponents. U.S. officials noted that "such danger as does exist, however, [Bustamante] is prone to take advantage of."[16]

Americans also urged that the hemispheric context not be overlooked. Although Washington approved of Jamaican developments, these did not suffice to exorcize the demons British Guiana had loosed, of which communism was not the only one. The British intervention, which had U.S. approval, had complicated inter-American relations by eliciting a new surge of Latin American anticolonialism. An NSC report, detailing U.S. attempts to convince the western-hemisphere governments to view the British intervention favorably, acknowledged that:

> [the] Latin Americans consider the British...action in breaking the control of local political leaders in British Guiana unjustified, [creating] increased dissatisfaction with the U.S. position on colonialism in the Americas, and [making] the Caribbean area...a subject of increased interest to the rest of the Continent.[17]

In part this grew out of a general Latin American stance of anti-interventionism. In part, though, it owed to the political cover the British action provided for other regional actors to covet European holdings. As had occurred at the OAS founding at Bogotá, the colonies pitted the inter-American system against the Anglo-American one, as Latin American governments had staked claims on adjacent territories from the Falklands/Malvinas to the Dutch Antilles to British Honduras. After the British Guiana intervention in late 1953, the problem re-emerged.[18]

Two events in 1954 brought these issues to a head. At the meeting in March of western-hemisphere Foreign Ministers at Caracas, Venezuela—called principally in a U.S. effort to secure Latin American support for action against what Washington saw as the "communist-leaning" government of Jacobo Arbenz Guzman in Guatemala—Secretary of State Dulles cajoled his counterparts into signing the Caracas Declaration. The document affirmed hemispheric anticommunist solidarity, although less resoundingly than Dulles had hoped. Critics have noted that the Declaration gave the Eisenhower administration license to employ aggressive anticommunist tactics in Latin America. Arguably as important was the symbolic statement it made. It formed the backdrop to Bustamante's renewed pressure for anticommunist action, to which the governor responded with a speech, the consul reported, "probably timed to show local solidarity with [the Caracas] resolution...calling for collective action against Communist infiltration of the hemisphere." The consul added that a Bustamante interview on his anticommunism in the 8 March 1954 *Daily Gleaner* was similarly timed to take "advantage of prominence of Communist issue at Caracas."[19] Both the governor and Bustamante no doubt understood the import of the Declaration and were speaking as much to each other as to Washington and London. Jamaica thus offered a counterexample to British Guiana, showing colonial resolve—not vulnerability—in the face of communism in the Americas.

The high-water mark of that threat during Eisenhower's first term was the June 1954 Guatemala intervention, seen as representative of New Look methods. Suspicion of Arbenz's true ideological colors led to CIA intrigues ending in his ouster. The signal to radical forces around Latin America was as unmistakable as the bitterness it engendered. What is less appreciated is the role of the British colonies.[20] At the OAS founding at Bogotá, Guatemala had reiterated century-old designs on British Honduras and nearly made annexation a part of its revised constitution. The colony next door held rich timber- and farmlands and was essentially a political vacuum. British Guiana had shown that a Caribbean colony could fall to internal forces; British Honduras might fall in like manner to external ones, if Arbenz pressed Guatemalan claims. In the phrase Eisenhower contemporaneously coined for Southeast Asia, should British Honduras prove to be as fragile as British Guiana, then an Arbenz triumph might represent not one domino but two.

Jamaican observers both pro- and anticommunist saw the Guatemala episode as highly relevant to their respective efforts. Editorial comment pressed the need to keep Guatemala noncommunist. "If President Arbenz can defeat this challenge," wrote a columnist for the Jamaican *Daily Gleaner* as the conflict raged, the "underground cells of Communism in this hemisphere will take fresh heart, creating a new danger to all anti-Red regimes this side of the Atlantic."[21] After Arbenz's fall, Hamlin reported that Jamaican communists such as Hart, faltering after a string of failed strikes and police raids, had been "given a further setback by the overthrow of the Arbenz government. Local leaders, however, show no signs of giving up."

Hamlin relayed the colonial view that "while it is a conflict between Guatemalans, [it will determine] whether Communism will take a firmer hold in the western hemisphere."[22] Hamlin noted the failure of a Hands-Off-Guatemala rally, which only attracted about two hundred and which was "devoted to denunciations of the United States and United Fruit." The Eisenhower administration had made its point in Guatemala, and interested parties around the littoral grasped it. The next autumn, U.S.-owned bauxite facilities in Jamaica were sabotaged, demonstrating the continuing threat.[23] It was, however, much reduced. The Anglo-American anticommunist compact—abetted by colonial leaders such as Butler and Bustamante—had achieved at least short-term success. It bears emphasizing that in both of the 1954 events—the Caracas meeting in March and the Guatemalan intervention in June—communism was the main concern, but colonialism hovered in the background. The connection should not be overlooked; it draws needed attention to the simultaneous, parallel nature of the challenges the United States and Britain perceived in the region. Caracas and Guatemala are inevitably and rightly linked in inter-American relations under Eisenhower. Yet, although Caracas prepared the ground for the Guatemala intervention, it also merits a place on the timeline of West Indian decolonization, following British Guiana and coinciding with the cresting of Jamaican anticommunism.[24]

Such a "united front," however, carried long-term risks, as Eisenhower noted in preparing for talks with Winston Churchill in late 1953.[25] For the United States, the danger was in being cast as just another imperial oppressor, hostile to Third World nationalism. In the Caribbean, that danger hinged on a tenuous reputation. On the one hand, West Indians were generally "strongly oriented toward the United States psychologically."[26] This owed not only to contacts with the black mainland but also to U.S. support for colonial reform. On the other, America's reputation was not helped by its support for the British Guiana and Guatemala interventions, nor by its racial regime. Compared to military and ideological operations, the administration's diplomatic initiatives regarding race and reform were slight indeed. These did, however, offer at least some chance to leaven the American image in an area that knew the reality well.

When Smith had arrived in Jamaica in 1952, officials noted that his "color makes him acceptable to West Indians."[27] Although the issue of race—specifically, of American racial practices—was then muted, it was never far below the surface. In Trinidad, the consul noted that "occasionally the color issue is raised" in communist propaganda; and there, as in Jamaica, Kenya's Mau Mau had attracted popular interest. Communist propaganda in the West Indies made liberal use of Jim Crow.[28] Truman's State Department had organized counter-propaganda campaigns to combat these charges in the Caribbean. Under Eisenhower the United States sustained many of these efforts to manage the American racial image, although the American reputation arguably suffered most from a law signed by his predecessor: the 1952 McCarran Immigration Act restricting nonwhite immigration.[29] Especially for radicals like Smith, U.S. efforts at racial "image management" went for naught. It is telling that the African-American icon with whom they identified was not one of the mainland lynched, but rather Paul Robeson.[30]

If the Eisenhower administration found itself hamstrung by the U.S. racial record, there were two other vehicles that could nonetheless help to improve the American reputation. The first was the Caribbean Commission, which now included the Netherlands and France as well as founders Britain and the United States. The Commission, especially since the death of its prime mover Charles Taussig, had drifted into limbo. First conceived of as a forum for pooling resources to address shared Caribbean problems, the body had been overtaken by events. In particular, the spread of popularly elected governments made the very idea of "representative" metropolitan Commission members, speaking *for* the Caribbean colonial territories, problematic.

Early in the Eisenhower administration, Taussig's successor as chief of the U.S. section, Ward Canady, brought the body to the president's attention. He proposed that Washington use the Commission to accelerate Caribbean progress and asked why it was not already doing so.[31] Canady had proven a worthy heir to Taussig by almost single-handedly getting Congress to authorize technical assistance and development aid under the Point Four program to the Caribbean territories. Eisenhower forwarded Canady's question to his State Department, which assured the president it shared Canady's zeal.

Despite the rhetoric, the department found that the best way to use the Commission was as a symbol. A report prepared for Dulles confirmed that the body "at present has a distinctly colonial flavor about it," and it was in American interests to remove this foul taste.[32] In practice this meant revising the Commission Agreement to remove the word "colony" from its text and to make the body's membership more representative. In addition, Washington should build on the well-regarded Operation Bootstrap to make further unilateral improvements in Puerto Rico, setting an example for continued progress. U.S. initiative there would defuse the "ever-present threat" of communism and demagoguery and place the United States in the right on decolonization, even if it fell short of the reformism Canady had suggested.[33]

One reform eclipsed all others and received strong Eisenhower administration support: federation. It offered an opportunity to show American support for the transition to self-rule, with which federation was bound up in many minds. As Richard B. Moore put it during Bustamante's 1954 Harlem visit, "federation would lead to sovereignty and independence, [and] the Caribbean people could achieve their proper destiny only through federation."[34] In a sense federation was a vehicle on which the United States was catching a free ride; Washington had little to do with a reform that the British and the nationalist leadership were going to proceed with anyway. Yet the American stake was considerable and not only as a means of polishing the U.S. reputation.

In April 1953 the Standing Closer Association Committee (SCAC), in charge of planning the union, returned its first report. The committee envisioned the federation—whatever its final shape and size, both matters yet to be decided—as a kind of halfway house en route to full independence. Universal suffrage would elect parliamentary democracies at both the unit and federal levels. The member units would have internal political sovereignty, minus whatever powers were conferred upon the federal center, such as the responsibility for some as yet undetermined form of regional economic organization. The federation's external affairs would be handled by London until independence was achieved, at which time the halfway house would become fully sovereign and a member of the Commonwealth.

The SCAC conceded, however, that federating would be an uphill struggle, facing both logistical and sentimental difficulties. Some of these were already manifest. The selection of a federal capital site, for example, revealed the gap between pan-colonial and provincial loyalties. It also underscored the "imbalance" factor that would haunt the federal project—namely, the yawning gap in size, population, wealth, and political culture between the two "bigs" (Jamaica and Trinidad), the "littles" (the smaller British possessions of the lesser Antilles), and Barbados in between. Accommodating such a range is the challenge of any federal system, but one made harder in this case by geographic and psychological insularity. The question of where to put the capital encapsulated the dilemma. The colonies lacked an obvious and shared "leading city" that could play that role, and the breadth of the archipelago made the Brasilia option of a neutral-site federal district logistically impractical. Each of the "big" island options, moreover, brought problems of its own, and reading between the lines of the first SCAC report hinted at the ways in which the capital-site question foretold dilemmas about the federation's structure. But despite the dilemmas, which most nationalists and the Colonial Office were sure could be surmounted by compromise and their shared commitment to the federal project, the SCAC report served as a stepping-stone to a federal destiny that seemed increasingly inevitable.

Events in British Guiana the next month cast a shadow over federal deliberations. British Guiana and British Honduras were the odd men out in most schemes of union. Even plans that included them—which the SCAC report did not—did so less because of kinship than because of the assets they offered, notably abundant land for surplus populations. The election of Jagan cast doubt on British Guiana's suitability for federation of whatever shape, seeming one part contagious neighbor and one part cautionary tale. If radicals could take power there, a federal link could infect other members of the union. At the same time, the radicals' triumph underlined the importance of a British-supervised transition to federal self-government.

Washington had long supported federation, but the events of 1953 added urgency. In July the United States communicated to London its desire to assist. Worried by the "communist tendencies" in the region, the State Department "feels a federal British-Caribbean dominion is much more to U.S. advantage."[35] In 1954 U.S. officials reiterated their support, in a conversation that named Trinidad as the key obstacle due to its displeasure over the capital-site issue. Colonial Office personnel predicted a quick resolution and then federation perhaps as early as 1956. Their American counterparts expressed high hopes for the project and the expectation that the new state would be the key to Caribbean stability.[36] When a compromise on the capital-site issue was reached, satisfying Trinidad's concerns, the State Department's Europe desk confirmed that momentum for federation was now unstoppable and that it had the United States' blessing:

[Federation] is in the United States interest and [is] the best hope for orderly and stable progress towards self-government...A self-governing dominion composed overwhelmingly of colored people will also have great psychological advantages both here and abroad and be a dramatic counter to Soviet propaganda on Colonialism. The self-governing aspect should also ease the problem with the American Republics of Colonialism in the Western Hemisphere....We should...lend all possible assistance, moral and economic, to the achievement of Federation [in] the British West Indies.[37]

The West Indian union, in short, held great importance to U.S. foreign policy; it offered concrete and symbolic benefits on issues of race, colonialism, communism, and national security.[38]

The analysts failed to note, however, that West Indian progress toward federation and self-government had a potential downside for the United States. As Britain gradually abjured its sovereignty, the hegemon would inevitably assume a larger role in West Indian affairs. This would add pressure to existing points of contact, especially American military facilities. Already these were causing static, especially in Trinidad, where conflict over the U.S. base would soon emerge. For the moment, though, the tensions were in check, as national-security pursuits predominated and trumped other American, British, and nationalist concerns, even as the latter matured and expanded into the federal vessel.

Nationalism, Federation, or Both? Slouching toward Union, 1955–1956

After Guatemala, the Eisenhower administration adjusted its relations around the hemisphere only at the margins. The promotion of trade and military pacts with the countries to the south signified the belief that communism, while still a threat, was more or less in abeyance. So too in the West Indies, where the British Guiana intervention and the colonial anti-communism pioneered in Jamaica suggested that radicalism in the embryonic West Indies Federation had been defanged. The challenge now for sovereign Britain and the witness-participant United States was to channel nationalist momentum in constructive, pro-Western ways.

That momentum in 1955 continued to gain steam. In January, Manley and the PNP at last won a victory over Bustamante and the JLP. With characteristic humility, Bustamante conceded defeat: "Without any boast whatever, I am positively confident that what my government has done for the last ten years no other government will be able to do within thirty years!" Speaking for many, Williams felt differently, writing Manley to salute his victory over the "mountebank."[39] The result was taken as Jamaican endorsement of the West Indian nationalism, self-government, and federation Manley championed. As the consul put it, "Manley has become a symbol of Jamaican nationhood and self-reliance, the prophet of a federated West Indian dominion," unlike Bustamante whose followers were "mostly devoid of a sense of national pride in Jamaica."[40] Given the bitter campaign and close result, though, observers could not be sure that this was the full picture. Bustamante had blasted the PNP as communist shills. Despite his purge of the party three years earlier, Manley could not quite bleach its red tint so long as Bustamante had the full use of his voice. Now that Bustamante's diatribes had failed to keep the PNP from power, Manley and his associates set about conveying their anticommunist sincerity.

Throughout 1955 they pursued this mission. Soon after his victory, Manley made a trip to New York to thank supporters and to emphasize Jamaica's ties to the United States. Minister of Labour Florizel Glasspole called at Washington, after informing Hamlin that "his main mission was to convince the U.S. government that the PNP government is not communistic." At every turn, Manley disavowed nationalization, including in his victory speech.[41] Acknowledging that the campaign might have caused "some disquiet in...England and America...let me say categorically that we recognise that nationalisation is not the present answer to our problem." In August, Hamlin parsed the differences between Manley and his rival. Bustamante was more "intensely pro-American" and better grasped the need for a strong anticommunist hand lest another Jagan arise, but ultimately both Manley and he were "firmly anticommunist." The governor confirmed that eight months after the victory of the party accused of radicalism, "communism [was] at its lowest ebb in Jamaica." The consul went further, remarking that "while this island is still some stage removed from complete self-government, it is already much closer to that goal in practice. . . . And much of that advance has taken place, without fanfare, [since] the present government of Mr. Manley has been in office."[42] Manley's mission, in short, was a success, and his reign satisfied American observers.

The implications for U.S. conduct were mostly but not fully clear. As national-security concerns held priority, Washington looked first to the impact of Manley's win on remaining U.S. bases and on bauxite extraction. The latter in particular involved the new government. Manley had promised not to nationalize, but he had attacked Bustamante's and Britain's acceptance of a "sellout" bauxite royalty. Mining had benefited the island, through high wages, an enviable rate of capital formation, and infrastructure additions. Manley was mindful of this. At the same time, he held a high card—his island held 62 percent of all potential North American reserves—and he had a point. The companies had locked in a low rate for twenty-five years, depriving Jamaica of needed revenues during the crucial transition to independence. Moreover, the U.S. tariff on alumina discouraged any on-site refining, foreclosing a local opportunity to add value.[43] Manley made successful bauxite renegotiation a priority of his government. He launched an elaborate campaign of publicity and diplomacy—and of what U.S. observers, had they known of it, would no doubt have called "collusion" with other Third World nationalists such as Kwame Nkrumah, with whom Manley quietly strategized about the renegotiations—to that end.[44]

Manley sent Finance Minister N. N. Nethersole to Washington to discuss changes in the bauxite arrangements. Nethersole sought Washington's help in persuading American companies to build plants for processing ore into alumina, and to raise the royalty rates. He pointed out that the U.S. government had the needed leverage; if it would cancel the alumina tariff, then the companies would have an incentive to build alumina plants in Jamaica. Washington declined and advised Nethersole not to press too hard lest the companies move elsewhere—an empty threat, given that Jamaican reserves dwarfed all others. Two months later, the consul alerted Washington that Manley was leaning toward requesting a higher royalty.[45] Soon after, he did so. The request was resolved rapidly—and in Jamaica's favor, as Manley reported on the radio after his return that the island's royalty take would rise tenfold in four years, from £352,000 in 1956 to £3.6 million in 1960. As Munroe records, "the agreement...produced a more equitable formula for tax payments and, generally, resulted in considerable increase in the Government's revenue intake."[46] Even so, Washington had to be pleased. Haggling over the royalty was a minor nuisance compared to the range of latent or ongoing conflicts over raw materials elsewhere in the Third World, such as oil in Iran, rubber in Indochina, or uranium in Africa.

The Asian-African Conference at Bandung, Indonesia in April 1955, moreover, showed that the Third World was here to stay. The Bandung meeting brought together representatives of twenty-nine emerging nations; Western-white nations were pointedly not invited. Conferees, including Jawaharlal Nehru and Abdel Gamal Nasser, called for neutralism, an end to colonialism, and racial progress. The symbolic power of the event resonated around the globe. Eric Williams spoke to West Indians about it in one of his first public addresses and added a historian's perspective: "Bandung symbolized...the profound revolution [of] the past century. A hundred years or so ago such a conference would have been unthinkable." Participants reveled in "a newfound sense of 'belonging' and...'solidarity' against racial domination and discrimination," according to scholar Paul Gordon Lauren. "The Bandung Conference immediately sent waves rushing across the world.... [Senegalese nationalist poet] Leopold Senghor even went as far as to describe [it] as the most important event since the Renaissance."[47]

The Eisenhower administration recognized the conference's importance but was unsure how to respond.[48] At first Washington hesitated even to issue a statement, for fear of raising hopes of a Third World Marshall Plan. Later Dulles suggested a "Bandung conference in reverse," at which the imperial powers would offer leadership in guiding the Third World independence movements to fruition. Eisenhower and Dulles both had been quietly pressing the British to make such a move for some time, but they could point to few concrete results.[49] One of the few, though, was West Indian progress. Indeed, the State Department seized on the region to score post-Bandung points. The U.S.-backed revision of the Caribbean Commission agreement "puts [us] in the proper column [on] the colonial issue [and will] receive the overwhelming approval of native leaders in the Caribbean." State went on to urge heavy press coverage worldwide, "since this U.S. position should be (and can be made to be) of interest to peoples everywhere who feel strongly about colonialism."[50]

Ironically, one such person who would play a large role in U.S.–West Indian relations rose to fame in part because of an embittering experience with the Commission. Eric Williams had served that body for years in various research positions. His tenure had not always been a smooth one, and his work at times embarrassed British interests. Moreover, though Williams was hardly hard Left, some of his scholarship employed a variation on Marxist analysis that rendered him suspect to anyone unfamiliar with the difference between Marx, Lenin, and Stalin. This left him, as he later reported to his fellow Trinidadians, vulnerable to false charges of being a communist. Such charges, combined with the Labour Party's loss in the 1955 British elections, cost Williams his protectors, and his contract with the commission was not renewed.[51]

Williams returned to his homeland and pondered a political career. In a famous public lecture in June 1955 in Port of Spain, he launched one. His addresses at what he called "the University of Woodford Square" rallied a coherent Trinidadian nationalism in a way nothing else had since the 1937 riots and was the foundation on which he built his People's National Movement (PNM) party. His choice of subject for that first lecture was telling: "My Relations with the Anglo-American Caribbean Commission, 1943–1955."[52]

If this topic seemed unlikely to stimulate West Indian nationalism, Williams nonetheless succeeded in making it do so. He launched searing attacks not only against his British antagonists but against his American ones too. His enmity for the British was unconcealed; a lesser antipathy toward the United States was unconfirmed but suspected. An American analyst wrote that "Williams is a brilliant scholar and politician whose influence...is already large and will continue to grow. His attitude toward the United States is uncertain and there is a danger that he could be pushed into a position of consistent anti-Americanism."[53] Both powers, Williams charged, shared an anticommunist paranoia and a disdain for Caribbean agency: "If West Indians are to think only when Britain and the U.S. consider it is the right time for them to do so, we will never think at all!" Williams returned to the podium often, giving voice to an inchoate nationalism that had been seeking expression since World War II. Unlike Jamaica, where energy coalesced around Bustamante and Manley, Trinidad's politics had never taken stable, bipolar form, except roughly and ominously around the black–East Indian racial division.

Williams entered politics in the hopes of leading an irresistible—and ideally, interracial—nationalist movement. U.S. officials reported his out-of-the-blue political strength; Williams wrote excitedly to Manley that "the pot here is boiling!" Not everyone was impressed; his rival Ashford Sinanan dismissed him as an "educated but rather shallow individual who was seeking to organize the Indian and Negro populations on a racial basis."[54] But the founding of the PNM in January, and its electoral victory in September, were milestones not just in Trinidadian politics but in the broader story of Caribbean decolonization. Unlike most of its regional peers, the PNM did not grow out of the 1930s. The organizations of labor leaders such as Butler and Gomes had roots in the unrest, but had not spun off full-fledged political parties à la Jamaica. Williams's challenge was to foster a political nationalism without alienating the labor groups. Manley saw this from Jamaica and wrote Padmore to request that he second Manley's counsel "advising [Williams] him to make alliances with the best Trade Union groups."[55] This had to be done on a scene shaped not just by local issues but by uneven progress toward federation as well.

Indeed, federation would prove a powerful catalyst of internecine West Indian tensions and battles, and even more so as the prospective union jelled. The 1956 London Conference on Federation had laid out the basic structure of the union, with important details deferred to a Standing Federation Committee (SFC). Shortly after the conference, Parliament passed the British Caribbean Act to create a federal union of a "semi-colonial" nature.[56] The entity was premised on regional cooperation and unity as the road to self-rule, but its proposed structure instead deepened divisions among its member units. The conflicts centered on fundamental questions regarding constitutional structure, taxation, movement of people and goods, and other basic matters that pitted member-unit prerogatives against one other as well as against the federal power. Further complicating all of these conflicts was the fact that some territories had already taken long strides toward self-government. Far from being the means to that end, federation now appeared to threaten to undo those advances. Even fervent believers in the federal dream were reluctant to give up what self-rule they had won, albeit now to a central West Indian government instead of the distant British one. Uncertainty over these issues grew as the prospective launch of the federation drew nearer by the day.

For the United States, the regional union remained the focus of Caribbean policy, even though Washington could do little more than cheer from the sidelines. There were indications that a pan-colonial identity was taking root. The West Indian Federal Labour Party, launched in 1956 in an attempt to unify colonial labor organizations, selected Manley as its leader in hopes of forging a federal political party. The nominally socialist W.I.F.L.P. was an umbrella group of the left-labor parties of Jamaica, Barbados, Antigua, St. Kitts, Grenada, Montserrat, and St. Lucia. Williams and the PNM "at first hesitated to join a professedly socialist national party" but joined in May 1957 once their concerns were addressed. As of early that summer, Manley, Williams, and Grantley Adams (chief minister of Barbados and soon first federal prime minister) thus all belonged to the same "party," one that spanned the Caribbean. The W.I.F.L.P. was not the only "national" party to take shape; in response to it, Bustamante organized the Democratic Labour Party (DLP), and Gomes formed an affiliate, the Federal Democratic Party. But the W.I.F.L.P. was the only one to unite the ruling parties of Caribbean territories.[57] Recurring clashes among the party leaders, however, raised American worries that the enterprise might be doomed. Indo-Trinidadians remained unreconciled to any union with a trans-colonial black majority and worked instead to foster bonds with India abroad and political strength at home. Jamaicans, Manley and his inner circle notwithstanding, ranged from ambivalent to apathetic.[58] In mid-1955, American officials had second thoughts as to whether federation would serve U.S. interests: "on [its] face, the principle of federation seems acceptable, but...a new political structure in the area may...not add up to an advantage for the U.S. It might be easier to deal with individual units than to be faced eventually by a larger grouping."[59]

However, political and strategic considerations won out, and despite signs of the union's weakness, Washington continued to endorse it. Key leaders appreciated this support, including Manley and Adams. Visiting New York, Adams declared that "the U.S. is equally the 'mother country' to the West Indies Federation."[60] Beyond showcasing "progressive" decolonization, the new state would strengthen U.S. security, help to stabilize the hemisphere, and perhaps even benefit U.S. relations with Latin America. As a State Department analyst put it:

> The Latin American countries have repeatedly [called for] elimination of colonialism from this hemisphere...it seems reasonable to suppose that federation of the West Indies will meet with mixed reaction in Latin America [but] in the balance it would appear that Federation would be consistent with our foreign policy objectives and not detrimental—perhaps even beneficial—to our relations with Latin America.[61]

In early 1956 the USIA offered advice on how to use the emerging federation in the hemispheric and world press. Aside from propaganda, the union assumed a central place in U.S. plans.[62] The Embassy in London relayed the torturous progress at the Caribbean Union Conference there and confirmed doubts about the proposed state's weaknesses.[63] Still, despite misgivings, the United States continued to support the project.

The limits of that support would soon become clear. The argument over the federal capital reached a crescendo in September 1956, coinciding with Williams's victory and with the report of Sir Francis Mudie's Capital Site Commission. The report recommended Barbados, Jamaica, and Trinidad, in that order. Barbados took first place in large measure because it represented a "third party" choice whose selection showed no favor in the innate rivalry between the other two, which were the largest and richest West Indian islands. In addition, Barbados was as logistically accessible as, and more politically stable than, the two "bigs" or for that matter almost any of the "littles." The commission justified Trinidad's ranking in blunt terms, citing "corruption" and "the instability of that island's politics and the low standard accepted in its public life," all oblique references to the black–East Indian racial division.[64]

The timing was important. When Williams had launched his party in January, he had done so partly in response to the corruption and instability to which the Mudie report referred. In September, though, that same observation—coincident with the victory of Williams's avowedly interracial and incorrupt nationalist movement—sparked Trinidadian anger, as it now seemingly rebuked the PNM's achievement. One result was the redoubling of Williams's resolve to win the capital for the island. Even before the report, the Colonial Office had debated the sites there. Routinely among the top few was Chaguaramas and the Northwest Peninsula, site of the major U.S. military base on the island. A hive of activity during the war, it now functioned as a maintenance facility and missile-tracking station with around 250 personnel. The site was close to Port of Spain, included the city's nearest recreational beach, and had an infrastructure convertible to civilian purposes. This characteristic was found at several U.S.-leased areas. The presence of such facilities, of which the United States might make gifts to the new country, was what made Chaguaramas so appealing.[65] British officials in early 1956 had begun sounding out the United States on the possible release of Chaguaramas and nearby areas for use as a capital site.

The State Department warmed to the idea. Provided that such an act was "consistent with other national interests," the United States should release whatever area the West Indians requested, given the "obvious...need for [us] to take a positive interest in the federation's development...in light of our strategic interests in the area" and the need to avoid resentment and build goodwill. The military, however, was less convinced. Washington notified London that its decision would await the capital-site committee's report.[66] Although events would soon disprove this, Williams's victory seemed a good omen. Aware of latent West Indian resentment of the original Bases Agreement, Williams nonetheless reiterated the PNM position that it and other such "legacy" accords must be honored. Observers concluded that this would be the position of the new PNM government, which was not expected to be a radical one.[67] This helped to balance the uncertainty over the capital-site question, which awaited the next SFC meeting in January 1957.

That uncertainty arose at the same time as the major international event of that fall: the Suez crisis. Prior to Suez, the British sensed that American anticolonialism was fluctuating. Between Bandung and Suez, the Policy Planning Staff had wrestled with the dilemma European colonialism posed, concluding that trends after Bandung were rendering the matter acute. The British were ahead of the other powers, in the U.S. view, but still frustrated officials watching the tide rise against the empires.[68] U.S. conduct at Suez, though driven by the contingencies there, took place within this re-evaluation of Anglo-American relations regarding the colonial question.

Caribbean developments of late 1956 were also positioned within these colonial currents. Although Williams, Bustamante, and Manley all commented on the Suez crisis, most islanders showed little interest. For Washington and London, the contrasts were reassuring. There was little evidence of Soviet interest in the federation, à la the Aswan Dam project. Nor was there reason to think that among West Indian nationalists there lurked a Nasser. Finally, despite similarities regarding access to a vital canal and the presence of Western troops, few involved yet drew parallels between the Mideast crisis and the Caribbean struggle to federate. Yet both similarities, especially the latter regarding "uninvited" troops at a sensitive site, formed the backdrop as the United States, Britain, and the West Indies sorted out the Suez aftermath on the eve of federal nationhood.

Born under a Bad Sign: Federation and Chaguaramas, 1957–1958

Unbeknownst to American and British officials meeting at Bermuda to clear the post-Suez air, the year 1957 would drive home the change in the racial-colonial dynamics of the Cold War. Events in the United States and abroad produced a sea change in relations between the superpowers, the Western allies, and nonwhite peoples the world over. The achievement of independence in Ghana that spring sparked a new wave of decolonization and galvanized the anticolonialist bloc in the United Nations. The Little Rock crisis focused attention on American racial practices, building solidarity between nonwhites in the United States and the Third World, and complicating American diplomatic efforts everywhere.

While this "second Cold War" did not immediately touch developments in the West Indies, it furnished the backdrop against which the intertwined federation and Chaguaramas crises unfolded. Colonialism and its denouement shaped the agenda at Bermuda. British Prime Minister Harold Macmillan avowed that "the process [of decolonization] could not be stopped." Nor need the two powers be so far apart; despite British resentment at "smug," not to say disingenuous, American anticolonialism, Dulles emphasized its limits in U.S. diplomacy.[69] For London, this was a start: "The objective of the Bermuda conference [is] to get the U.S. to overhaul its attitude toward British colonialism." American thinking was colored by "prejudice on the subject," Colonial Secretary A. T. Lenox-Boyd wrote Macmillan; the United States did not see that it was "a constructive job of nation-building."[70] This despite the fact that a premier example—the anti-Suez, as it were—lay right on the U.S. doorstep:

> The Caribbean Federation [is] a step toward self-government [but] there is still a tendency to believe that we are clinging on to our colonial possessions as long as we can. On the contrary, we are launching them out as soon as we can.... Our failures (e.g. British Guiana) are the result of going too fast rather than too slow.[71]

Events would soon call the dependability, especially regarding U.S. concerns, of this premier example into question. But as of the Bermuda conference, the WIF occupied the "model area" role in which London was long comfortable casting it.

Washington agreed with the casting. A group of diplomats and scholars studying the colonial problem—"THE problem for future United States foreign policy"—reaffirmed in early 1957 the long-held U.S. conviction that the Caribbean Commission offered a model for the decolonizing world. That body, in addition to other American initiatives in the region, was of great significance to the rest of the world as a laboratory for proving American bona fides.[72] Federation was to consummate this progress, all to the credit of West Indian nationalists, British officials, and the supportive northern neighbor.

Yet this was not to be the case. The United States, looking on the emergent union with approval, would soon find itself caught up in a bitter dispute with its neighbor. At a moment already complicated by Little Rock, Sputnik, and the anticolonial surge, U.S. relations with the federation threatened to break down. Suddenly not only was the American image at risk, but a planned bulwark of hemispheric security was too. The proximate cause of the crisis was the ongoing dispute over the WIF capital site. The immediate cause was the proposed use of Chaguaramas for that site. The resulting clash dominated U.S. relations with the nascent federation in 1957–58 and helped to hobble the new state at birth.

Prior to 1957, the capital site had been far from the only issue splitting colonial opinion. As federation loomed, colonial leaders faced a hard choice: to risk positions won at home or to seek office in the federal arena. Manley, in particular, agonized over the decision. On the one hand, the new state needed men of his stature in order to succeed. On the other, leaving home meant abandoning the office he had sought since 1944 and only held since 1955. The decision, like that of the capital site, involved insular pride; questions over whose leader would head the union, and whose island would host the capital, undercut West Indian unity. Racial-political tensions also continued to rend the regional fabric.[73] For the general public, federation was—at least in most colonies—as yet barely on the political radar, though its launch was imminent. In most islands, interest in the project was top-heavy; nationalist leaders, journalists, intellectuals, and local elites followed and supported it much more evidently at this point than did the colonial masses. The capital-site question, however, *had* registered in Trinidad, where the Mudie report had prompted a storm of protest. Williams had vowed to fight: "[He] is now more than ever assured that all Trinidad is with him in the fight for a federal capital."[74] At the 1957 SFC meeting, he lived up to his word. Following his rebuttal of the Mudie insults, the committee voted to place the capital in Trinidad. That colony was asked to name a local committee to make recommendations "on all suitable sites."

The committee concluded its work in April. Three of the potential sites were areas leased by the American military: Waller Field, Tucker Valley, and Chaguaramas. The first was an all but deactivated airbase; the second was mostly inactive but accessible only via Chaguaramas. The third, however, was home to an active U.S. base—and was the enthusiastic first choice, due among other reasons to its proximity to Port of Spain and its extensive infrastructure. The SFC was to vote on these findings at its next meeting. This put Williams in a very tough position. He remained publicly committed to the PNM's campaign position that agreements to which Trinidad was party—including especially the Bases-for-Destroyers Deal that had leased the Chaguaramas acreage to the United States during the war—must be honored. He reiterated this position at the SFC meeting and abstained from votes on the matter.[75] Other leaders such as Gomes expressed wariness about Chaguaramas given likely repercussions, most of all the American wrath that a demand for the base would surely incur. In Trinidad and London alike, several members thought it would be embarrassing to Trinidad and, worse, irritating to the United States to ask for the area. However, in the end, a divided committee voted to do just that, and a delegation was appointed to go to London and Washington to press the case for Chaguaramas.[76]

The State Department told the British Embassy that the vote was a "painful surprise." The United States had quietly made clear to London before the committee's vote that Chaguaramas could not be released, although Waller Field might be.[77] Despite State support for release, the military had concluded that it must keep Chaguaramas. In view of this, the committee's decision was "provocative" and "did not augur well for the United States' future relations with the W.I.F." Washington could take comfort in the fact that the request did not have diplomatic force; London had not endorsed it. Moreover, although the vote had generated excitement in Trinidad, this was less evident in the rest of the WIF. As Trinidadian calypso-singer Atilla the Hun sang in honor of the capital decision and of federation, and of West Indian nationalists' long-stated hope about where that union would ultimately lead:

> When the news came over the air that night
> That Trinidad was selected as the Capital site
> There was jubilation all over the land
> And songs of rejoicing on every hand ...
> For now that we have set up our Federation
> The next step will be full Dominion
> And then to take our place, our greatest ambition
> In that galaxy of peoples, a Commonwealth nation.[78]

The consul noted that Williams was refraining from public comment on the committee's vote. His rivals held that the prestige and jobs Trinidad gained from the U.S. base made it imperative to put the capital elsewhere. Local businessmen deduced, and hoped, the United States would not release the base. "Unless there is a complete and presently unforeshadowed reversal of local public opinion," the consul reported, "it would appear that in Trinidad we should have little to fear from a polite, well-reasoned but firm refusal to release [Chaguaramas] for use as the capital site."[79]

From all points on the diplomatic triangle—Washington, London, and the West Indies—the situation was seen to have cross-cutting ramifications. The United States genuinely sought good relations with the WIF, seeing it as a pro-West pillar in the hemisphere. Yet Washington faced a potential no-win situation if the Chaguaramas claim were pressed. For the WIF to be that pillar, it had to host key U.S. bases to defend against external threats. Here was a scenario in which one of those bases might create an *internal* threat, by generating anti-American instability. Furthermore, beyond just the federation, surrender of base areas might encourage claims against other U.S. holdings, most crucially the Panama Canal Zone.[80]

Nor would a surrender necessarily bring any lasting goodwill to offset the strategic losses, given that West Indian leaders were far from unified on

Chaguaramas. For them, the matter was a political football. The parliamentary oppositions in Jamaica and Trinidad blasted the idea of demanding the base, while Manley, for his part, asserted that Waller Field was unsuitable, voiced confidence that the United States would be generous, and appeared to be seeking longer-term political capital for future use against Washington.[81] London felt caught in the middle. The United States had conveyed its unwillingness to release Chaguaramas and expected London to set the terms of debate for its West Indian subjects accordingly. The West Indians, by the same token, expected the British to represent their capital-site claims even if these included the base. The Colonial Office knew that the Bases Agreement had always been resented in Trinidad, given the 1940 protests of then-Governor Hubert Young. Whitehall urged that this be strongly considered and confidentially seconded the notion that Chaguaramas was the best site in Trinidad. But the Colonial Office had also argued to the WIF that U.S. goodwill was more important to the new state than was the capital site and had warned the committee that London would not support a request for the whole area.[82] However, Manley informed Williams that he had a source in Foggy Bottom who assured him that State was "sympathetic to us"; should a confrontation arise, the State–Defense split might be exploited in the hopes of State winning. In the event, the British strategy became to give a "friendly warning" to West Indians and the committee and to take no public stand until the latter made its decision in London that July.[83]

That meeting, to the shock of all involved, produced the "unforeshadowed reversal" the U.S. consul had dismissed as unlikely. The reversal was not one so much of that island's public opinion as of the position of its chief minister. It became clear early in the meeting that the U.S. delegation had come not to negotiate but to convey that the base's military value was paramount and that the United States would not give an inch. Williams leapt to battle. Abandoning his previous rhetoric and his party's stance, Williams launched an attack on the 1941 Bases Agreement and its Chaguaramas offspring as a rank continuation of colonialism. "In a tense monotone," according to scholar-participant John Mordecai, he cited chapter and verse of then-Governor Young's opposition to the Agreement, averring "that I could not possibly put myself in a position in 1957 of being less [protective] of the fundamental interests of the people of Trinidad" than Young had been in 1940.[84] It was bad enough, he argued, that a soon-to-be-sovereign country should have a foreign military installation imposed without consent on its soil. Worse still that the installation should occupy the chosen spot for the new country's capital. Cost, he suggested, was little object:

> It would cost, we are told, $100 millions to move Chaguaramas.... This is equivalent to 34 cents a year per head of the Federation for the unexpired portion of the lease. One would have thought this a small price to pay for West Indian goodwill and avoidance of friction. Certainly no amount of money would be able to buy that goodwill if the West Indian people learn how the rights of Trinidad were trampled in 1940. For friction there will be.... What appears to the Americans only as a base, what the SFC sees as the only capital, I see as an explosion of the first order.[85]

While stating his desire to find a mutually acceptable site for an American base elsewhere on the island, he concluded with an ultimatum: the United States must vacate Chaguaramas.

Williams's about-face surprised his colleagues and critics alike. Months before, he had reassured Washington that the capital-site deliberations did not indicate West Indian antipathy toward the United States. He had held to his campaign position when the Site Committee and the SFC had pressed the issue. Yet he *did* have the Committee's recommendation behind him, and a confrontation might serve Williams in two ways. First, it would test the sincerity of the two powers' support for West Indian autonomy. Second, it could potentially rally opinion at home and ratify his place at the head of a new generation of West Indian leadership. In effect, he made Chaguaramas the defining issue of U.S.–West Indian Federation relations.[86]

The London meeting was at a deep impasse. The West Indians, with Williams's stunning turn, had essentially declared it was all of Chaguaramas or nothing. The United States had made the now-rejected offer of Waller Field on grounds of Chaguaramas' strategic indispensability, and now dug in around the latter. Britain, torn between its colonial clients and its Atlantic ally, had not committed to a position but had leaned toward the latter, with some misgivings: "if Britain could give up Suez," one official put it, "surely the U.S. could give up Chaguaramas." As neither diplomats nor nationalists could bridge the gap, the committee turned to the highest levels. A request was sent to Macmillan, asking that he secure the intervention of the president.[87]

The prime minister did so immediately. He detailed the capital-site problems and the committee's impasse. "These [West Indian leaders] are not very easy to handle," he lamented, but there are "strong feelings in the West Indies and I am anxious there may be a breakdown." Macmillan underlined the need for cooperation and asked that the United States agree to a commission to settle the issue. In his response the next day, Eisenhower stated that the United States did not want to be where it was not wanted and would depart if London insisted. However, he warned that the base was vital to U.S. defense commitments, as per "the [findings] of the Inter-American Defense Board, [which] has expressed its concern lest the United States deactivate the base." The cost of replacing the base would be prohibitive, assuming another site could be found. The president closed by agreeing to a joint commission provided that this would not, in Eisenhower's words, "virtually commit [the U.S.] to leave."[88]

Moreover, Eisenhower pointed out that Congress would be disinclined to support losing and then replacing Chaguaramas, given the manner in which Williams had raised the issue: "The fact that this problem was forced upon us by the West Indies Federation would undoubtedly affect the attitude of the Congress toward it." Eisenhower was right. Except for the odd mention of the West Indies by members with a connection to the area, such as Representative Powell or Senator George Smathers, the colonies rarely made the congressional radar screen. However, any part of the Third World challenging the United States could expect to raise, if nothing else, at least some isolationist ire. Chaguaramas did so when Senator Randolph Wiley inserted articles from the *Milwaukee Journal* and the *New York Times* into the Congressional Record. The articles frustrated the State Department because they "hew[ed] the Navy line," thus complicating U.S. diplomatic efforts.[89]

What is remarkable, though, is not how much anger Chaguaramas raised among the American public but how little. The crisis remained largely confined to involved parties. Even Williams's blistering about-face—easy grist for anyone seeking to demonize Third World anti-Americanism—hardly made the papers. The *Times* piece does not mention Williams by name, although it did prompt one of his former students to write a letter to the editor in his defense: "He is far from the fire-eating anti-imperialist we might think him."[90] This image would change over the next two years, as Williams turned the behind-closed-doors crisis into a public crusade. For the moment, though, what American sentiment existed—outside of the Executive branch—tended to waver between warmth and apathy.

Even diasporan circles did not display the degree of active involvement seen in those moments of crisis of the previous two decades. The African-American–West Indian Harlem nexus showed some signs of its old self. The Caribbean League of America held an October 1957 rally in Harlem for "conciliation in the interest of West Indian–American Harmony, for an amicable settlement of the Embryo West Indian Federal Capital Site (Chaguaramas) now occupied by the United States as a naval base." Years earlier, on the eve of the 1953 Federation Conference, Moore had spoken for mainland West Indians when he affirmed that "federation is the *sine qua non* of progress for the Caribbean people."[91] Expatriates were the prime movers of activities like this in Harlem and elsewhere, as West Indians and well-wishers in Detroit, Chicago, and Washington all planned events to fete the federation.

Participation by African-Americans—Powell spoke at the 1957 rally—was important, but it was usually individual rather than institutional. The NAACP, for example, was not officially represented at the event, which in the 1940s it undoubtedly would have been. That organization still kept some contact with the West Indies; the leadership made it something of a tradition to go on a speaking tour of the islands every winter.[92] This controversy, though, attracted little of the group's attention. Especially after the Little Rock crisis further cemented the NAACP's domestic turn, outside of transnational Harlem black America had little attention to spare.[93]

The announcement of a joint Chaguaramas commission concluded the London meeting, although the impasse lingered throughout the autumn of 1957, threatening to last into the scheduled launch of the federation the following spring. The United States struggled to balance base needs with the need for a strong, friendly federation; Britain sought a compromise between its Caribbean constituents and its American partner; and West Indian leaders jockeyed for position as the union's birth drew near. In American eyes, this triangulation traced contours seen elsewhere in the decolonizing world, with two major differences. First, the WIF's proximity added a geostrategic dimension. This included security concerns—indistinguishable from bullying in many minds—and symbolic ones too, as American racism rose to global attention. Second, the communist menace seemed muted, having failed to graft itself to West Indian nationalism.

However, American officials perceived that some combination of these forces might fuse into a legitimately organic strain of anti-Americanism should Williams choose to nurture it. His about-face had "materially altered the local situation," wrote the U.S. consul. This was thanks in part to his "superb [confidence] that the U.S. will eventually agree to release Chaguaramas." Close surveillance and deft intriguing were required:

> It is hard to believe that two such seasoned campaigners as Manley and Adams would be prepared to stick with Williams...to the point of going along with him in stirring up a hornets nest of anti-Americanism throughout the West Indies and inviting the inevitable backfire....The only way...for us to hold on to Chaguaramas and at the same time to avoid an eventual explosion of anti-Americanism in Trinidad is through the other two members of the West Indian triumvirate—Manley and Adams.[94]

Williams averred to Manley that "the population is with us on Chaguaramas," although Canadian observers found that island opinion was divided. Some felt the base should stay in U.S. hands, since this would serve long-term regional defense; many felt that they should fight for an area given away without their consent. This tension had not yet translated into strong feelings against the mainland or action against Americans in the colony, but this could well result should Williams and his supporters hold fast to the hard-line.[95]

American efforts thus aimed simultaneously to support federation and to defuse anti-Americanism. Aside from the commission, officials pursued this goal in several ways, seeking to exploit the divisions between Williams and other leaders, the apathy toward Chaguaramas and federation, and the pro-American sentiment evident in many of the colonies.[96] Another was to emphasize the financial importance of American goodwill, by confidentially linking the base question to future U.S. aid. Attempts were also made to dissuade Williams from his crusade, to no avail. In one such meeting, Williams argued that if U.S. intransigence caused the capital to be moved outside Trinidad, Trinidad would leave the WIF, in which case the union would fail and the United States would be responsible. A consular analysis disagreed, but did detail the considerable costs and marginal benefits of acceding to Williams and abandoning the base.[97]

At the center of the Chaguaramas dispute was unmistakably the matter of prestige, for both sides. For Williams, facing down the United States as an equal was an essential step in shedding the colonial legacy. In "An Open Letter to Mr. Eisenhower," federation-supporter and University of Puerto Rico Professor Gordon Lewis expressed reason and respect. "Chaguaramas will not become another Suez," he declared, but postwar base negotiations elsewhere showed that sober discussion was possible, and Lewis insisted this was all that was sought: "The [WIF] asks for no more than this....It simply requests that agreements affecting its interests shall be arrived at through the ample use of its own diplomatic treaty-making power."[98]

The practical matter of siting the capital was inseparable from the psychological matter of becoming a legitimate nation by standing up for "national" interests. As Manley put it in a 15 May 1958 letter to the *Daily Gleaner*, the West Indies were confronting "the usual arrogance and contempt of an Imperial power. . . . It is an insult and an outrage to the people of the West Indies." A similar duality existed for the United States. Prestige and credibility were never far down the list of American concerns. Holding the base would testify that the United States would honor its written commitments and its unwritten stakes in the decolonizing world. The pursuit of national security and hemispheric defense was inextricably tied to both.

The actual shape of that pursuit had evolved by the time of the Chaguaramas dispute. By then, bauxite shortages had turned into surpluses. This meant that Jamaican bauxite's greatest importance was no longer its role in American military industries but rather its role in the economic development of Jamaica and, by extension, the WIF.[99] As for the traditional foundation of U.S. hemispheric defense doctrine—protection of the approaches to the Panama Canal—this too had evolved, partly due to the Trinidad dispute and partly in response to improved Soviet capabilities. After Chaguaramas, Eisenhower's national security team explored the possibility of building a second isthmian canal—discussions that continued, perhaps only coincidentally, into 1958, more or less in step with the Chaguaramas dispute.[100]

The federation came into being on 3 January 1958, with the question of Chaguaramas or, for that matter, any permanent capital site unresolved. If the American message of welcome at inauguration lauded the "historic step," all parties nonetheless knew it was a shaky one. The British governor-general to the federation was to preside over an interim administration while the new state prepared its first elections, slated for March. As important to the union's future, of course, were the deliberations of the Chaguaramas joint commission. There, as Manley warned Williams, "It is obvious . . . that the Conference is running into enormous difficulties."[101]

The Chaguaramas and federation questions continued to preoccupy regional leaders, as well as dominate cable traffic in and out of Foggy Bottom. In March, the joint commission affirmed one of the key facts on which Williams had built his case: technically, Chaguaramas was indeed the best location, largely because no other site could be developed without spending millions of dollars. This did not include estimates for rebuilding the military facilities, which ran up that cost a hundredfold. The base had originally cost one hundred million dollars to build and, assuming an alternate site could be found, it would cost even more to replace. This prompted a blunt interdepartmental question from the Navy: "Do we want the Federation to survive?" If the cost of its survival was that high, that is, U.S. interests might be better served by splitting rather than uniting the Caribbean.[102]

This idea, however, never received serious consideration, because the joint commission's findings were only one piece of the puzzle. The other was the federal election campaign, which was dominated by Chaguaramas. Familiar divisions crosscut the region. The election heartened U.S. officials; Williams's associates in the W.I.F.L.P. performed worse than expected. The party took only a slim majority of seats against the rival DLP, and more crucially, failed to win majorities in Jamaica and Trinidad. Most analysts agreed that Chaguaramas had hurt the party. A shocked Manley, having predicted a big win, commiserated with Williams that "we have done very badly indeed" for reasons he found unclear. C. L. R. James lamented that "the new Federation government is in a crisis before it has begun."[103] In a way, this merely added to the mystery: Chaguaramas apathy and even "pro-Americanism" in most colonies coexisted with what seemed to be burgeoning anti-Americanism spearheaded by Williams. Discerning whether pro- or anti-American sentiment represented "real" West Indian opinion befuddled U.S. and British officials. This had been the case before and continued to be after the Chaguaramas controversy erupted, but now with a key difference: the election results. These indicated a slight pro-American tilt. Before the elections, Under-Secretary of State Christian Herter, in discussing inter-American security arrangements, had cautioned that some leading candidates in the WIF were hostile to the United States, and their victory might jeopardize those arrangements.[104] But those candidates had lost. Now, although Williams might eloquently rally his PNM followers, and although his party held the upper hand in Trinidad, his was the minority position at the federal level.

This prompted a shift in U.S. tactics. Both at the joint commission and in conversations with federal winners and losers, the United States began increasingly to link settlement of the Chaguaramas dispute to American aid. Such economic aid was vital to the WIF. London had committed to continue grants-in-aid for a period of years, but this would not come close to meeting the new nation's needs. The United States was the obvious replacement. Aid held both real and symbolic value, as a sign of Washington's blessing on the new state. With Chaguaramas still unresolved after the election, however, the administration made sure that West Indian leaders grasped the tacit linkage between the base dispute and American aid to the federation.[105]

West Indian leaders, not least Williams, understood this very well. The chief minister may have seen his own and his allies' standing hurt on the federal level, but he was still in power at home and could make Chaguaramas a chronic problem if it were not settled to his satisfaction. As of April, when the federal government was installed, it was still an open question. Thus, the union was born into a kind of limbo. Long rent by internal fissures, it faced strained external relations, channeled through London, with the United States over aid and Chaguaramas.

From Panacea to Pandora: The Federation Arrives

To the disappointment and surprise of those who had long dreamed of such a union, the West Indies Federation raised more questions than it answered.

Williams phrased the problem in a December 1957 speech: "What sort of nation will we be?"[106] The issues encapsulated therein were difficult. Was there a common West Indian identity—amid the regional welter of race, culture, and history—strong enough to sustain a geographically dispersed nation-state? Could the interests of the larger, richer territories be balanced with those of smaller, poorer ones within the federal structure? Considering that some territories had on their own seen terrific political and economic development since union was first planned, did the federation still have a compelling reason for being?

These issues would have haunted the federation even if the Chaguaramas crisis had never occurred, though the crisis did not help matters. Moreover, in U.S. and British eyes, its flaws notwithstanding, the federation did have a reason for being: to serve as a bulwark in the Cold War western hemisphere. True, the two allies had different designs for their bulwark. London saw it as a vessel for British influence, envisioning a regional "European bloc" via closer ties with the French and Dutch islands. Washington, for its part, integrated the WIF into its security plans. Besides bolstering the hemispheric perimeter, the WIF also made a statement to the Third World: that the West could be trusted to sponsor "progressive" decolonization. Yet for these same reasons the United States could not afford to look like a bully over Chaguaramas. Hence the dilemma: how simultaneously to keep U.S. assets, and win over those angry about them, in a new and shaky state that could not be allowed to fail?

In this sense the Chaguaramas crisis revealed some of the basic diplomatic challenges of the Eisenhower years. The administration's quest for cheaper means of waging the Cold War led it to covert operations and reliance on allied or local proxies in areas, like the Caribbean basin, where this was possible. It also meant managing the epochal, geopolitical earthquake whose tremors officials began feeling in the mid-1950s: the racial-colonial awakening that would bring new Third World nations to life, First World minorities to fuller citizenship, the Atlantic alliance to headache, and the Cold War to complication. The West Indies offered perhaps the most favorable landscape anywhere for the smooth accommodation of these tectonic forces. Yet even there, as Chaguaramas showed, "smooth" was too much to hope for. If the dispute was an inauspicious start for the federation and American relations with it, its temporary resolution a few months hence did little to solve U.S. problems to the south. These appeared to be growing in ways that made the West Indian bulwark simultaneously less dependable and more vital to Washington's changing approach to an increasingly turbulent region.

5

The American Lake or the Castro Caribbean?

As if its geographical, constitutional, and logistical troubles, its leaders' infighting, and the Chaguaramas crisis were not bad enough, the West Indies Federation also had exquisitely bad timing. The April 1958 seating of the new federal government was sandwiched between Castro's March call to revolt in Cuba and Vice President Richard Nixon's ill-fated Latin American tour in May. These events prompted the Eisenhower administration to undertake a deep revision of U.S. policy. Eisenhower and his diplomatic team had always pursued a focused, if unevenly effective, strategy in Latin America and the Caribbean. The events of spring 1958 brought changes to that policy, in hopes of heading off further disaster. Many of these, including the Alliance for Progress and the interventionism that would culminate at the Bay of Pigs, would be continued under the Kennedy administration.[1] Together, the late Eisenhower and early Kennedy years marked a change from most of the dominant postwar policy directions regarding Latin America.

The West Indies could not help but be affected by developments emanating from both the northern colossus and its southern neighbors.[2] Indeed, the career of the West Indies Federation coincides almost precisely with this key phase in regional affairs: from the turn in spring 1958, to the WIF collapse in summer 1961 after the Bay of Pigs, to its largest members' independence in summer 1962 before the Cuban Missile Crisis. The British Caribbean had always been affected at least indirectly by U.S. relations with the area, but it became even more so as the regional stakes rose. Whether the West Indies would prove a decolonized, pro-Western bulwark or the seedbed for a second Castro was the key question. For most of the period, the former was the obvious and welcome answer. Yet at crucial moments, the latter could not be ruled out.

Changes in the dynamics of global race relations and the Cold War around this time were intimately connected to Caribbean developments. The second great wave of decolonization began to crest around 1960. In that "Year of Africa," seventeen new nations joined the continent's atlas. But the question of what shape such new nations ought to take had in almost every case haunted the years leading up to independence. Lines drawn on the map long before to suit metropolitan convenience rarely corresponded to ethnic, cultural, religious, linguistic, and other "nationalist" identity realities on the ground. The Cold War overlaid and distorted most attempts to reconcile these dynamics and raised the stakes of the decolonization transition. One popular solution was federal union. In this respect, the West Indies Federation marched in step with a half-dozen other federated political units constructed out of the British empire—from South and Southeast Asia (the Pakistans and Malaya/Malaysia) to East and West Africa (Rhodesia-Nyasaland and Nigeria)—toward nationhood. As an answer to the most basic questions of sovereignty and anticolonial-*cum*-national identity, the federations erected amid the empires' retreat represented a middle ground between imperial calculations, Cold War imperatives, and nationalist visions. In the West Indies and most other cases, that middle ground trembled ominously as independence approached. If the quickening of racial-colonial justice movements signaled a new era in world affairs, as white supremacy became more international liability than domestic or colonial peculiarity for the West, it was nonetheless left unclear what form that quickening would ultimately take. These years of the global "race-revolution," added to renewed crises in the superpower conflict, thus added up to a pivotal stretch of the Cold War.

These crosscurrents were especially treacherous in the Caribbean. In many ways, the Eisenhower and Kennedy administrations broke the "benign neglect" of preceding U.S. relations with the British West Indies. If the United States did not resume Roosevelt-era reforms, they still bespoke concern that the integrity of the "American Lake" had been breached and aroused more of Washington's interest than had recently been the case. In addition to its traditional hegemony in the Spanish-speaking hemisphere, the United States began assuming a similar role in the West Indies as British sovereignty there receded. The controversy over whether to site the federal capital on land occupied by the U.S. naval base at Chaguaramas, Trinidad—a crisis nearing its first anniversary—made this abundantly clear. The American response attempted to solve that crisis and to support the fledgling federation. The result—a deceptive resolution—created more problems than it solved, distorting WIF affairs internally and externally just as the region as a whole seemed to begin unraveling.

A Resolution Quick and False: Chaguaramas and the WIF, 1958–1959

Among the plethora of players in the ongoing battle over a capital site for the West Indies Federation, the British were the only side presenting any noticeable unity despite their initial hesitation to take a position. Their hesitation stemmed from fear of offending their colonial clients on the one hand, and their Atlantic ally on the other. The provocateur of the Chaguaramas crisis, Chief Minister Williams of Trinidad, had turned the cause into a crusade to evict the Americans: "I [will] break the Chaguaramas problem or it [will] break me!"[3] As a matter of interstate affairs, Williams had made the base/ capital-site into an "issue central to West Indian and Trinidadian national- ism" and the defining issue of U.S.–West Indian relations.[4] This is not to say that it reached as far into American as into West Indian public opinion; while the *Saturday Evening Post* fumed about Trinidad's abuse of U.S. good- will, neither of two *New York Times* editorials welcoming the federation even mentioned the dispute.[5]

The matter did, however, animate relations within and without the federation, and Williams's counterparts did not all share his passion. The Trinidadian, Jamaican, and federal oppositions denounced the crusade, and the issue would soon divide Williams and his ally Manley from their erstwhile comrade, Prime Minister Grantley Adams. Why the issue pulled West Indian leaders apart is a complex question. On the surface, such an issue had the power to unite West Indians against the "imperialists." The oppositions' role should not be overlooked; Bustamante argued that press- ing on Chaguaramas was "lunacy," a nonissue outside of Trinidad—and asserted that even there a majority favored U.S. retention of the base.[6]

The answer also lies partly in structural dynamics that pitted Trinidadian versus federal versus British sovereignty, partly in the clash of personalities, and partly in the tactics chosen.[7] For example, before Adams had been chosen fed- eral premier, most observers had thought Manley the leading candidate. Neither man, moreover—nor Williams, seen as a rising star—ruled out the possibility of being the first leader of an independent union when that status arrived. Williams's difficult personality complicated matters as well, at times alienating the other two men from the July 1957 launch of his crusade onward, though Manley remained his ally for the time being. The split between the three, and with their oppositions, also reflected that all had as many conflicting interests as shared ones—and all meant to manipulate the United States to secure them. In this sense they were determined that their islands would not be mere pawns but instead deft players of the imperial devolution.

On the American side, the State and Defense Departments were at odds, the former open to surrendering some base areas and the latter dead set on keeping them. Both agreed, though, that Williams posed a problem aside from the base-area dispute, even if that was the most obvious manifestation. Consular officials met with opposition leaders, even going so far as to furnish them with damaging material about the chief minister's marital woes. "Accepting the policy to erase Williams from political power," U.S. Consul- General Walter Orebaugh wrote, "[this] is the opportunity to put another nail in [his] political coffin."[8] This, though, was likely to be a slow-motion process, and the Chaguaramas dispute needed quicker resolution.

At this stage in early 1958, the Defense view—that Washington could not give up the base—predominated. The U.S. reputation of "bullying" on the issue was not helped by the leak, before the release of the report of the joint commission convened to settle the matter, that the Navy was planning to shift its South Atlantic headquarters to Chaguaramas.[9] But this position was not just "bullying." The case for keeping the base, while arguable, had strong merits. This position was seconded by the May 1958 report, which confirmed the impracticality of relocation. "Objective in every detail," writes scholar-participant Mordecai, "the report knocked the bottom out of the West Indian case." The British with "execrable timing [then] forced a posture of defiance on the West Indies" by announcing that they would not support a request that the United States move.[10] The West Indian leadership, stung by this rebuke, sought ways to protest.

The Chaguaramas crisis had always called into question the scope of federal sovereignty. Put simply, who had the jurisdiction to press for a capital in Trinidad— the federal government or its member and prospective host? The question exposed the weaknesses of the federal structure. Manley had stated bluntly that the capital-site decision was up to the units, not the federal seat; Williams insisted on a Chaguaramas Conference to be run in and by Trinidad. Tensions between local and federal officials rubbing elbows in Port of Spain—since the city was both the colonial and temporary federal capital—further strained federal–Trinidad relations. Mere weeks into the life of the WIF, federal sovereignty was, at best, challenged and, at worst, fictional.

This state of affairs was not unusual in "federated" areas of the decolonizing world. The WIF was the third of six federations created out of the British empire. Federal entities took shape amid a variety of circumstances, from white supremacy in Rhodesia-Nyasaland to guerilla war in Malaya to multiethnic-communal antagonism in Nigeria. Nor were the British the only promoters of the federal solution; the French and Dutch also did so, as did various African and Middle Eastern entities both colonial and postcolonial.

As R. L. Watts showed in his landmark 1966 study *New Federations*, written while many of the federal experiments were still underway, until World War II most thinkers believed the very idea of federalism dead.[11] But the future breakup of Europe's empires revived the idea during the war. Its practical virtues appealed to metropolitan administrators, but its romantic dimensions should not be overlooked. Given, for example, the rise in race consciousness and left-international class consciousness in the interwar African diaspora, it is fair to say that the federal idea appealed as much to radicals as to bureaucrats. Strategists could see in it a path to viable integrity against military, ideological, and economic challenge; visionaries could see in it an identity grounded in race or ethnicity against outsiders or, alternately, of class-conscious "outsiders" together transcending race and ethnicity. The six British-empire entities emerged from negotiation between imperial administrators, nationalist leaders, and also in some cases the *amicus curae* participation of an interested third party, such as the United States or Canada.

The main challenge in establishing a federation lay in translating the above into a sound constitutional structure. For some areas, this challenge was made easier in the design stage by pre-existing state or societal arrangements that could be integrated into the federal schema. In most cases, though, pre-existing and often unchangeable conditions made the creation of such a structure difficult, if not impossible. Ethnicity, religion, or geography might theoretically be accommodated. But none could be easily altered, and any or all might pose an insurmountable obstacle to a union's success. Some combination of these elements, plus the factors of leadership and personality, afflicted all federations to some degree with the plague of infighting within and among the federal units. This was true in the West Indies, which unlike the other unions had to deal with the added variable—at times a boon, at times a burden—of U.S. interest. In the case of Chaguaramas, it was certainly the latter, straining both the question of West Indian sovereignty and the dialogue, in the joint commission and elsewhere around the region, meant to settle it.

In June the federal government officially rejected the joint-commission report and urged the resumption of talks. But the message included a subtle disclaimer from Adams, which in Mordecai's view "must have given the United Kingdom and United States ideas."[12] The line in question affirmed the WIF's stand that any decision must not endanger "the defence of the Western world." There is no explicit evidence that this phrase prompted the U.S. response, but the timing was indeed suspicious. Just after its appearance, Orebaugh spoke on the matter publicly for the first time, stating that there was no point in further talks. Chaguaramas was an internal question between London and its possessions, and the former had made no formal request to the United States on the matter. Some months later Orebaugh was summoned home for this intrusion into the "internal" conflict, but the damage was done. The British government followed the announcement by proposing a ten-year "amnesty" on Chaguaramas, after which Washington promised to revisit the issue, with an eye to changes in defense needs that might make the base obsolete. Also, any mutually acceptable arrangements concerning ad hoc modifications were allowed. But formal talks would be shelved for the immediate future.

Adams made his move. Seeing that events had placed in his hand one stone, he looked to kill not two but three birds. He saw his chance, namely, to reassert federal primacy, to save his government, and to settle the capital-site question all at once. Without consulting his ostensible allies and partners, and using parliamentary legerdemain to disarm the opposition in camera, Adams declared the WIF's acceptance of the amnesty. Chaguaramas would therefore stay American, at least for ten years, and the capital would find another home.

An incensed Williams savaged the deal as "a stab in the back." Manley concurred. Yet Adams, as prime minister, had authority on his side. Washington and London knew Williams could continue to make trouble, but Adams had given them an opening: "Williams is becoming a very damaging element in our relations," wrote one State official, but Washington could now act "as though Adams's [action] solved Chaguaramas for the next 10 years."[13] The United States and Britain soon announced that the amnesty was in effect. Williams vowed to continue to fight. He swore that Chaguaramas would become "a running sore" and launched a "campaign of irritants" to evict the Americans and "end Trinidad's position as an 'exploited cipher.'"[14]

Williams's local popularity, and the base's location on his territory, gave him leverage. If it proved insufficient to dislodge the Americans, it might nonetheless suffice to extract aid from them. American officials had long known that as British authority devolved, West Indian eyes would look northward for economic assistance. The Eisenhower administration had sought to detach the aid and Chaguaramas questions. An implicit link was plain to perceive, though U.S. diplomats never admitted as much, and worked hard at public "de-linkage." American offers of aid remained closely guarded leading up to the WIF's inauguration.[15] At that event, the U.S.'s public offer of assistance improved the climate, and "it had become difficult for the Federation to [continue] a hard demand for Chaguaramas in the face of US willingness to provide assistance."[16] The new climate soon evaporated, though, and following what he saw as Adams's betrayal, Williams showed renewed determination to exploit Chaguaramas.

However, Williams's leverage had a shifting fulcrum. In part this owed to the fact that aid and Chaguaramas could not really be separated, public assertions to the contrary notwithstanding. In part too it owed to the kinds of aid being considered and the strings attached thereto. The United States, for example, had offered to fund construction of a capital at a site other than Chaguaramas, which was difficult not to see as a bribe. Variations on this offer had figured in discussions since the initial colonial decision to ask for the base in 1956. U.S. proposals to build public housing in Trinidad were seen the same way and indeed were designed to undercut Williams's crusade.[17]

Most of all, though, Williams's leverage shifted because of his own unsteady hands. In October, a Canadian official reported that Orebaugh lost patience with Williams's attempts to make explicit links between U.S. aid and his Chaguaramas agitation: "[Orebaugh] evidently admitted that the U.S. could not be expected to give aid to a country where there did not exist a climate of friendly co-operation." The Canadian diplomat concluded that Williams's intransigence and unpredictability hurt his cause:

> [Williams's] actions throughout the aid conversations could hardly have been designed to make negotiations more difficult. Nor is it possible to understand how [he] can imagine that such tactics can arouse the support of Trinidadians in particular or West Indians in general...Chaguaramas is such an obsession with him that he [seems] incapable of thinking clearly of the effects of his actions.[18]

The chief minister's idiosyncrasies were widely remarked upon by observers of all stripes: American, African-American, British, Canadian, and Caribbean. These personal qualities were born as much of temperament as of biography. As Colin Palmer writes, Williams's energy and brilliance were unfortunately matched by his "distressing tendency to alienate his colleagues with his sharp tongue, his difficulty in absorbing criticism or dealing with opposing points of view, and his marked intellectual arrogance."[19] When it came to dealing with the United States, Williams's personal and professional experiences in that country could thus only amplify any slights he felt done him by the hegemon—to say nothing of his mainland experience with Jim Crow, which left him understandably suspicious of American promises.

In this, Williams was hardly alone among West Indians—or among non-whites the world over. West Indians' long contact with Americans had made race the single greatest sore point in otherwise generally smooth relations. Race-fraternity acted in two specific ways on African-American–West Indian ties. The first was the contribution of expatriates and their sympathizers to the Caribbean struggle. This took the form of rhetorical and financial support, grounded in the multinational Harlem nexus but not limited to it. The West Indian community in Chicago, for example, marked the birth of the WIF with a series of social events.[20] Back in Harlem, expatriates and the mainland-born also organized celebrations, accompanied by a fundraising drive to send Adam Clayton Powell to the WIF inauguration.[21] Smaller than collaborations during the 1940s, these nevertheless constituted one positive way in which race could continue to unify West Indian and African-American activists in northern urban centers of the United States.

The other way in which race entered the equation was the negative contribution of Jim Crow to the American image. West Indian admiration for the United States ended at the Mason-Dixon line, and the 1950s saw this condition become ever more global. The civil rights movement and especially the Little Rock crisis changed the worldwide dialogue on race, as they drew attention to the racial regime that contradicted the claims of the "land of the free."[22] International outrage over post–Little Rock "race" events generated hundreds of letters of protest to Secretary Dulles and to U.S. embassies abroad. The West Indies joined this chorus. Letters came from all walks of island life, and from Manley, Bustamante, their parties, and groups such as the Afro-Caribbean League. Demonstrators bore placards inscribed "Blacks Unite," "Cold Blooded Slaying Sam," and "Cease Robbing the Rights of the Negro."[23] The importance of the global audience could only rise as the civil rights movement and the Cold War wove race and America's reputation together. Race per se was rarely decisive in Washington's 1950s West Indies policy; national-security concerns almost always outranked it. However, with the cresting of the civil rights movement, the Cold War contest for Third World loyalties guaranteed that the race factor could never be simply ignored.

The United States was not the only racial reference point for emerging nations. Manley's government, for example, passed a 1959 resolution boycotting trade with South Africa.[24] Such solidarity was not limitless; no other islands nor the federal government nor British Guiana duplicated the Jamaican gesture, although many island leaders did voice support for it. In general, though, local tensions simply loomed larger. In Trinidad, where the black plurality and the large Indian minority cohabited uneasily, attention tended to focus more on that divide than on any white actions. However, the United States was rarely forgotten when race matters were discussed. The changing diplomatic dynamic led Washington to intensify efforts to manage its racial image.[25] With many West Indians, Williams included, this was a lost cause. Awareness of this fact reached the highest levels of the Eisenhower administration: "U.S. actions and attitudes with respect to racial frictions and rights, especially in Africa and in the U.S. itself, are closely observed by the predominantly Negro population of the West Indies."[26]

Even well apart from overarching racial dynamics, Williams's quirks complicated the issues underlying the Chaguaramas dispute, issues that were thorny enough without him. How did the Bases Deal apply if the West Indies were no longer British wards? Should not the West Indies have a say over a foreign presence on its soil? To what extent were London and the federation—recognized as sovereign entities by the United States, which Trinidad was not—the valid voices on the issue? Was Williams speaking for himself, for Trinidad, for the federation, or all of the above? Legitimate questions all—and all made more difficult by the difficult man who refused to stop asking them.

Williams's crusade ensured that Chaguaramas would continue to dominate intra-federal affairs, all strained by the clash of personalities. London agreed, blaming structural problems: "the present federal constitution in the West Indies...means that the federal government is hardly worthy of the name." Unless these flaws could be corrected, "we run a grave risk of the Federation failing, with all that implies to our policy."[27] Damaged British prestige would be only one such casualty. A failed union also held implications for West Indian economic development. Aside from its use as a means to self-government, federation was envisioned as a mechanism for economic planning. But the fact that most islands' economies were competitive rather than complementary—most grew sugar and similar commodities, and all wanted to diversify and industrialize—made this quixotic. In 1958, for example, Manley won his island a contract for an oil refinery, putting Jamaica at odds with Trinidad's monopoly on that sector within the West Indies. Perhaps more importantly, wrote the U.S. consul, the action "represents...the apparent determination of an 'industrialized' territory to ignore the possibility of Federal planning."[28] On the political plane, suspicion spread; one of Manley's key allies wondered if the Chaguaramas crusade was not simply a maneuver to keep Manley out of the federal premiership.[29]

The continued weakness of the federation, and the unspoken prospect of its failure, posed problems for American interests as well. Other brewing threats made the federation key to defending those interests. In early 1959, Williams continued to press the cause of Chaguaramas, and the matter of U.S. aid to the federation had not been fully settled. But these paled beside the dramatic events in Cuba. Fidel Castro's seizure of power in January 1959 was initially seen by the United States not as a communist revolution but a popular one. However, things seemed to spin out of control as the year went on, and Castro moved increasingly leftward. Various contacts reported the serious possibility that his revolution might reach the West Indies. In March, Jamaican authorities caught seven hundred Castro men planning to use the island as a base for operations, while the local business community warned that such events were causing a local rise in communism—which was "now a force in Jamaica. With Castro's victory in Cuba the field for Communist endeavour here is much more promising than it ever was."[30] En route to a victory tour of South America, Castro stopped briefly in Trinidad where he was greeted by Williams, although the revolutionary did little to endear himself when he revealed his total ignorance of the Chaguaramas controversy.[31] Still, as the British role continued to shrink and Castro's shadow lengthened, U.S. plans made good relations with a strong federation simultaneously more difficult and more urgent. "As [British rule] recedes," one American diplomat noted, "the U.S. [with Chaguaramas] is rapidly assuming the posture of the colonial power against which the resentments of a newly independent nation may be exercised."[32] The Eisenhower administration expected the West Indies Federation to gain full independence within the next few years and planned to draw the new state's orbit closer to the mainland and the inter-American system.[33]

Yet the Chaguaramas knot tied up this policy and seemed impossible to cut. Months after Adams's compromise, Williams continued his charge. In March 1959, Orebaugh—soon reassigned partly for his inability to make progress with Williams—reported that "Williams intends to carry forward his campaign against the U.S. for Chaguaramas to the bitter end." In keeping with Foggy Bottom's view—still the minority position in Washington—that some of the base acreage should be surrendered for the sake of good relations, Orebaugh warned that "the U.S. cannot ignore the significant changes occurring in the West Indies and it is unthinkable to consider a policy of 'standing pat.'" But "regardless of what we do or don't do, the U.S. is going to have further serious trouble with Williams.... [We] can ill afford to leave a man of this stamp in power at the very portals of the United States."[34] An intelligence report attributed all of the Trinidadian instability to Williams; and despite the fact that "the relatively moderate quality of [West Indian] nationalism makes it unlikely that agitation for US withdrawal will assume critical proportions," the "unreconciled" Williams could place Chaguaramas and regional defense at risk. Proposals included "plotting...to bring about Williams's political downfall" and propaganda to counter him by stoking latent West Indian admiration for the mainland.[35]

Through the summer of 1959, these efforts proved singularly ineffective. State–Defense conversations described the dilemma. Stonewalling on Chaguaramas and on revising the Bases Agreement that fathered it would only increase West Indian discontent and "make us the principal whipping boy in the future."[36] Worse, State's legal experts were reaching the conclusion that the original Bases Agreement would be null and void upon the federation's full independence. That left the United States with two main options for revision. Washington could negotiate with Williams now through Britain, which was party to the agreement and responsible for the

West Indies' foreign relations, and take a chance on an unfavorable result. Or, the United States could wait for independence and negotiate bilaterally from a position of weakness, since the base would technically be in Trinidad illegally. There was also the option of "plotting [Williams's] downfall." The military contended that there could be no progress as long as he was in power. Why not then "drag things out until elections, in the meantime try-ing to bring about Williams's political defeat," through continued collusion with the opposition, and perhaps seeking British permission to mobilize the CIA against him? The latter option was not taken, and the former was already being done, to little effect. Such was the dilemma that an exasper-ated State official suggested the United States rethink its support for the WIF, which "represented a serious political and economic problem...on our doorstep."[37] He was countered by State and Defense officers who agreed that the federation might not prove ultimately successful, but until that was clearly the case it was in America's interest to assist it. How best to do so, given the federation's internal battles and Williams's crusade, remained entirely unclear.

That crusade soon intensified, as Williams launched a fusillade of charges. The most incendiary came in June when he accused the United States of exposing islanders to radiation.[38] This, he blasted, was merely the latest "great-power" use of the region as fortress and fiefdom. In a speech at Woodford Square, Williams put Chaguaramas in a context that began with the 1493 *Asiento*, and after spending two-thirds of the speech just getting to the present day, he concluded:

> When we deal with Chaguaramas, we are not merely dealing with what has become the symbol of...independence. [It] means...that we...have begun a long overdue attempt which India has started, which Ghana has started...We are the standard bearers of the nationalist movement. But more than that, in fighting for Chaguaramas [we are] stating our claim to what our calypsonian puts simply but so forcefully: 'We want back we lan'![39]

Given this broader and oft-repeated purpose, in American eyes Williams's charges seemed more like tactical moves than causes in their own right. But some of the charges stuck. The radiation matter gained attention from the local press to Westminster.[40] The Eisenhower administration informed London that the radar facility, one of the largest in existence, could not pos-sibly pose a radiation threat, since it was not yet even operational. American reassurances, though, were insufficient to assuage Trinidadian worries, and the latter redounded into U.S. concerns "over the fears that Williams may have aroused by his intemperate and irresponsible statements."[41]

This buttressed U.S. perceptions of an unfavorable climate in Trinidad. According to the USIA, "Williams's campaign of harassment and harangue against the U.S. in general and the base at Chaguaramas in particular has been turned on and off to suit his political purposes." One of the latter was to secure not just a renegotiated Bases Agreement but also a place for Trinidad at the negotiating table separate from the federation.[42] His campaign thus pitted him against both Washington and the federal government. That campaign was entering its third year, and neither the federation's launch nor the U.S. carrot-and-stick approach had brought about resolution.

Many American and British officials at different points during the crisis had concluded that the problem—that is, Williams—was unsolvable. The notion that U.S. interests might be better served by ending support for federation gained ground every time the Trinidadian—"a Nasser and a racist," according to State Department official James Swihart, and the "absolute monarch of Trinidad," according to one opposition leader—took to the podium.[43] The troubling fact was that Williams, six months before and now eighteen months after the federation's birth, was—despite repeated protestations that he was not expressing anti-Americanism but merely West Indian nationalism—gambling his government on a confrontation with the United States. The symbolism of a colonial coalition demanding the return of land for a quasi-independent federal capital escaped no one, and raised questions about the advisability of pinning American hopes on the new West Indian union.

Yet each time, and ever more so as the Cuban situation deteriorated, Washington came back to support its Caribbean bulwark. The stakes in doing so were illustrated by the fact, as one diplomat observed, that Chaguaramas had received the attention of the "British Prime Minister and U.S. President, the Secretary of State and Foreign Secretary, Under-Secretaries of State, and miscellaneous Foreign Office and Colonial Office officials."[44] None of these had been able to settle matters, although it is unclear what any leader might have been able to achieve, given the vexing questions of sovereignty, nationalism, and hegemony manifest in the crisis. But the personality clash made a hard situation more difficult, and given the gathering regional clouds, Williams, as former Consul-General Philip Habib put it, had simply "GOT to be lived with."[45]

Thinking Twice: The United States and the WIF in the Castro Caribbean, 1959–1960

The festering Chaguaramas affair, falsely solved by Adams's June 1958 compromise and inflamed by Williams's subsequent campaign, not only pitted a West Indian leader against the United States. It also pitted West Indian leaders against each other—or more correctly, deepened the existing gaps between them. For every prominent figure such as Manley weighing in on Williams's side, another came out against it; and even Williams's supporters tended to fall short of his position that "the Federation itself will stand or fall on the Chaguaramas issue."[46] In this respect the federal arena saw not a sequence of new, regional political battles, but simply provided a new venue in which "local" politics were fought out.[47]

The active role of the United States meant too that a "new" player was included. The colonial opposition cannily milked the situation. The Trinidadian East Indian party, its leader told Swihart, opposed Williams "on the grounds that his approach to Chaguaramas seriously endangers the friendship of the U.S. [which] Trinidad needs."[48] However, the five-foot tall professor whom U.S. officials derisively called the "little doctor" was in power and was not backing down. Washington looked for a fine line between mollifying Williams, addressing legitimate West Indian concerns, retaining national-security assets, and showing firm resolution.

The importance of these latter qualities rose in tandem with the progress of Cuba's revolution. After consolidating power in April, Castro had instituted a series of drastic reforms. Although these were not technically matters of foreign affairs, insofar as they involved U.S. property in Cuba they were not entirely domestic either. Moreover, Cuba was hardly alone in being host to conditions favorable to social upheaval and even communism. Should the latter penetrate the Caribbean perimeter, U.S. interests as defined since the beginning of the Cold War would be compromised. As 1959 drew to a close, a British official caught the irony of the U.S. position: "After being exhorted to show less favor to dictators and having tried a moderate policy with Castro, Cuba now seems heading for disaster under a violently anti-American regime with Communist leanings. In addition, Castro's efforts to stir up revolution [around] the Caribbean, even if they now appear ineffective, must give cause for concern."[49]

Rising anti-Yankee hostility in the hemisphere seemed epidemic. As Stephen Rabe puts it, "in early 1960, the [United States] suddenly feared [it] could lose the cold war in Latin America."[50] In this light, the problems that the federation presented to Washington, especially Williams and Chaguaramas, became more serious. Beyond Williams loomed constitutional collisions; one official predicted that by mid-1960 "the showdown between Jamaican separatism and federal centralism [would] take place."[51] Not only was the federation, a supposed anticommunist bulwark, looking shaky but U.S. involvement with Chaguaramas was evidently making it even more so. At the end of 1959, Williams's agitation had temporarily ceased, although analysts believed this to be a "tactical silence" and not a serious shift toward a more reassuring position.[52]

This, combined with Cuban events, led the Eisenhower administration to revamp regional policy, including the creation of the first-ever policy document to deal exclusively with the West Indies. That paper, NSC-6002, had several objectives. Implicit among them was reconciling the two skirmishes within the American government: between State and Defense over which base areas were essential to security and which could be sacrificed for the sake of better foreign relations; and a lesser conflict between State and Treasury over the appropriate amount of aid.[53] Explicit, and of greater importance, was the need to retain security assets and to win over West Indian leaders and masses alike, thus solidifying defense plans and U.S.–West Indian relations. This effort would, it was hoped, create a stable federation secure against communism.

The good news, as policy-makers sat down to draft NSC-6002, was that Castroism seemed to pose little threat to the British Caribbean. As Habib put it, "most political leaders in the West Indies take it for granted that the Federation will pursue a pro-West policy.... There is not much chance the West Indies will align itself with Castro."[54] West Indian communists through whom Castro might work were thin on the ground. But if communism had seemingly little appeal, the same could not be said for anti-Americanism. As things looked from Washington, Williams had, after all, arguably hitched his immediate political future to this star. He had paid little domestic penalty, aside from strained relations with the federation, which, given structural and personality issues, might have happened anyway. Williams and his anti-American moves "provide a short AND long-run danger to U.S. interests."[55]

The first discussion of NSC-6002 was slated for January 1960, but other pressing matters forced postponement until March. In the interim, U.S. policy-makers brainstormed with their counterparts abroad. The British confirmed that they were working with Manley behind the scenes to shore up the federal structure. They maintained that the federation was strong enough, that Jamaica would not leave it, and that Manley had been advised of the U.S. need for both to be true. Manley himself said that, despite the unsettled matter of federal power-sharing, Jamaica would almost certainly stay in the union, which Washington saw as a sine qua non of federal stability. "Manley said he thought there was 70% probability that Jamaica would stay [in]," recorded Swihart. "Our feeling... is that the percentage is higher than that."[56]

The trust American officials tended to place in Manley—and not to place in Williams—merits comment. In both cases, the U.S. estimation of these leaders, which largely corresponded with British opinion, seems to have had deep roots. Neither man was particularly well known to the general public, outside of diasporan circles and foreign-relations specialists. The Chaguaramas controversy briefly gave Williams a platform for attracting some press and congressional attention in summer 1957 and late 1959. Congressman Robert Walter, for example, blasted Williams for the base crisis and accused him of stoking anti-Americanism while seeking aid. Senator George Smathers kept an eye on Caribbean developments, including the Chaguaramas crisis, although he made few waves about them outside his home state of Florida. Yet Williams rarely reached a mass U.S. audience, and when he did, he was likely to follow a harangue with kind words for historical figures such as the abolitionists.[57]

It was among specialists that the Williams–Manley contrast was starkest. Beginning in his 1955 lecture that reinvigorated Trinidadian nationalism, Williams had regularly excoriated Anglo-American duplicity. His startling rise and thorny disposition made diplomats permanently suspicious of him. In contrast, Manley's restrained public presence worked enormously to the Jamaican's benefit. Manley mostly agreed with Williams on the substance of Chaguaramas, if not always on tactics, but rarely did he arouse the suspicions Williams did. Moreover, Manley had been long and falsely rumored to be anti-white, communist, or both, as credibly as Williams ever had been—but he refused to play the anti-American card in response. Finally, for specialists, both men cast long shadows, and their respective causes—Chaguaramas and federation—determined diplomats' views of each. They were both invested in both issues and usually on the same side. However, as each one came to a head—Chaguaramas with Williams's eviction campaign, federation with Manley's Jamaican referendum—one of the two became more associated with it.

Regarding Chaguaramas, there were indications, especially Williams's silence, that a threshold had been crossed. British MP Hugh Gaitskell, sympathetic to the West Indian leaders, asserted Britain's agreement with the United States that "Chaguaramas was an essential military base in case of global war." Moreover, in meetings with British-Caribbean leaders other than Williams:

> [They] made it quite clear they had no wish to continue to demand Chaguaramas for the capital site, but would much rather settle for somewhere else. However, the issue has now become very much involved with internal West Indian rivalries and controversies, above all between Williams and the federal government.[58]

Here was confirmation of what several U.S. officials had surmised. "As far as Chaguaramas was concerned," Gaitskell said, "the only real problem the U.S. faces is Williams," and his political isolation provided an opening. If the United States and Williams could settle their other disputes—of which there were many, often overlooked by Washington but never by Williams—then the chief minister might "be induced to relax pressure" on Chaguaramas.

When at last the NSC convened to discuss the draft of NSC-6002 in March, it laid out a broad framework with the overarching goal of a stable WIF that would serve hemispheric security. "Because [the WIF] is on [our] doorstep [it is] of more direct importance to us than any other emerging state. Retention of military installations is our major immediate goal, [especially] Chaguaramas.... Economic interests are also large [and growing]."[59] Key to achieving these goals, and to winning over West Indian leaders and peoples, was a combination of goodwill gestures and financial assistance. A drop in British support meant that U.S. aid could be used to entrench the ex-colony in the Western camp. The United States would package these benefits in ways that would inoculate the federation from the Castro virus next door.

That changed regional framework shaped the discussion. Although a colonial area, NSC-6002 argued, the federation lay in Latin America for the strategic purposes of U.S. aid. The president stated that the United States "would find it wise not to be indifferent to the West Indies. Cuba should be a warning to us.... We need not be paternalistic but we should be benevolent."[60] Williams "was trying to evict us," the president said, and maybe the United States could give up the base except for the money that had been poured into it. The low estimate of the base's cost was one hundred million dollars. The pure financial terms of quitting Chaguaramas thus would have constituted a gift to the West Indies twenty times greater than the highest aid amount ($5 million) under discussion. The fact that U.S. rights to the base would end when the WIF became independent—tentatively slated to occur within the next few years—increased its present value as a bargaining chip. Both the president and Secretary Herter argued for putting U.S. policy on a "broader basis" than just the narrow matter of bases. "In fact," Eisenhower allowed, "[I] would be willing to trade several military bases for a strong OAS determined to hang together."

However, the financial investment in Chaguaramas, Williams's volatility, and security interests outweighed the idea of using the base as a bargaining chip. This was not least because those interests went beyond the base itself to include trade routes, among them the lifelines of some vital raw materials. One discussant noted, for example, that Jamaica furnished half of the bauxite used by the U.S. aluminum industry. Chaguaramas not only protected that sea-lane but also was a transshipment point for southern-mainland ores. Eisenhower felt this to be crucial: "we must have access to the South American continent. The U.S. was getting to be more and more a 'have-not' as far as raw materials were concerned." Trinidad's role as an oil producer was not mentioned, as it had been in previous administrations' discussions of hemisphere resources; the island's production had been eclipsed by the Middle East. But its role guarding Venezuelan oil and regional minerals figured in the NSC's calculations about the continued need for Chaguaramas. Beyond bases, a strong federation was vital given the Cuba situation, Eisenhower argued: "[the WIF] is not our responsibility but [it is] in our interest." CIA Chief Allen Dulles doubted the viability of the federation, given its internal flaws, even with American support. He agreed with the president that the NSC, which favored a relaxed approach and greater aid, was being overly optimistic about the WIF's prospects. The president and Dulles "believed the situation in the West Indies was more serious than the Planning Board thought it was."[61]

The gravity of this belief is underscored by the date on which it was expressed: 17 March 1960 was also the day Eisenhower authorized clandestine operations against Fidel Castro.[62] If Cuba could fall, were the West Indies, under weakening British rule, truly secure? Jamaica was, after all, as close to Cuba as Cuba was to Miami. With Williams stoking anti-Americanism, and the fissures in the federation, nothing could be taken for granted. However, the urge to bolster the federation and block communism clashed with the traditional U.S. policy of deferral to the British. NSC-6002 made two changes to this policy: First, observers would closely track West Indian opinion and anti-U.S. sentiment, in addition to surveillance of communist activity. Second, Chaguaramas renegotiations, set to begin in late 1960, would proceed with an eye to the changed context of the Castro Caribbean.

An April event called the "March in the Rain" brought these two tracks together. Calling Chaguaramas "the supreme example of colonialism," Williams organized a march on the base. British and American officials grew nervous. Both powers joined West Indians in hoping for a peaceful march but fearing a violent one. James spoke to the incendiary potential of the event: "[with] Chaguaramas you need only a highly nervous Southern boy with his finger on the trigger to start off something."[63] Williams claimed to see the same potential. Just before the March, he asked the consul if guards would shoot into the expected crowd of fifty thousand if it got unruly. The flabbergasted consul said of course not and replied that, on the contrary, he hoped Williams would let him address what he expected would be a peaceful crowd.[64]

On 22 April, the march came off peacefully. Williams led a rally of several thousand in a driving rain, then marched a dwindling contingent across Port of Spain to the Consulate gates. There he reiterated demands for Chaguaramas, self-government for Trinidad, and independence for the West Indies. He blasted Britain and the United States, blaming both for the problems of Chaguaramas and racialism. He also skewered his opposition and declared West Indians free:

> We have beaten our heads in vain against the forces and agents of colonialism—against the unswerving and often discourteous hostility of the British and American governments on the one hand, and on the other, against the...inferiority complex bred among some West Indians by centuries of colonial rule....We march [now] to show and tell the world that if we are not yet independent in law, we today and after today are independent in fact.[65]

Williams preceded his address with the ceremonial burning of "the seven sins of colonialism," including the federal and Trinidad constitutions and the 1941 Bases Agreement.[66] Each was served to the fire with the declaration: "I consign it to the flames. To hell with it!"[67] Williams then elected not to continue the march to the base seven miles away, as he had threatened.

With a line of people stretching a mile, the demonstration was among the largest Trinidad had ever seen. Williams himself counted it a historic success—but given the threatened turnout, a peaceful march of just several thousand in an ostensibly anti-American cause actually reassured Washington. Other islands, such as Jamaica, evinced no anti-Yankee feeling over Chaguaramas and not nearly enough to eclipse intra-federation tensions.[68] Still, if the United States took comfort that West Indian antipathy was less than Cuban, policy remained focused on winning over island opinion, where possible using Chaguaramas to do so. In June the United States made known its view that Williams held "almost exclusive bargaining rights" in the base dispute, at the jurisdictional expense of the WIF.

This necessarily undermined the standing of the federal government, although no more so than Williams's actions already had. After this, he became "far easier to deal with," a welcome relief in Washington where Williams had been seen as among the most likely to become a "West Indian Castro." The chief minister addressed this point in a June speech affirming that Trinidad would be "part of the West for good."[69] This contradicted his ongoing flirtation with neutralism, but it was seen as at least a step in the right direction. Momentarily reassured about the aim of his influence, the United States resumed watching and waiting.

Shadows of communism and anti-Americanism abounded in the mid-1960 Caribbean. Against this backdrop, the changed tone in U.S.–West Indian relations was most satisfying in Washington and beyond. The West Indies—although not the WIF—did harbor a figure who in American eyes was becoming a "second Castro," one now more worrisome than Williams.

Cheddi Jagan, in 1953 the subject of the first anticommunist intervention of the Cold War Caribbean Basin and now in somewhat tempered power in British Guiana, lauded Castro's revolution as the "path to progress" for the colonies in the hemisphere.[70] The Eisenhower administration, watching that revolution turn harder to the Left, sped up its Latin American policy review given that "the Caribbean [was now] an area with numerous specialized problems."[71]

In its West Indian section, however, the problems seemed if not solved then at least contained. A Jamaican commentator reminded the United States in July that Williams was far from the only voice and Chaguaramas far from the only cause, going on to chastise Washington's lack of fortitude in dealing with the Trinidadian, and urged not only that Chaguaramas be kept but that more U.S. bases be built. Earlier in the year, one of Manley's ministers had told U.S. officials that Castro might evict the Americans from their base at Guantanamo Bay—and that if they did so, the United States should consider reopening deactivated facilities in Jamaica to replace it.[72] While most vocally expressed in Jamaica, similar sentiments, and growing awareness of the Castro threat, could be traced elsewhere in the West Indies as well.

Castro—"the very devil...he is your Nasser," Macmillan wrote Eisenhower—endangered West Indian and American in addition to British interests in the region.[73] Although the British role was changing, it continued to offer parallels to the West Indies' experience. When the Chaguaramas crisis had erupted in 1957, all sides compared it to the still-fresh Suez debacle. Williams had only recently ceased being dubbed "Nasser," that title having passed to Castro. But as the latter consolidated his gains, Chaguaramas changed labels as well. It was no longer Suez but "the Gibraltar of the Caribbean," suggesting not the loss of a strategic imperial garrison to Third World nationalism but its negotiated retention amidst such sentiment.[74] The battle over it with Williams was in ceasefire, not conclusion, which was to come via renegotiations at year's end. Nor could that affair be isolated from events in Spanish-speaking areas, nor from Anglo-American attempts to parcel out regional responsibilities. In March, "[British officials said that] anything the U.S. could do to lessen difficulties in Panama and Cuba would make [Chaguaramas] more susceptible of solution. [A U.S. official] said Washington saw this the other way around."[75]

At a review of NSC-6002 in September 1960, the NSC Working Group on the West Indies recommended no policy changes.[76] The two-track approach—that is, close surveillance of anti-Americanism and communism, and progress on Chaguaramas—was deemed adequate for protecting stated American interests. It bears note, however, that those interests had been evolving before Castro. Defined as securing two kinds of Caribbean assets—military facilities and raw materials—U.S. needs had changed considerably since Eisenhower's inauguration. Some elements, such as geography, obviously had not. A study prepared for the Chaguaramas renegotiations reaffirmed that "the strategic position of Trinidad is the only suitable one in the area as 'anchor' to the Caribbean island-chain."[77] In addition, Chaguaramas had taken on another role beyond that of naval outpost, as new technologies in missiles, radar, and spacecraft had created additional uses for this and other U.S. bases in the Caribbean. These uses bolstered the desire for a settlement that would allow a continued American presence.

The more mundane aspect of the bases—protecting the trade in vital materials—could not be overlooked either. Yet this had evolved as well. By 1960, shortages in key strategic materials had turned to surpluses, and aluminum in particular had gone from being one of the least available metals to one of the most abundant. U.S. stockpiles were glutted. In 1960, Manley pressed Washington to keep Jamaican bauxite on the list of needed goods despite this surplus. This would limit the damage to the Jamaican economy, which had been planned around continued production. The importance of that production was difficult to overstate. Population growth and economic development were in a race in Jamaica: between 1943 and 1960, its population grew 30 percent. The governor remarked on the similarity of such conditions to those which had produced Castro's revolution.[78]

With stockpiles full, Jamaican bauxite became less important to immediate American military needs than to longer-term Jamaican economic needs. Meeting the latter would serve American security by helping to stabilize Jamaica and the federation. It would, in Senator J. William Fulbright's words, support islanders who had "made a valiant effort to 'help themselves.'"[79] Washington agreed to continue listing bauxite on a year-to-year basis on these grounds, effectively creating a hidden aid program to Jamaica and, by extension, to the WIF. More aid was urged before renegotiations began, in order to ensure good relations, retention of bases, and "access [to] bauxite and oil," as well as to block "penetration by foreign ideologies."[80] For his part, Williams had refrained from agitation since June, although officials did not rule out the possibility of a resumption. An October intelligence report blasted Williams's history of "opportunistic...'Hate-US'" campaigns, and feared that rising resentment of the United States might tempt him to renew the fight.[81] As talks approached, Chaguaramas, aid, Williams, federal prerogative, intensifying American and receding British interest, and—for good measure—a new U.S. president, all combined to draw a very complicated picture.

A confidential paper prepared for the incoming administration spelled out the American rationale and position as base talks got underway:

> Refusal to talk now would result in serious agitation in West Indies, especially Trinidad, and Castro could capitalize on growing anti-American sentiments.... At the same time a majority of West Indians are pro-U.S. An unsatisfactory resolution of the base problem would adversely affect our position [with them].[82]

The three-stage talks would be nearly complete by Kennedy's inauguration on 20 January, but as with other aspects of American hemispheric policy, the new president continued his predecessor's approach in most respects. In this case that meant that the first stage of the talks would focus on the Bases Agreement, and specifically on settling Chaguaramas. Once this "obsolescent" arrangement, the "chief obstacle [and] major political irritant" in relations, was removed, the remaining two stages would lay out the planning and implementation of the officially unrelated matter of U.S. economic aid and technical assistance.[83]

The U.S. delegation to the Phase I talks in London was notable for whom it excluded. Going into the talks, and in line with NSC-6002 and evolving security needs, the long-running State–Defense split over how much land should be surrendered was much in evidence. Yet on closer inspection it appears that State, perhaps taking cues from Eisenhower's willingness to surrender some acreage, had taken the upper hand. State intrigued to leave out of the delegation a military representative infamous for taking the hardest line: "we [State] have felt it essential to keep a certain admiral out of London. Though the price has been heavy from our standpoint, we have succeeded in that effect."[84] State delegates meant to seize the chance to give up nonessential acreage, which would all but guarantee a successful outcome to the talks.

Defense had not given up, however. "In limited areas of [the Pentagon]," a State analyst noted, "there is lingering distaste at our having entered negotiations prior to independence [for fear] that after it we will be forced into a second negotiation and demands for more concessions. This is coupled with a personal dislike of Williams who is labeled another Castro."[85] The State position was that whatever his faults, Williams was key, leaving the United States no alternative but to deal with him. But Defense delegates held the line. "Even over drinks," their British counterparts reported, "[they] would not admit they could let go more land [even when] our defense expert pointed out that Gibraltar took up six hundred acres and Chaguaramas twelve thousand."[86] The replacement admiral made a muddled case for retaining all of Chaguaramas as a possible nuclear submarine base, outraging State delegates who saw that this would kill chances of an accord.

In the end, State representatives were able to sustain the initiative. Phase II of the talks ended in December, resulting in what Manley wrote Williams was a "significant achievement... your stand has been vindicated."[87] The final phase of the talks at Port of Spain sealed this success in February 1961. Washington agreed to release four-fifths of all lands obtained in the original Bases Agreement, which translated to all Trinidad holdings even including some of the Chaguaramas acreage outside of the base proper. This the military would keep for seventeen years, at which time an independent WIF and the United States would jointly review the arrangement. Finally, Phase III filled in the details of the Phase II aid discussions: more than seven million dollars in aid, technical assistance, and programs from housing to harbor dredging to expansion of the University of the West Indies.[88] Given the principles, personalities, and history involved, on all points of the Anglo-American-Caribbean triangle, even cynics breathed a sigh of relief at news of this settlement.

"Vague in Its Origin and Thin as Belief": Federation and Decolonization in Castro's Shadow

Derek Walcott was not writing about the West Indian union when he penned that verse, but it captures the source of continuing anxiety about the federation: the fear that it would prove ultimately artificial, endangering the Chaguaramas settlement along with everything else. The settlement thus did not evict the United States, but it placated Williams even as some of his associates, like James, felt he had let Washington off easy. Historian Elisabeth Wallace notes that James was not alone; "the [West Indian] press gave only grudging acknowledgment of the [United States'] conspicuous generosity."[89] Soon after the talks, and in continued pursuit of Caribbean goodwill, the State Department told the British that the promised U.S. aid would be doubled. London correctly read into this decision: "The reason is their unease about the [Caribbean] situation. They reckon that an independent West Indies, as yet untainted by Communism and unimpressed by Castro, may be one of the few stable countries in the area."[90] Even military officials occasionally acknowledged that the real threat was not external assault but internal unrest.[91] If the reworked Bases Agreement could pre-empt the latter, the goal of an anticommunist WIF would be served as well by that as by nuclear submarines.

This was a large "if" given Williams's unpredictability and the federation's weaknesses. Still, no other course of action had brought progress, and Washington was willing to try almost anything that could conceivably head off another Cuba. By early 1961, there was cause to wonder if federation might be no better than the "least-worst" option for the West Indies; certainly as the record of federal unions elsewhere came in, Caribbean fingers were crossed tighter. In Asia, India was holding together thanks to Nehru and a heavily centralized federal structure; Pakistan's federation had not survived the decade, having been replaced by military rule in 1958; and Malaya had reached independence riven by insurgent war and ethnic tension. In Africa, Nigeria displayed similar tension but also an encouraging unity strong enough to cope with a regional-constitutional crisis; Rhodesia-Nyasaland showed little prospect of overcoming conflict between settlers and Africans, as the latter rebelled against an unjust arrangement. From one viewpoint, the WIF had advantages that could enable it to overcome these sorts of obstacles. Yet from another angle, those federal experiments raised the worry that the WIF would not be any different from its faltering brethren around the ex-empire.

For now, Williams seemed placated, but the listing federal edifice was worrisome. Both would soon be put to the test. In Jamaica, Bustamante, who was sometimes a proponent of union and was leader of the opposition in Jamaica, railed against federation as a raw deal for Jamaicans. His agitation coincided with a rise in "racialist" politics and in fear of Cuban-communist infiltration on the island. This pressure forced Manley to call a referendum on Jamaican participation in the WIF. Manley and British officials assured all parties that the vote would pass—"I have the greatest confidence about it," Manley wrote C. L. R. James that summer—offering an endorsement of West Indian union by its largest member.[92] Manley was not without reason; a Canadian diplomat reported that Castro's revolution seemed to stir pro-federation sentiment, as it led Jamaicans to wonder whether they could indeed go it alone. Not all Jamaicans, nor all the island's other nationalist intellectuals such as Domingo, were as sanguine—"my confidence in Manley has been ebbing for some time," he wrote Roberts—but most signs pointed toward the affirmative.[93] The referendum would settle the issue, and the expected "yes" result would show all parties that the WIF was the solid anti-Castro bulwark it was meant to be.

6

Collapse: The Broken Bulwark

The Castro earthquake and its aftershocks kept rumbling in the weeks following the January 1961 inauguration of John F. Kennedy. The new administration continued or expanded most of the hemispheric-policy revisions that its predecessor had initiated after the Nixon trip south and the Castro push left. In the West Indies, the matter of Chaguaramas would be at last put to rest just weeks into Kennedy's term. This was an especially welcome prospect given what Washington saw as the deterioration of the neighborhood, where Castro was helping to turn Latin America into, in Kennedy's words, "the most dangerous area in the world." The Bay of Pigs debacle would redouble again the West Indies' importance, as well as the Kennedy team's relief that Chaguaramas had been settled just in time. Beyond the ongoing crisis in the western hemisphere, the Third World generally was to take center-stage in the Kennedy administration's diplomacy. In part this owed to the unstoppable momentum of decolonization, as vast colonial areas won independence. In part, an intensified civil rights movement in the United States brought race issues to a position of commensurate importance. These developments, and the fear that the Soviets might take decisive advantage of them, made smart diplomacy in the Third World imperative for the new administration.

This was all the more important given the diplomatic dilemmas in the Third World at the time—namely, that several of the two-pronged efforts to manage the decolonization transition and block the communist advance were in the process of failing. One did not necessarily lead to the other, but areas such as Southeast Asia showed Washington that the two could well be linked. Nor was colonial status alone the only sign of vulnerability. As Castro was demonstrating, poverty and oppression—universal across the Third World, whether colonial or not—counted too. Hence, efforts at decolonization, such as federations and economic development, gained greater importance within the perilous matrix of the Cold War.

Federations were of vital importance in another way as well. All of them, whether crafted by decolonizing or post-colonial entities, were multiethnic. They manifested the quest for a structure that harbored national identity but that also transcended "tribal" ones. Yet given that a main engine of the global race-revolution was the twentieth-century surge in race consciousness, any attempt to contain subnational communities within a national one seemed to guarantee constant struggle. This was true in the First World as well, as nations from the United States to South Africa began confronting the injustices within their own structures of race, citizenship, and governance. As multilateral attempts to answer crosscutting questions of strategy and stability, imperial withdrawal, and political, national, and racial identity, federations thus drew together the two main dynamics—Cold War and race-revolution—of postwar global history. The West Indian union was especially important because it stood in the overlapping tides of decolonization, of transnational race relations, and of Castroism in the American backyard.

In the West Indies, as around the region, this meant that "smart diplomacy" would come to mean a combination of carrot and stick. However, in contrast to Latin America, where as Rabe notes, U.S. initiatives "bolstered regimes and groups that were undemocratic, conservative, and frequently repressive," in the West Indies carrot and stick were used to bolster an emerging democratic ally.[1] The former took the form of assistance as outlined in the Alliance for Progress, as well as of concessions on issues like Chaguaramas. The latter took the form of covert and not-so-covert operations against anti-American regimes. In some cases, this involved transitions away from pro-American dictators, in, for example, the Dominican Republic. In others, the transition was from British rule to some degree of independence, such as the WIF and British Guiana.[2] In both, the core objectives were the same: contain Castroism, bolster pro-Western sentiment and assets, and ensure regional security and stability. The West Indies Federation, though it faced a crucial referendum eight months hence, was intended to do all of these.

Peace at Last? Chaguaramas, Referendum, and Castroism

As the new administration settled into office and the Bases Agreement talks concluded, the Jamaican referendum was still months away. Despite intermittent misgivings about the strength of the federation and the wisdom of supporting it, Washington had always in the end done so. The Policy Planning Staff anticipated that the West Indies Federation would continue to face internal problems but that Castroism and communism were not major internal threats.[3] Both were, however, on the minds of the American public and its diplomats, who had followed Caribbean events closely since Castro's revolution. The United States, most agreed, needed to maintain good relations with the federation—and keep its military bases there. To this end, the Kennedy team continued the policy of integrating the WIF into the OAS and into U.S. aid programs, especially the Alliance for Progress.[4] Public discussion of the future prospect of OAS membership offered the new administration political advantages. The OAS had been founded on an inter-American pact avowing anticommunism and anti-interventionism, and implying anticolonialism. The peaceful accession of the West Indies Federation would vindicate all three, shedding colonial rule to achieve independence neither communist nor the victim of intervention, in an organization that in 1961 was wrestling with the collision of communism and interventionism in Castro's Cuba. The new president, in short, made no basic changes to his predecessor's approach, pressing on with bases talks and keeping longer-term policies in place.

Success at the Bases Agreement talks seemed to herald an era of good feeling. True, the new administration had played virtually no part in them, save for a statement Kennedy made ten days into his term. According to an African-American member of the U.S. delegation, though, this—and the caliber of his West Indian counterparts—made the talks a historic event:

> [To many here] the Agreement represents implementation of your...pledge to eliminate obsolescence on our bases [and this] should provide a model world-wide....The most significant thing was...Williams['s] and Manley['s] unequivocal stand with the West [since Manley] is considered by many English-speaking African leaders as the 'Nehru' of West Indies.[5]

Instability around the region confirmed the federation's importance, but Washington could now rest assured that with the bases question settled, the United States was helping rather than hurting the emerging state. Jamaica, via the referendum, was expected soon to do its part as well, proving the WIF's readiness to play the Cold War role written for it.

The concurrent leadership of Manley and Kennedy added a new dimension to relations. Manley and the PNP had ties, more than two decades old, to the Democratic Party. The bond had originated in the 1930s via African-American groups such as the NAACP, but now, for the first time, Manley and the American party with which he most identified were both in power. There is little evidence that Kennedy knew much about these ties, although Manley of course did. If the bond did little to alter the general contours of relations, it may nonetheless explain why Manley was among the first Third World leaders to visit the new president in Washington.[6]

Manley's trip followed on the heels of the visit of British Prime Minister Macmillan to the West Indies. Neither man, alas, was the bearer of entirely good news. Macmillan wrote Kennedy that he was "impressed with [West Indians'] responsibility and awareness of the part they could play in this hemisphere."[7] He relayed West Indian leaders' request for U.S. consideration of several issues—especially aid, terms of trade for sugar and bauxite, and U.S. immigration policy—as independence approached. Privately, however, Macmillan expressed concern over the "deep feelings against Federation" he detected brewing in Jamaica. These currents were inseparable from the "racialism [being] stirred up by irresponsible factions" and surging through island politics.[8] Macmillan urged a joint statement avowing "our identical interest in the emergence of the West Indies as a dominant and new Negro nation in the western hemisphere."

Kennedy and the Jamaican premier covered much the same ground. They discussed some of the issues, such as bauxite barter and sugar quotas, that Macmillan had raised.[9] Immigration policy also loomed large. The mainland was a traditional safety valve for emigrants fleeing stagnant economies, but restrictive U.S. laws had sharply curtailed West Indian access to it. Greater West Indian access to Britain had offset some of these losses, but in the wake of 1958 race riots in Nottingham and London's Notting Hill neighborhood, Parliament reduced immigration to a trickle. This damaged island economies. West Indian advocates like Arthur Lewis put it bluntly to U.S. officials in 1961: the "single best thing the U.S. could do" for the islands was to admit 250,000 West Indians.[10] Manley pressed the issue with Kennedy, who as a senator had championed immigration reform as a historic duty and a concrete example of American beneficence.

However, federation and the referendum were central to Manley's visit. Reports besides Macmillan's had suggested that the WIF's flaws were becoming irreparable.[11] Now Manley told Kennedy, in effect, that Macmillan was right—the referendum, and hence the federation, was in trouble. Should it collapse, the United States would be no less affected, since the result would be a scattering of "ten small, weak states" in its backyard.[12] The president asked what the United States could do. Manley encouraged Kennedy to make a strong, pro-federation statement declaring U.S. intent to provide aid along the same lines as to Latin America. Kennedy assured Manley of the federation's importance to the United States and agreed in principle to make a statement, but hedged on a public promise of aid until the regional picture was clearer.[13]

That regional picture, however, was at that precise moment murky and getting murkier. On the day of Manley's first meeting at the State Department, 17 April, U.S.-supported guerillas were launching their doomed assault at the Bay of Pigs. That fiasco could not help but influence relations between the United States and the West Indies. As Ambassador Harold Caccia reported after a conversation with State's Ivan White, "White did not speak [about] Cuba, but it is not difficult to sense that the situation there underlies all American thinking about the Caribbean." The stakes rose further when Castro weeks later revealed the Soviet presence in Cuba. This led U.S. officials to argue for the growing need to integrate the WIF into revised security plans, noting "mounting uneasiness in Jamaica," and that "the West Indies might welcome a 'protective arm.' "[14] The coincidence of Manley's visit and the Bay of Pigs disaster strengthened his plan for the West Indies to be, like Puerto Rico, a "showcase" of free-world progress. Manley assured Kennedy of Jamaica's stand with the West, in welcome contrast to current events.[15]

The next day, State Department testimony to Congress regarding a separate issue drew the same connection. The issue was the conversion of the Caribbean Commission into the Caribbean Organization.[16] That body's history was a microcosm of regional events since World War II; launched as a joint Anglo-American forum for reform, it had been made irrelevant by the rise in self-rule among its "subject" peoples. In the revised entity, the metropolitan powers except for France were observers instead of members, and combined with "native" participation from the American, British, French, and Dutch territories, this offered a comforting counterpoint:

> The Caribbean is only minutes away from the U.S. The disturbing and unhappy events...in Cuba have shocked Americans. While violence and Communism have been at work there, orderly progress and peaceful, democratic development have been at work in other parts of the Caribbean. The run-away...forces of nationalism, racism, and separatism [seen] in Africa are not paralleled in the non-independent...Caribbean.[17]

The rise of Castro and the decline of regional stability added to the strategic importance of the "non-independent" Caribbean. There, even most challenges to the evolving status quo—such as Bustamante's push against Manley and for the referendum—came not from copycat Castros on the Left but from loyal oppositions to the Right.[18] Certainly the absence of hard-left agitation did not necessarily mean a lack of West Indian interest in that end of the spectrum. Scholar Trevor Munroe, for example, blames authorities' repression of activists for the dearth of leftist alternatives.[19] But it bears note that, *pace* Munroe, the West Indian Left was not gone, even if its hardest-liners were sidelined. Its Fabianist wing was in power both in Jamaica and the federation, a circumstance, contrasting Castro, which the United States welcomed.

Three months after his visit, Manley thanked Kennedy for his support: "I do not have to tell you how much U.S. interest in the West Indies means to us." The feeling was very mutual. Manley reported to London that "[the United States] is deeply concerned that the Federation should not break down. From their point of view the West Indies has become an important political and geographic entity." London thought Manley's performance "masterful" and saw that events in Cuba added to American esteem of him. He, and Jamaica and the WIF, were a "fundamentally steady, hardworking, friendly element in the Caribbean [which] came as a much needed comfort to U.S. audiences."[20] Indeed, especially after the Bay of Pigs, the United States predicated its regional policy on a soon-independent WIF.[21] This included quick incorporation into the OAS, which both countries plus Britain were urging, albeit for complementary reasons of "enlightened self-interest...[for the federation] the desire [was] to participate in the Alliance for Progress. [For the United States, it was] hemispheric stability by having the Federation offset Cuba."[22]

Indeed, if all went according to plan, Washington would acquire, thanks to the heavy lifting done by the British and West Indians, a regional ally which would not only offset Cuba but help to surround it. Yet the geographic spread of the WIF was only one of several "structural" difficulties that the federation's authors were having trouble resolving. As the referendum loomed, there were, in a sense, two main sets of differences within the union: first, Jamaica versus Trinidad in a battle of the two "bigs," and second, Jamaica and Trinidad versus the "little eight." Both sets of differences had haunted the federal idea since Grenadian T. A. Marryshow had in 1938 urged that the imperative was to "federate or disintegrate."[23] The first set of differences was the axis along which most of the battles were fought.

This was understandable, if not inevitable, given the structural imbalance of the union. The imbalance could be alleviated to a degree by, for example, increasing the number of seats in the Federal House of Assembly and allocating them by a formula of unit-plus-population. The Assembly was the elected half of the bicameral federal parliament—a nominated Senate was the other half—and its sixty-four seats split roughly two-to-one between Jamaica and Trinidad on the one hand and the "little eight" on the other. But the question of what precise powers that government possessed proved less easy to calibrate. In particular, the leaders divided over who had the power to set policy regarding economic and demographic matters, and left the center irredeemably weak. This was in part because some insular interests could not be reconciled—and in part because of the opportunism of insular oppositions when attempts were made to do so. Federal systems by design organize tensions by distributing powers to assigned mechanisms and polities. But if unwisely distributed, those powers can destroy the mechanisms and rend the polities to which they are assigned. This proved to be the case in the WIF, as tensions led to a too-weak center, commanding no loyalty, save perhaps that of a quasi-ideological minority. The center's weaknesses, in the end, serrated the ties that might have bound the union together.

Three issues—taxation, development, and migration—cut the deepest. On tax policy, for example, the two big islands accounted for 80 percent of federal GNP and total revenues. The remaining eight not only contributed little but were in much greater need of development aid. Hence the large islands, whose own development needs were themselves quite dire, insisted that the central government not have the power to tax individual units, who retained primary authority for taxation. They feared, not unreasonably, that their own progress would be hostage to disbursements to their neighbors. But this meant, in effect, a unit-level veto on federal tax policy. In a related manner, the federal seat was to have relatively little power to dictate industry and development, or to establish a customs union. A dedicated federalist like Williams could make the case that centrally planned development would be in the collective interest. But one less impassioned like Manley, or more cynical like Bustamante, could point—again, not without reason—to cases in which a preferred industrial project in one island might be sent to another, in a zero-sum fashion not easily explained to insular voters back home. As with taxation, the federal constitution avoided this problem by enshrining another: a unit-level veto. Finally, the two "rich" islands—especially Trinidad given its relatively high level of income and industrialization—feared unrestricted internal migration. They figured that if the federation embraced "free movement" among units, migrants from the poorer, smaller units would flood the larger, richer ones in search of work. The final constitution attempted to split the difference, by affirming that freedom-of-movement should be delayed and installed within a decade of the attainment of independence.

Williams thought that Jamaica had gotten all it wanted, and more—he termed the federal constitution a "total sell-out" to that island—but even this was not enough to dissuade Bustamante from his campaign. Convinced that on all counts Jamaica would come out the loser—and believing, apparently, that in continuing the campaign he himself would come out a winner—he maintained the pressure as the referendum drew near. He relentlessly charged that Jamaica was getting a raw deal: carrying an unfair share of the cost burden, while receiving too little of the benefits. As his campaign progressed, it revealed other signs of federation weakness. For one, it fed a growing sense that the Chaguaramas settlement had brought an unintended consequence. Meant to bolster the WIF by removing a "major irritant," it instead weakened it by exposing the federation's utter dependence on its two most powerful members, Jamaica and Trinidad. This, in turn, combined with Bustamante's charges of a federal structure unfair to Jamaica to guarantee that internal and bilateral Jamaican and Trinidadian battles would have an outsized impact on federal stability.[24]

Beyond Bustamante, for example, Jamaica's racial-*cum*-political turmoil was becoming a major force in the referendum. Although the consul detected no "general spirit of revolt" beyond these disruptive politics, he did suspect Cuban agitators were trying to stir one up.[25] Manley did too, warning that although the situation was reasonably well in hand, there was evidence that the flow of Cuban funding to island radicals had increased.[26] An American businessman in Kingston was more blunt: "Communism, via Castro [and] African glorification, is moving smoothly and confidently. Jamaicans prefer to sweep it under the rug. No one is fighting back!"[27]

This was an overstatement—the colonial government was indeed "fighting back" against subversive influences, Cuban and otherwise—but the sense that the federation was in trouble was not inaccurate. The British perceived it too. At a London meeting intended to iron out remaining problems before full independence, a Colonial Office representative outlined the stakes:

> If our plans for Federation were now to break down...we would have contributed to the Balkanization of the Caribbean...leaving us with a gaggle of small islands to grant-aid forever...subject to all the malign influences in the Caribbean.... Serious though the results would be for us, I believe they would be worse for the U.S. The Caribbean is an area of acute anxiety to her at the moment and to fail to create a Federation now would surely have disastrous effects on our relations with the United States.[28]

Everything hung on the referendum, the campaign for which, Manley wrote Williams, was "a non-stop all-out battle." A State Department analyst urged stronger statements of support for federation in an effort to sway the vote, in addition to better use of USIS resources to counteract anti-WIF currents and to make the case for federation.[29]

Not all the signs were bad. A month before the 19 September vote, Manley predicted—despite some private doubts—that the racial-political turmoil would calm in time for the measure to pass and with support from Bustamante's rural strongholds to boot. Most of the colonial and metropolitan press predicted and endorsed victory for federation. Colonial Secretary Ian Macleod told Consul-

General Robert McGregor that "approval of Federation in the Jamaican referendum [was] practically assured" and that London now considered Williams—slipping back into combative mode, this time against Manley and Jamaica rather than against Adams or the United States—as but a "stumbling block."[30]

On the eve of the election, the consul reported that it was "generally expected Jamaicans will decide by substantial majority in the referendum tomorrow to remain in Federation." He added that the British strongly supported Manley but could not take a public stance beyond pro-federation platitudes. This put them in the same position as the United States: "it might be at least as delicate for US to indicate in any public way our interest in outcome of referendum."[31] Both Washington and London stayed offstage as the vote approached. Speeches by Manley and Bustamante made few references to either, citing instead new nations like Ghana. Manley called the vote Jamaica's "last river to cross, like Jordan of old, like the day when brave men with vision and faith crossed the water to a better land." As an eerie silence covered Jamaica—the result of a late ban on "street campaigning," a partially effective effort to pre-empt partisan violence—West Indian observers predicted "that pro-Federation sentiment will tip the scales."[32]

Yet on election day, Jamaicans voted their island out of the union by a 54–46 margin. Observers all around the Atlantic were stunned. British Colonial Attaché J. D. Hennings reported from Washington that State Department personnel were "both disappointed and bewildered by [the] result."[33] James, one of many former allies with whom Williams had broken, blasted the vote as "the most desperate crisis [since] emancipation." To Manley, James was equally blunt: "It is a disaster."[34] The *New York Times* agreed, giving editorial space to a topic of special interest to many of its Harlem readers and calling the vote a "great disappointment." The *Trinidad Guardian*, antagonistic to Williams but supportive of union, expressed "profound shock" and warned that "our friends abroad are watching" to see how the West Indies responded to the difficult questions that the vote raised.[35] Some replied in the local idiom. A calypso by Trinidad's Mighty Zebra dismissed Jamaica's action; another, by Lord Yul Brynner, asked "Jamaica Why You Run Away?" Officials and the press in the "little 8" bemoaned the result and pondered possible future scenarios, most of them grim. While the vote was not a landslide, it was convincing, and its main consequence from calypso club to diplomatic desk was uncertainty.

The U.S. consul in Kingston blamed the result on several factors: a sense that federation thwarted Jamaican nationalism; Bustamante's campaign to capitalize on this feeling; the fear of financial sacrifice to islands with whom little kinship was felt; and the cross purposes and uneven leadership of Adams, Williams, and Manley.[36] Caribbean and Canadian analysts agreed, but the latter added that Britain and the United States bore some blame too; both had undermined the federation by, respectively, "rushing" independence and negotiating with unit governments, namely Trinidad. Nor had it gone unnoticed that "only following the threat posed by Castro [did the United States] talk in terms of substantial aid."[37] The governor, in a sign of desperation, pondered discreetly asking the Jamaican leaders, especially Bustamante, somehow to reconsider. Other British officials, though, recognized that "the Jamaican decision to quit the W.I.F. must be taken as final [and] the U.S. will be extremely concerned about this development."[38]

Picking up the Pieces: From Federal Bulwark to Twin Pillars, 1961–1962

At a stroke, American plans were all but obsolete. No contingency plan was in place for the new situation. Nor were all the implications immediately clear, beyond the obvious one that Manley was fighting for his political life. Foggy Bottom determined that Jamaica was probably out of the WIF for good and likely to "go it alone," becoming independent next year.[39] Some Jamaican voices were calling for closer ties to the United States, possibly along the lines of commonwealth status à la Puerto Rico. Jamaican nationalism made this unlikely. But closer ties of some kind were needed; "because this island is defenseless [and] tempting to adventurers," offered the consul, "we should be particularly vigilant in regard to the spread of Castroism." He concluded that the United States should accept the referendum, continue aid projects, bolster intelligence-gathering, and prepare to deal with Jamaica as an independent entity.

As for the remainder of the WIF, things were even less certain. Without Jamaica the union's prospects looked poor indeed. Washington thought a "rump" federation of Trinidad and the Eastern Caribbean to be the principal remaining option, albeit one problematic at best: "a weak and decentralized W.I.F. will probably fragment next year." Manley agreed that "hope for the survival of the federation lays with Trinidad."[40] His PNP anticipated that the next step for Jamaica was to prepare for independence under a unitary constitution, making the "necessary adjustments...with our neighbours."[41] Trinidad's place atop the new, smaller heap brought mixed feelings. Williams and other Trinidadian leaders had long resisted proposals that would tap the island's resources for the benefit of other colonies. A revised structure would have to balance this concern, perhaps with a strong central government that had an effective Trinidadian veto over taxation and migration. But the smaller islands, as one analyst ironically put it, would never accept a structure that would "weaken [their] ability to resist Trinidadian 'imperialism.'" In any case, to the irritation of those who had dealt with him before, "Williams [was] the key to federation now."[42]

Further unraveling the West Indian situation, Jamaica's withdrawal prompted Williams to claim that the renegotiated Bases Agreement was now invalid. It was bad enough, for Washington, that West Indian policy had been sent back to square one at a time when chaos loomed not only from Cuba but now, following the assassination of Rafael Trujillo, from the Dominican Republic as well. Worse yet that Williams resumed beating the Chaguaramas drum. Accusing Manley, Macleod, Adams, and the United States of conspiring to engineer a PNM defeat in upcoming Trinidad elections, Williams even threatened to lead another march on the base.[43]

Weariness and cynicism pervade correspondence on the subject. Most officials saw Williams as renewing his crusade both on anticolonial principle and to gain leverage to extort more aid. His intimation that Castro was "looking at Jamaica" reinforced the latter conclusion.[44] U.S. Consul-General Ed Moline also noted that Williams was nervous about upcoming elections and surmised that he was seeking ways to use the renegotiated agreement to his domestic advantage. In any event, Washington gratefully declared the base issue moot after London—which still controlled West Indian foreign policy—stated that the renegotiated Bases Agreement would stand despite the Jamaican withdrawal. In December 1961, Williams and his PNM won re-election.[45] This, and the British statement, restrained Williams on Chaguaramas at the end of 1961 but could not guarantee he would not raise the matter again.

By that time, the implications of the post-referendum "federation" for American policy had become clearer. The first imperative was not to meddle, lest this inadvertently complicate the British and West Indian job of picking up the pieces. The second was not to let go of the remaining Chaguaramas facilities should Williams renew his crusade. In addition to its new role as a tracking station for the U.S. space program, the base retained its traditional uses. As a British study put it, "with a major oil producer at its back door the importance of Trinidad needs little stressing....Any [hostile] attempt to take Trinidad over will be resisted by the U.S."[46] Third, U.S. and British thinking was beginning to diverge. London held that even a rump union "would provide more security against the growth of Castroism than would separate and weaker island governments. [Since] Williams is the most promising leader in the area [he] should be exploited in interests of stability in the Eastern Caribbean."[47]

The Americans were not so sure. "Given his demonstrated willingness to blackmail [us]," argued Moline, Williams's "control of [the Eastern Caribbean] could be used by him as leverage for U.S. aid." Moreover, a Trinidad-led WIF "was only an outside possibility." Manley agreed, partly because of the timeframe: "it is inevitable that the present Federation will come to an end long before a new Federation is devised."[48] But the Embassy in London felt that Williams "was the strongest leader on the horizon" and that for all his flaws he was anticommunist enough and had brought Trinidad good government. For their part, the British were broke and wanted out. They had told Washington that "[large U.S. aid] might be a major factor in achieving some kind of Eastern Caribbean Federation." However, lamented the Colonial Office, "so far the Americans have given no indication of biting." Hence, it was still Britain's problem, "unfortunately for [our] interest in reducing the financial burden...by progressively transferring it to the shoulders of the U.S."[49] Moline grasped that the problem was more than financial. As he put it following the referendum and Williams's threats, "the British government must be most anxious to divest itself as soon as possible of its remaining vestiges of responsibility for this troublesome island."[50] The analysis was correct, and the implication clear: U.S. aid decisions would loom large in whatever course Trinidad and "federation" chose and should be made judiciously.

It is noteworthy that as late as December 1961 the NSC had not revised NSC-6002—a policy premised on a federation—in the wake of the Jamaican vote that all but killed that entity. This appears to have owed to the conclusion that the WIF per se might not be so crucial if its members could be counted on to toe the Western line. Washington thus became agnostic about federation. The "little 8," even Barbados, were years away from independence and thus would remain London's problem for the immediate future. The Kennedy administration decided that, given the post-referendum landscape, "U.S. aid would achieve the greatest return in Jamaica and Trinidad. Based on that, the U.S. should neither promote nor discourage an Eastern Caribbean Federation but along with Canada and the U.K. should funnel aid to Jamaica and Trinidad."[51]

Along with this conclusion, the conviction took root that Williams's outbursts of anti-Americanism were expedients—and unevenly effective ones—meant for domestic consumption. Chaguaramas in this light was indeed only a means to leverage U.S. aid. It was not, in short, proof of a proto-Castro, although that specter still loomed: "Williams gives the impression of being against allowing [Castroism] to take root here [but] in view of his cynical and erratic behavior, I would not...say with any certainty where he is going."[52] But he was the best that could be hoped for at the moment, and he was a "good enough" anticommunist. Manley was a better one; despite his wrong instincts on the referendum, "he takes an almost exemplary attitude on development aid, foreign investment, and western-hemisphere defense."[53] Unfortunately, he was damaged by the vote and now faced a daunting campaign against an energized Bustamante.

Leading up to that election set for April 1962, Washington reverted to pre-Chaguaramas form: deference to British and West Indian initiative. The exception to this was the fine-tuning and expansion of aid programs to select areas of the West Indies. In January Williams put an end to the speculation, announcing that Trinidad would not lead a rump federation but would instead, like Jamaica, "go it alone." Perhaps "alone" was not the correct term; a Canadian diplomat remarked that as of that month, the United States had "committed aid on a considerably greater per capita basis [to Trinidad] than [was] now committed to South America."[54]

In part this funding was an effort to pre-empt Williams from renewing Chaguaramas claims, as he had threatened to do after the referendum. In part it was an effort to strengthen him politically, lest Trinidad, as the British put it, "go sour on us and become another British Guiana."[55] The analogy had two dimensions: Cheddi Jagan's flirtation with communism and the black–Indian racial split shared by the two colonies. British Guiana had an Indian plurality and black minority; Trinidad had the reverse. Jagan headed an interracial party leadership, although street-level clashes were constant. The same was true for Williams, and when he gave a speech entitled "Massa Day Done," it appeared the clash might become permanent. Arguing that "Massa" was not dead—and need not be white—and thus making a larger point about the lingering impact of colonialism on the colonized, Williams's speech also attended to his more immediate political battles by comparing the rival East Indian Democratic Labour Party to colonial slave masters. He accused them of fomenting racial discord and vowed to fight "these imps of Satan."[56] American solicitousness, it was hoped, would help to contain Williams's fire.

On the whole, the targeted increase in aid reflected the American decision to support the "twin pillars" of Jamaica and Trinidad rather than the "federal bulwark." As Consul-General James Donovan in Barbados put it to Colonial Under-Secretary Hugh Fraser, the rump federation was Britain's problem; "the U.S. was just an interested observer."[57] Fraser argued that, given the chaos in Latin America, the United States should be more than that. But his plea missed the mark, for reasons the Foreign Office had noted:

> [The United States] saw the W.I.F. as offering an example of political stability to the western hemisphere [and as such] they were ready to back it strongly. These hopes have been sharply disappointed by the Jamaican referendum; [the United States] are now likely to be less forthcoming in aid to these islands than we had at one time hoped because they no longer feel that they can extract from them the same arguments in support of their Latin American policy.[58]

The American decision to support the "twin pillars" of Jamaica and Trinidad offset its broader pattern of inactivity, that is, of deferral to the British and West Indian attempt to sort out the ex-colonies' and ex-federation's future.

A Canadian analyst criticized this approach as short-sighted. "One of the real tragedies of [the WIF] breakup," he wrote, "is that an area that had a blueprint for stability and progress is threatened with...degeneration into a number of petty states run by ruthless, corrupt power-seekers." Supporting the "pillars" would not halt this degeneration and might accelerate it. Yet no obvious alternative existed. The West Indies Federation as originally envisioned was no more. Castroism and instability had not abated. Jamaica and Trinidad were more advanced politically than the rest of the West Indies and seemed ready for the independence soon to come. As for the other islands, they and Britain were still trying to build a future from the rubble. As the Canadian noted in April when Manley lost to Bustamante, "relieved spitefully for a moment by [Manley's] defeat, the Federation drags painfully and almost disgracefully to its end. Let it be said that it all adds up to a sorry and unedifying end to a brave experiment in nation-making.... [In the aftermath] the 'Haitianization' of the area is at least a possibility."[59]

Besides "Haitianization," the "twin pillars" approach carried with it other risks. In May Williams began—again—making vague threats regarding Chaguaramas to Consul-General William Christensen, who resigned himself to the situation. As long as Williams is in power, he sighed, "Chaguaramas will remain as the whipping boy to stir up [local] agreement at [our] expense."[60] Williams renewed his threats because he believed that the United States was working with the opposition to unseat him, and that it was also reneging on the aid agreements so painstakingly negotiated in talks at Tobago in 1960. Although the United States had indeed worked with his rivals in the first two years of the Chaguaramas crisis, there is scant mention of any such plots after the Jamaica referendum, and even less after Williams's late 1961 re-election forced any remnants of that strategy to the sidelines.

Regarding the funds, it seemed Williams was reading the Tobago aid pacts creatively and was not above blunt threats to Christensen. The consul-general suspected, "People in his own party were dissatisfied with the Chaguaramas agreement and [Williams] was tired of restraining them. He said, 'There is one way out—to accept everything agreed on at [Tobago].'"[61] The problem was that this was exactly what the consul-general thought he was doing; different interpretations of what had been "agreed on" now moved Williams to fan the Chaguaramas embers. "Williams's deep bitterness," Christensen added later, "shows through...in short he seems not to expect much more from us except the worst, i.e. U.S. military imperialism," although Washington could take comfort in Williams's reiteration of a pro-Western Cold War stance.[62]

Bustamante's return to power in Jamaica, from Washington's perspective, was more promising. Bustamante's hyperbolic anticommunism was well-known and welcome. Soon after his victory, he proclaimed his intent to secure a defense treaty with the United States. Two months later, he made a state visit to Washington. Many of the topics of conversation the premier initiated with Kennedy were the same ones that Manley had raised the previous year. The biggest exception was federation, of which Jamaica was now observer rather than participant. This entailed new discussion about strategic matters, such as military assistance and OAS membership, meant to fill the gap that the West Indies Federation's collapse had left. Bustamante "emphasized...his belief that Jamaica's natural affinity was not toward the...Caribbean, but rather to Canada and the United States." His stand reassured Kennedy that, WIF or not, Jamaica was no domino. "Of the colonies in the Caribbean," Secretary of State Dean Rusk wrote Kennedy after the visit, "Jamaica seems to be best prepared to play a responsible role in the...hemisphere after independence."[63]

Intra-Caribbean ties, however, did brush up against Cold War dynamics. At about the same time the new premier visited Washington, Bustamante's government was debating whether to invite Cuban representatives to the independence ceremony slated for 6 August. Bustamante feared negative repercussions for the forty thousand Jamaicans in Cuba if no invitation were extended. The U.S. Consulate, predictably, warned against it: "if Jamaica began formulating its hemispheric foreign policy on the premise of avoidance of Castro blackmail it was starting a long, slippery slope. Almost any solution was preferable to one which would provide propaganda for Cuba." Reporting to Washington, McGregor noted the "paradox[ical] timidity [of a] government as staunchly anti-Communist as that of Jamaica" agonizing over such an issue. For geographic and demographic reasons, Trinidad was less concerned about the matter, but the State Department elected not to take chances. Drawing a lesson from the Jamaican experience, Washington asked London to discourage Trinidad from inviting Cuba to its independence ceremony.[64]

Such protocol matters, however, hardly rated as speed bumps in the twin pillars' progress into the American ambit. An administration "Scope Paper" on Jamaica laid out the benchmarks of that progress.[65] The two months leading up to independence saw almost every one met. Early in June, for example, Jamaica concluded its defense agreement with Washington, which provided American equipment for use by Jamaican patrols against Cuban adventurism. Securing Jamaican entry into the OAS proved tougher and took longer than planned.[66] The United States voiced support and Jamaica voiced desire, but the island's application was not submitted until a year after independence. In part this owed to Jamaica's other priorities and limited means as independence approached. However, it also owed, in an echo of the way that colonialism had long complicated the inter-American system, to Guatemalan resistance. Guatemala calculated that Jamaican entry would pave the way for other ex-British areas—such as British Honduras, which Guatemala had long coveted—to do the same. This calculation was correct and was part of the American rationale for pushing Jamaica's OAS entry. Jamaica's delay in securing entry was the exception; in other respects, the shared goals of the Kennedy and Bustamante governments were becoming reality as independence approached. An updated Scope Paper stated the U.S. plan "to encourage the Jamaican government to continue its resolute anticommunist policy, with particular reference to Cuba." No encouragement was needed. A month before independence, Bustamante declared that Cuba and Jamaica were "geographically close but politically distant."[67]

Pro-American sentiment in the new nation was less endangered by Cuban communism than by a continued rise in racialist politics, about which Macmillan had warned Kennedy in April 1961 for its potential to destabilize Jamaican society and to stoke West Indian resentment of American racial practices. Although a fringe presence electorally, Millard Johnson's radically pro-black People's Political Party (PPP) and the growing Rastafari movement were changing the terms of Jamaican debate. The former was an offshoot of Marcus Garvey's black-nationalist party of the same name founded in 1928.[68] The latter, a small faction self-exiled to the Jamaican margins since its founding in the 1930s, bore only passing resemblance to the post–Bob Marley image of the Rasta. Its members shunned societal conventions, proclaiming that their salvation would one day come via repatriation to Africa. Their worldview, loosely modeled on Christianity, was equal parts utopian, communitarian, and millenarian. The Rastafarians blasted the injustices of colonial Jamaican society. These attacks, added to their sacralization of marijuana, led them into repeated clashes with the government between 1954 and 1959.

American and British authorities, as well as most Jamaicans, viewed the Rastas as little more than a cult and little less than a fifth column. Manley was something of an exception, taking the group more seriously than did most of the rest of the island leadership. In 1960, some senior Rastafarians went to the University of the West Indies to clear their name. These meetings produced a study that recommended that the Jamaican government sponsor a "back-to-Africa" mission to explore repatriation. "This was regarded by the general public as far-fetched," writes scholar Rex Nettleford, but Manley enacted it. "Manley understood the implications and indulged the Rastafarians in their quite valid demands...despite the fact that such demands were made from a [worldview] which grated on Jamaican nationalist sensibilities."[69] What made that worldview ever more grating in the late 1950s was its roots in black consciousness—at a time when racialist politics had been loosed by the federation referendum. Pro-federation Jamaican nationalism asserted that not just in the island itself but across the region, phenotypical and cultural-ethnic differences within the British Caribbean were artificial and thus no obstacle to either Jamaican or federation unity. But just as the East Indian plurality in Trinidad called this conclusion into question, so too did black radicalism do the same in Jamaica. Black radicalism, combined with the Rastafarians' antiestablishment bent, thus created a destabilizing element in Jamaican politics.[70] Indeed, American intelligence in January 1961 had found that the Rasta movement was a greater threat to Jamaican stability than were island communists. Even more troubling, the Rastafarians had scurrilous ties to the mainland; several were involved in crimes in New York City for the purpose of raising money for subversive activities back home. Some members of what appeared to be the same gang engaged in a dramatic June 1960 shootout with Kingston police—but these men, it turned out, were in fact African-Americans from New York, led by the son of a local messianic con man.[71]

This episode was a bitter, insulting echo of the "Harlem nexus" that had nurtured the West Indies' political emergence in the 1930s. Whereas Manley continued to get moral and financial support from black New York, his government now faced a disaffected minority that moved among the same mainland nodes for much more unsavory purposes. Black New York, and its Caribbean contingent, had not fully turned its back on the West Indies. Manley, Adams, and other leaders could still draw crowds there and at other familiar venues such as Howard University.[72] However, by the 1950s, major groups such as the NAACP had distanced themselves from most black-internationalist projects. This left a vacuum where the axes of the black hemisphere used to intersect. As one result, radical, race-based appeals such as Rastafarianism and the PPP—minor presences but ones which, if left unchecked, seemingly had the potential to ignite the black masses—gained a higher profile in internal and external West Indian relations.

This changing dynamic affected the way islanders saw not only each other and their (former) fellow citizens of federation but also the United States.[73] The short life of the WIF coincided with something of a lull in the U.S. civil rights movement. However, race-based island–mainland exchanges transpired across a continuum of race, ranging from cooperation to contentiousness, that underlay U.S.–West Indian relations both before and after independence. This "Achilles Heel" had been revealed in the drafting of NSC-6002. The NSC warned that "anti-white sentiment could be directed against countries with predominantly white populations including the U.S.," the report stated. "West Indians are aware [of U.S.] discrimination....The result-ing antagonism creates difficulties for us in retaining the friendship of the new country and...our installations there."[74] An intelligence report early in the Kennedy administration contended that American racism was the single biggest obstacle to friendly relations.[75] Although West Indians admired American accomplishments and took cues from "Hollywood and Harlem," the treatment of black Americans impeded good feelings. Jamaica's leading newspaper answered its own rhetorical question regarding the idea of feder-ating with its northern neighbor:

> The [United States] has a large Negro population, but we doubt whether Jamaicans would wish to belong to the United States. The freedoms [and] sophistication of the Jamaican people have reached a level of urbanity far ahead of anything achieved in the United States, in any part of it, in the way of racial relations.[76]

Civil rights clashes in the South received extensive coverage in the island press. Discrimination at American-patronized tourist sites confirmed the view of Yankee racism. Onerous restrictions on immigration, correctly seen as of a piece with Jim Crow, entrenched the perception. This was more the case for Jamaica than for Trinidad. In the latter, sensitivity on race matters never lost sight of the distant mainland, but tended to focus more on the black–Indian split at home. Ultimately, America's "image" burdens, the Kennedy administration concluded, were not sufficient to derail relations, since, as the *Gleaner* put it, the islands had "looked to the U.S. to help make federation a success." But they were real liabilities in a decolonizing Caribbean shot through with race consciousness and American preoccupation with Castroism.

Vocal, mutual support and solidarity between West Indian and African-American activists was less visible near the end of the road to independence than it had been at the start of it. This did not mean that such solidarity had vanished; West Indians followed the civil rights movement with great inter-est, and African-American luminaries were honored guests at the indepen-dence celebrations.[77] It may be most accurate, if perhaps oversimplified, to say that the Harlem nexus had shifted from active to passive mutual support. In this view, African-American and West Indian activists increasingly real-ized that while their broad cause—black freedom—was the same, their spe-cific enemies and objectives were different. Jim Crow in the U.S. South and John Bull in the empire shared a bloodline, but not a body. This meant that, as white Southern resistance stiffened and imperial devolution proceeded, different tactics were needed for each. Shelving idealized visions of solidarity was necessary if concrete progress was to be made.

This was as true within the West Indies as it was in the islands' ties to the wider world—as witnessed, to take the easiest example, in the collapse of the federation. Following the Jamaican referendum and Trinidad's subse-quent withdrawal, the Canadian Commissioner at Port of Spain bitingly assessed the "racial hypocrisy" of the situation:

It is to the everlasting discredit of the politicians in Jamaica and Trinidad that the fate of the "little 8" did not enter into their calculations *at all*, when they considered whether or not [to] break the Federation. These are the people who shed tears (crocodile as it turned out) for...South Africa, suffering under the burden of Apartheid...yet who callously took decision to abandon their own West Indian brothers without so much as a 'by-your-leave' nor a thought of what the destruction of the Federation meant to them in terms of humiliation, despair, and economic stagnation.[78]

The decline in active cooperation between mainland black groups and colonial nationalists, and the Jamaican and Trinidadian retreat from federation, marked points on the same curve. Both were, in a basic sense, simply a matter of picking battles and pressing advantages. Diasporan groups could cheer each other on in their respective fights for freedom, but neither mainland nor island could do much more if it hoped to devote scarce resources to more immediate interests.

If mutual support between the islands and the black mainland was thus more or less confined to symbolism, that element nonetheless still held some power as independence day arrived. This was not least because leading African-Americans, inside and outside the Kennedy administration, pressed for official involvement in the celebrations. The State Department obliged, suggesting to the president that he name a speaker to address the New York Jamaica Progressive League in conjunction with the independence ceremony set for 6 August.[79] Expatriates in New York, in cooperation with the USIA, organized a calypso and steelband festival to mark Trinidadian independence day on 31 August. Racially mixed contingents featuring luminaries such as Ralph Bunche, William Hastie, Adam Clayton Powell, NAACP Secretary Roy Wilkins, Urban League official Nelson Jackson, and high-ranking white officials including Vice President Lyndon B. Johnson and National Security Advisor McGeorge Bundy attended one or both of the Jamaican and Trinidadian ceremonies.[80]

Outside official gestures, African-Americans and expatriates weighed in on the occasion. The black press ran flattering stories on Williams and other West Indian leaders and took note of sister ceremonies on the mainland.[81] The Bajan firebrand and longtime advocate of independence Richard B. Moore was less sanguine, publishing a series of articles in which he concluded that independence, shaped by federation's failure and achieved within a context of economic subservience to Britain and the United States, was a sham.[82] But most of those involved were more positive. Black participation in the ceremonies was not limited to islanders and African-Americans; emerging African nations such as Nigeria sent emissaries, though neighbors such as Barbados, presumably in reply to Jamaica's withdrawal from the federation, did not. The presence of Hastie, Bunche, and Powell established continuities in both race and time. All three had long involvement with West Indian nationalism, as witness, cheerleader, and participant, dating back more than two decades. Seeing their old ally Manley was bittersweet; black America's longtime favorite in the region, Manley bore the blame for the lost referendum and had consequently been turned out of power. His African-American fans at the independence celebration, though, distinguished the man who was by rights the father of the occasion.

Manley acquitted himself brilliantly during the festivities, given the irony of his situation: "his grand design [having] faltered (with a fatal referendum)," the *Gleaner* reflected, "his rival [Bustamante] was left to make the final heroic battle cry of independence." The father of his country was now the Leader of the Opposition. Independence Week, he noted in his diary, thus "demanded great inner reserves."[83] These Manley had. He spoke graciously at all occasions, understanding that his rivalry with Bustamante must not be allowed to poison the atmosphere. He did not slight the challenges Jamaica faced, but his tone was optimistic and resolute. In remarks at the opening of the independence Parliament, Manley noted that Jamaica was "by far the oldest of all the British colonies to achieve independence this century.... You, Princess," he said with a nod to nearby Princess Margaret, "have handed us the formal title deeds to our heritage. For us the task is to plough the land and gather the fruit."[84]

The actual "handing back of the deeds" took the form of a midnight ceremony at the National Stadium, at which the new Jamaican flag was unfurled. The green triangles represented hope and agriculture, the black ones hardships overcome and upcoming. The diagonal gold bars stood for natural wealth and sunlight. The flag's unique design, a point of pride to the thousands of Jamaicans waving it, was meant to encapsulate the island's history and future alike. At midnight on 6 August, the two converged, and cheering throngs exulted. Observers and participants were by turns wary and confident at what would come next.[85] But for the moment, all was jubilation unbound.

Following closely in Jamaica's footsteps, Trinidad's independence was set for 31 August. The governor described an "air of unreality" surrounding its approach and feared the celebration might come off badly.[86] His fears were unfounded. At the ceremony in front of Red House, solemnity reigned over the midnight lowering of the Union Jack and the raising of the red, white, and black banner of Trinidad and Tobago. The only music heard was the Last Post played by the British Band of Royal Marines; steelbands and calypso were banned until after the ceremony. At that point, however, began "a nine-day independence party designed to top the birth-of-a-nation celebration in nearby Jamaica 26 days earlier."[87] Churches' "freedom bells" pealed across the island, and ships' sirens wailed the length of the Gulf of Paria. Rockets and flares speckled the sky. Trinidadians let out the raucous hurrahs of a people finally free.

Even the *Guardian*, often antagonistic toward him, declared that it was "Dr. Williams's hour" since "it was [he] who led us on to claim the prize that others had lacked the vision and the genius to garner." Opposition leader Rudranath Capildeo sounded a similar note: "Let the Healing Begin!"[88] Williams, like Manley, rose to the occasion. Setting aside his often-biting rhetoric, he, like Manley, stressed the possibilities and responsibilities of nationhood. "I have given to the Nation," he told a youth rally, "as its watchwords, Discipline, Production, Tolerance. They apply as much to you the young people as to your parents." The next day he took the same message to the elders, also charging his fellows with the high duties of democracy and unity. As a scholar he was inclined to the long view, and he put the matter bluntly: "You [Trinidadians] are nobody's boss and nobody is your boss. What use will you make of your independence? What will you transmit to your children five years from today? Other countries have ceased to exist in that period. Some, in much less time, have become totally disorganised, a prey to anarchy and civil war."[89] Given the state of the region, American observers were perhaps waiting for some reference to a different kind of threat. None came in that speech, but Williams later that day reaffirmed that his nation was "unequivocally west of the Iron Curtain."[90]

A small contingent from the American delegation stayed after the celebrations to plumb this affirmation and to size up the post-independence Williams. The Chaguaramas settlement, now added to Trinidad's passage to independence, must have given American officials hope that the proverbial chip would now be off Williams's shoulder. If true, this would support the conclusion that Trinidad would finally be the reliable ally Washington had planned on, whether in or out of a federation, as a counter to Castro. While not the vocally pro-American leader Bustamante was, Williams, Hastie assured Kennedy, was on the right side. "The new nation will be politically stable in the years immediately ahead [and] can become a significant influence in the Caribbean, offsetting...the unwholesome influence of Cuba and British Guiana."[91]

More Lucky Than Good: The United States and the Life and Death of the WIF

It has been said that in the Cold War, the United States was fortunate in its enemies. It might be argued that the country was just as lucky in its friends. Consider the foreign policy challenge the WIF presented. After Castro's revolution punctured American hegemony in the Caribbean, the United States supported the creation of the WIF as a counter-model for regional progress. At virtually the moment of its launch, this Western-oriented "model of decolonization" imploded. If not quite a second Bay of Pigs, the episode nonetheless drove home just as plainly as that fiasco the limited dependability of U.S.-supported action in the archipelago; Washington could not count on getting its regional way in the new age of Castro. After the implosion, thanks to, by turns, genuinely and sufficiently pro-Western leadership in the federation's remnants, a bulwark was built from them, and the regional drift toward communism was countered if not halted. Indeed, the return of British Guiana to the leftist camp after 1961 underlined in American and British eyes the importance of inoculating the West Indian colonies against the Cuban contagion and their good fortune that the two major ones willingly did so.

In retrospect, the collapse of the West Indies Federation was logical, if unfortunate.[92] It sought to build a nation of islands which shared problems but, paradoxically perhaps, not interests. Differences in size, location, economy, and population strangled the decades-old vision of a pan-West Indian identity, which even its champions admitted was more ideal than reality.[93] It is difficult in the best of circumstances to create a democratic polity, but harder still, in the ideological and geostrategic blast furnace of the Cold War Caribbean, to forge a nation out of diffuse longings. Sooner or later these must contend with the challenges of basic survival, and absent a powerful unifying agent, they lose. The architects of the West Indies Federation both in the Colonial Office and in the islands built a structure at once too ambitious and too modest to have a serious chance at success.

In fairness to the West Indies, "too ambitious and too modest" was true for most of the new federations. Yet the failure of the WIF resonated far and wide. It was the one whose chances of success, on paper, had been greatest. Its racial-ethnic challenges, as conventionally understood, were largely confined to one unit and seemingly under control there. To the extent that insular island identities were "ethnic," even these were seen as minor differences that could be subsumed within a pan-island identity. None of its religious, linguistic, and "tribal" frictions compared to those of South Asia or West Africa. Its most significant obstacle—geography—was formidable, but seen as manageable given advances in transportation technology and the asset of a longstanding de facto "capital of the Caribbean" in New York. Yet with all these advantages, the union could not hold. Its collapse shook the confidence of even the stoutest Third World nationalists. The "founding father" of pan-Africanism, Nkrumah, wrote to Manley, Williams, and their fellow Caribbean leaders in June 1962, imploring them to reconsider and rebuild:

> I hold the sincere conviction that success in the establishment of a powerful West Indian nation would substantially assist the efforts we are making in Africa to redeem Africa's reputation in world affairs and to re-establish the personality of the African and people of African descent everywhere.[94]

Nkrumah acknowledged the "immense difficulties" of rebuilding. He nonetheless insisted on the importance of trying to do so, arguing that a West Indian Federation would boost efforts to create a united Africa. Yet while he may have been right about the particular symbolism of the WIF, as he undoubtedly knew, that union's implosion was only remarkable among Third World federations in the speed at which it happened. Most of the others, shaky at best, looked as of 1962 to be facing a similar fate.

Among the lot, however, only the West Indies Federation stood at the crossroads of Third World nationalism, Western anticommunism, inter-American and Anglo-American relations, and Cold War geostrategy. The West Indies, Britain, and the United States had all counted on it. On the eve of its full independence, it fell. That independence still came to the West Indies was unsurprising, as European empires were almost everywhere in retreat. In that context the end of British rule in the Caribbean was as momentous, if not more so, as in East Africa or Malaya. After all, the West Indies had spent three centuries under such rule, while those areas were still working on their second. Certainly the Caribbean carried greater weight as far as the United States was concerned; as Kennedy put it in his independence day message to Bustamante, "the American people are always gratified to see a newly independent state...but in this instance we must be permitted an extra measure of satisfaction on seeing a near neighbor attain full self-determination."[95] Yet the epochal end of empire in the British Caribbean came at a moment when, thanks to the breach of the federal vessel, it could have brought disaster. External affairs, notably those with Britain and the United States, figured prominently in this collapse, but internal affairs loomed at least as large. The collapse constituted a crisis for all parties, not least Washington, whose navigation of it was equal parts prudent and lucky.

Conclusion

The West Indian colonial situation is unique because the West Indies, in all their racial and social complexity, are so completely a creation of Empire that the withdrawal of Empire is almost without meaning. In such a situation nationalism is the only revitalizing force.

V. S. Naipaul, *The Middle Passage*

The fireworks smoke from the independence celebrations had hardly dissipated when U.S. policy toward the West Indies had its first payoff. Mere weeks after the ceremonies, Washington discovered the construction of Soviet nuclear-missile sites in Cuba. The subsequent Missile Crisis left no doubt that the Caribbean had become a significant Cold War battleground. In that crisis, the West Indian islands stood resolutely with the United States. When it was over, Kennedy sent a word of thanks to Bustamante and Williams, reaffirming hemispheric determination to keep Castroism at bay. The collapse of the West Indies Federation had not left its largest constituent parts wobbly, but rather solid when Castro and Khrushchev tested the region and its hegemon. The same was true of the "little 8"—where British rule continued until 1966 for Barbados, and until a decade or more later for the other members of the failed union—to the relief of a Kennedy administration deeply worried about a "second Castro" in British Guiana.[1]

If external relations after independence had brought the hoped-for result, the transition was nonetheless no panacea for the two big islands. Both—Jamaica more than Trinidad—suffered from debilitating partisan and/or racial conflict in the years after the British flag came down. Internal stability had, of course, always been a matter of great concern and continued to be. As in most societies transitioning from imperial rule to self-government, pre-existing social divisions tended to grow rather than subside, and the absence of a unifying imperial enemy meant that factions aimed instead at one another, even more so than they had before.

Here again, though, the West Indies had better fortune than many decolonizing areas. Political violence after independence was widespread enough to spark a new exodus following U.S. immigration reform in 1965.[2] This exodus, in turn, had a profound effect on the formation of West Indian identities in independence. It is estimated, for instance, that a third of all Jamaicans alive reside abroad, in places where "West Indianness" does not always fit easily into local racial dynamics, and where that identity has evolved into what, with apologies to DuBois, one might call a "triple consciousness"—metropolitan, diasporan, and island-specific all at once.[3] Yet compared to the postcolonial prices paid, for example, in the violence that marked the transition in Southeast Asia or the Indo-Pakistani partition, this was a bearable burden. Few other new nations had such relatively good Cold War fortune. Although internal stability continued to pose a problem for independent West Indian nations and their diplomacy, communism was a negligible factor in that instability.

The contrast with the surrounding area was striking. The United States had not left its neighbors to their own political fates; far from it. But U.S. interventions—as was historically the case going back a hundred years—were largely confined to the Spanish-speaking parts of the hemisphere. In the Dominican Republic a few years later, and not long afterward in Central America, U.S. arms enforced U.S. norms. In contrast, the American military presence dwindled to nothing in the former British possessions. Even in "essential" Trinidad, the 1970s saw the last U.S. military officials leave Chaguaramas. In that same period, American prestige ebbed along with its military presence, notably when the Michael Manley government led Jamaica to a kind of *rapprochement* with the Castro regime. Washington responded with harsh words but little more. Only in pre-independence British Guiana in the early 1960s, and in 1983, when the Reagan administration decided that the revolutionary government in Grenada was becoming too friendly toward the Soviet bloc, did the United States intervene in the territory of the British West Indies.

This relative restraint in territories which, prima facie, presented similar capacity to that of their neighbors for unrest and instability, grew from an array of factors. That restraint, though, goes far in explaining why U.S.–British–West Indian affairs were on the whole more constructive than destructive. At those points in time when the United States was unrestrained—that is, in an active rather than passive policy stance—it encountered resistance from one or both of the British and West Indian sides of the triangle. Hence the simplest explanation is that restraint made policy sense. Not only was it conducive to good relations with Washington's British ally and West Indian neighbors, it also rarely endangered U.S. objectives.

Most important among these, and chief among the group of geostrategic themes guiding relations, was the pursuit of national-security assets. These were, in varying order over the long course of decolonization: bauxite and oil from the West Indies; military facilities in the West Indies; the stability of the West Indies as a buffer against communism; and good relations with the West Indies to ensure all of the above. A rough form of this approach became worldwide American doctrine in the early Cold War, but before that it had guided U.S. policy toward the West Indies since the 1930s. Even the salient features of relations under Roosevelt, most of all the push for reform, stemmed less from anticolonial principle than from national-security priorities. The former was genuinely held, but the latter were more highly held. Reform would serve the larger purpose of a stable Caribbean, which in turn would help secure strategic assets.

One reason this did not cause more friction than it did was that it often harmonized with British and West Indian objectives. Indeed, each side could use the American pursuit to its own ends. U.S. efforts to expand civil aviation by winning concessions for U.S. airlines clashed with British and Dutch efforts to protect a Euro-monopoly. But they also met a need for inter-island communications, a need that U.S., British, and joint commissions had all declared pressing. U.S. pressure for the expansion of the Jamaican bauxite industry profited North American companies and assured Washington a material vital to the Truman defense buildup. But Jamaica had desperately sought to add industry to its economy, and the bauxite operations were the largest such addition in its history. The initiative also widened the gulf between London and the colonial nationalists, who chafed at the restrictions placed on their islands' economic development. Even if the bauxite operations were designed to maximize U.S. supply rather than stimulate Jamaican development, the capital infusion they represented brought a long-called-for if short-term benefit.

To be sure, American pursuit of national-security assets more than once caused friction with one or both of the other parties. Chaguaramas generated the most heat, pitting not only the United States against a vocal West Indian nationalism but also one American need against another. That was not the first time U.S. facilities had caused tension; revulsion against Jim Crow around them during World War II and after, despite officials' best efforts, was difficult to neutralize once loosed. Away from the bases, the U.S.-directed expansion of bauxite operations first met fierce and successful resistance by British imperial interests, only finally overcome some years later. When it was, the expanded operations contributed to the revival of Jamaica's labor movement, including its communist wing. Hence, acquisition of a military asset (bauxite) endangered retention of a political asset (a noncommunist local government).

In the end, though, Jamaican communists paid for their newfound influence with official banishment, an act applauded by Washington but organized and executed by West Indian leaders and colonial authorities. These episodes of controversy and crisis were among the only times that U.S.–West Indian affairs rose to high-level attention, further underscoring the central role of national-security concerns in relations. However—with the signal exception of British Guiana, an outlier in this and other senses, as viewed from Washington, London, and West Indian capitals alike—it bears repeating that the general tenor of those relations, whether directly or indirectly touched by the security imperative at a given moment, was positive. Controversies and crises were the exception, not the rule.

American policy toward and resulting relations with Britain's Jamaican and Trinidadian colonies might thus be described as "benign neglect." The phrase cuts two ways. For critics of the U.S. interventions so abundant elsewhere in the hemisphere and century, the emphasis is on "benign." Certainly the comparisons with Guatemala in 1954 or the Dominican Republic in 1965, not to mention Cuba in between, were stark. For critics of U.S. self-interestedness, the emphasis is on "neglect." The shift from official British to unofficial American supremacy, in this view, carried with it the duty to see that the decolonizing Jamaican and Trinidadian economies and polities developed well.

Both views have some merit regarding relations whose chief characteristic was a pattern of deferral to the British, itself the fruit of strategic choices about Anglo-American relations. Those choices dictated that British sovereignty over, and initiatives in, the West Indies not be challenged more than necessary. When they were challenged, it was in the direction of colonial self-rule, not of replacing British with American writ. All of this, however, was conditioned on continued access to, or at least the last word regarding, national-security assets. Provided that this could be assured by a policy of deferral to the British, or by concessions to West Indian nationalism, this was the path Washington took.

This path was not without risk. Deferral left British authorities in charge of events on the ground, even those touching American interests, which did not always match British ones. Concessions, especially on Chaguaramas, came almost too late. Most of all, "benign neglect" regarding federation was not technically neglectful—U.S. policy sought to bolster the union with moral, financial, and military support—but neither was it deeply involved, except negatively on Chaguaramas. This left much to chance. American action would likely have ultimately done little to offset the internal weaknesses of the federation, or to influence the Jamaican referendum that killed it. Yet American plans for the hemisphere counted on the union, and its implosion in a crisis-torn Caribbean invited dire possibilities. That these were mostly avoided—that is, the fact that the benignly neglectful pursuit of American national-security interests was on the whole successful—owed as much to diplomatic prudence as to dumb luck.

Yet the good fortune and American restraint summed up in "benign neglect" are at best only part of the story. Among other flaws, the phrase does not encompass the intermittently intense American interest which broke the pattern of deferral to British and West Indian action. Nor can it convey the vital point that the story is not only the one-sided relation between neglector and neglectee, but of multiple actors and agendas evolving over time. Among the latter must prominently be included West Indians themselves, whose agency in shaping their own national futures was much greater than in many parts of the global South. Thus, a better and fuller description is that of a U.S.–West Indian "protean partnership," which can accommodate the waxing and waning of reciprocal interest between mainland and island, as well as the British and West Indian influences on these fluctuations. It also properly credits the role of West Indian agency in shaping Anglo-American–Caribbean affairs. Moreover, it transcends the purely official dimension of those affairs, expanding to include at key moments the transnational, race-based networks that allowed the black mainland and the colonies to offer mutual support.

The protean partnership did not operate without limits, and the discovery of such limits could make for either pleasant or unpleasant surprises. The strength of "organic" West Indian anticommunism, for example, and the high caliber of the leadership championing it, came as an acute relief to American officials, and to a lesser extent their British counterparts, fearful of communism's spread. Even a cursory contemplation of other Third World statesmen with whom Washington and London dealt—from Sukarno to Nehru to Nasser to Nkrumah to Perón—suggests the comfort that the non-dictator, pro-West, anticommunist likes of Manley, Bustamante, and even Williams provided. Although often at odds with one another, they steered a sensible, realistic road to independence. Except for Bustamante, their intellectual strengths often exceeded their political acumen. Miscalculations, occasionally grave, complicated relations among them, and between their nations and Washington and London. However, they fostered what a majority of their constituents as well as the Atlantic powers found to be a responsible nationalism. In so doing, they gave that sentiment peaceable, anticommunist shape en route to independence.

Their most visible unpleasant surprise—the blame for which does not fall on their shoulders alone—was the failure of the federation. "Failure" is perhaps not even the right word, given that for Bustamante it was a political success, and that the collapse resulted not from violence but from Jamaica's democratic (and then Trinidad's semi-democratic) decision to withdraw. The inability of the two largest colonies and their smaller cousins to unite around an abstract nationhood, moreover, went deeper than just their key leaders. Indeed, this phenomenon was present in West Indian relations with the broader Third World. Racial-ethnic solidarity, though genuinely expressed, rarely went beyond rhetoric. Leaders like Manley and Williams voiced unfeigned outrage at South Africa and eloquent solidarity with its sufferers. They spoke for most of their countrymen and -women. But given the chance to give pan-national solidarity a concrete form in the regional federation, West Indians ultimately declined.

This phenomenon—a rhetoric of solidarity that exceeded its practice— also characterized the ties linking West Indian nationalism with the black mainland. In the black-consciousness hothouse of the 1930s, Caribbean expatriates and African-Americans in New York forged strong and uniquely influential bonds. The Harlem nexus provided a conduit to a receptive Roosevelt administration. It also provided key nationalists, Manley most of all, with moral and financial support. An undeniable race-based solidarity, in short, produced the "diaspora diplomacy" that was a key feature of both official and unofficial island–mainland relations.

However, the limits of that solidarity were just as remarkable as its strengths. Black-mainland support for Manley, for example, came from both expatriate and native-born black individuals and organizations. It only rarely, though, extended to his opponent Bustamante, who had arguably greater claim to the title of leader of the black Jamaican masses. Expatriates and African-Americans, moreover, often had different ideas about how decolonization should proceed, although all agreed that it must. A similar division extended into the Cold War. West Indians and African-Americans spoke in support of each other's struggle, but organizationally had different objectives and directed their resources to them. Freedom from white rule was the shared cause, but freedom from John Bull in Kingston was not the same mission, requiring the same tactics, as freedom from Jim Crow in Montgomery. Symbolic, mutual support fluctuated but never disappeared, and indeed intensified after independence as the U.S. civil rights and Black Power movements resonated in the increasingly race-conscious West Indies. But concrete cooperation declined after the first half of the 1940s.

This was not the full extent of the influence of race, broadly defined, on Anglo-American–Caribbean relations. Both British and West Indian figures used America's racial reputation against it. The specter of Jim Crow hovered from the Bases Deal forward, and officials tried with varying success to exorcize it in day-to-day dealings with West Indians. During the postwar racial-colonial awakening, and especially after its quickening in Bandung, Montgomery, and Ghana, neutralizing Jim Crow held high priority in U.S. propaganda and diplomatic efforts. This was as true of the West Indies as of anywhere else in the nonwhite world, indeed arguably more so given West Indians' intimate knowledge of the American racial regime.

Race was often an unsubtle factor in American foreign relations, as friends and foes alike asked how the United States could claim to stand for freedom and equality while the mobs howled in Little Rock. Yet race was, as U.S.–British–West Indian relations showed, also unpredictable. Its most recognizable, and reprehensible, manifestation was white terrorism in the South. Somewhat less visibly, black cooperation in solidarity's name had an important influence on West Indian nationalism. Practically unseen, that cooperation for a time found a sympathetic ear in white Washington, some of whose agents pressed British authorities for greater black freedom than London wanted to give. It would be a mistake, however, to presume that even the deeply unpredictable race factor was either independent or decisive. Race was a consistent, important, and multivalent consideration, but never the paramount one.

American, African-American, British, and Caribbean navigation of the route to West Indian independence suggests several such conclusions in addition to this one. Some reach beyond the Caribbean to join similar currents elsewhere; others are confined to the area's unique historical and geographical position. One is the useful comparison and striking contrast with the rest of the hemisphere. With episodic exceptions, such as the Good Neighbor Policy and the Alliance for Progress, Washington tended to see Latin American nationalism as potentially dangerous, especially when it was oriented to the left. Most West Indian nationalism, on the other hand, won the support of interested U.S. parties provided that it met a few basic conditions. It had to adhere to noncommunist political norms; be channeled through appropriate institutions such as federation; and not jeopardize American access to national-security assets.

In this respect the West Indies were both like and unlike their Latin American neighbors, a paradox pointing to another conclusion. The British possessions posed more or less the same strategic challenge that independent western-hemisphere areas did: Washington could allow neither to fall into enemy hands, Nazi, communist, or otherwise, and could not allow much internal instability in them either. More than once the United States intervened militarily on these grounds in Latin America, but it never did so in the British areas, which thus stand as a partial exception to the Monroe Doctrine. The reason was that sovereignty, and responsibility for orderly change, belonged to trusted London. This was, in effect, the difference between informal and formal empire, and it explained the absence in the West Indies of the American interventions so historically promiscuous around the littoral. The British areas had, in the crown, a mediator between their wishes and American power, not to mention a sometime rival to that power. Spanish-speaking areas in the region, having no such entity, were at the mercy of U.S. imperatives in time of crisis.

The contrast with the rest of the hemisphere is instructive in another way as well: it helps to reposition, relative to the Cold War, both the early version of the national-security doctrine practiced in U.S.–West Indian relations and the history of U.S. interventionism in the Americas. The superpower conflict made that doctrine the centerpiece of global American strategy. But U.S. relations with the West Indies suggest that the doctrine, at least in prototype, antedated the Cold War. American strategic priorities in the Caribbean during World War II were virtually indistinguishable from its priorities worldwide after 1945. In that respect, the real change in the search for the "preponderance of power" was its application to a global rather than a regional or hemispheric scale. Moreover, the search for the resources that made preponderance possible also fits a long-standing pattern of acquisitive American behavior in the hemisphere. As historians Kyle Longley, Jeff Taffet, and others have noted, scholars of inter-American relations can be forgiven for thinking the Cold War was nothing new in their neck of the woods; that is, rather than creating a wholly new dynamic, the conflict superimposed an anticommunist veneer atop a pre-existing hegemony. The history of Anglo-American–Caribbean relations adds another dimension to this approach. Without its inclusion, the historiography of inter-American affairs is incomplete, especially regarding such crises as Castro's Revolution, U.S. policy responses to which placed notable importance on the West Indies.

This "repositioning" suggests another. Proximity to informal U.S. empire in the New World thus helped to shape American responses to formal European empire there, and to make those responses unique in the Third World. The dilemma that European colonialism, and its decline, posed for U.S. policy prompted different and conflicting American answers in various parts of the globe. Preventing communist gains and promoting orderly decolonization were Washington's overarching goals, but local dynamics demanded tailored responses. These, often, were not forthcoming. Vietnam most vividly, but hardly uniquely, would suffer the U.S. failure to maneuver among communism, declining European empire, and Third World nationalism.

The variables contained in each of these three elements complicated Cold War diplomacy the world over—but arguably less so in Jamaica and Trinidad than anywhere else. A combination of American restraint, anticommunist West Indian leadership, and British reform made this so. The dilemma colonialism posed for U.S. policy was real: how could a nominally anticolonial superpower promote decolonization, thereby winning the friendship of the Third World, if this ran the risk of inviting instability and producing enemy gains? The dilemma in its Caribbean incarnation was solved, however imperfectly, by a mix of pressure on and accommodation of the colonial regime, anticommunist vigilance, a focus on security-related objectives, and sensitivity— albeit often insufficient—to emerging racial and national identities.

Yet the dilemma was not one for U.S. policy alone and leads to another "repositioning" within the historical literature more broadly. Reconciling strategy, security, and identity in the postwar era meant navigating the interplay of superpower competition and Third World assertion. Contemporary actors were imperfectly aware of these dynamics; even today, scholars struggle to grasp the full dimensions of that interaction. How did the Cold War arrest or abet the "race-revolution" of the second half of the twentieth century? What does it mean for the earlier decades of "nationalist" action and thought—whether acquisitive U.S. interventions, nationalist agitation, or diasporan promotion of race-inflected independence—that they only came to fruition in the middle of the bipolar standoff? If not for the Cold War, would those pre-existing trends have still culminated in the demise of imperial white supremacy and the achievement of Third World independence in more or less the same manner and timeframe they did?

This study suggests that in the Caribbean, the Cold War had a decisive effect on the timing, and ultimate shape, of decolonization; first slowing and then speeding the process, via the "protean partnership" of U.S.–West Indian relations. But this study also suggests the broader and deeper forces at work. The brief, ill-fated career of the West Indies Federation and most of its federated siblings gives one hint. Some of these federations remained Cold War backwaters, while others became Cold War battlegrounds, and among the latter the WIF had the greatest geostrategic immediacy to a superpower. None of them survived more than a generation in their original form, and only a few in any form at all—and none fell victim to Cold War, which at most could be called an accessory to their murder. Rather, these unions foundered most of all on the rocks of the particularist racial-ethnic identities contained within them. Much more study is needed to flesh out a comprehensive comparative picture, especially now that the documentary record of the federations has become available. John Lewis Gaddis has observed that one paradox of the modern era is the simultaneous impulse to federate at the supranational level and to disintegrate at the subnational level. Thus, for example, the United Kingdom joined the European Union even while London supports the diffusion of its authority to, say, a newly created Scottish Parliament. Whether Gaddis' insight will prove to apply across the First World remains to be seen. But the basic trajectory of postwar Third World federations is clear and suggests he is right. Whether jointly organized by Colonial Office–colonial nationalist cooperation or by post-colonial pan-nationalist initiative, very few of these new nations could fully overcome the parochial, pre-national and sub-national forces within them.

Racial-ethnic nationalism in the Third World had thus helped drive the effort to end rule by imperial outsiders—and in many areas, subsequently prevented the formation of a viable polity to take its place. Even in areas gaining independence under unitary rather than federal charters, the continuation of long-running racial-ethnic antagonism was more the norm than intra-national unity. The pattern is pregnant with implications, and none are necessarily foregone conclusions. The work of scholar Shalini Puri, for example, on the post-independence appearance of the "Dougla's"—half-Afro-, half-Indo-Trinidadians—suggests that a fusionist, "federated" national identity can replace parochial ethnic ones, transcending colonial-era antipathies over time.[4] But as far as the Cold War was concerned, the rise of racial-ethnic consciousness constituted a powerful and multivalent force at odds with the Manichean division of the world seen from both Moscow and Washington. It points to an irresolvable tension between the Wilsonian ideal of democratic self-determination and the multiethnic realities of the Third World, a tension that persists into the post-colonial and post–Cold War era of globalization. As the legal scholar Amy Chua's insightful study *World on Fire* argues, the rapid spread of democracy and markets serves to energize a given society's racial-ethnic identities, pitting them against each other to frequently destructive effect.[5] True, the Cold War could and did aggravate such clashes, but as Chua suggests, this dynamic predated and outlasted the superpower conflict.

At the time Washington tended not to agree, seeing decolonization through "Cold War Lenses."[6] This alone could be sufficient to inject the Cold War into the local-colonial bloodstream. It could create, as with Jamaican bauxite, organic connections to distant theaters of the struggle such as Korea. Unquestionably, there was significant interaction between the Cold War and decolonization; at a given site, one could irretrievably warp the other. But as the experience of the West Indies Federation and its fellow Third World unions suggests, the forces driving the creation of nation-states from the shards of empire did not ultimately depend on the bipolar clash either for their genesis or their demise. The sources of both flowed from much deeper, even if the Cold War, once begun, could channel them in new directions.

The changes and adaptations that this interplay wrought upon the U.S.–West Indian relationship sketch its protean character. It is worth recalling, though, the story behind the term. Proteus was a minor sea god with the ability to shape-shift, which he used to escape the clutches of any who tried to hold him. But aside from this, he was powerless to defend himself. Once in the clutches of one more powerful, he could only thrash about changing shapes, in hopes of scaring off the aggressor. One so determined as Menelaus would hold fast because the reward for doing so was that Proteus had to share his other gift: the ability to see into the future. The United States had no such grandiose goal as it brought the islands within its grasp after the 1930s. But the imbalance of power between the American Menelaus and shape-shifting West

Indies—and the way in which, at key points, the relationship foretold future paths—counts as protean in more than just the usual sense of the term.

For Jamaica, Trinidad, and most of the rest of the West Indies, the transition to independence was all the more dramatic for being so long in coming. With three centuries under the Union Jack, only a handful of places were European colonies longer. However, that transition occurred amid intense worldwide conflict and high regional tension, and given the particular timing of the collapse of the federal entity meant to complete it, it might have gone much worse. In most respects, and relative to what might have been, U.S.–British–West Indian relations en route to independence take a measure of their significance because they are a rare story of "what went right," compared not only to nearby British Guiana but to so many other stories in U.S.–Third World relations at the crossroads of the Cold War and decolonization. That things "went right" was thanks above all to prudence and restraint—and no small measure of luck—in the decisions and actions taken by the chief actors in the drama.

What is striking about their decisions and actions is that all parties in this history answer Cain's question in more or less the same way. This suggests a dynamic that transcends even those overarching ones of Cold War and decolonization, and reaches beyond to touch the "permanent" nature of interstate affairs. Cain asked "Am I my brother's keeper?" to divert attention from the fact that he was his brother's killer. But even without such a specific crime or cover-up, the question as cynical rhetoric rings true in the Anglo-American–Caribbean triangle, and in the larger geometry of North–South relations during the last century. In the British Caribbean, the United States answered the question three times—twice from Washington and once from Harlem. Britain answered in several parts. The West Indies unexpectedly faced the question and surprised themselves with their answers. In each case, the short answer was "yes" in theory and "no" in practice. Or put another way, it was "yes," to the extent that "keeping" my brother benefits me, regardless of what it does to or for him. The fact that this answer was embraced by each of the players in the U.S.–British–West Indies drama despite their vastly different levels of power relative to one another is cause for contemplation.

As with Cain, the rhetoric of all parties belied their actions. In a sense this vindicates the classical Realist interpretation of diplomacy: states pursue their self-interest with little regard to anything resembling brotherly responsibility for their neighbors. In this view, they are ultimately responsible to their own citizens, not responsible for the effects of their policies on those of other nations. Yet such a view is intuitively at odds with the sorting out of the historical developments encapsulated within Anglo-American–Caribbean relations, and within the broader stories of the Cold War and decolonization. The matter of moral, historical, and humanitarian responsibility for the transition and aftermath of centuries of slavery, exploitation, and domination is not so easily settled. It remains relevant in a time of globalization barely two generations removed from the independence struggle, however fortunate and peacefully or cursed and violently any given theater of that struggle unfolded, in the West Indies and elsewhere across the global South.

Notes

Abbreviations

BDA	Barbados Department of Archives, St. Michael, Barbados
BDEE	*British Documents on the End of Empire*
CAB	Cabinet Office
CNA	Canadian National Archives, Ottawa, Canada
CO	Colonial Office
DDEL	Dwight D. Eisenhower Library, Abilene, Kansas
FDRL	Franklin D. Roosevelt Library, Hyde Park, New York
FO	Foreign Office
FRUS	*Foreign Relations of the United States*
HSTL	Harry S. Truman Library, Independence, Missouri
JA	Jamaica Archives, Spanish Town, Jamaica
JFKL	John F. Kennedy Library, Boston, Massachusetts
JLP	Jamaica Labour Party
JPL	Jamaica Progressive League
LOC	Library of Congress
MSRC	Moorland-Spingarn Research Center, Howard University
NA	U.S. National Archives, College Park, Maryland
NLJ	National Library of Jamaica, Kingston, Jamaica
OAS	Organization of American States
PNM	People's National Movement (Trinidad)
PNP	People's National Party (Jamaica)
PREM	Prime Minister's Office Records
PUL	Seeley Mudd Library, Princeton University Library
RG 25	Record Group 25, Records of the Department of External Affairs (Canada)
RG 38	Record Group 38, Department of the Navy

RG 59   Record Group 59, State Department Records
RG 84   Record Group 84, Records of Foreign Service Posts of the Department of
            State
RG 218   Record Group 218, Records of the Joint Chiefs of Staff
RG 273   Record Group 273, Records of the National Security Council
RG 306   Record Group 306, Records of the United States Information Agency
RG 319   Record Group 319, Records of the Army Chief of Staff
RG 353   Record Group 353, Records of the Department of State, Interdepartmental
            and Intradepartmental Committees: State-War-Navy Coordinating Com-
            mittee
RG 469   Record Group 469, Records of U.S. Foreign Assistance Agencies
SC   Schomburg Center for Research in Black Culture, New York, New York
UCLA   Young Library Special Collections, University of California-Los Angeles
UKNA   United Kingdom National Archives (formerly PRO), Kew, Richmond, UK
USIA   United States Information Agency
UWIM   University of the West Indies, Mona, Jamaica
UWISA   University of the West Indies, St. Augustine, Trinidad
UWICH   University of the West Indies, Cave Hill, Barbados
WIF   West Indies Federation
WINC   West Indies National Council
WO   War Office Records

Introduction

1. "Conversation with Norman Manley in New York," 16 March 1954, in Robert J. Alexander, ed., *Presidents, Prime Ministers, and Governors of the English-Speaking Caribbean and Puerto Rico: Conversations and Correspondence* (Westport, 1997), 20.

2. For an analysis that places the American, Haitian, and Latin American revolutions in insightful relation to one another—and which underlines the anomalous status of the European-ruled areas—see Lester Langley, *The Americas in the Age of Revolution, 1750–1850* (New Haven, 1998).

3. When French demographer Alfred Sauvy coined the phrase in 1952, the "Third World" was meant to denote, however imperfectly, those areas that were neither in the Liberal-Capitalist "First" World nor the Communist "Second" World—i.e., Africa, Asia, Latin America, and the Caribbean. (For an exploration of the term, see Arturo Escobar, *Encountering Development: The Making and Unmaking of the Third World* (Princeton, 1995), esp. chaps. 1 and 2.) This study means no disrespect by its use of the outdated, Cold War phrase "Third World" as a term of convenience for the decolonizing, predominantly nonwhite areas it explores.

4. Odd Arne Westad, *The Global Cold War: Third World Interventions and the Making of Our Times* (New York, 2005), is a recent and superlative example.

5. Matthew Connelly, "Taking off the Cold War Lens: Visions of North–South Conflict during the Algerian War for Independence," *American Historical Review* (*AHR*)105/3 (June 2000): 739–769.

6. Despite the West Indies' importance as a crossroads of black consciousness and a security liability in the "American Lake," only Cary Fraser has ventured a study of U.S.–Caribbean relations during decolonization. Little else has appeared on the subject; for a recap of earlier work, see Fraser, *Ambivalent Anti-Colonialism: The United States and the Genesis of West Indian Independence, 1940–64* (Westport, 1994), 4–6. Fraser's path-opening work covers the whole British Caribbean and emphasizes geostrat-

egy over race, although the latter does appear as an influence on policy, especially in Fraser's exploratory sketching of African-American–West Indian ties during World War II. Also of note on this period are one recent book and two older articles: Gerald Horne, *Cold War in a Hot Zone: The United States Confronts Labor and Independence Struggles in the British West Indies* (Philadelphia, 2007); Howard Johnson, "The United States and the Establishment of the Anglo-American Caribbean Commission," *Journal of Caribbean History (JCH)* 19/1 (1984): 26–47; and "The Anglo-American Caribbean Commission and the Extension of American Influence in the British Caribbean, 1942–1945," *Journal of Commonwealth and Comparative Politics* 22/2 (1984): 180–203. But most ostensibly "regional" scholarship overlooks the English-speaking areas. Lester Langley's influential study, for example, focuses overwhelmingly on the Spanish Caribbean, as indeed most of the literature does. See Langley, *The United States and the Caribbean in the Twentieth Century*, 4th ed. (Athens, 1989); *America and the Americas: The United States in the Western Hemisphere* (Athens, 1989); and *The Americas in the Modern Age* (New Haven, 2003). The overview by Robert Freeman Smith, *The Caribbean World and the United States: Mixing Rum and Coca-Cola* (New York, 1994), does the same. In similar fashion, most works on U.S.–Third World relations during decolonization focus overwhelmingly on non-Caribbean areas, tending to be either country-specific or devoted to the Asian or African theaters. See David Ryan and Victor Pungong, eds., *The United States and Decolonization: Power and Freedom* (New York, 2000); and Peter Hahn and Mary Heiss, *Empire and Revolution: The United States and the Third World Since 1945* (Columbus, 2001). The partial exception to this tendency is in the literature on Anglo-American relations, although here too—except for William Roger Louis's magisterial *Imperialism at Bay: The United States and the Decolonization of the British Empire, 1941–1945* (New York, 1978), and Charlie Whitham's recent *Bitter Rehearsal: British and American Planning for a Post-War West Indies* (Westport, 2002)—the inclusion of the West Indies tends to be an afterthought.

7. See Irma Watkins-Owens, *Blood Relations: Caribbean Immigrants and the Harlem Community, 1900–1930* (Bloomington, 1996).

8. This is not to understate the importance of other individual colonies. Barbados staked a claim to leadership of the West Indies Federation; British Honduras, bordering Guatemala, most complicated the inter-American system; British Guiana came closest to being a "second Cuba" and endured two interventions, the second of which was abetted by the CIA. Indeed, British Guiana's difficult relationship with both metropole and hegemon demands book-length treatment itself, which it has finally received in Stephen Rabe's excellent *U.S. Intervention in British Guiana: A Cold War Story* (Chapel Hill, 2006). As Rabe makes clear, if British Guiana was not exactly sui generis in U.S.–Third World relations—suffering intervention and animosity that badly warped its society—it was nonetheless the outlier in U.S.–British Caribbean relations. Its Indian-majority demographics, its mainland location, its ecological misfortune, and its provocative (to Anglo-American eyes) leadership left it outside the West Indian mainstream defined by Manley, Bustamante, Williams, and Adams. British Guiana is thus too complex to be adequately treated in the present study, which focuses on Jamaica and Trinidad, with reference to neighboring colonies only when they affected the two islands in question and the region in general. Finally, the term "Trinidad" is used rather than the official "Trinidad and Tobago," since the narrative focuses entirely on events physically centered in the big island (such as the Chaguaramas controversy). No disrespect to Tobago, or to Trinidad and Tobago's full composition, is thereby intended.

9. Melvyn Leffler, *A Preponderance of Power: National Security, the Truman Administration, and the Cold War* (Stanford, 1992).

10.　One can make a similar argument for pre–World War II U.S. policy in Pacific areas such as the Philippines. But U.S. relations with the "American Lake" areas — because of transnational racial ties to the mainland and because of the contrast with U.S. behavior around the littoral—offer the closest antecedent to the national-security doctrine later applied in the Cold War.

11.　For a compelling iteration of this overarching argument, see William Roger Louis and Ronald Robinson, "The Imperialism of Decolonisation," *Journal of Imperial and Commonwealth History (JICH)* 22 (September 1994): 462–511. For a Caribbean-specific iteration, see Bridget Brereton, "Independence and the Persistence of Colonialism in the Caribbean," in *Crossroads of Empire: The Europe–Caribbean Connection, 1492–1992,* ed. Alan Cobley (Mona, 1994), 53–63.

12.　These individuals were also, as Dennis Benn shows, the heirs to a deeply rooted intellectual tradition. Benn, *The Caribbean: An Intellectual History, 1774–2003* (Kingston, 2004).

13.　This analysis is in keeping with a growing trend in the study of inter-American relations, noted in Max P. Friedman, "Retiring the Puppets, Bringing Latin America Back In: Recent Scholarship on United States–Latin American Relations," *Diplomatic History (DH)* 27 (November 2003): 621–636. The West Indian side of this trend is somewhat longer-standing. Given the quasi-hagiographic sheen of much West Indian scholarship on the nationalist generation, such as Colin Palmer's *Eric Williams the Making of the Modern Caribbean* (Chapel Hill, 2006), it stands to reason that "agency" would not be lacking in these accounts. But the fundamental insight of the reality of that agency is most apt and most welcome in broader histories of inter-American relations.

14.　Interest in race in foreign relations began in earnest in the 1980s, thanks to works such as Gerald Horne, *Black and Red: W. E. B. DuBois and the Afro-American Response to the Cold War* (Albany, 1986); Michael Hunt, *Ideology and U.S. Foreign Policy* (New Haven, 1987); Paul Gordon Lauren, *Power and Prejudice: The Politics and Diplomacy of Racial Discrimination* (Boulder, 1988); and Thomas Noer, *Cold War and Black Liberation: The United States and White Rule in Africa, 1948–1968* (Columbia, 1988). This interest has gotten stronger since then, as shown by titles such as Alexander DeConde, *Ethnicity, Race, and American Foreign Policy* (Boston, 1992); Brenda Plummer, *Rising Wind: Black Americans and U.S. Foreign Affairs, 1935–1960* (Chapel Hill, 1996); Penny Von Eschen, *Race Against Empire: Black Americans and Anticolonialism, 1937–1957* (Ithaca, 1997); Michael Krenn, *Race and U.S. Foreign Policy*, 5 vols. (New York, 1998); Mary Dudziak, *Cold War Civil Rights: Race and American Democracy* (Princeton, 2000); Thomas Borstelmann, *The Cold War and the Color Line* (Cambridge, 2001); Carol Anderson, *Eyes off the Prize: The United Nations and the African American Struggle for Human Rights, 1944–1955* (New York, 2003); James Meriwether, *Proudly We Can Be Africans: Black Americans and African, 1935–1961* (Chapel Hill, 2002); and Brenda Plummer, ed., *Window on Freedom: Race, Civil Rights, and Foreign Affairs, 1945–1988* (Chapel Hill, 2003).

15.　See Jason Parker, " 'Capital of the Caribbean': The African American–West Indian 'Harlem Nexus' and the Transnational Drive for Black Freedom," *Journal of African American History (JAAH)* 89 (Spring 2004): 98–117.

16.　Jonathan Rosenberg, *How Far the Promised Land? World Affairs and the Civil Rights Movement from the First World War to Vietnam* (Princeton, 2005).

17.　Hardly a month goes by that the West Indian press does not refer at least in passing to the federation's ghost, regarding issues ranging from the Caribbean Court of Justice to the proper roster of "Windies" cricket. It continues to engage scholarly attention as well; see the special issue of the Caribbean journal *Social and Economic*

Studies 48/4 (1999): 1–286. More colloquially, the term "federation" has become a slang synonym for chaos. In a post discussing the November 2007 earthquake in the Eastern Caribbean, Bajan blogger and writer "Caribbean Lionesse" phrased things this way: "when the quake hit, it was just federation—people running up and down shrieking" (http://caribbeanlionesse.blogspot.com/2007/11/earthquake-update-4-and-happy.html, viewed 20 December 2007).

18. Nikhil Pal Singh, *Black is a Country: Race and the Unfinished Struggle for Democracy* (Cambridge, 2004), 14.

19. Thomas Borstelmann, *Apartheid's Reluctant Uncle: The United States and Southern Africa in the Early Cold War* (New York, 1993), 195.

20. For one recent analysis of the "race revolution" as a factor in U.S. foreign-policy thinking, see Jason Parker, "Cold War II: The Eisenhower Administration, the Bandung Conference, and the Re-periodization of the Postwar Era," *DH* 30/5 (November 2006): 867–892.

Chapter 1

Portions of this and the subsequent chapter were previously published in the *Journal of African American History*; I gratefully acknowledge the journal's permission to reproduce them here.

1. Chief of Naval Operations, 13 June 1928, folder: Study of Attack and Capture of Jamaica, Box 51, RG 38, Strategic Plans—Miscellaneous Subject Files, NA. See also Christopher Bell, "Thinking the Unthinkable: British and American Naval Strategies for an Anglo-American War, 1918–1931," *International History Review (IHR)* 19/4 (November 1997): 789–808.

2. Winston James, *Holding Aloft the Banner of Ethiopia: Caribbean Radicalism in America* (New York, 1996), 12.

3. Fraser, *Ambivalent*, chapter 2 and *passim.*

4. British Embassy-Washington to FO, 26 January 1939, FO 371 /22827, UKNA. "The Anglo-American Naval Staff Talks of 1938–39 . . . helped to define a new defense framework for the Caribbean." Fitzroy Baptiste, *War, Conflict, and Cooperation: The European Possessions in the Caribbean, 1939–1945* (Westport, 1988), 3. Richard Harrison dates this process to 1936, in "Testing the Water: A Secret Probe towards Anglo-American Military Co-operation in 1936," *IHR* 7/2 (May 1985): 214–234.

5. Fitzroy Baptiste, "The British Grant of Air and Naval Facilities to the United States in Trinidad, St. Lucia, and Bermuda in 1939 (June–December)," *Caribbean Studies* 16 (1976): 5–43; David Reynolds, *The Creation of the Anglo-American Alliance, 1937–1941: A Study in Competitive Co-operation* (Chapel Hill, 1982), 64–65.

6. British Consulate-Panama to FO, 18 February 1939, FO 371 /22831, UKNA.

7. British Embassy-Washington to FO, 30 May 1939, FO 371 /22802, UKNA. David Haglund emphasizes that the geographic context was key, in Haglund, *Latin America and the Transformation of U.S. Strategic Thought* (Albuquerque, 1984), 2, 16.

8. Meriwether, *Proudly*, 27–56; Plummer, *Wind*, 40–43; Joseph Harris, *African-American Reactions to War in Ethiopia, 1936–1941* (Baton Rouge, 1994), 34–38; William R. Scott, *The Sons of Sheba's Race: African-Americans and the Italo-Ethiopian War, 1935–1941* (Bloomington, 1993), 100–101.

9. MacDonald to Cabinet, #26 (38), 25 May 1938, CAB 23/ 93, cited in D. J. Morgan, *The Origins of British Aid Policy, 1924–45*, 1:24.

10. Harvey Neptune, *Caliban and the Yankees: Trinidad and the United States Occupation* (Chapel Hill, 2007), 38–41.

11. Von Eschen, *Race Against Empire*, 11, 17. West Indians were prominent in these groups, with Trinidadian George Padmore helming the IASB.

12. James, *Holding Aloft*, 184. West Indian immigrants and their descendants who have stoked black consciousness in the United States are too many to list, but a sample would include the following along with Garvey: Sylvester Williams, Hubert Harrison, C. L. R. James, Claude McKay, Richard B. Moore, and George Padmore. The tradition continued later in the century in figures such as Stokely Carmichael and Louis Farrakhan. James, *Holding Aloft*, 1.

13. Program, JPL Mass Meeting, 14 January 1937; program, JPL Bi-Weekly History Class, "December 1937–June 1938," MS 234—JPL, NLJ.

14. Program, JPL Mass Meeting, 23 January 1938, Box 5, MS 353—W. Adolphe Roberts Papers, NLJ.

15. Program, 3rd Mass Meeting of JPL, 14 January 1937, MS 234—JPL, NLJ.

16. Resolution, JPL, 13 December 1937, MS 234—JPL, NLJ.

17. Roberts to Garrett, 15 January 1937; Roberts to Garrett, 9 February 1937, folder: Correspondence between W. A. Roberts and Clara Maude Garrett, 1937–1938, Box 2a, MS 353—Roberts Papers, NLJ. See also Ken Post, *Arise Ye Starvelings: The Jamaican Labour Rebellion of 1938 and its Aftermath* (The Hague, 1978), 221–224. Richard Hart, writing many years later, agreed regarding the key role of the "intellectual ferment" in New York. Hart, *Rise and Organize: The Birth of the Workers and National Movement in Jamaica, 1936–1939* (London, 1989), 23.

18. Manley to Kirkwood, 22 June 1938, folder 4/60/2B/2, Norman Manley Papers, JA.

19. *West Indies Royal Commission, 1938–39: [Moyne] Report*, Cmd 6607 (microfilm), 440–445. On the 1930s island economies, see Fraser, *Ambivalent*, 38–41, and "The Twilight of Colonial Rule in the British West Indies," *Journal of Caribbean History* 30/1–2 (June 1996): 1–27.

20. Cited in Post, *Arise*, 96. See also O. Nigel Bolland, *On the March: Labour Rebellions in the British Caribbean, 1934–39* (Kingston, 1995), 132.

21. Bolland, *March*, 135; Lauren, *Power*, 120. See also the chapter "The Origins of Rastafari" in Noel Leo Erskine, *From Garvey to Marley: Rastafari Theology* (Gainesville, 2005), 59–84.

22. Governor of Trinidad to CO, 26 June 1937, CO 295 /599 /70297 part II; Memorandum of Conversation, Deputation of West India Committee, 3 July 1937, CO 295 /599 /70297 part I, UKNA; Post, *Arise*, 321–322; Lloyd Braithwaite, "Introduction," in *Trinidad Labour Riots of 1937: Fifty Years Later*, ed. Roy Thomas (St. Augustine, 1987), 10.

23. The sequence of unrest ran as follows: 1934: British Guiana, British Honduras, Trinidad; 1935: Jamaica, St. Kitts, Trinidad, British Guiana, St. Vincent, St. Lucia; 1936: British Guiana; 1937: Trinidad, the Bahamas, Barbados; 1938: Jamaica; 1939: Antigua, British Guiana.

24. Kelvin Singh, "The June 1937 Disturbances in Trinidad," in Thomas, ed., *Riots*, 58–59.

25. Kafra Kambon, *For Bread, Justice, and Freedom: A Political Biography of George Weekes* (London, 1988), 14–15, cited in Paul Buhle, *Tim Hector: A Caribbean Radical's Story* (Oxford, MS, 2006), 56.

26. Neptune, *Caliban*, 42.

27. Ken Post, *Strike the Iron: A Colony at War: Jamaica, 1939–1945*, 2 vols. (Atlantic Highlands, 1981), 1:74.

28. U.S. Consulate-Bridgetown to Department of State, 17 August 1935, 844C.504/1, RG 59, NA.

29. "Patriotic Pioneer," *Plain Talk*, cited in Post, *Arise*, 209–210.

30. Singh, "June 1937," in Thomas, ed., *Riots*, 66. Singh puts it bluntly: "The 'disturbances'…opened the way to British West Indian internal self-government, [which] had been sought in Trinidad, with limited success, [for] more than eighty years." Singh, "June 1937," in Thomas, ed., *Riots*, 74. Bolland notes that Caribbean intellectuals, such as C. L. R. James, recognized this, and he seconds their conclusion. Bolland, *March*, 190–191.

31. Timeline of Strike, Governor of Trinidad, no date, CO 295 /599 /70297-I; Report, "Disturbances," 1938 (no month given), CO 137 /826 /68868, UKNA. This is not to suggest that Manley did not eventually take on "messianic" status, only that in comparison to Bustamante—who seemed born to it—Manley had it thrust upon him. Rex Nettleford, "Introduction," in *Norman Washington Manley and the New Jamaica: Selected Speeches and Writings 1938–68*, ed. Nettleford (New York, 1971), xcii.

32. Cripps to Manley, 9 September 1938, folder 4/60/2B/2, Manley Papers, JA.

33. Report, "Labor Troubles and Riots in Trinidad," 2 July 1937, U.S. Consulate-Port of Spain to State Department, 844G.5045/7, RG 59, NA.

34. U.S. Embassy-London to State Department, 1 June 1938, 844G.00/26, RG 59, NA.

35. Interview, *Daily Worker*, 9 June 1938, cited in Post, *Arise*, 358.

36. Cranbourne to Eden, 16 September 1942, FO 371 /30718; Colonial Secretary to Eden, December 1943, CO 448 /2; *Moyne Report*. For an overview of the Moyne findings, see Fraser, *Ambivalent*, 42–49.

37. Holt, *Problem*, 397. A book published shortly after one of the first (and mildest) of the riots made this case to the British public: W. M. Macmillan, *Warning from the West Indies: A Tract for Africa and the Empire* (London, 1936).

38. Minute, CO (Campbell), 23 May 1938, CO 318 /433, 71168, UKNA.

39. Huggins to Maffey (CO), 24 June 1937; Memorandum of Conversation, Deputation of West India Committee, 3 July 1937, CO 295 /599 /70297 part I, UKNA.

40. Huggins to Chamberlain (PM), 3 July 1937, CO 295 /599 /70297 part I; Vice Admiral and C-in-C/West Indies Meyrick to Secretary of the Admiralty, 2 August 1937, CO 295 /599 /70297 part II, UKNA.

41. U.S. Consulate-Port of Spain to Department of State, 1 March 1937, 844G.00/17, RG 59, NA.

42. Interview, *Trinidad Guardian*, 14 March 1937, cited in U.S. Consulate-Port of Spain to Department of State, 16 March 1937, 844G.6363/54, RG 59, NA.

43. Hartley Fuel Committee to Oil Board, 13 January 1939, #1504B, CAB 4/29, UKNA; Report, "Labor Troubles and Riots in Trinidad," 2 July 1937.

44. Cited in Neptune, *Caliban*, 74. For a discussion of "America" as seen by Trinidadians, see Neptune's chapter, "The American Preoccupation: Assessing the United States before the War."

45. U.S. Consulate-Port of Spain to State Department, 3 August 1938, 844G.7962/9, RG 59, NA. The British from early on determined that "the use of bases [granted under the bases deal] to be leased . . . should be limited to defensive purposes," for fear that the United States would extend the concession to commercial use by U.S. or third-party carriers. Memorandum, War Cabinet Committee on U.S. Bases, 4 October 1940, Box 2, folder: Greensdale [*sic*] Papers, Fitzroy Baptiste Papers, Special Collections, Main Library, UWISA.

46. "Future Provision for Colonial Development and Welfare," Colonial Secretary to War Cabinet, 15 November 1944, CO 852 /588 /11 /60303; CO to FO, 30 December 1942, FO 371 /34132, UKNA. See also Whitham, *Bitter Rehearsal*, 11–12.

47. U.S. Embassy-London to Secretary to State, 8 March 1940, 844C.50/7, RG 59, NA.

48. Hoover to Berle, 17 March 1944; 844.00B/1, RG 59, NA. This prospect had struck some observers even before the Nazi blitz through Western Europe. For example, Howard University student Vincent Byas, a Martiniquan, wrote in the student newspaper that "many Martiniquans are convinced that regardless of the eventual outcome, the end of that war will leave Martinique an American possession." Byas, "Martinique and the War," 13 October 1939, *The Hilltop*, Microfilm M07—fiche Mi2578, Reading Room, MSRC.

49. "It would also be unwelcome to the upper-class Jamaicans of mixed blood," the writer went on, "for they fear that their social equality with the whites would be impaired." Draughon to Attorney General, 17 June 1940, 844D.014/9, RG 59, NA.

50. Hoover to Berle, 15 February 1944, 844.00B/1, RG 59, NA; Letter, Domingo to Roberts, 27 May 1940, folder "Correspondence Between Roberts and Domingo," Box 2B, MS 353—Roberts Papers, NLJ.

51. Cordell Hull, *The Memoirs of Cordell Hull*, 2 vols. (New York, 1948), 1:365.

52. The name change also marked, according to informers, both a broadening of the West Indian independence agenda and Jamaica's assuming leadership of it. Hoover to Berle, 17 March 1944; Hoover to Berle, 31 May 1944, 844D.00B/2, RG 59, NA.

53. Domingo to Roberts, June 4, 1940, "Correspondence between Roberts and Domingo," Box 2b (#14–19), Box 2B, MS 353—Roberts Papers, NLJ.

54. Roberts to Domingo, June 14, 1940, "Correspondence between Roberts and Domingo," Box 2b (#14–19), Box 2B, MS 353—Roberts Papers, NLJ.

55. Hoover to Berle, 31 May 1944.

56. Domingo to Walter White, 6 November 1940; folder Labor—British West Indies—1940–49; Box A332, NAACP Papers, LOC.

57. Richard B. Moore, "Reply to Cordell Hull," in *Richard B. Moore: Caribbean Militant in Harlem, Collected Writings 1920–1972*, ed. W. Burghardt and Joyce Turner (Bloomington, 1988), 267–268.

58. See Jason Colby, "'Banana Growing and Negro Management': Race, Labor, and Jim Crow Colonialism in Guatemala, 1884–1930," *DH* 30/4 (September 2006): 595–622; see also Eric T. L. Love, *Race Over Empire: Racism and U.S. Imperialism, 1865–1900* (Chapel Hill, 2003).

59. Manley, "Selling the British West Indian Islands?" *Public Opinion*, 22 June 1940, folder: 4/60/2A/2, Manley Papers, JA.

60. Domingo to Manley, 23 August 1940, folder: 4/60/2A/2, Manley Papers, JA; Domingo to Logan, 9 November 1940, folder: Correspondence—WINC, Box 166–23, Rayford Logan Papers, Manuscript Division, MSRC.

61. Roberts to Domingo, 29 July 1940, "Correspondence between Roberts and Domingo," Box 2B, MS 353—Roberts Papers, NLJ.

62. Post, *Arise*, 223. Other activists concurred on the importance—for good or ill—to Jamaica's future of the "capitalist colossus." Ibid., 230.

63. Post, *Strike*, I, 118. Manley lauded WINEC's Havana efforts, since none of the attending countries had insisted that West Indian voices be heard. "The Act of Havana," Manley, 14 September 1940, *Public Opinion*, Microfilm #2682, West Indian & Special Collections, Main Library, UWIM.

64. Winston James, "Migration, Racism, and Identity Formation: The Caribbean Experience in Britain," in *Inside Babylon: The Caribbean Diaspora in Britain*, ed. James and Clive Harris (Verso, 1993), 255.

65. Reynolds, *Creation*, 118.

66. Baptiste notes that "Havana...tested the patience of the British government," which saw it as an American vote of no confidence. Baptiste, *War*, 47.

67. Welles to Roosevelt, 8 October 1940, Official File (OF) 4318 "Charles Taussig, 1937–42," FDRL; C-in-C/West Indies Bailey to Balfour, 29 January 1941, FO 371 /26155, UKNA.

68. "Memorandum Concerning the Caribbean Area," Taussig to FDR and Hull, 12 September 1940, folder Caribbean Commission—U.S. Section [Taussig]—Report: Committee on B.W.I. 1940, Box 35, Taussig Caribbean Files, Charles W. Taussig Papers (CWTP), FDRL.

69. Taussig to Roosevelt, 25 February 1937, President's Personal File (PPF) 1644; Taussig to Tugwell, 22 August 1947, folder: AACC #3, Box 43, Rexford Tugwell Papers, FDRL.

70. Memorandum, "Memorandum Concerning the Caribbean Area," 12 September 1940.

71. Roosevelt to Greenslade, 16 September 1940, PPF 1644; Welles to Roosevelt, 8 October 1940, OF-4318, FDRL.

72. Report of Taussig Mission, December 1940, folder: Caribbean Commission— U.S. Section [Taussig]—Report: Committee on British West Indies, 1940, Box 35, Taussig Caribbean Files, CWTP, FDRL. However, the text of the report makes clear that Taussig was taking notes for future projects and/or commission work even on this initial trip.

73. White to Reid, 15 October 1940, folder: British West Indies, 1940–49, Box A155, NAACP Papers, LOC. For a sense of the tight-knit universe of that intelligentsia, see Jonathan Scott Holloway, *Confronting the Veil: Abram Harris Jr., E. Franklin Frazier, and Ralph Bunche, 1919–1941* (Chapel Hill, 2002).

74. See for example Roberts to White, 15 March 1941, folder: British West Indies, 1940–49, Box A155, NAACP Papers, LOC. The letter expresses admiration for the NAACP, and the writer's intent to join when he comes to the United States. Many similar documents can be found in the NAACP papers.

75. See Cabot to White, 13 December 1940, folder: Staff—Walter White—Good Neighbor Policy 1940–41, Box A609, NAACP Papers, LOC.

76. White To Whom It May Concern, 7 November 1940, folder: British West Indies 1940–49, Box A155, NAACP Papers, LOC.

77. White to Duggan, 7 December 1940, folder: Staff—White, Walter—Good Neighbor Policy 1940–41, Box A609, NAACP Papers, LOC. Taussig concurs in the importance of White's letter. Report of Taussig Mission, December 1940.

78. Report of Taussig Mission, December 1940.

79. Ibid.

80. Taussig to Welles, 4 December 1940, Attached as Appendix to Report of Taussig Mission, December 1940.

81. Report of Taussig Mission, December 1940. Taussig asked Rienzi if he ever tried "to repudiate the support of apparently irresponsible organizations in the United States," such as the West Indian National Party. Rienzi shrugged; "he looked with favor on almost any organization that could give [West Indian labor parties] publicity in the United States." Among these were WINC, Ethelred Brown's Watch Tower, and the Progressive Leagues. Report of Taussig Mission, December 1940.

82. Whitehead to Evans, 26 December 1941; FO 371/ 30673, UKNA; Report of Taussig Mission, December 1940.

83. Post, *Strike*, 1:224.

84. Reynolds remarks that "Welles and Berle, architects of the 'Good Neighbor' Policy, probably saw the agreement [the formal result in 1941 of the bases deal] as an opportunity to extend American influence in the Caribbean." Reynolds, *Creation*, 174.

85. Post, *Strike*, 1:138.

86. Report of Taussig Mission, December 1940; Lloyd quoted in Reynolds, *Creation*, 170.

87. Jamaica Governor to CO, 23 December 1940, FO 371 /26175, UKNA.

88. Trinidad Governor to FO, 22 January 1941, FO 371 /26152; Trinidad Governor to FO, 22 January 1941, FO 371 /26152, UKNA. See also Whitham, *Rehearsal*, 45–46, and Palmer, *Eric Williams*, 85–87.

89. See Michael Conniff, *Black Labor on a White Canal: Panama, 1904–1981* (Pittsburgh, 1985).

90. Trinidad Governor to FO, 22 January 1941; Jamaica Governor to Colonial Secretary, 15 January 1941; FO to British Embassy-Washington, 2 January 1941, FO 371 /26152, UKNA; Palmer, *Eric Williams*, 86.

91. Trinidad Governor to CO, 18 January 1941, PREM 3 /464/1, UKNA; Trinidad Governor to Colonial Secretary, 22 October 1940, folder: Trinidad, Box 1, Baptiste Papers, UWISA.

92. Colonial Secretary to War Cabinet, 27 December 1940, (CAB 66/14 /1726), folder: Greensdale [*sic*] Papers, Box 2, Baptiste Papers, UWISA.

93. Ibid.; Attale to M.P. Liddall (to Churchill), 22 August 1940, PREM 43A/2, UKNA.

94. Domingo to Campbell, 4 December 1940, folder: 4/60/2A/2, Manley Papers, JA.

95. Taussig to Welles, 12 December 1940, Box 35, folder: Caribbean Commission—U.S. Section [Taussig]—Report: Committee on British West Indies, 1940, Box 35, Taussig Caribbean Files, CWTP, FDRL.

96. Memorandum of Conversation, Roosevelt, Governor Lethem, and Butler, 23 January 1941, FO 371 /26155, UKNA.

97. See Steven High, "The Racial Politics of Criminal Jurisdiction in the Aftermath of the Anglo-American 'Destroyers-for-Bases' Deal, 1940–50," *JICH* 32/3 (September 2004): 77–105.

98. Taussig to Welles, 6 March 1941, folder: #2, Box 46, Taussig Caribbean Files, CWTP; Roosevelt to Knox and Stimson, 19 March 1941; OF-4101 ("Naval Bases 1940–43"), FDRL.

99. White to Cordell Hull, 23 April 1941; Taussig Caribbean Files, Box 35, folder: Caribbean Commission—US Section—Correspondence—Duggan, Lawrence, FDRL.

100. Letter, Roberts to Edna Manley, 27 January 1941, folder: "Correspondence—Edna Manley, Norman Manley, & W. A. Roberts," Box 2b, MS 353—Roberts Papers, NLJ.

101. Domingo to Manley, 25 March 1941, folder: 4/60/2A/2, Manley Papers, JA.

102. Tugwell to Ickes, 10 April 1941, folder: Ickes, Harold & Jane, 1939–1965, Box 11, Tugwell Papers, FDRL. Ickes forwarded this message to the president. Berle recorded a similar sentiment: Entry, 21 March 1940, Berle Diaries, Adolph Berle Papers, FDRL.

103. Manuscript, attached to Amidon to Taussig, 6 March 1941, folder: Caribbean—General—Manuscripts—Correspondence, Box 36, Taussig Caribbean Files, CWTP, FDRL.

104. Handbill, "Will United States [*sic*] Take Over the West Indies?", American–West Indian Association on Caribbean Affairs," 1 July 1942, in fiche #005,732–1, SC Clipping File.

105. Amidon to Taussig, 6 March 1941. Domingo agreed on the unlikelihood of an American takeover: "I still am unconvinced that the US really want the islands. It suits them better to have the bases and not be responsible for the economic wellbeing of the populations." Domingo to Campbell, 4 April 1941, folder: 4/60/2A/2, Manley Papers, JA.

Chapter 2

1. A joint commission was also a precursor of the "trusteeships" Washington would later propose, which London saw as a "cloak for American expansion." Louis, *Imperialism*, 8. See also Johnson, "The Anglo-American Caribbean Commission," and Whitham, *Rehearsal*. "A Jamaican at the Base," Fitz Clarke, *Public Opinion* (Jamaica), 9 May 1942.

2. Halifax to Cadogan, 14 April 1941, FO 371 /26175, UKNA. However, "betterment" and U.S. reformism generally fell well short of British fears. Roosevelt told Hull that winter that he had no desire to assume the "headaches" the British faced in the islands. Reynolds, *Creation*, 174.

3. Memorandum of Conversation, Taussig, Stockdale, et al., 18 April 1941, 844C.50/13, RG 59, NA.

4. Emphasis added. Tugwell to Ickes, 24 April 1941, folder: Ickes, Harold & Jane, 1939–1965, Box 11, Tugwell Papers, FDRL. Ickes forwarded this message to Roosevelt. Jules Benjamin describes this as the "reform expansionism" of Roosevelt's (and Welles's) Good Neighbor diplomacy, as well as of Truman's Point-Four programs. Cited in Gail Hanson, "Ordered Liberty: Sumner Welles and the Crowder–Welles Connection in the Caribbean," *DH* 18/3 (Summer 1994), 329. For a deeper view into this topic, see Elizabeth Borgwardt, *A New Deal for the World: America's Vision of Human Rights* (Cambridge, Mass., 2005).

5. British Embassy-Washington (Edwards) to Churchill, 14 April 1941; FO 371 /26175; telegram, Martin to Mallet, 7 May 1941; FO 371/ 26175, UKNA.

6. This was in spite of what an organizer puzzlingly described as the "unbelievable anti-Domingo feeling in Harlem." Letter, Brown to Roberts, 17 July 1941, folder: "Correspondence between Roberts and Domingo," Box 2B, MS 353—Roberts Papers, NLJ.

7. FBI Report, "West Indies National Council: Subversive Activities in the West Indies," 11 April 1942, 844.00B/3, RG 59, NA; Manley to Domingo, 24 February 1941, and Domingo to Manley, 3 March 1941, folder: 4/60/2A/2, Manley Papers, JA. The island's divisions reached Harlem, as a comparison of the New York reactions to the Bustamante and Domingo detentions makes clear. See Parker, " 'Capital of the Caribbean,' " 109–110. On the turbulent politics of wartime Jamaica, see Post, *Iron*; George Eaton, *Alexander Bustamante and Modern Jamaica* (Kingston, 1975); and Hart, *Towards Decolonisation: Political, Labour, and Economic Development in Jamaica, 1938–1945* (Mona, 1999).

8. His comrade Ken Hill extended the point: "The United States has assumed 'joint responsibility' with Great Britain . . . For good or ill, our future destiny is interlocked with the United States." Manley and Hill cited in Post, *Iron*, 1:259–260.

9. White to Taussig, 19 September 1941, folder: Caribbean Commission—U.S. Section—Miscellaneous 1941; Reid to Taussig, 31 July 1941, folder: Caribbean General Manuscripts—Taussig—Colonies, Box 36, Taussig Caribbean Files, CWTP, FDRL.

10. Hevenor to Clark, 11 July 1941, folder: Caribbean Commission—US Section—Reports & Memoranda, 1941–42, Box 34, CWTP, FDRL. Domingo noted that U.S.–islander friction had already developed in Trinidad, and he anticipated more of the same elsewhere. Domingo to Manley, 12 March 1941, folder: 4/60/2A/2, Manley Papers, JA. Memorandum of Conversation, Taussig and Roosevelt, 23 September 1941, folder: Caribbean Commission—Reports & Memoranda, 1941–42, Box 34, CWTP, FDRL.

11. Kirkwood to Taussig, 8 October 1941, folder: Kirkwood 1941, Box 36, CWTP, FDRL.

12. Letter, duBois to Welles, 10 December 1941, folder: duBois 1941, Box 36, CWTP, FDRL. Steven High offers a close analysis of the racially charged nature of the jurisdiction question, by comparing the Caribbean bases with that of "white" Newfoundland, in High, "The Racial Politics of Criminal Jurisdiction." Neptune cites "one of the rare openly reported" violent incidents, in which "a U.S. army private attending a dance hall party in Arima found the antics of a drunken 'native' patron annoying and simply shot him to death." Neptune, *Caliban*, 88. On the collision of base labor, the American presence, and the British and nationalist responses, see Neptune's chapter "Laboring over the Yankee Dollar: Work in Occupied Trinidad."

13. Memorandum, FO, 27 December 1941, FO 371 /30673, UKNA; Fraser, *Ambivalent*, 67.

14. CO to FO, 26 January 1942, FO 371 /30673; Colonial Secretary to British Embassy-Washington, 17 February 1943, FO 371 /34132, UKNA.

15. CO to Anthony Eden, 23 December 1943, FO 371 /38536, UKNA.

16. Taussig to FDR, 23 June 1942, FW 844.00/98½, RG 59, NA.

17. Halifax to Eden, 11 May 1943; Campbell to Eden, 20 October 1943, FO 371/ 34192, UKNA.

18. Early to FDR, 7 February 1942, folder: Sumner Welles, Box 21, Stephen T. Early Papers, FDRL; Colonial Secretary to West Indian Governors, 7 March 1942, FO 371 /30673, UKNA. FO commentators wanted a disclaimer in writing as well. Halifax to FO, 22 March 1942, FO 371 /30673, UKNA. Curiously, the governors and Foreign Office were not mollified by the assurance that the commission was strictly advisory, even though that was precisely the line they gave the PNP when the party protested the absence of West Indians on the AACC. Rogers to Evans, 23 March 1942, FO 371/ 30673, UKNA.

19. U.S. Naval Commander-Jamaica to U.S. Consulate-Kingston, 25 May 1942, folder: Confidential File January–December 1942, Box 2, RG 84: Kingston, NA. Baptiste, *War*, 144.

20. U.S. Consulate-Kingston to Hull, 13 February 1942, folder: Confidential File January–December 1942, Box 2, RG 84: Kingston, NA; COMCAR-NCF to Navy Operations, 27 December 1941, folder: #16—Central America & West Indies, Box 36, Map Room Files; COMCARIBSEAFRON to Navy Operations, 17 April 1942, folder: #3—Central America & West Indies, Box 39, Map Room Files; FDR to Welles, 9 April 1942, folder: State: Welles, January–April, 1942, Box 77, President's Secretary's File, FDRL.

21. Taussig to Welles, Attached to Note, Welles to Halifax, 28 May 1942, folder: #16: AACC 1942, Box 75, Sumner Welles Papers, FDRL. Taussig suggested this on behalf of a goal he and the president shared; the breakup of the plantations was a prominent feature of his and Roosevelt's discussions. See, for example, Memorandum of Conversation, Taussig and Roosevelt, 19 March 1942, folder: Coert Dubois, 1942–44, Box 36, CWTP, FDRL.

22. Welles to Halifax, 28 May 1942; Stockdale to FO, 15 May 1942, FO 371/30673, UKNA. London got the same message when Ambassador John Winant addressed the Royal Empire Society and urged the adoption of AACC/Moyne reforms. Winant to Hull, 29 July 1942, folder: Caribbean Commission—US Section, Miscellaneous, 1942–43, Box 36, CWTP, FDRL.

23. Fraser, *Ambivalent*, 74–75.

24. As Howard University professor Alain Locke would argue in a variety of settings, "It is not as many racialists think a war of races or color war, but since color differentials correspond so largely to those of empire and colony, dominant and subject peoples, there is essential truth in saying that the parity of peoples is the main moral issue of the world conflict." Notes for essay, undated, folder: Colonial Connections, Imperialism (#12), Box 164–42, Writings by Locke: Notes, Alain Locke Papers, MSRC. Gunnar Myrdal observed this too. Myrdal, *An American Dilemma*, vol. 2 (New York: Harper, 1944), 1006. Recent elaborations on this theme can be found in Meriwether, *Proudly*, chap. 2; Von Eschen, *Race Against Empire*, chap. 2; Plummer, *Wind*, chap. 3; and Singh, *Black is a Country*, chap. 3.

25. U.S. Consulate-Kingston to State Department, 7 January 1942, folder: Confidential File January–December 1942, Box 2, RG 84: Kingston, NA. Post, *Iron*, 1:226, 245.

26. Jamaica-Base Command to U.S. Consulate-Kingston, 9 May 1942; U.S. Consulate-Kingston to State Department, May 1942, folder: Confidential File January–December 1942, Box 2, RG 84: Kingston, NA.

27. Chief of Naval Operations-Jamaica to State Department, forwarded in State Department to U.S. Consulate-Kingston, 20 August 1942, folder: Confidential File January–December 1942, Box 2, RG 84: Kingston, NA.

28. Report, unsigned, to U.S. Consulate: Port of Spain, 17 June 1942; on Axis agents' activity, see Naval Operations to U.S. Consulate: Port of Spain, 25 June 1942, folder: Confidential Correspondence, Confidential File 1939–1942, Box 1, RG 84: Port of Spain, NA. As Max Friedman shows in *Nazis in Good Neighbors: The United States Campaign Against the Germans of Latin America in World War II* (New York, 2003), however, caution is required when it comes to American records showing Nazi "infiltration" of the western hemisphere.

29. Taussig to Roosevelt, 22 April 1942.

30. Williams to Johnson, 21 September 1944, folder #019, Eric Williams Memorial Collection, UWISA.

31. Hoover to Berle, 17 March 1944, 844.00B/1; Hoover to Berle, 10 November 1942, 844D.00B/3; Hoover to Berle, 30 March 1943, 844.00/148, RG 59, NA.

32. Whitehead to Evans, 26 December 1941, FO 371 /30673, UKNA.

33. Cranbourne et al. to Eden et al., 16 September 1942; Memorandum, 31 October 1942, FO 371 /30718, UKNA.

34. Cranbourne to Eden, 21 October 1942; Eden to Cranbourne, 19 October 1942; Cranbourne to Eden, 16 September 1942, FO 371 /30718, UKNA. On British "p.r." efforts, see Susan Brewer, *To Win the Peace: British Propaganda in the United States during World War II* (Ithaca, 1997).

35. "Summary of Opinion and Ideas on International Post-war Problems," State Department, 4 November 1942, folder: #01, Postwar Foreign Policy Files, 1940–43, Summary of Opinions and Ideas on International Postwar Problems, Box 190, Welles Papers, FDRL.

36. Memorandum of conversations, Taussig and Welles, "Preparatory to my Trip to London," 30 November 1942, folder: London Trip, 1942, Box 35, CWTP, FDRL.

37. Memorandum of conversations, Taussig and Welles, 30 November 1942; "Discussion between Stanley and Taussig," Report of the Visit of Taussig and de la Rue to London, December 1942, "PSF Subject File: Taussig Visit to London, December 1942," Box 166, President's Secretary's File, FDR Papers, FDRL. The "reactionary" islands were the Bahamas, Bermuda, and Barbados, all three of whose regimes enshrined the anachronistic but continuing power of the planter class.

38. "Discussion between Stanley and Taussig;" Creech-Jones to Cranbourne, 30 October 1942, CO 137 859/68714/1/44, UKNA.

39. "Luncheon with Winston Churchill," 17 December 1942, in Report of the Visit of Taussig and de la Rue to London, December 1942.

40. CO to FO, 30 December 1942, FO 371 /34132, UKNA.

41. Assessing the London meeting, Fraser concludes that it "marked a decisive shift in British colonial policy in the West Indies. American pressure had helped to create the context in which this shift could occur." Fraser, *Ambivalent*, 77. For a thorough account of the London meetings, see Whitham, *Rehearsal*, 97–105.

42. Report, Law Committee, 27 January 1943, FO 371 /34087, UKNA.

43. "Summary of Opinion," State Department, 4 November 1942, Box 190, Welles Papers, FDRL.

44. Domingo to Manley, 12 March 1941. Domingo also pointed out the protective utility of the new constitution in the new Caribbean power balance: "Self-government must give us the power to defend ourselves against the Americans in Jamaica."

45. CO to FO, 7 January 1944, FO 371 /38522, UKNA. See also Annette Palmer, "Black American Soldiers in Trinidad, 1942–44: Wartime Politics in a Colonial Society," *JICH* 14/3 (1986): 203–218. On the gender dynamics the black soldiers introduced, see Neptune, *Caliban*, 174–178.

46. U.S. Consulate-Kingston to State Department, 20 April 1946, folder: Confidential Correspondence, Box 6, RG 84: Kingston, NA.

47. CO to Paul Mason, 18 September 1943, WO 95/ 1351, UKNA.

48. Air Ministry to British Embassy, 9 April 1943, WO 95/ 1351, UKNA.

49. Halifax to FO, 23 May 1945, FO 371 /44640, UKNA.

50. Memorandum, Combined Chiefs of Staff, 26 June 1943, folder: Caribbean Area, Box 25, RG 218, Geographical File 1942–45, NA. Memorandum of Conversation, Taussig and Hull, 22 July 1943; Taussig to Roosevelt, 15 July 1943, "OF 48p— Jamaica 1940–44," Box 12; Entry, 20 July 1943, "Diary, July–December 1943," Box 33, Diary, Tugwell Papers, FDRL.

51. Entry, 20 February 1943, "Diary, January–June 1943," Box 33, Diary: 1942– June 1944, Tugwell Papers, FDRL.

52. Taussig to FDR, 10 April 1943, folder: 1942–44, Box 34, CWTP, FDRL.

53. "The Political Situation in Jamaica," Report by Paul Blanshard, 20 September 1943, 844D.00/56, RG 59, NA. Domingo described Blanshard to Edna Manley as "a man of advanced, liberal opinions and, to me, an agreeably surprising choice." Domingo to Manley, 11 February 1943, folder: Correspondence [#17], Box 2B, MS 353—Roberts Papers, NLJ.

54. Memorandum of Conversation, Taussig and FDR, 14 February 1944, folder: 1942–44, Box 34, CWTP, FDRL. At Casablanca, Roosevelt and Churchill cited the AACC as a model for Pacific territories. Memorandum of Conversation, Taussig and Roosevelt, 18 February 1943, folder: Miscellaneous 1939–44, Box 52, CWTP, FDRL.

55. Memorandum of Conversation, Taussig and Roosevelt, 24 June 1943, folder: Miscellaneous 1939–44, Box 52, CWTP, FDRL.

56. See Clifford Muse, "Howard University and U.S. Foreign Affairs during the Franklin D. Roosevelt Administration, 1933–1945," *JAAH* 87 (Fall 2002): 403–415; and Tony Martin, "Eric Williams and the Anglo-American Caribbean Commission: Trinidad's Future Nationalist Leader as Aspiring Imperial Bureaucrat," *JAAH* 88 (Summer 2003): 274–290.

57. Harris to Logan, 23 November 1942, folder: #031, Williams Collection, UWISA; Entries 9 February, 9 May 1943, Rayford Logan Diary, Box 4, Diary 2, Logan Papers, LOC.

58. The proceedings were published in 1944 as E. F. Frazier and Eric Williams, eds., *The Economic Future of the Caribbean*, republished with introduction by Tony Martin (Dover, 2004).

59. Petioni quote from Entry, 27 June 1943, Logan Diary, Box 4, Diary 2, Logan Papers, LOC. On cooperation, as Domingo put it, "It is my long-held belief that American Negroes...demanding Self-Government for the West Indian peoples... could exert a tremendous influence on world affairs." Domingo to White, 7 February 1941, folder: Labor—British West Indies—1940–49, Box A332, NAACP Papers, LOC.

60. Hoover to Berle, 14 November 1944, 844D.00/11–1444, RG 59, NA; Manley, "Presidential Address to Annual Conference of PNP," August 1945, in *Manley*, ed. Nettleford, 87.

61. Neptune, *Caliban*, 65.

62. Resolution, All-Jamaican Conference, sent to Colonial Secretary, 11 June 1943, CO 137 859/68714/1/44, UKNA; Blanshard to State, 9 March 1943, 844D.011/6; Winant to Hull, 27 February 1943, 844D.011/4, RG 59, NA. Evidence of FDR's reputation can be found in West Indian materials meant for domestic consumption. See, for example, "W.I.N.P. Statement of Policy," attached to Richards to Manley, 26 August 1943, folder: 4/60/2B/7, Manley Papers, JA.

63. Winant to Hull, 27 February 1943.

64. "I outlined to the President the racial situation in the West Indies, the tie-in between [WINC] in Harlem and certain...groups in Jamaica, Trinidad, and British Guiana. I told him of the study that we were making to try to bring into focus the...whole situation." Memorandum of Conversation, Taussig and FDR, 14 February 1944, "1942–44," Box 34, CWTP, FDRL.

65. Post, *Iron*, 2:420.

66. Ibid.

67. Ibid.; Memorandum and *Manchester Guardian* clipping, U.S. Embassy-London to Secretary of State, 18 March 1944, 844.00/244, RG 59, NA.

68. Report of Henry Field and Paul Blanshard, December 1944, Henry Field Papers, FDRL. Manley regularly wrote asking for money. Manley to Roberts, 16 October 1943, folder: Correspondence [#17], Box 2B, MS 353—Roberts Papers, NLJ. They answered the call as the campaign began. Manley to Brown, 26 January 1944, in folder: 4/60/2B/9, Manley Papers, JA.

69. McFarlane to Brown, 14 January 1943, MS 234—JPL, NLJ; Department of State to U.S. Consulate-Kingston, 26 April 1944, folder: Confidential Correspondence 1944, Box 4, Consulate Files 1944, RG 84: Kingston, NA; Brown to Manley, 6 June 1944; Manley to Brown, 26 June 1944, folder: 4/60/2B/9, Manley Papers, JA.

70. Lord to Hull, 16 December 1944, 844D.00/12–1644, RG 59, NA; Padmore to James, 19 August 1945, George Padmore Letters, SC.

71. Lord to Hull, 16 December 1944, 844D.00/12–1644, RG 59, NA. See Post, *Iron*, and Munroe, *Decolonization*, for analysis of class and race in the election.

72. Eaton, *Bustamante*, 119.

73. U.S. Consulate-Kingston to State Department, 8 January 1943, folder: Confidential Correspondence 1945 [*sic*], Box 3, Confidential File 1943, RG 84: Kingston, NA. Adolf Berle was in charge of coordinating the surveillance. In early 1944, J. Edgar Hoover collected all dossiers on WINC, Domingo, and other West Indians at home and in the United States for Berle's inspection. Hoover to Berle, 31 March 1944, 844.00B/3, RG 59, NA.

74. Taussig to Berle, 5 January 1944, folder: #1, Box 49 (Caribbean Commission Photostats), CWTP, FDRL; U.S. Consulate-Kingston to State Department, December 1943, folder: Confidential Correspondence 1945, [*sic*] Box 3, Confidential File 1943, RG 84: Kingston, NA. The ad was quickly withdrawn. Violence between Americans and islanders inevitably took on racial overtones, but rarely owed to these alone. Naval Intelligence to State Department, 18 June 1943, 844D.4016/10, RG 59, NA.

75. Memorandum of Conversation, Taussig and Hull, 8 February 1944, folder: #1, Box 49; Memorandum of Conversation, Taussig and FDR, 14 February 1944, folder: 1942–44, Box 34, CWTP, FDRL. U.S. Consulate-Kingston to State Department, March/April 1944, folder "Confidential Correspondence 1944," Box 4, Confidential File 1944, RG 84: Kingston, NA. See also Cindy Hahamovitch, *The Fruits of Their Labor: Atlantic Coast Farmworkers and the Making of Migrant Poverty, 1870–1945* (Chapel Hill, 1997), 175–180, 200–202.

76. "Self Determination for the West Indies," H. P. Osborne, *Congress Vue*, March 1944, 3. The editorial board of *Congress Vue* included Ferdinand Smith and NNC luminaries such as Max Yergan and Alphaeus Hunton. Hoover to Berle, 3 April 1944, 844.00B/4, RG 59, NA. Hoover to Berle, 26 April 1944, 844.00B/5, RG 59, NA. The meeting was a qualified success, raising $300 for the PNP, a useful sum but one only half the amount raised the previous month.

77. Hoover to Berle, 26 April 1944; Memorandum, Hoover to Berle, 19 June 1944, 844.00B/6–1944, RG 59, NA. Powell, whose base included Harlem West Indians, had met with Taussig and Hastie in 1942 to place himself at the forefront of expatriate concerns. FBI Report, 30 March 1943, 844.00/148, RG 59, NA, cited in Fraser, *Ambivalent*, 72.

78. Field undertook his study on behalf "of the AACC" according to Hoover to Berle, 22 March 1944, 844.00B/1, NA. But Field does not appear on official AACC lists. Roosevelt approved, calling him "a very good man." Memorandum of Conversation, Taussig and FDR, 14 February 1944, folder: 1942–44, Box 34, CWTP, FDRL. On the AWIA, see Hoover to Berle, 22 March 1944, 844.00B/1, RG 59, NA.

79. Report of Henry Field and Paul Blanshard, December 1944.

80. Lord to Hull, 16 December 1944, 844D.00/12–1644, RG 59 NA.

81. See Post, *Iron*, 2:346, 468. The drive to acquire Jamaican bauxite was part of a complicated transformation of business–government relations regarding mineral extraction, as recounted in George D. Smith, *From Monopoly to Competition: The Transformations of Alcoa, 1888–1986* (New York, 1988). See also Alfred Eckes, *The United States and the Global Struggle for Minerals* (Austin, 1979). On the shortage, see FDR to Phillip Murray (CIO), 21 August 1941, OF 1050—Aluminum Production 1933–41, Box 1, FDRP, FDRL; Arnold to Nelson, 9 February 1942, folder: Aluminum, Box 130, Hopkins Papers, FDRL.

82. Hull to Winant, 23 March 1944, 844D.6359/27; Eden to Winant, 14 July 1944, 844D.6359/7–1744, RG 59, NA.

83. Memorandum of Conversation, "Development of Jamaican Bauxite," 8 December 1944, 844D.6359/12–844; Rice to Hull, 9 November 1944, 844D.6359/

11–944, RG 59, NA. Memorandum of Conversation, Taussig, FDR, Governor Lethem, 10 November 1944, folder: #1, Box 49, CWTP, FDRL.

84. See Post, and to a lesser extent Fraser: Post, *Iron*, 2:346–349; Fraser, *Ambivalent*, 81.

85. MP De Rothchild, in Winant to Hull, 17 March 1943, 844D.011/5, NA. For insight into the conflict over aviation as it extended into the postwar era, see Jeffrey Engel, *Cold War at 30,000 Feet: The Anglo-American Fight for Aviation Supremacy* (Cambridge, 2007).

86. Law Committee to FO, 7 January 1944, FO 371 /38522, UKNA. The report summed up American inroads: "It is not so much that all the goods in the shops will be American, but the economic pattern of the community tends to be largely influenced by American ideas and methods...On the whole...the Americans do not regard the British colonies as an important field for economic [but rather for] strategic penetration."

87. Lee to Butler, 9 February 1944; Butler to Winant, 30 March 1944, FO 371 /38569, UKNA; Halifax to FO, 9 August 1943, folder: 4047–40C, Box 3031, RG 25, CNA.

88. Lee to Butler, 9 February 1944, FO 371 /38569, UKNA.

89. Memorandum, no author given, 7 August 1943; Bateman to Robertson, 11 September 1943; Robertson to Prime Minister, 15 September 1943; Robertson to Canadian High Commissioner for U.K., 26 October 1943; Bateman to Wilson, 8 April 1943, folder: 4047–40C, Box 3031, RG 25, CNA.

90. Fraser argues that the United States and the AACC "retreated" from an activist stance by 1945. This was true to a degree, but it shortchanges the "prototype" role that the body and region nonetheless played. Louis, *Imperialism*, 345, 435, 440–441.

91. Meeting Notes, Taussig, 16 January 1945, folder: #2, Box 48, CWTP, FDRL.

92. Bunche to Taussig, 7 January 1945, folder: #2, Box 48, CWTP, FDRL.

93. "A Meeting of the Fabian Colonial Bureau," Report by LeRoy for Brown, 24 February 1945, folder: January–June 1945, Box 52, CWTP, FDRL.

94. Report, "The General Election and the New Government of Jamaica," Paul Blanshard, 23 January 1945, 844D.00/1–2345, RG 59, NA.

95. Excerpt from Manley to Blanshard, January 1945, cited in ibid.

96. In an election postmortem, Domingo crystallized PNP disappointment in the black masses: "[They] are desperately ignorant [and] superstitious. The simple principles of logic . . . are alien to the thought processes of [most] Jamaicans." That said, Domingo remained "a determined optimist regarding black democracy." Report, "The General Election," 23 January 1945.

97. Ibid.

98. Report, "The General Election," 23 January 1945.

99. Report of Henry Field and Paul Blanshard, December 1944.

100. "The Economic Lure of Colonial Trusteeship," Frank Hill in *The Masses* (Jamaica), 9 June 1945, cited in Post, *Iron*, 2:531.

101. Report of Henry Field and Paul Blanshard, December 1944.

102. Memorandum of Conversation, Taussig et al., 14–15 December 1944, [no folder], Box 47, CWTP, FDRL.

103. Louis, *Imperialism*, 436.

104. Memorandum of Conversation, 13 March 1945, folder: #1, Box 48, CWTP, FDRL; Memorandum of Conversation, Taussig et al., 13 January 1945.

105. Meeting Notes, Taussig, 16 January 1945, folder: #2, Box 48, CWTP, FDRL.

106. Manley to France, 8 September 1945, folder: 4/60/2B/10, Manley Papers, JA; Speech, "Possibilities of West Indian Federation," Rayford Logan, Division of Social Sciences of Howard University Graduate School, 24 June 1943, folder: Speeches—June 21, 1943—Possibilities of West Indian Federation, Box 166–23, Logan Papers, MSRC.

107. Entry, 2 March 1946, "Diary, January–June 1946," Box 34, Diary: July 1944–June 1946, Tugwell Papers, FDRL.

Chapter 3

Portions of this chapter were previously published in *International History Review*; I gratefully acknowledge the journal's permission to reproduce them here.

1. Leffler, *Preponderance*.

2. Fraser labels the period one of "[U.S.] disengagement and imperial reassertion." Fraser, *Ambivalent*, 91–122.

3. Fraser recounts that Taussig argued for "an express commitment in the U.N. Charter to the objective of independence for colonial territories" but "bowed before [British and French] opposition.... [This] reflected the ascendancy of collaboration with the colonial powers in American foreign policy and the abdication of the role of champion of anticolonialism." Fraser, *Ambivalent*, 92; *FRUS*, 1945, 1:792–797.

4. Taussig to Welles, 12 April 1945, Box 4, RG 59 Lot Files, Lot 65D140, Records Relating to Caribbean Dependencies Affairs 1941–1962 (RG 59 Lot Files: Caribbean Dependencies), NA.

5. Fraser, *Ambivalent*, 92–93. However Herbert Corkran notes that despite a weakened Taussig, the Commission continued to make contributions, producing "over a period of fifteen years.... substantial achievements in agriculture, trade, fisheries, education, health, and related areas of special concern to the peoples of the West Indies." Corkran, *Patterns of International Cooperation in the Caribbean, 1942–1969* (Dallas, 1970), xii.

6. Memorandum of Conversation, Taussig, Bunche, et al., 4 December 1945, Box 4, RG 59 Lot Files: Caribbean Dependencies, NA, cited in Fraser, *Ambivalent*, 92.

7. Quotation is by Secretary of War Robert Patterson, cited in Leffler, *Preponderance*, 60.

8. Beyond the change of direction signaled by the new Labour government, the signs in Kingston and New York were positive too. Creech Jones to Manley, 12 February 1946; Nethersole to Manley, 6 March 1946, folder: 4/60/2B/11, Manley Papers, JA; Memorandum of Conversation, 4 December 1945. On the mutual influence between Jamaica and Puerto Rico, see Pico to Manley, 14 October 1946; and Manley to Pico, 26 October 1946, folder: 4/60/2B/11, Manley, JA.

9. Truman to Taussig, 7 February 1946, Box 4, RG 59 Lot Files: Caribbean Dependencies, NA. Fraser notes that Taussig's statement provoked intransigence among the Europeans, who were determined to resist links between the Commission and U.N. or other instruments by which the world might harshly judge Europe's handling of Caribbean affairs. Fraser, *Ambivalent*, 96–97.

10. Manley to Marryshow, 24 January 1946; Manley to Powell, 23 March 1946, folder: 4/60/2B/11, Manley Papers, JA. On the "evolving" black dialogue, see Von Eschen, *Race*.

11. Manley to Graham, undated; Manley to Young, 30 March 1946; Manley to "Comrade," 31 May 1946, folder: 4/60/2B/11, Manley Papers, JA; Invitation list, 11 October 1945, folder: American Committee for West Indian Federation, 1945–48, Box A356, NAACP Papers, LOC.

12. White to Membership, 11 January 1946, in fiche #005,719–1, SC Clipping File; Staupers to White, 29 October 1945, folder: American Committee for West Indian Federation, 1945–48, Box A356, NAACP Papers, LOC.

13. White to Hoover, 16 November 1945, folder: American Committee for West Indian Federation, 1945–48, Box A356, NAACP Papers, LOC; Hoover to Lyon, 16 October 1945, 844D.01/10–1645, RG 59, NA. In New York, Manley met with Ferdinand Smith, Max Yergan, and other suspected "reds." Hoover to Lyon, 16 October 1945.

14. National Council of Negro Women (NCNW), "West Indies Night to be First International Night Event," 28 January 1946, folder: Coterie of Social Workers of Trinidad and Tobago 1946, Series 5, Box 8, NCNW Papers, Bethune Museum, Washington, D.C. See also Memorandum on By-laws, undated (1945), folder: #013, Williams Collection, UWISA.

15. Intelligence Review, 14 February 1946, Naval Aide Files—Alphabetical Files, Box 15; Intelligence Review, 23 May 1946, Naval Aide Files—Alphabetical Files, Box 16, Harry S. Truman Papers (HSTP), HSTL.

16. Quoted in Elisabeth Wallace, *The British Caribbean: From the Decline of Colonialism to the End of Federation* (Toronto, 1977), 95–96.

17. U.S. Consul: Port of Spain to State Department, 4 September 1947, 844.00/9–447, RG 59, NA, cited in Fraser, *Ambivalent*, 107. See also Munroe, *Decolonization*, 118. On federations as vessels of continued influence, see Louis, "The Imperialism of Decolonization." On Montego Bay, see Fraser, *Ambivalent*, 106–110.

18. John Mordecai points out that the British provided a "federal" template as well: the Colonial Development and Welfare Organization. "Here for the first time was a West Indian-wide administrative unit [acting] as if the West Indies were already a single political [being]." Mordecai, *The West Indies: The Federal Negotiations* (London, 1968), 31.

19. Manley to Marryshow, 24 January 1946, folder: 4/60/2B/11, Manley Papers, JA.

20. Report, *Conference on Closer Association of the British West Indian Colonies*, Montego Bay, 11–19 September 1947, (mfilm), 26–27. Manley saw that even with support from London, Washington, and the West Indian center-left, building a viable federation would be—as he confessed to Williams—"a far harder fight with a far more doubtful outcome than I would care to admit in public." Manley to Williams, 23 May 1946, folder: #114, Williams Collection, UWISA.

21. Munroe, *Decolonization*, 118–121; McFarlane, "The History of Self-Government in Jamaica," June 1950, MS 1893—Walter McFarlane Papers, NLJ.

22. Bridget Brereton, *A History of Modern Trinidad, 1783–1962* (Kingston, 1981), 214; Selwyn Ryan, *Race and Nationalism in Trinidad and Tobago: A Study of Decolonization in Multiracial Society* (Toronto, 1972), 70–73.

23. Munroe, *Decolonization*, 61. See also Ryan, *Race*, 76.

24. Leffler, *Preponderance*, 475; John Lewis Gaddis, *We Now Know: Rethinking Cold War History* (New York, 1997), 154.

25. Speech sent with Ambassador to FO, 14 January 1947, FO 371 /60998, UKNA.

26. A February 1947 report observed that the Labour government had committed to ultimate self-rule. Intelligence Review, 13 February 1947, Box 18, Naval Aide Files—Alphabetical Files, HSTP, HSTL. See also Ritchie Ovendale, ed., *The Foreign Policy of British Labour Governments, 1945–1951* (Leicester, 1984).

27. Intelligence Review, 13 February 1947; Report, "Review of World Situation as it Relates to the Security of the United States," CIA, 26 September 1947, Box 20,

Asst. Chief of Staff—Intelligence Division—Reports/Messages 1918–1951, CIA, ORE 1–49 thru 69–49, RG 319, NA.

28. Roger R. Trask, "The Impact of the Cold War on United States–Latin American Relations, 1945–1949," *DH* 1 (Summer 1977), 284.

29. Cabot to Kennan, 7 November 1947; Kennan to Butler, 18 November 1947, folder: Communism, Box 8, RG 59 Lot Files, Lot 64D563 Records of the Policy Planning Staff (RG 59: PPS) 1947–1953, NA.

30. Hartley to Notter, 21 November 1945, folder: Caribbean Conference—July 1946, Box 28—Misc. Subject Files, 1939–50, RG 59: Harley A. Notter Files (RG 59: Notter), NA; Report, State Committee on Colonial Problems, 11 February 1948, folder: Colonialism, Box 8, RG 59: PPS 1947–1953, NA.

31. U.S. Embassy-London to Undersecretary of State Lovett, 4 March 1948, Box 3, RG 59: PPS 1947–1953, NA.

32. How these would be affected by the Truman Doctrine was not very clear; indeed, the Doctrine's main effect on the Caribbean military balance was uncertainty. As the U.S. consul put it, "the ARMY DOES NOT YET KNOW WHAT IT WANTS IN TRINIDAD" [emphasis in original]. U.S. Consul-Trinidad to State Department, 11 April 1947, folder: Clara Borjes (Confidential Letters) 1946, 1947, Confidential File: Correspondence between Bonnet and Borjes, 1947–48, Box 1, RG 84: Port of Spain, NA.

33. CO to West Indian Governors, 29 May 1948, CO 537 /3824/1149597, UKNA; Munroe, *The Cold War and the Jamaica Left, 1950–1955: Re-Opening the Files* (Kingston, 1992), 149.

34. This was a point of repeated contention in Manley's relations with expatriates who as seen in chapter 2 were split over communism in their ranks. McFarlane to Manley, 20 February 1947, folder: 4/60/2B/12; Manley to McFarlane, 5 March 1947; Manley to Domingo, 19 July 1948, folder: 4/60/2B/13, Manley Papers, JA.

35. *Jamaica Daily Gleaner,* 23 December 1949. This justified Bustamante's refusal to join the PNP in a coalition government, since Manley had not yet shed the PNP's extreme left wing, and helped to give Jamaican politics its Manichean shape.

36. Report, "Jamaica—Constitutional Problems, Political Scene," Jamaica Governor to CO, 16 August 1947, CO 137 /875/68714/6/47; Report, Jamaica Governor to CO, 20 November 1948, CO 537 /3808, UKNA. On the worsening labor relations, see Munroe, *Decolonization,* 55–60.

37. Police Report, forwarded from Trinidad Governor to CO, 16 April 1948; Report, Trinidad Governor to CO, 16 August 1948; Report, Trinidad Governor to CO, 25 December 1948, CO 537 /3816, UKNA. For an extended and widely researched look at the CLC, see Horne, *Hot Zone.*

38. Intelligence Review, 13 March 1947, Box 18, Naval Aide Files (Alphabetical), HSTP, HSTL.

39. Report, "US Policy Regarding Non-Self-Governing Territories," State Department Committee on Dependent Areas, 15 December 1947, Box 4, RG 59 Lot Files: Caribbean Dependencies, NA.

40. Memorandum, unsigned, 4 June 1947, Box 2; Memorandum of Conversation, "U.S. Policy on Colonial Questions," 9 September 1948, Box 4; Memorandum of Conversation, Caribbean Commission Working Committee, 26 October 1948, Box 2, RG 59 Lot Files: Caribbean Dependencies, NA; Memorandum of Conversation, Acheson et al., 4 May 1949, folder: May–June 1949, Box 64, Memoranda of Conversations: January–July 1949, Acheson Papers, HSTL.

41. Report, "ORE 25–48," CIA, 3 September 1948, Box 23, Asst. Chief of Staff—Intel. Div.-Reports and Messages 1918–1951, CIA, ORE 1–49 thru 69–49, RG 319, NA.

42. Trevor Munroe, *Jamaican Politics: A Marxist Perspective in Transition* (Kingston, 1990), 128.

43. Plummer, *Wind*, 98; Manley to Williams, 6 August 1947; Domingo to Manley, 25 August 1947; folder: 4/60/2B/12, Manley Papers, JA.

44. Barnett to Wilkins, 20 April 1946; Reid to White, 21 September 1948, folder: British West Indies 1940–1949, Box A155, NAACP Papers, LOC.

45. Noyes to NAACP, 15 May 1947; McDowall to NAACP, 27 October 1947, folder: British West Indies 1940–1949, Box A155, NAACP Papers, LOC.

46. U.S. Consulate-Kingston to State Department, 1 December 1948; U.S. Consulate-Kingston to State Department, 7 December 1948, folder: Confidential Correspondence 1948, Box 8 (1948), RG 84: Kingston, NA.

47. U.S. Embassy-Panama to State Department, 11 September 1947, 844D.504/9–1147, RG 59, NA; Domingo to Manley, 15 August 1947. Manley to Domingo, 2 October 1947, folder: 4/60/2B/12; Memorandum, "Political Conditions in the Caribbean Area," 17 February 1949, Box 4, RG 59 Lot Files: Caribbean Dependencies, NA; Cyrus to Manley, 11 April 1949, folder: 4/60/2B/14, Manley Papers, JA.

48. Pabst to Chamberlin, 13 May 1948, Box 4, RG 59 Lot Files: Caribbean Dependencies, NA.

49. Nor was this the first time Robeson's reputation clashed with Caribbean interests. Fraser tells of a 1947 CLC rally at Madison Square Garden, at which Robeson was slated to appear with Manley and Barbados' Grantley Adams. Manley's and Adams' appearance was canceled under what Fraser sees as pressure to "de-radicalize." Fraser, *Ambivalent*, 114–15. It was certainly not due to skittishness on Robeson's part; he had been trying to arrange an appearance with Manley for some time, although he would be unsuccessful until the 1949 event. Robeson to Manley, 1 May 1946, folder: 4/60/2B/11, Manley Papers, JA. See also Nicholson to Labouise and Borjes, 22 August 1950, Box 4, RG 59 Lot Files: Caribbean Dependencies, NA; JPL to PNP, 30 April 1947, MS 234—JPL, NLJ.

50. Speech, Harry Truman, February 1948, folder: 1948, Feb. 20–21, Puerto Rican Speeches, Box 31, Presidential Speech File, Clark Clifford Papers, HSTL.

51. Taussig to Truman, 12 October 1945, folder: OF-106, Box 593, White House Central File-Official File (WHCF-OF), HSTP, HSTL. On Bunche being seen as "out of touch," see Von Eschen, *Race*, 76–77, and Kenneth Robert Janken, *Rayford W. Logan and the Dilemma of the African American Intellectual* (Amherst, 1993), 206–207. Pickens to Bunche, 7 September 1945, folder: OF-106, Box 593, WHCF-OF, HSTP, HSTL. Emphasis added.

52. Cunningham to Barnes, 25 February 1944, folder: White House File—Negroes—Conference of Negro Democratic Leaders, Box 53, Philleo Nash Papers, HSTL; Excerpt, *Congressional Record*, 1 May 1946, Vol. 92, Part 4, 4296–97, in folder: Internal Security File—Civil Rights—Negro file, Box 42, Stephen Spingarn Papers, HSTL.

53. Kemp to Byrnes, 25 June 1946, 844D.00/6–2546, RG 59, NA. Manley wrote Williams that he was deeply honored to receive the Howard degree. Manley to Williams, 23 May 1946, folder: #114, Williams Collection, UWISA.

54. Lohman to Chapman, 26 March 1947, folder: Racial Minority Groups, Box 38, Oscar Chapman Papers, HSTL; article, *Opportunity* (Urban League), Winter 1947, folder: Internal Security File—Civil Rights—Negro File, Box 42, Assistant to President File, Spingarn Papers, HSTL. Dudziak confirms that the administration got the message, using the same argument in *amicus curae* briefs supporting the NAACP's desegregation effort. Dudziak, *Civil Rights*, 96, 99.

55. Report, "ORE 25–48," CIA, 3 September 1948.

56. Borjes to Allen, 24 March 1950, Box 4, RG 59 Lot Files: Caribbean Dependencies, NA.

57. U.S. Consul-Port of Spain to State Department, 14 May 1947, 844G.504/ 5–1447, RG 59, NA.

58. Oakley to Price, 25 November 1949, Box 4, RG 59 Lot Files: Caribbean Dependencies, NA; "British West Indies—Threat of Communist Activity," Office of Naval Intelligence, 14 February 1949, 844G.00/2–1449, RG 59, NA, cited in Fraser, *Ambivalent*, 116.

59. U.S. Consul-Kingston to State Department, 23 June 1950, Box 4, RG 59 Lot Files: Caribbean Dependencies, NA; Elliott to Acheson, 4 May 1950, 741H.00/ 4–2750, RG 59, NA.

60. U.S. Consul-Kingston to State Department, 12 November 1947, 844D.101/11–1247, RG 59, NA. See also Memorandum of Conversation, "Colonial Policy Talks with U.K.," Acheson et al., 5 July 1950, Box 13, RG 59 Records of Assistant Secretary/Undersecretary Acheson (RG 59: Acheson), NA.

61. Memorandum, "Political Conditions in the Caribbean Area," 17 February 1949. The NSC concluded that Jamaica and Trinidad by 1950 showed a "moderate degree of communism," Bustamante notwithstanding. Report, NSC, 19 May 1950, folder: Reports—Current Policies of Government Relating to National Security—Vol. 1—Geographic Area Policies—#2, Box 194, PSF—Subject File: NSC (Memoranda. & Reports -1), HSTP, HSTL.

62. Even the "exceptions"—transport and minerals—must be qualified. The Colonial Office fought longer than any other entity against Reynolds's efforts to develop Jamaican bauxite even after the island government had signed on. CO argued that the deal failed to protect British investors, and thus set a harmful precedent. Fraser, *Ambivalent*, 102–106.

63. British Embassy-Washington to FO, 1 January 1947; Jamaica Governor to CO, 5 March 1947, FO 371 /61005, UKNA.

64. British Embassy-Washington to FO, 1 January 1947.

65. Memorandum of Conversation, Consul Bonnet and General Stamford, 27 March 1947, folder: Clara Borjes (Confidential Letters) 1946–1947, Box 1, Correspondence between Ellis Bonnet and Clara Borjes 1947–48, RG 84: Port of Spain, NA.

66. Intelligence Memorandum 142, CIA, 5 April 1949; Intelligence Memorandum 235, CIA, 13 October 1949, folder: NSC/CIA (5–11)—Intelligence Memoranda, December 1948–December 1949, Box 2, NSC Records, CIA File, HSTP, HSTL.

67. "Report by Joint Strategic Plans Committee to JCS Overall Base Requirements of Caribbean Command," 5 January 1949, folder: CCS 360, Box 146, RG 218, NA.

68. Report, "Military Requirements for Base Rights," 5 March 1949, folder: CCS 360, Box 146, RG 218, NA.

69. Report, "Importance to U.S. of Latin American Civil Air Transport," ORE 22–49, folder: ORE 1949, Box 256, PSF—Intelligence File, HSTP, HSTL.

70. Report, "Technical Cooperation—Point Four: Caribbean Dependent Areas," State Department, November 1950, folder: Caribbean Area—General, Box 64, RG 469—Institute for Inter-American Affairs (IIAA) 1948–61, NA; Report, "ORE 31–48," CIA, 14 May 1948, Box 23, Asst. to Chief of Staff, Intelligence—Reports and Messages 1918–51, CIA/ORE, RG 319, NA; Memorandum, Interior Secretary (Chapman) to Bureau of Mines Director, undated, folder: Interior Department 1946–1950, Box

20, WHCF-Confidential File, HSTP, HSTL; Memorandum, "Overall Base Requirements of the Caribbean Command," Ridgway to Joint Chiefs of Staff, 22 October 1948, folder: CCS 360, Box 146, RG 218, NA.

71. Report, Joint Chiefs of Staff, 14 April 1948; Report, Joints Chiefs/Joint Logistics Plans Committee, 4 May 1948, folder: U.S. Petroleum Situation, Box 128, RG 218, NA.

72. Report, "ORE 34–49," CIA, 14 November 1950, Box 24, Asst. to Chief of Staff, Intelligence—Reports and Messages 1918–51, CIA/ORE, RG 319, NA; Report, "Estimate of Soviet Capabilities in Latin American Area in a War Commencing July 1952," Joint Intelligence Group, June 29, 1951, folder: CCS 381—Section 7–12, Box 117, Geographic File 1951–53, RG 218, NA.

73. Palmer to Vanderburg, 6 January 1945; Clipping, "Shortage of Aluminum Sheet May Affect Aircraft Production," *Wall Street Journal*, 23 January 1945, folder: Materials—Aluminum, Box 8, National Aircraft War Production Council Files—Correspondence; Draft Report, Interior Department, 6 July 1948, folder: Correspondence—Commission—Aluminum, Box 56, President's Materials Policy Commission (PMPC) Files, HSTL.

74. Hull to Stimson, 28 March 1945, 844D.6359/1–3145, RG 59, NA.

75. U.S. Consulate-Kingston to State Department, 24 March 1949, 844D.6359/3–2449, RG 59, NA; see also Eberstadt to Hill, 4 June 1948, folder: Re NSRB: Report by [Eberstadt] to Arthur Hill, Chairman of NSRB, Box 113, Ferdinand Eberstadt Papers, PUL.

76. Memorandum of Conversation, State Department, Rice et al., 16 March 1949, 844D.6359/3–1649; "Reynolds Bauxite Proposal," Jamaica Governor, 6 April 1949, attached to U.S. Consul-Kingston to State Department, 12 April 1949, 844D.6359/4–1249, RG 59, NA.

77. U.S. Embassy-London to State Department, 28 April 1949, 844D.6359/4–2749, RG 59, NA. CO opinion was not unanimous, even after Korea made the U.S. argument unanswerable. Fraser, *Ambivalent*, 104; see also Memorandum of Conversation, 17 December 1945.

78. Truman's Korean War defense budget envisioned a 58-group Air Force. By 1953, this spending was producing one thousand warplanes per month. Hogan, *A Cross of Iron: Harry S. Truman and the Origins of the National Security State, 1945–1951* (New York, 1998), 305, 364.

79. Report, PMPC, 11 August 1951.

80. Memorandum of Conversation, State Department, Rice, et al., 16 March 1949.

81. Minutes of 11 a.m. Meeting, 7 January 1952, folder: Churchill–Truman Meeting in Cabinet Room, January 1952, Box 18, NSC Records—Chronological List of Policies, HSTP, HSTL; Lay to NSC, 6 March 1952, folder: P-25, Box 1—Policy Papers, RG 273, NA; Draft Report, PMPC, 7 April 1952, folder: Aluminum, Box 21, PMPC Files, HSTL.

82. Report, Department of Trade & Commerce, 14 March 1951.

83. Munroe, *Decolonization*, 57–64.

84. Jamaica Governor to CO, 1 December 1951, CO 1031 /132, UKNA.

85. Jamaica Governor to Colonial Secretary, 6 January 1950; Jamaica Governor to Colonial Secretary, 1 July 1950, CO 537 /6142; Trinidad Governor to CO, 27 April 1950, CO 537 /6149, UKNA.

86. Jamaica Governor to Colonial Secretary, 1 January 1951, CO 537 /6142, UKNA.

87. Jamaica Governor to Colonial Secretary, 1 July 1950; Jamaica Governor to Colonial Secretary, 1 September 1950; Report, Jamaica Governor to Colonial Secretary, 1 August 1950, CO 537 /6142, UKNA.

88. Jamaica Governor to Colonial Secretary, 14 August 1951, CO 537 /7391; CO to Commonwealth Relations Office (CRO), November 1952, CO 1031 /129, UKNA.

89. The DuBois case stirred anger in Jamaica, including from Hart who wrote Truman in protest. Hart to Truman, 3 November 1951, MS 126a—PNP Pamphlets Vol. 1, NLJ. This reflected the comradely relationship Hart and DuBois had. DuBois to Hart, 18 September 1946, folder: CLR 7—Pan African Federation, Richard Hart Papers, Institute of Social and Economic Studies, UWIM.

90. Memorandum, "Point Four Programs in the West Indies," 26 January 1951, Box 4, RG 59 Lot Files: Caribbean Dependencies, NA.

91. Memorandum of Conversation, Acheson, White, Randolph, Bethune, Logan et al., 13 April 1951, folder: April 1951, Box 68, Memoranda of Conversation, Acheson Papers, HSTL; Letter, Chapman to Hoffman, 24 July 1951, folder: NAACP Miscellaneous Correspondence 1945–1952, Box 114, Ralph J. Bunche Papers, UCLA. Also see Dudziak, *Civil Rights*, 47–77, especially regarding the USIA pamphlet *The Negro in American Life*.

92. Brown to White, 3 February 1951, folder: BWI 1950–1953, Box A155, NAACP Papers, LOC. Correspondence from West Indians suggests that White remained known as sympathetic to their cause. Rapley to White, 8 August 1951; Swaley to White, 11 October 1951; West Indian Day Association to White, 31 August 1952; White to Mitchell, 2 September 1952, folder: BWI 1950–1953, Box A155, NAACP Papers, LOC.

93. Handbill, "Public Meeting—Mr. Norman Manley and 'The Birth of a Nation,'" JPL, 11 February 1951, fiche #002,488–1; "Americans and West Indians Are Invited to Unite with the [JPL] . . . We Work Better if We Work Together!", Handbill, JPL, 29 April 1951, fiche #005,719–1, SC Clipping File.

94. Memorandum, "Manley Speech at Howard University," no author, 2 February 1951, Box 4, RG 59 Lot Files: Caribbean Dependencies, NA. On Manley as a "closet communist," see Memorandum, "Political Conditions in the Caribbean Area," 17 February 1949.

95. Church House (Trinidad) to CRO, March 1952, CO 1031 /129, UKNA.

96. Brodie to Ronning, 26 May 1952, folder: 10824-E-40 / #1, Box 4063, RG 25, CNA; CO to CRO, October 1952, CO 1031 /129, UKNA.

97. Church House (Trinidad) to CRO, March 1952.

98. The decisive marginalization of "an authentic worker opposition movement under Marxist leadership," according to Munroe, came in December 1953–January 1954, when Bustamante engineered a formal ban on communist activity in Jamaica. Munroe, *Cold War*, 169. For an overview of the trajectory of Caribbean Leftism, see Perry Mars, *Ideology and Change: The Transformation of the Caribbean Left* (Detroit, 1998).

99. "West Indies Colonial Intelligence Report," Commissioner—London to Undersecretary of External Affairs, July 1952, folder: 10824-E-40 vol 1, Box 4063, RG 25, CNA.

100. Acheson to McGregor, 27 March 1952, 741H.00/12–2352; U.S. Consulate-Port of Spain to State Department, 6 October 1952; U.S. Embassy-London to State Department, 3 March 1952, 741E.00/3–352, RG 59, NA.

101. TCA Staff to Cramer, 18 August 1952, folder: Development Projects in British West Indies, Box 64, RG 469—IIAA Country Files 1942–53 / Caribbean Area, NA.

102. Booklet, State Department, March 1952, folder: Memoranda on 'Our Foreign Policy,' Box 4, Subject File, Kenneth Hechler Papers, HSTL. Hickerson to Matthews, 13 May 1952, attached to Secret Report, "U.S. Policy Toward Colonial Areas and Colonial

Powers," State Department, folder: Colonialism 1952–1959, Box 2, RG 59 Lot Files, Lot 64D369, Office Files of the Deputy Assistant Secretary for Inter-American Affairs—Regional-Bloc Affairs, NA; Secret Report, "Re-examination of U.S. Foreign Policy on Colonial Problems," SANACC, folder: Documents: Working Group on Colonial Problems, Box 4, RG 353, NA.

103. Report, "Problems of U.S. Policy Regarding Colonial Areas," Policy Planning Staff, 2 October 1952, folder: Colonialism, Box 8, RG 59: PPS 1947–1953, NA.

Chapter 4

1. Borstelmann, *Cold War*, 93; Cary Fraser, "Crossing the Color Line in Little Rock: The Eisenhower Administration and the Dilemma of Race for U.S. Foreign Policy," *DH* 24 (Spring 2000): 233–264; and Parker, "Cold War II," 867–892.

2. Stephen Rabe, *Eisenhower and Latin America: The Foreign Policy of Anticommunism* (Chapel Hill, 1988), 174.

3. Washington took comfort in the West Indies' disposition, as 1952 saw signs of communist activity in the French West Indies, Puerto Rico, and Cuba. State Department to U.S. Consulate-Martinique, 28 November 1952, Box 4, RG 59 Lot Files: Caribbean Dependencies, NA; Report, "Jamaican Economic and Political Situation," 23 December 1952, 741H.00/12–2352, RG 59, NA. On Smith's career, see Gerald Horne, *Red Seas: Ferdinand Smith and Radical Black Sailors in the United States and Jamaica* (New York, 2005).

4. State Department to U.S. Consulate-Kingston, 4 March 1953, 741H.001/12–2652, RG 59, NA; Avery to Cramer, 27 February 1953, folder: Caribbean Area—General, Box 64, RG 469—IIAA, Country Files 1942–53, NA; U.S. Consulate-Port of Spain to State Department, 12 February 1953, 741M.001/2–1253, RG 59, NA; CO to CRO, April 1953, CO 1031 /129, UKNA.

5. U.S. Consulate-Kingston to State Department, 20 January 1953, 841H.2569/1–2053; Kingston to State, 17 February 1953, 841H.2541/2–1753, RG 59, NA; Tosswill to Jamaica Governor, 10 April 1953, WO 336 /12, UKNA.

6. U.S. Consulate-Kingston to State Department, 29 May 1953, 841H.00/5–2953, RG 59, NA.

7. Thomas J. Spinner, *A Political and Social History of Guyana, 1945–1983* (Boulder, 1984), 41–43. See also Rabe, *British Guiana*, 38–46.

8. U.S. Consulate-Kingston to State Department, 1 May 1953, 741H.00/5–153; Kingston to State, 5 June 1953, 741H.00/6–553; Kingston to State, 3 July 1953, 741H.00/7–353, RG 59, NA.

9. NSC 163/1, "Security of Strategically Important Industrial Operations in Foreign Countries," 1 October 1953, Box 7, Office of the Special Assistant for National Security Affairs (OSANSA) Papers: NSC Series—Policy Papers Subseries, White House Office (WHO) Files, DDEL.

10. U.S. plants would have had to be massively retooled to equal the Canadian ones. "We would be idiots," the president observed, not to use them. Discussion of "Aluminum Supply in Time of War," NSC, 22 October 1953, folder: 167th Meeting of NSC, Box 4, Ann Whitman File: NSC Series, Dwight D. Eisenhower Papers as President (DDEP); Brief, "Source of U.S. Aluminum Supply in Time of War," OCB, 12 October 1953, folder: Aluminum Supply, Box 1, NSC Staff: Papers 1948–61—Special Staff File Series; Memorandum, Executive Office of President to NSC, 16 October 1953, Box 7, OSANSA Papers, WHO, DDEL; Eisenhower to Barnes, 26 October 1953, folder: Eisenhower Diary October 1953 #2, Box 3, Eisenhower Diary Series, Whitman File, DDEP, DDEL.

11. U.S. Consulate-Kingston to State Department, 14 October 1953, 741H.001/ 10–1453; U.S. Consulate-Kingston to State Department, 19 November 1953, 741H.00/ 11–1953; U.S. Consulate-Kingston to State Department, 14 October 1953; Kingston to State, 11 December 1953, 741H.5/12–1153, RG 59, NA.

12. U.S. Consulate-Port of Spain to State Department, 8 December 1953, 741M.5/12–853, RG 59, NA; Despatch, Kingston to State, 11 December 1953, Box 4, RG 59 Lot Files: Caribbean Dependencies, NA; Report, "Actions Taken by the United States Information Agency in the Guatemalan Situation," 27 July 1954, *FRUS, 1952–1954*, 4:1212–1217.

13. U.S. Consulate-Kingston to State Department, 13 November 1953, 741H.00/ 11–1353, RG 59, NA. Intelligence Report, November 1952, folder: 10824-C-40 / #2, Box 4291, RG 25, CNA; Jamaica Governor to Colonial Secretary, 25 September and 5 October 1953, CO 1031 /124, UKNA.

14. U.S. Consulate-Kingston to State Department, December 22, 1953, 741H.00/ 12–2253; Kingston to State, 23 December 1953, 741H.00/12–2353; U.S. Consulate-Kingston to State Department, 22 January 1954, 741H.00/1–2254, RG 59, NA.

15. U.S. Consulate-Kingston to State Department, 5 March 1954, 741H.00/3–554, RG 59, NA; CO to Jamaica Governor, 5 February 1954, CO 1031/1961, UKNA. "By 1955," Munroe writes, "the Jamaican Left had been effectively isolated." Munroe, *Cold War*, 190.

16. Minutes, CO discussion, 22 June 1954, CO1031 /1961, UKNA; U.S. Consulate-Kingston to State Department, 20 May 1954, 741H.00/5–2054, RG 59, NA.

17. Intelligence Digest, "Nationalism," NSC, 23 October 1953, Box 5, OCB Secretariat Series, NSC Staff: Papers 1948–61, WHO, DDEL; NSC 144/1, 20 November 1953, Progress Report on "US Objectives and Courses of Action in Latin America," *FRUS, 1952–1954*, 4:37–38.

18. U.S. Embassy-Buenos Aires to State Department, 4 January 1954, 741H.022/ 1–454, RG 59, NA. The embassy forwarded a *La Prensa* editorial, which raised the issue for the upcoming Inter-American Conference. Months later, Dulles noted the continued quandary: "the remnants of colonialism in the Western Hemisphere have become an appreciable cause of disturbance to Pan-American relations." Memorandum, Dulles, 16 May 1954, folder: General Foreign Policy Matters, Box 8, White House Memoranda Series, John Foster Dulles Papers (JFDP), DDEL.

19. U.S. Consulate-Kingston to State Department, 11 March 1954, 741H.00/ 3–1154; U.S. Consulate-Kingston to State Department, 18 March 1954, 741H.00/ 3–1854, RG 59, NA.

20. Some authors note the connection but little more. See Wood, *Dismantling*, 201 n. 48; Smith, *Last Years*, 181; Schlesinger, *Fruit*, 121. Richard Immerman gives the matter greater weight in his analysis, though Piero Gleijeses disputes this assessment, noting that the Arbenz regime's rhetoric at the time gave the issue short shrift. Immerman, *The CIA in Guatemala: The Foreign Policy of Intervention* (Austin, 1982), 94, cited in Gleijeses, *Shattered Hope: The Guatemalan Revolution and the United States, 1944–1954* (Princeton, 1991), 118–119.

21. "Red Threat to the Americas," E. H. J. King, *Daily Gleaner*, 23 June 1954; Editorial, *Daily Gleaner*, 19 June 1954; Editorial, *Trinidad Guardian*, 19 June 1954.

22. U.S. Consulate-Kingston to State Department, 8 July 1954, 741H.00/7–854; U.S. Consulate-Kingston to State Department, 24 June 1954, 741H.00/6–2454, RG 59, NA.

23. U.S. Consulate-Kingston to State Department, 19 August 1954, 741H.00/8–1954, RG 59, NA; Jamaican Constabulary to CO, 2 December 1954, CO 1031 /1961, UKNA.

24. The Eisenhower administration noticed the tandem currents in English- and Spanish-speaking parts of the Caribbean littoral. See NSC 144/1, 20 November 1953,

Progress Report on "US Objectives and Courses of Action in Latin America," *FRUS*, 1952–1954, 4:29–30, 37–38.

25. Notes of meeting, Eisenhower and Churchill, 4 December 1953, folder: Bermuda—President's Notes Dec. 1953 #1, Box 3, Intl. Series, Whitman File, DDEP, DDEL.

26. U.S. Consulate-Kingston to State Department, 21 September 1953, 841H.00 TA/9–2153, RG 59, NA.

27. Avery to Cramer, 27 February 1953.

28. U.S. Consulate-Kingston to State Department, 24 April 1953, 741H.00/ 4–2453, RG 59, NA; CO to CRO, November 1952, CO 1031 /129, UKNA. Communist literature confiscated by authorities, for example, blasted the "mass Negro pogroms" in the United States. See e.g. U.S. Consulate-Kingston to State Department, 10 July 1953, 741H.00/7–1053, RG 59, NA.

29. For Caribbeans, the McCarran Act was a bitter insult. The Jamaican magazine *Spotlight* made this point and caught the consul's eye; "such expression by a conservative organ inspires leftist magazines, newspapers, and agitators to exploit color question to disadvantage of U.S." U.S. Consulate-Kingston to State Department, 3 April 1953, 741H.00/4–353, RG 59, NA.

30. U.S. Consulate-Kingston to State Department, 15 July 1954, 741H.00/ 7–1554; U.S. Consulate-Port of Spain to State Department, 28 December 1953, 741M.001/12–2853, RG 59, NA.

31. O'Connor to Stephens, 12 March 1953, folder: Chronological File— O'Connor & Hanes, 2–18 March 1953 #2, Box 2, Special Assistant Chronological Series, JFDP, DDEL.

32. McIlvaine to Dulles, 7 April 1954, folder: Caribbean Commission, Box 13, Subject Series, Confidential File, White House Central File (WHCF), Dwight D. Eisenhower Records as President (DDER), DDEL. The "colonial flavor" quote is from Memorandum, McIlvaine to Adams, 18 October 1954, in ibid.

33. In naming a team of experts for a West Indian visit, Washington sought Puerto Rican personnel because "the example of Puerto Rico . . . is so highly regarded and so well known" in the British Caribbean. Laidig to O'Connor, 4 November 1953, folder: Caribbean Area—General, Box 64, RG 469 IIAA—Country Files 1942–53, NA. The administration sought to use the island to symbolize American anticolonialism. Sears to Lodge, 8 January 1954, folder: Puerto Rico, Box 45, International Series, Whitman File, DDEP, DDEL; McIlvaine to Dulles, 7 April 1954.

34. "Federation: West Indians in U.S. Look to Jamaica," *Daily Gleaner*, 26 June 1954.

35. Barbados Governor to CO, 30 July 1953, CO 1031 /1082, UKNA.

36. Memorandum of Conversation, Barbour, Luke et al., 15 October 1954, Box 2, RG 59 Lot Files: Caribbean Dependencies, NA.

37. Merchant to Dulles, "Federation of the British West Indies," 21 December 1954, Box 2, RG 59 Lot Files: Caribbean Dependencies, NA.

38. Memorandum of Conversation, 18 October 1954, Box 2, RG 59 Lot Files: Caribbean Dependencies, NA.

39. "Bustamante Rule in Jamaica Ended," *New York Times (NYT)*, 14 January 1955; Williams to Manley, 18 January 1955, folder: #039, Williams Collection, UWISA.

40. U.S. Consulate-Kingston to State Department, 18 August 1955, 741H.00/ 8–1855; U.S. Consulate-Kingston to State Department, 10 January 1955, 741H.00/ 1–1055, RG 59, NA.

41. U.S. Consulate-Kingston to State Department, 10 March 1955, 741H.00/ 3–1055; U.S. Consulate-Kingston to State Department, 7 April 1955, 741H.00/4–755; U.S. Consulate-Kingston to State Department, 24 June 1955, 741H.00/6–2455, RG 59, NA. Manley repeated this assurance from Kingston to New York to London. "Victory Speech 1955," in Nettleford, ed., *Manley*, 195.

42. Kingston to State, 18 August 1955; U.S. Consulate-Kingston to State Department, 22 September 1955, 741H.00/ 9–2255, RG 59, NA; U.S. Consulate-Kingston to State Department, 7 December 1955, 741H.00/ 12–755, RG 59, NA.

43. U.S. Consulate-Kingston to State Department, 18 February 1955, 841H.00/ 2–1855; Kingston to State, 6 October 1955, 841H.05/10–655, RG 59, NA; Bloch to Nethersole, 28 February 1956, folder: 4/60/2A/12, Manley Papers, JA.

44. Nethersole to Bloch, 23 March 1956; Manley to Nkrumah, 25 January 1956; Nkrumah to Manley, 23 February 1956, folder: 4/60/2A/12; Nethersole to Manley, 20 June 1956, folder: 4/60/2A/13, Manley Papers, JA.

45. Memorandum of Conversation, Nethersole, et al., 30 June 1955, 841H.2569/ 6–3055; U.S. Consulate-Kingston to State Department, 28 April 1955, 841H.2569/ 4–2855; U.S. Consulate-Kingston to State Department, 25 August 1955, 841H.2569/8– 2555, RG 59, NA.

46. Radio script, Manley, undated (1956), folder: 4/60/2A/12, Manley Papers, JA; Munroe, *Decolonization*, 100.

47. "The Bandung Conference," Eric Williams, 23 February 1956, in *Forged from the Love of Liberty: Selected Speeches of Dr. Eric Williams*, ed. Paul K. Sutton (Port of Spain, 1981), 404; Lauren, *Power*, 213.

48. See Matthew Jones, "A 'Segregated' Asia? Race, the Bandung Conference, and Pan-Asianist Fears in American Thought and Policy, 1954–55," *DH* 29/5 (November 2005): 841–868; and Parker, "Cold War II." For their part, the British were more sure how to respond; see Nicholas Tarling, "'Ah-Ah': Britain and the Bandung Conference of 1955," *Journal of Southeast Asian Studies* 23/1 (March 1992): 74–112.

49. Memorandum of Telephone Conversation, Hagerty and Dulles, 11 April 1955, folder: White House Telephone Conversations, May–December 1953 #1, Box 10, Telephone Calls Series; Dulles to Hoover, 23 November 1955, folder: Chronological File: Dulles November 1955 #1, Box 12, Chronological Series 1951–59, JFDP, DDEL. H. W. Brands recounts the short career of the "reverse" idea in Brands, *The Specter of Neutralism: The United States and the Emergence of the Third World, 1947–1960* (New York, 1989), 117–118. Eisenhower to Churchill, 22 July 1954, folder: Eisenhower Diary—Churchill July–Dec. 1954 #1, Box 19; Eisenhower to Gruenther, 30 November 1954, folder: Eisenhower Diary—November 1954, Box 8, International Series, Whitman File, DDEP, DDEL.

50. Hanes to McCardle, 6 December 1955, folder: Macomber-Hanes Chronological File December 1955 #3, Box 9, White House Memoranda Series, JFDP, DDEL.

51. "My Relations with the Caribbean Commission, 1943–1955," Eric Williams, 21 June 1955, in *Eric E. Williams Speaks: Essays on Colonialism and Independence*, ed. Selwyn Cudjoe (Wellesley, 1993), 111–165. The final stages of Williams's Commission career had foreshadowed his future battles with the United States and Britain. Williams to Secretary-General, 27 April 1953; Williams to Smith, 28 April 1953; Williams to Secretary-General, 28 April 1954 folder: #054, Williams Collection, UWISA.

52. Politics was not an entirely new option; Williams had earlier told Manley that he was mulling it over. Williams to Manley, 17 June 1954, folder: #039, Williams Collection, UWISA. "My Relations with the Caribbean Commission," Williams, 21

June 1955. See also Palmer, *Eric Williams*; and Kirk P. Meighoo, *Politics in a Half Made Society: Trinidad and Tobago, 1925–2001* (Kingston, 2003), 25–61.

53. Lister to Cameron, 15 October 1956, 741M.00/10–1556; U.S. Consulate-Port of Spain to State Department, 22 December 1956, 741M.00/12–2256, RG 59, NA.

54. U.S. Consulate-Port of Spain to State Department, 18 May 1956, 741M.00/ 5–1856; U.S. Consulate-Port of Spain to State Department, 28 June 1956, 741M.00/ 6–2856, RG 59, NA; Williams to Manley, 3 January 1956, folder: 4/60/2A/18, Manley Papers, JA; Memorandum of Conversation, Douglas et al., 20 December 1955, folder: Political Affairs 1953–55, Box 1, Classified General Records 1953–63, RG 84: Port of Spain, NA.

55. Manley to Padmore, 13 February 1956, folder: 4/60/2A/18, Manley Papers, JA.

56. The term is Wallace's, indicating that the federation did not confer full internal self-government, though that was expected within a few years. Wallace, *Caribbean*, 119.

57. Wallace, *Caribbean*, 139–140. See also position papers of the Antigua and Jamaica branches of the W.I.F.L.P., undated (ca. October 1957), folder: Z17/3/8, Grantley Adams Papers, BDA.

58. U.S. Consulate-Barbados to State Department, 1 September 1955, 741E.00/9–155; U.S. Consulate-Port of Spain to State Department, 16 March 1955, 741M.00/3–1655, RG 59, NA; Report, "Jamaica 1955," Department of Trade & Commerce to Department of External Affairs, 3 July 1956, folder: 10824-E-40 / #1, Box 4063, RG 25, CNA; Luke to CO, undated, CO 1031 /1749, UKNA.

59. Murphy to Holland, 12 May 1955, FW-741E.022/5–955, RG 59, NA.

60. British Consulate-New York to British Embassy-Washington, 22 April 1955, FO 371 /114385, UKNA.

61. Holland to Murphy, 25 May 1955, 741E.022/5–2555, RG 59, NA. This was optimistic; two years before, anti-federation propaganda was such a staple of the Latin American press that the CO considered running samples in West Indian papers to stimulate pro-federation feeling. Thompson to CO, undated; CO to Barbados Governor, 26 October 1953; Barbados Governor to CO, 5 January 1954, CO 1031 /773, UKNA.

62. USIA to U.S. Consulates-Caribbean, 31 January 1956, folder: Federation 1956–58; State Department to Western Hemisphere and European Consulates/ Embassies, 2 February 1956, folder: Federation 1956–57, Box 1, Classified Records 1956–58, RG 84: Kingston, NA. A planning document counted on integrating the WIF into the OAS within ten years. "Objectives 1966," Policy Planning Staff, 14 May 1956, Box 106, RG 59: PPS 1956, NA.

63. U.S. Embassy-London to U.S. Consulates-Port of Spain et al., 29 February 1956, folder: Political Affairs—W.I.F.—1956–58, Box 2, Classified General Records 1953–63, RG 84: Port of Spain, NA.

64. Report, *British Caribbean Federal Capital Commission*, Col. No. 328 (London, 1956), cited in Mordecai, *Negotiations*, 67.

65. St. Lucia Governor to CO, 20 March 1956, CO 1031 /1226; "For Secretary of State for Colonies and UK Delegation [to British-Caribbean Federation Conference 1956]," 30 January 1956, CO 1031 /1750; Trinidad Governor to CO, 28 February 1956; Trinidad Governor to CO, 28 February 1956; CO to FO, 19 April 1956, CO 1031 /1226.

66. Murphy to Gray, 22 May 1956, FW-741E.022/5–2256, RG 59, NA; U.S. Embassy to Foreign Secretary, 5 June 1956, CO 1031 /1226, UKNA.

67. Trade Commissioner to Department of Trade & Commerce, 13 November 1956, folder: 10824-F-40 / #2, Box 4063, RG 25, CNA.

68. British Embassy-Washington to FO, March 1956, FO 371 /120328, UKNA; "U.S. Foreign Policy and the Problem of Social-Political Change," Policy Planning Staff, 28 January 1956; "A Reconsideration of U.S. Policy Toward Colonialism," Policy Planning Staff, no date, Box 106, RG 59: PPS 1956, NA.

69. Memorandum of Conversation, Bermuda Conference, 21 March 1957 10:30 a.m., in *FRUS* 1955–1957, 27:710. Still, on the eve of Bermuda, CO analysts said the "unconstructive American attitude toward 'colonialism'...is one of the main stumbling blocks to a fruitful understanding between our two countries, not only on colonial issues but [all] of international politics." CO to Prime Minister, 17 March 1957, PREM 11 /3239, UKNA; High Commissioner-New Delhi to CRO, 23 February 1957 FO 371 /126679, UKNA. At Bermuda, Dulles told Lloyd "he hoped the British won't think we are exerting pressure for premature independence." Memorandum for the Record, Goodpaster, 25 March 1957, folder: Bermuda Meeting (March 1957), Box 2, International Trips and Meetings—Official Staff Security Files, WHO, DDEL.

70. CO to British-Africa Governors, 29 May 1957; Memorandum, Attached to Minute, "British Colonial Policy—United States Attitude," Colonial Secretary to Prime Minister, 23 February 1957, PREM 11/3239, UKNA.

71. Appendix to "British Colonial Policy," PREM 11/3239, UKNA.

72. Jessup to Bunche, 17 October 1956; Working Paper, January 8, 1957, Council on Foreign Relations Study Group on Colonial Problems, folder: CFR—Study Group on Colonial Problems, Box 107, Collection 2051—Bunche Papers, UCLA; Digest of discussion, Rusk, Bunche, Jessup et al., 17 April 1957, in ibid.

73. U.S. Consulate-Kingston to State Department, 14 February 1957, folder: Federation 1956–57, Box 1, Classified Records 1956–58, RG 84: Kingston, NA. Report, USIA Inspector, 11 February 1957, folder: Jamica [*sic*] Feb. 11–6, 1957, Box 5; Report, USIA Inspector, 18 March 1957, folder: Trinidad March 18–22, 1957, Box 9, Records of Inspection Staff, RG 306, NA.

74. "All Trinidad" was not with him, as Sinanan's DLP fought him at every step. But Williams held both momentum and power. U.S. Consulate-Port of Spain to State Department, 7 January 1957, 741H.02/1–757, RG 59, NA. See also Report, Canadian Commissioner to External Affairs Under-secretary, February 1957, folder: 10824-C-40 / #2, Box 4291, RG 25, CNA.

75. Mordecai, *Negotiations*, 109.

76. Trinidad Governor to Colonial Secretary, 1 March 1957; Jamaica Governor to Colonial Secretary, 18 April 1957; Trinidad Governor to Colonial Secretary, 12 April 1957, CO 1031 /2024, UKNA; Mordecai, *Negotiations,*109.

77. Colonial Attaché (Washington) to Colonial Secretary, 9 May 1957, CO 1031 /2024, UKNA; Secret Report, unsigned, 25 April 1957, folder: International Political Relations, Box 1, Classified Records 1956–58, RG 84: Kingston, NA.

78. *NYT*, 7 April 1957.

79. U.S. Consulate-Port of Spain to State Department, 13 May 1957, 741M.00/ 5–1357, RG 59, NA.

80. Whiteman to Price, 15 May 1957, 711.5634j/5–1557, RG 59, NA.

81. U.S. Consulate-Kingston to Taylor, 29 May 1957, folder: Chaguaramas, Box 1, Classified Records 1956–58, RG 84: Kingston, NA.

82. CO to FO, 20 May 1957, FO 371 /126701; FO to Minister of Defense, 3 June 1957, CO 1031 /2024; Colonial Secretary to Trinidad Governor, 13 May 1957, CO 1031 /2024, UKNA.

83. Manley to Williams, 17 June 1957, folder: 4/60/2A/18, Manley Papers, JA; CO to FO, 20 May 1957.

84. Mordecai, *Negotiations*, 113–114; Document #64: Annex E, "Memorandum by Dr. Williams," 18 July 1957, CO 1031 /2024 168, in *BDEE: The West Indies*, ed. S. R. Ashton and David Killingray (London, 1999), 184; Palmer, *Eric Williams*, 85–87.

85. "Memorandum by Dr. Williams," *Documents*, Ashton and Killingray, eds., 183.

86. "Memorandum by Dr. Williams," *Documents*, Ashton and Killingray, eds., 115; Fraser, *Ambivalent*, 147–148.

87. Discussion, Colonial Secretary and U.S. Ambassador, 17 July 1957, CO 1031/2024; Ormsby-Gore to Prime Minister, 19 July 1957, PREM 11 /2880, UKNA.

88. Macmillan to Eisenhower, 19 July 1957, folder: Macmillan, President, May 29–November 30, 1957 #2; Eisenhower to Macmillan, 21 July 1957, folder: Macmillan, President, May 29–November 30, 1957 #6, Box 23, International Series, Whitman File, DDEP, DDEL.

89. *Congressional Record*, 15 August 1957, A6686; Dale to U.S. Consulate-Kingston, 21 August 1957, folder: Chaguaramas, Box 1, Classified Records 1956–58, RG 84: Kingston, NA.

90. *NYT*, 16 August 1957, in fiche #005,307–4, SC Clipping File.

91. Handbill, "Hands across the Seas Rally," 13 October 1957, in fiche #005,726–3, SC Clipping File. Cyrus to Logan, 22 November 1957, folder: American Friends of the WIF, Box 166–7, Logan Papers, MSRC; "On Caribbean Federation at the Luncheon Meeting for Lord Listowel," Richard B. Moore, in Turner and Turner, *Moore*, 288.

92. See "Speaking Engagements in the Caribbean," in Report of NAACP Executive Secretary, January 1954, fiche 2:0551; and "Secretary on Caribbean Tour," in Report of NAACP Executive Secretary, January 1955, fiche 2:0719, NAACP Papers.

93. Jonathan Rosenberg confirms that American civil rights leaders did not avert their eyes from the global scene. However, as a tactical matter their organizations for the most part focused their resources on domestic targets. Rosenberg, *Promised Land*.

94. U.S. Consulate-Kingston to State, 13 August 1957, folder: Chaguaramas, Box 1, Classified Records 1956–58, RG 84: Kingston, NA.

95. Williams to Manley, 14 August 1957, folder: 4/60/2A/18, Manley, JA; "Colonial Intelligence," Canadian Commissioner to External Affairs Undersecretary, September 1957, folder: 10824-C-40 / #2, Box 4291, RG 25, CNA.

96. Moline to Ringwalt, 6 September 1957; U.S. Consulate-Kingston to State Department, 13 August 1957; U.S. Consulate-Port of Spain to State Department, 20 December 1957, folder: Chaguaramas, Box 1, Classified Records 1956–58, RG 84: Kingston, NA.

97. Williams stated that after the British retreat from Suez and Cyprus, "if Chaguaramas had been a UK base [he] could have evicted the British in a week." U.S. Consulate-Port of Spain to Dulles, 12 October 1957; U.S. Consulate-Port of Spain to State Department, 20 December 1957, folder: Chaguaramas, Box 1, Classified Records 1956–58, RG 84: Kingston, NA

98. "Chaguaramas: Open Letter to Mr. Eisenhower," Gordon Lewis, *Daily Gleaner*, 13 February 1958, in fiche #005,721–6, SC Clipping File; Palmer, *Eric Williams*, 91, 94.

99. U.S. Consulate-Kingston to State Department, 14 November 1957, 841H. 2569/11–1457, RG 59, NA. Dulles noted "the world is richer in aluminum than in any other basic metal." Dulles to U.S. Consulate-Kingston, 23 December 1957, 841H. 2569/11–1457, RG 59, NA.

100. Memorandum, "National Security Aspects of Existing Panama Canal and Alternatives to it," Cutler to Adams, 19 November 1957, folder: November 1957 #2, Box

3, Chronological Subseries—Special Assistant Series, OSANSA, WHO; Memorandum, Brucker to Eisenhower, March 1958, folder: Department of Army #9; Report, "Panama Canal Traffic," Stanford Research Institute to Army, March 1958, folder: Department of Army #10, Box 5, Subject Series, Confidential File, WHCF, DDER, DDEL.

101. Dulles to Hailes, 2 January 1958, folder: Re: West Indies Federation 1958, Box 137, Duplicate Correspondence, JFDP, PUL; Manley to Williams, 13 January 1958, folder: 4/60/2A/18 Manley Papers, JA.

102. Wallace, *Caribbean*, 117–118; Memorandum of Conversation, Moline, et al., 14 February 1958, folder: Chaguaramas #2, 1958, Box 1, Classified Records 1956–58, RG 84: Kingston, NA; Eisenhower to Macmillan, 21 July 1957.

103. Arneson to Dulles, 28 March 1958, 741E.00/3–2858, RG 59, NA; Report, "Colonial Intelligence," Canadian Commissioner to External Affairs Undersecretary, 24 March 1958, folder: 10824-C-40 / #2, Box 4291, RG 25, CNA; Manley to Williams, 13 February 1958; Manley to Williams, 27 March 1958, folder: 4/60/2A/18, Manley Papers, JA; James to Mohamed Omar, 17 March 1958, folder: #105, Box 5, C. L. R. James Collection, UWISA.

104. Notes of Meeting—Discussion of Nash Report, NSC, 13 March 1958, folder: 358th Meeting of NSC, Box 9, NSC Series, Whitman File, DDEP, DDEL.

105. U.S. Consulate-Port of Spain to State Department, 1 May 1958; Dulles to U.S. Consulate-Kingston, 14 May 1958, folder: Chaguaramas #2, 1958, Classified Records 1956–58, RG 84: Kingston, NA.

106. Eric Williams Speech to Convention of Village Councils, cited in Report, Canadian Trade Commissioner to External Affairs Undersecretary, 16 December 1957, folder: 10824-F-40 / #2, Box 4063, RG 25, CNA. See also James to Adams, 28 July 1957; and James to Adams, 12 December 1957, folder Z17/3/6, Grantley Adams Papers, BDA.

Chapter 5

1. Rabe, *Eisenhower and Latin America*, 148–152.

2. Baptiste makes this point in "The Federal Process in the West Indies as Seen by the United States, 1947–1962," *Social and Economic Studies* 48 (1999): 185–210. Recent works such as Rabe's *British Guiana*—which shows that the unhappy fate of that colony stands in stark exception to the "West Indies" covered in this study—amply confirm this insight.

3. Williams used this line in public lectures all over Trinidad. Cited in "Massa Day Done," Eric Williams, 22 March 1961, in Cudjoe, *Eric E. Williams Speaks*, 261.

4. Fraser, *Ambivalent*, 148. Chaguaramas would help to demonstrate, however, that the two nationalisms—Trinidadian and West Indian—were not the same thing.

5. Editorial, "Now We're Supposed to Give Up Our Trinidad Navy Base!" *Saturday Evening Post*, 11 January 1958, fiche #005,307–4, SC Clipping File; "Birth in the Caribbean," 4 January 1958, and "Birth of a Nation," 24 April 1958, *NYT*. Most pieces on the federation took the *Times'* tack, making only short mention of Chaguaramas. See "New Federation in the Sun," *NYT Magazine*, 10 August 1959, and *Newsweek*, 5 May 1958, in fiche #005,726–4, SC Clipping File.

6. U.S. Consulate-Port of Spain to State Department, 8 May 1958, folder: BWI Federation, Box 1, Classified Records 1956–58, RG 84: Kingston, NA.

7. For extended descriptions of these dynamics, see Wallace, Mordecai, and Fraser, and for a view through the eyes of Williams and with an eye to his impact, see Palmer, *Eric Williams*.

8. Orebaugh to Dale, 14 May 1958, Box 1, RG 59 Lot Files, Lot 66D43, Records Relating to Trinidad and Tobago 1955–63 (RG 59 Lot Files: Trinidad & Tobago), NA.

9. State Department to U.S. Embassy-London and U.S. Consulates-Kingston/Port of Spain/Bridgetown, 27 March 1958, 841J.00-TA/3–2758; U.S. Consulate-Port of Spain to State Department, 1 May 1958, 841J.00/5–158, RG 59, NA.

10. Mordecai, *Negotiations*, 116.

11. R. L. Watts, *New Federations: Experiments in the Commonwealth* (Oxford, 1966). No study comparable to this contemporary one has been recently attempted, despite the new availability of archives making the subject an inviting one.

12. Mordecai, *Negotiations*, 118.

13. Dale to Orebaugh, 26 June 1958, Box 1, RG 59 Lot Files: Trinidad & Tobago, NA. Adams sought to leverage his now-strengthened international position over the course of the first year of his premiership. See Adams, *The First Year: Six Broadcasts*, Pamphlet Collection, West Indies Collection, UWICH.

14. Mordecai, *Negotiations*, 123. For a contemporary recap and analysis of this campaign as it neared its first birthday, see James to Adams, 18 May 1959, folder Z17/3/6, Grantley Adams Papers, BDA.

15. State Department to U.S. Embassy-London and U.S. Consulate-Kingston/Port of Spain, 27 March 1958; State Department to U.S. Embassy-London and U.S. Consulates-Kingston/Port of Spain/Bridgetown, 9 April 1958, 841J.00-TA/4–958, RG 59, NA.

16. U.S. Consulate-Port of Spain to State Department, 1 May 1958, 841J.00/5–158.

17. U.S. Consulate-Port of Spain to State Department, 30 July 1958, 841J.00TA/8–858, RG 59; Lightbourne to U.S. Consulate-Port of Spain, 23 December 1958, folder: BWI Federation, Box 1, Classified Records 1956–58, RG 84: Kingston, NA.

18. Intelligence Report, Commissioner/Port of Spain to Under-Secretary of State for External Affairs, 8 October 1958, folder: 10824-K-40 / #1, Box 7323, RG 25, CNA.

19. Palmer, *Eric Williams*, 75. Opinion regarding Williams's prickly personality is impressive in its unanimity. A sampling would include: Port of Spain to Under-Secretary of State for External Affairs, 21 April 1962, folder: 10824-K-40 / #7, Box 5398, RG 25, CNA; U.S. Consulate-Port of Spain to State Department, 11 October 1961, folder: Trinidad, General, 1961–63 (2), Box 165a, NSC Files—Countries, John F. Kennedy Papers (JFKP), JFKL. FO to British Embassy, 27 August 1959, FO 371/139792, UKNA; James to LaCorbiniere, 23 October 1961, folder: 105, Box 5, James Collection, UWISA.

20. "Local West Indians Salute Birth of Federation at Gala Reception," 26 April 1958, *Chicago Defender*; editorials, 4 January and 11 January 1958, *Pittsburgh Courier*.

21. Handbill, "Caribbean Federation Celebration Rally," 22 April 1958, in fiche #005,726–4; American Friends of the West Indian Federation to "Dear Friend," 1 April 1958, in fiche #005,726–3, SC Clipping File.

22. Dudziak, *Civil Rights*, 115–151.

23. U.S. Consulate-Kingston to State Department, September 9, 1958; Resolution, Afro-Caribbean League, 7 September 1958, attached to ibid.; Memorandum of Conversation, Bottomley, Dale, Huyler, 4 September 1958, folder: People, Popular Problems, Box 2, Classified Records 1956–58, RG 84: Kingston, NA.

24. Commissioner/Port of Spain to Under-Secretary of State for External Affairs, 13 August 1959, folder: 10824-K-40 / #1, Box 7323, RG 25, CNA.

25. Dudziak, *Civil Rights*, 47–78; see also Krenn, " 'Unfinished Business': Segregation and U.S. Diplomacy at the 1958 World's Fair," *DH* 20/4 (Fall 1996): 591–613.

26. "Operations Plan for the West Indies," OCB, 22 June 1960, in *FRUS* 1958–1960, 5:444–446.

27. "We knew this," the writer admits, "[but] it was a price we had to pay to get West Indian agreement." Lennox-Boyd to Secretary of State/Commonwealth Relations, 5 November 1958, PREM 11/ 2880, UKNA.

28. U.S. Consulate-Kingston to State Department, 18 August 1958, 841J.3932/ 8–1858, RG 59; Memorandum of Conversation, U.S. Consul et al., 24 February 1959, folder: Political Affairs 1959, Box 3, Classified Records 1959–62, RG 84: Kingston, NA

29. Issa to Manley, 16 September 1959, folder: 4/60/2B/17, Manley Papers, JA.

30. U.S. Consulate-Kingston to State Department, 12 March 1959, folder: Cuban Activities 1959–1961, Box 4, Classified Records 1959–62, RG 84: Kingston, NA; U.S. Consulate-Kingston to State Department, 31 August 1959, folder: Communism 1959, Box 5, Classified Records 1959–62, RG 84: Kingston, NA; "Memorandum on Communist Penetration—The First Phase," unsigned, sent in Issa to Manley, 13 August 1959, folder: 4/60/2B/17, Manley Papers, JA.

31. Intelligence Report, Commissioner/Port of Spain to Under-Secretary of State for External Affairs, 6 May 1959, folder: 10824-K-40 / #1, Box 7323, RG 25, CNA.

32. Minutes of Discussion, State-JCS Meeting, 8 May 1959, folder: 1959, Box 1, RG 59—State-JCS Meetings, NA.

33. Discussion Paper, NSC Planning Board, 15 April 1959, folder: New Independent Countries, Box 6, OSANSAP: NSC Series—Policy Papers Subseries, WHO, DDEL.

34. Palmer, *Eric Williams*, 116; U.S. Consulate-Port of Spain to State Department, 18 March 1959, folder: General 1959, Box 3, Classified Base Agreement Files 1941–61, RG 84: Port of Spain, NA.

35. Intelligence Report, OIR, 24 March 1959, folder: General 1959, Box 3, Classified Base Agreement Files 1941–61, RG 84: Port of Spain, NA; Special National Intelligence Estimate (SNIE) 100–3-59, "Threats to the Stability of the US Military Facilities Position in the Caribbean and Brazil," in *FRUS* 1958–1960, 5:362–369; U.S. Consulate-Port of Spain to State Department, 18 March 1959; Report, "Country Plan for the West Indies and British Guiana," USIS-Port of Spain to USIA, 14 July 1959, folder: Latin America, Box 2, Despatches 1954–63, RG 306, NA.

36. Minutes of Discussion, State-JCS Meeting, 8 May 1959.

37. Ibid.; Report, "U.S. Policy toward the West Indies: Problems and Courses of Action," Author Unidentified, no date (1959), folder: Political—Federation 1959, Box 3, Classified General Records 1953–63, RG 84: Port of Spain, NA.

38. Talking Paper, prepared for Murphy–Caccia Meeting, (July 1959), Box 1, RG 59 Lot Files: Trinidad & Tobago, NA. See also Palmer's chapter on Chaguaramas in *Eric Williams*.

39. "From Slavery to Chaguaramas," Eric Williams, 17 July 1959, in *Forged*, ed. Sutton, 308.

40. FO to British Embassy, 10 June 1959, FO 371 /139789, UKNA.

41. FO to British Embassy, 7 July 1959, FO 371 /139789, UKNA; Dale to White, 6 August 1959, Box 1, RG 59 Lot Files: Trinidad & Tobago, NA. On the radiation dispute, see Palmer, *Eric Williams*, 121–128.

42. Inspection Report, USIA, 11 September 1959, folder: West Indies September 11, 1959, Box 10, Inspection Records and Related Records 1954–62, RG 306; Memorandum of Conversation, Logan, Swihart, et al., 18 September 1959, folder: Secret—

Chaguaramas July–December 1959, Box 5, Classified Base Agreement Files 1941–61, RG 84: Port of Spain, NA.

43. Memorandum of Conversation, U.S. Consul-Kingston at State Department, 30 July 1959, 741E.00/7–3059, RG 59, NA; "monarch" quote from Memorandum of Conversation, Capildeo, Rewinkel, et al., August 28, 1959, folder: Political—Trinidad 1959, Box 3, Classified General Records 1953–63, RG 84: Port of Spain, NA.

44. State Department to U.S. Consulate: Port of Spain, 23 September 1959, folder: Politics—Trinidad 1959, Box 3, Classified General Records 1953–63, RG 84: Port of Spain, NA.

45. Memorandum of Conversation, Habib, Swihart et al., 15 January 1960, folder: Political—Federation 1960, Box 3, Classified General Records 1953–63, RG 84: Port of Spain, NA.

46. Memorandum of Conversation, Irwin et al., 21 September 1959, folder: Secret—Chaguaramas July–December 1959, Box 5, Classified Base Agreement Files 1941–61, RG 84: Port of Spain, NA; Talking Paper, prepared for Murphy–Caccia Meeting, undated; Manley to Williams, 26 February 1960, folder: 4/60/2A/19, Manley Papers, JA.

47. Wallace, *Caribbean*, 138–142. See also Bustamante to Manley, 2 May 1960; Bustamante to Manley, 4 May 1960; Bustamante to Manley, 11 May 1960; Bustamante to Manley, 17 May 1960, folder: 4/60/2A/8, Manley Papers, JA.

48. Memorandum of Conversation, White, Swihart, Sinanan et al., 13 October 1959, Box 1, RG 59 Lot Files: Trinidad & Tobago, NA.

49. Letter, Caccia to Lloyd, 18 December 1959, FO 371 /139754, UKNA.

50. Rabe, *Eisenhower and Latin America*, 117. Both Rabe and Alan McPherson trace this conclusion from its first evidence in the 1958 Nixon trip. McPherson, *Yankee No! Anti-Americanism in U.S.–Latin American Relations* (Cambridge, 2003).

51. Memorandum of Conversation, Habib, Swihart et al., 15 January 1960; Letter, Moline to Swihart, 29 January 1960, Box 1, RG 59 Lot Files: Trinidad & Tobago, NA.

52. Report, "Country Assessment Report," USIS-Port of Spain to USIA, 24 February 1960, folder: Latin America, Box 2, Despatches 1954–63, RG 306, NA.

53. "Statement of U.S. Policy toward the West Indies," NSC 6002/1, 21 March 1960, in *FRUS* 1958–1960, 5:433–443. On the State–Defense clash, see Swihart to Moline, 16 December 1959; on the State–Treasury clash, see Swihart to Moline, 21 October 1959, folder: Political—Trinidad 1959, Box 3, Classified General Records 1953–63, RG 84: Port of Spain, NA.

54. Memorandum of Conversation, Habib, Swihart et al., 15 January 1960.

55. "U.S. Policy toward the West Indies," Author Unidentified, no date (1959).

56. U.S. Embassy-London to State Department, 22 January 1960, folder: Political—Federation 1960, Box 3, Classified General Records 1953–63, RG 84: Port of Spain, NA; Swihart to Moline, 10 February 1960, Box 1, RG 59 Lot Files: Trinidad & Tobago, NA.

57. *NYT*, 31 December 1959; Smathers to U.S. Consulate-Port of Spain, 19 December 1958, 841J.00/12–1958; State Department to Smathers, 8 January 1959, 841J.00/1–859, RG 59, NA; "Perspectives for Our Party," Williams, 22 March 1961, in Cudjoe, *Speaks*, 210, 228.

58. U.S. Embassy-London to State Department, 2 February 1960, folder: Politics—Federation 1960, Box 3, Classified General Records 1953–63, RG 84: Port of Spain, NA.

59. Kohler to Dulles, 16 February 1960, in *FRUS* 1958–1960, 5:425–426.

60. Note, State Department, 22 January 1960, folder: West Indies, US Policy Toward, 1958–60, Box 19, OSANSAP, NSC Series—Briefing Subseries, WHO, DDEL;

Memo of Discussion at the 437th Meeting of the NSC, 17 March 1960, in *FRUS* 1958–1960, 5:427–433.

61. Ibid.

62. Rabe, *Eisenhower*, 129.

63. Trinidad Governor to Colonial Secretary, 1 April 1960; FO to British Embassy-Washington, 5 April 1960; Clipping, *The Nation* (Trinidad), 8 April 1960, in CO 1031 /3058, UKNA.

64. Moline to Swihart, 11 April 1960, Box 1, RG 59 Lot Files: Trinidad & Tobago, NA. The consul predicted Williams would get at most ten thousand marchers.

65. "We Are Independent," Eric Williams, 22 April 1960, in *Forged*, ed. Sutton, 313–314.

66. Wallace, *Caribbean*, 168.

67. *Trinidad Guardian*, 23 April 1960.

68. West Indies Governor to CO, 5 September 1959, CO 1031 /2956, UKNA; U.S. Consulate-Port of Spain to Swihart, 29 January 1960, folder: Trinidad 1955–1963, Box 1, RG 59 Lot Files: Caribbean Dependencies, NA.

69. Mordecai, *Negotiations*, 303; U.S. Consulate: Port of Spain to State Department, 3 June 1960, folder: Politics—Trinidad 1960, Box 3, Classified General Records 1953–63, RG 84: Port of Spain, NA.

70. Belk to Gray, 6 April 1960, folder: Cuba Situation 1959–60 #1, OSANSAP: NSC Series—Policy Papers Subseries, WHO, DDEL.

71. Smith to Harr, 19 April 1960, folder: Latin America—US Policy Toward, 1954–60 #1, Box 12, OSANSAP: NSC Series—Policy Papers Subseries, WHO, DDEL. On British Guiana, see Rabe, *British Guiana*.

72. U.S. Consulate: Kingston to State Department, 28 July 1960, folder: Federation 1960–61, Box 5, Classified Records 1959–62, RG 84: Kingston, NA; McGregor to Willoughby, 22 March 1960, folder: Jamaica 1955–63, Box 1, RG 59 Lot Files: Caribbean Dependencies, NA. A State-JCS committee had pondered this same option. Meeting Notes, State-JCS Meeting, 11 March 1960, folder: State-JCS, 11 March 1960, Box 1, RG 59—State-JCS Meetings, NA.

73. Macmillan to Eisenhower, 25 July 1960; Letter, Macmillan to Eisenhower, 22 July 1960, folder: Macmillan, Harold, January 1—August 4 1960 (#3), Box 25, Whitman File—International Series, DDEP, DDEL.

74. U.S. Consulate-Port of Spain to Secretary of State, 17 August 1960.

75. Memorandum of Conversation, Canadian, FO, CO, CRO, and State officials, 28 March 1960, folder: 10824-E-40 / #2.2, Box 7322, RG 25, CNA.

76. "Semi-Annual Appraisal of Policy towards the West Indies (NSC-6002/1)," 16 September 1960, folder: West Indies, Box 8, OSANSAP: OCB Series—Subject Subseries, WHO, DDEL.

77. "Strategic Appraisal of Trinidad, B.W.I.," Author Unidentified, 19 October 1960, 741J.00/10–1960, RG 59, NA; Secretary of Defense to Special Assistant to the President, 18 July 1960, folder: Base Rights 1957–1960 #4, Box 12, OSANSAP: NSC Series—Policy Papers Subseries, WHO; Briefing, NSC, 19 December 1960, folder: Continental Defense, U.S. Policy On 1955–1961 #1, Box 5, OSANSAP: NSC Series—Briefing Subseries, WHO, DDEL.

78. Jamaica Governor to Colonial Secretary, 10 April 1961, CO 1031/3624, UKNA.

79. Fulbright to Eisenhower, 29 January 1960; Fulbright to Herter, 2 February 1960, both attached to 841J.2569/2–160, RG 59, NA.

80. Riddleberger to Mutual Security Program Coordinator, 6 October 1960; Atwood to White, 12 October 1960, Box 1, RG 59 Lot Files: Caribbean Dependencies, NA.

81. Report, "Strategic Appraisal of Trinidad," 19 October 1960, folder: West Indies Federation, Box 149, RG 59: PPS 1957–61, NA; Radio Interview of Ivan White, 23 November 1960, Box 1, RG 59 Lot Files: Caribbean Dependencies, NA.

82. Talking Paper, State Department, 8 December 1960, Box 1, RG 59 Lot Files: Caribbean Dependencies, NA.

83. Scope Paper for Base Talks, Author Unidentified, 3 October 1960, folder: Defense Affairs: DEF 15 Bases—British West Indies, Box 1, RG 59 Lot Files, Records of the Deputy Under-Secretary for Political Affairs: Correspondence Concerning the Establishment and Defense of U.S. Military and Naval Bases Overseas 1957–63, (Overseas Bases Records 1957–63), NA.

84. Swihart to Moline, 24 October 1960; Moline to Swihart, 14 November 1960, Box 1, RG 59 Lot Files: Trinidad & Tobago, NA. The admiral was Wellings, involved since July 1957.

85. Kohler to Merchant, 8 December 1960, Box 1, RG 59 Lot Files: Trinidad & Tobago, NA.

86. Minute, FO, 23 December 1960, FO 371 /156477, UKNA.

87. Manley to Williams, 15 December 1960, folder: 4/60/2A/19, Manley Papers, JA.

88. Whitney to Secretary, 16 December 1960, folder: Defense Affairs, Box 1, RG 59 Lot Files, Overseas Bases Records 1957–63, NA.

89. Wallace, *Caribbean*, 180. Even Williams sounded friendly notes, affirming publicly that "all had been satisfied with [the] talks." *Nation*, 6 January 1961, Mfilm #2855, West Indian & Special Collections, UWIM.

90. CO to Prime Minister, 14 March 1961, CO 1031 /3611, UKNA.

91. A British review concluded that the "only [post-independence] threat [will be] political unrest. We have discounted any limited or global war threat in view of U.S.... influence in the area." Defense Ministry to CO, 9 September 1959, CO 1031 /2956, UKNA.

92. Manley to Williams, 15 December 1960; Manley to James, 6 June 1960, folder: #105, Box 5, James Collection, UWISA. Most of the regional press echoed this line. *Nation*, 4 August 1961, Mfilm #2855, West Indian & Special Collections, UWIM. Manley had the option of contesting the issue in the legislature, but thought the chances of success were better in a referendum. See Minutes of W.I.F.L.P. Executive Meeting (Port of Spain), 16 June 1960, folder: Z17/3/13, Grantley Adams Papers, BDA.

93. Letter, Commissioner/Port of Spain to Under-Secretary for External Affairs, 18 October 1960, folder: 10824K-40 / #1, Box 7323, RG 25, CNA; Roberts to Domingo, 11 June 1960, folder: #18, Box 2B, MS 353—Roberts Papers, NLJ.

Chapter 6

1. Stephen Rabe, "Controlling Revolutions: Latin America, the Alliance for Progress, and Cold War Anti-Communism," in *Kennedy's Quest for Victory: American Foreign Policy, 1961–63*, ed. Thomas Paterson (New York, 1989), 111.

2. See Cary Fraser, "The New Frontier of Empire in the Caribbean: The Transfer of Power in British Guiana, 1961–1964," *IHR* 22/3 (September 2000): 583–611; and Robert Waters and Gordon Daniels, "The World's Longest General Strike: The AFL-CIO, the CIA, and British Guiana," *DH* 29 (April 2005): 279–307.

3. "Situation and Prospects in the West Indies Federation," Office of Intelligence and Research, 30 January 1961, folder: American Republics 1960–61, Box 149, RG 59: PPS 1957–1961, NA.

4. "Cuban Hurricane over the Caribbean," *NYT Magazine*, 7 May 1961; "Shadow of Castro's Cuba Bulks Large in West Indies," *New York Herald Tribune*, 11 January

1961, in Dossier, FO, 17 January 1961, FO 371 /156478, UKNA; and earlier coverage such as "America's Sea of Trouble: The Caribbean," *U.S. News & World Report* (*USNWR*), 10 August 1959, in fiche #005,721–6, SC Clipping File; and "Turmoil in the Caribbean: Will Communists Take Over Cuba?" *USNWR*, 27 July 1951, in fiche #005,732–1, SC Clipping File; OCB to Bundy, 1 February 1961, folder: Latin American—General January–February 1961, Box 215a, NSC Files (NSCF): Regional Security, JFKP, JFKL.

5. Weaver to Kennedy, 16 February 1961, folder: West Indies 1961, Box 128a, President's Official Files (POF): Countries, JFKP, JFKL.

6. During his tour, Manley also spoke at the National Press Club and met with Adam Clayton Powell to discuss the federation and U.S. immigration. "In the Nation: A Brighter Seascape in the Caribbean," Arthur Krock, *NYT*, 27 April 1961; British West Indies Caribbean Labour Office to Manley, 1 May 1961, folder: 4/60/2A/40, Manley Papers, JA.

7. Macmillan to Kennedy, 7 April 1961, folder: UK—Macmillan Correspondence January 26–April 7, 1961, Box 171a, NSCF: Countries, JFKP, JFKL.

8. U.S. Consulate-Kingston to State Department, 2 April 1961, folder: Jamaica—Security—1961–63, Box 120, POF: Countries, JFKP, JFKL.

9. Memorandum of Conversation at Inter-American Development Bank, Manley, MacFarlane, et al., 20 April 1961; Memorandum of Conversation, Manley, Berle, et al., 18 April 1961, folder: unlabeled, Box 1, RG 59 Lot Files, Lot 66D17, Records Relating to Jamaican Affairs 1955–63 (RG 59 Lot Files: Jamaican Affairs 1955–63), NA. Manley was unwilling to commit to the OAS until it was clear this would not affect British grants-in-aid. Manley's trip won him great esteem back home; a Jamaican Broadcasting Company (JBC) commentator opined that no other Caribbean leader "would have commanded the respect and attention he received." Transcript, JBC, 25 April 1961, folder: #98, Semi-Public Records 3/9/1 (JBC), JA.

10. On the Notting Hill race riots, see Edward Pilkington, *Beyond the Mother Country: West Indians and the Notting Hill White Riots* (London, 1988). Memorandum of Conversation, Lewis, White, et al., 17 October 1961, folder: Federation 1960–61, Box 5, Classified Records 1959–62, RG 84: Kingston, NA.

11. Aide-Memoire, "For President's Personal Secretary as Requested by the President at the White House When He Saw White and Manley," unsigned, undated, folder: 4/60/2A/40, Manley Papers, JA. Williams told U.S. Consul Moline that "he felt odds tipping slightly against...federation." Telegram, U.S. Consulate-Port of Spain to Secretary of State, 10 April 1961, folder: Jamaica January 1961–July 1962—A, Box 123, NSCF: Countries, JFKP, JFKL. See also Jamaica Governor to WIF Governor-General, 7 March 1961, folder: Z17/3/26, Grantley Adams Papers, BDA.

12. Memorandum of Conversation, Kennedy, Manley, and White, 19 April 1961, folder: Jamaica January 1961–July 1962—A, Box 123, NSCF: Countries, JFKP, JFKL.

13. Aide-Memoire, "For President"; White to Manley, 30 May 1961; Manley to White, 24 June 1961, folder: 4/60/2A/40, Manley Papers, JA.

14. Caccia to CO, 29 April 1961, CO 1031 /3890, UKNA; U.S. Consulate-Kingston to Secretary of State, 25 May 1961, folder: Cuban Activities 1959–61, Box 4, Classified Records 1959–62, RG 84: Kingston, NA.

15. British Embassy to Jamaica Governor, 8 May 1961, CO 1031/3624, UKNA; Memorandum of Conversation, White House, 19 April 1961; Manley to Goodwin, 26 April 1961, folder: 4/60/2A/40, Manley Papers, JA.

16. The Caribbean Organization, however, did not last long, going downhill from the collapse of the WIF to its final disbanding in 1965. See Wallace, *Caribbean*, 54–55.

17. Statement at Senate Hearings on SJ-Res. 75, State Department, 19 April 1961, folder: Caribbean Commission (1), Box 5, John W. Hanes Jr. Papers 1950–70, DDEL.

18. "Except perhaps in British Guiana," the U.S. Ambassador in London put it, "Castroism is likely to have little impact on the British West Indies." U.S. Embassy-London to Secretary of State, 26 April 1961, folder: Cuban Activities 1959–61, Box 4, Classified Records 1959–62, RG 84: Kingston, NA.

19. See Munroe, *Cold War*; and Munroe, *Politics*.

20. Manley to Kennedy, 10 July 1961, folder: Jamaica (January 1961–July 1962)—A, Box 123, NSCF: Countries, JFKP, JFKL; Manley to Macleod, 26 April 1961, CO 1031 /3624; British Embassy-Washington to Jamaica Governor, 8 May 1961, CO 1031 /3624, UKNA.

21. Fitzgerald to Bell, 16 June 1961, folder: Reading File January 1—June 30 (#1), Box 37, Dennis A. Fitzgerald Papers, DDEL.

22. High Commissioner/London to Under-Secretary for External Affairs, 30 May 1961, folder: 10824-K-40 / #1, Box 7323, RG 25, CNA.

23. Ashton and Killingray, *BDEE: The West Indies*, xlii.

24. Fraser, *Ambivalent*, 158; Mordecai, *Negotiations*, 122–23. Eric Williams, for example, had claimed that Manley and Bustamante were conspiring, both against him and to torpedo the WIF. Memorandum of Conversation, U.S. Consulate-Port of Spain, 8 April 1961, folder: Trinidad 1955–1963, Box 1, RG 59 Lot Files: Caribbean Dependencies, NA. In July, Moline reported another Williams rant against Manley. U.S. Consulate-Port of Spain to Secretary of State, 15 July 1961, folder: Trinidad—General 1961–1963 #1, Box 165a, NSCF: Countries, JFKP, JFKL. These were not the first times when personalities and interests had clashed, but by summer 1961 the leaders were not even on speaking terms. See Wallace, *Caribbean*, 149–153, 185–191.

25. U.S. Consulate-Kingston to State Department, 16 May 1961; U.S. Consulate-Kingston to State Department, 23 August 1961, folder: Political Affairs 1961, Box 4, Classified Records 1959–62, RG 84: Kingston, NA.

26. Manley to Goodwin, 26 April 1961.

27. Munroe to Jackson, 6 September 1961, folder: Mu–Misc, Box 72, C.D. Jackson Papers 1931–1967, DDEL.

28. Colonial Secretary to Prime Minister, 7 June 1961, PREM 11 /3236, UKNA.

29. Manley to Williams, 4 August 1961, folder: 4/60/2A/19, Manley Papers, JA; McGregor to State Department, 16 May 1961, Box 1, RG 59 Lot Files: Jamaican Affairs 1955–63, NA.

30. Jamaica Governor to CO, 21 August 1961, CO 1031 /3452, UKNA; Manley to Macleod, 25 August 1961, folder: 4/60/2B/24, Manley Papers, JA; U.S. Embassy to U.S. Consulates-Kingston & Port of Spain, 13 September 1961, folder: (unlabeled), Box 4, Classified Records 1959–62, RG 84: Kingston, NA.

31. U.S. Consulate-Kingston to Secretary of State, 18 September 1961, folder: (unlabeled), Box 4, Classified Records 1959–62, RG 84: Kingston, NA. Macleod and Manley agreed: "All the reports I see speak of your campaign gaining in strength. I am delighted to hear that you are in such good spirits about it and am eagerly awaiting the result." Macleod to Manley, 14 September 1961, folder: 4/60/2B/24, Manley Papers, JA; U.S. Consulate-Kingston to Secretary of State, 18 September 1961, folder: (unlabeled), Box 4, Classified Records 1959–62, RG 84: Kingston, NA.

32. *Daily Gleaner*, 18 September 1961; Editorial, 17 September 1961; "PNP Sure of Referendum Win," 19 September 1961, *Trinidad Guardian*.

33. Hennings to CO, 28 September 1961, CO 1031 /3278 #75, document 161 in Ashton and Killingray, *BDEE: The West Indies.*

34. Letter, James to LaCorbiniere, 23 October 1961, folder: #105, Box 5, James Collection, UWISA. He added, in contrast, that Williams was "no George Washington [nor even] a Kwame Nkrumah." James to Manley, 23 September 1961, folder: 4/60/2B/25, Manley Papers, JA.

35. "Jamaica Balks," *NYT*, 21 September 1961; Editorial, *Trinidad Guardian*, 21 September 1961.

36. U.S. Consulate-Kingston to Secretary of State, 27 September 1961, folder: (unlabeled), Box 4, Classified Records 1959–62, RG 84: Kingston, NA. Manley was wrong, for example, about the rural vote—2-to-1 against—and a U.S. postmortem interpreted this as a clear "protest vote against the PNP." Report, ICA/USOM-Kingston, 3 November 1961, folder: Political: Federation 1961, Box 4, Classified General Records 1953–63, RG 84: Port of Spain, NA.

37. The PNM publication *Nation* concluded that in Jamaica "federation as an abstract idea failed to prevail against starvation, a fact of daily life." "Why the PNP Failed," *Nation*, 22 September 1961, Mfilm#2855, West Indian & Special Collections, UWIM. For the Canadian analysis, see Summary of Report, Dept. of External Affairs, 7 November 1961, folder: 10824-F-40 / #6, Box 5398, RG 25, CNA. Commissioner/ Port of Spain to Under-Secretary of External Affairs, 9 October 1961, folder: 10824-F-40 / #6, Box 5398, RG 25, CNA.

38. "[Bustamante] is still a loyal subject of HMG and presumably would adhere to [its] advice." Jamaica Governor to Colonial Secretary, 22 September 1961; Prime Minister to Colonial Secretary, 22 September 1961, PREM 11 /4074, UKNA.

39. U.S. Consulate-Kingston to Secretary of State, 18 September 1961 (#2), folder: (unlabeled), Box 4, Classified Records 1959–62, RG 84: Kingston, NA. Manley was deeply hurt by the outcome, even apologizing to U.S. officials for it. Manley to Goodwin, 7 December 1961, folder: Jamaica, Box WH-12a, White House Files, Arthur Schlesinger Papers, JFKL. Some "federal" affairs involving Jamaica, such as the University of the West Indies, would continue.

40. Report, "Future of West Indies Federation in Doubt," prepared for Bundy, 25 September 1961, folder: West Indies, General 1/1/61–7/30/63, Box 204a, NSCF: Countries, JFKP, JFKL; *Nation*, 6 October 1961, Mfilm#2855, West Indian & Special Collections, UWIM

41. Isaacs to Manley, 22 September 1961, folder: 4/60/2A/21, Manley Papers, JA.

42. Message to Ottawa, Author Unidentified, 26 October 1961, folder: 10824-F-40 / #6, Box 5398, RG 25, CNA; U.S. Consulate-Kingston to Secretary of State, 29 September 1961, folder: (unlabeled), Box 4, Classified Records 1959–62, RG 84: Kingston, NA.

43. Memorandum of Conversation, U.S. Consulate-Port of Spain, 29 September 1961, folder: Trinidad 1961, Box 3, Classified General Records 1953–63, RG 84: Port of Spain, NA; U.S. Consulate-Kingston to Secretary of State, 2 October 1961, folder: (unlabeled), Box 4, Classified Records 1959–62, RG 84: Kingston, NA; U.S. Consulate-Port of Spain to State, 11 October 1961, folder: Trinidad, General, 1961–63 (2 of 2), Box 165a, NSCF: Countries, JFKP, JFKL.

44. U.S. Embassy-London to State Department, 22 December 1961, folder: Politics—General 1959–61, Box 3, Classified General Records 1953–63, RG 84: Port of Spain; Report, "Future of West Indies Federation," 25 September 1961; Memorandum of Conversation, U.S. Consulate-Port of Spain, 29 September 1961; Report, "Future of West Indies Federation," 25 September 1961; Memorandum of

Conversation, Moline, Williams, et al., 29 September 1961; U.S. Consulate-Port of Spain to Secretary of State, 30 September 1961, folder: Trinidad 1961, Box 3, Classified General Records 1953–63, RG 84: Port of Spain, NA.

45. White to Burdett, 17 November 1961, Box 1, RG 59 Lot Files: Trinidad & Tobago, NA; Commissioner/Port of Spain to Under-Secretary for External Affairs, 19 December 1961, folder 10824-F-40 / #7, Box 5398, RG 25, CNA.

46. Secretary of State to U.S. Consulate-Kingston, 12 October 1961; RN to WO, "Importance of Trinidad to NATO," 3 December 1961, WO 336 /18, UKNA. The United States agreed. Bundy to Burdett, 22 March 1962, folder: Defense Affairs—Defense 15 BWI, Box 1, RG 59 Lot Files, Overseas Bases Records 1957–63, NA.

47. Galbraith to State Department, 22 December 1961, folder: Political Affairs 1961, Box 4, Classified Records 1959–62, RG 84: Kingston, NA.

48. U.S. Consulate-Port of Spain to Secretary of State, 23 December 1961, folder: Trinidad, General, 1961–63 (2 of 2), Box 165a, NSCF: Countries, JFKP, JFKL; Manley to Blackburne, 16 December 1961, folder: 4/60/2A/52, Manley Papers, JA; Galbraith to Foster, 22 December 1961, folder: Political—General 1959–61, Box 3, Classified General Records 1953–63, RG 84: Port of Spain, NA.

49. Brief, CO for Colonial Secretary, January 1962, CO 1031 /3611, UKNA.

50. U.S. Consulate-Port of Spain to Secretary of State, 16 January 1962, folder: Trinidad, General, 1961–63 (2 of 2), Box 165a, NSCF: Countries, JFKP, JFKL.

51. Galbraith to Foster, 22 December 1961.

52. U.S. Consulate-Port of Spain to State Department, 11 October 1961, folder: Trinidad, General 1961–63 (#2), Box 165a, NSCF: Countries, JFKP, JFKL; Christensen to Burdett, 7 June 1962, Box 1, RG 59 Lot Files: Trinidad & Tobago, NA.

53. Galbraith to Foster, 22 December 1961.

54. Commissioner/Port of Spain to Under-Secretary of State for External Affairs, 23 January 1962, folder: 10824-F-40 / #7, Box 5398, RG 25, CNA.

55. Bundy to Burdett, 22 March 1962; Commissioner/Port of Spain to Under-Secretary of State for External Affairs, 28 March 1962, folder: 10824-F-40 / #7, Box 5398, RG 25, CNA.

56. "Massa Day Done," 22 March 1961, in Cudjoe, *Speaks*, 261. For an analysis of the speech and its importance, see Palmer, *Eric Williams*, 22–25.

57. U.S. Consulate-Bridgetown to Secretary of State, 16 March 1962, folder: West Indies—General January 1961–July 1963, Box 204a, NSCF: Countries, JFKP, JFKL.

58. British Embassy-Washington to FO, 2 January 1962, FO 371 /162586, UKNA.

59. Commissioner to Under-Secretary of State, 21 April 1962; Commissioner/Port of Spain to Under-Secretary of State for External Affairs, 12 April 1962, folder: 10824-F-40 / #7, Box 5398, RG 25, CNA.

60. Christensen to Burdett, 29 May 1962, folder: Political Affairs—Trinidad, Box 6, Classified General Records 1953–63, RG 84: Port of Spain, NA.

61. Memorandum of Conversation, Christensen and Williams, 23 May 1962, folder: Political Affairs—Trinidad, Box 6, Classified General Records 1953–63, RG 84: Port of Spain, NA.

62. Christensen to Burdett, 14 June 1962, Box 1, RG 59 Lot Files: Trinidad & Tobago, NA.

63. Memorandum of Conversation, Kennedy, Bustamante, et al., 27 June 1962, folder: Jamaica (January 1961–1962)-B; Rusk to Kennedy, 28 May 1962, folder: Jamaica 1961–62—A, Box 123, NSCF: Countries, JFKP, JFKL.

64. The compromise solution was to limit Cuban participation to the local Cuban consul already in Jamaica. U.S. Consulate-Kingston to State Department, 14 May

1962, folder: Jamaica 1961–62—A, Box 123; Secretary of State to U.S. Embassy-London, 9 August 1962, folder: Trinidad, General 1961–63 (#2), Box 165a, NSCF: Countries, JFKP, JFKL.

65. "Jamaica Scope Paper," State Department, 22 June 1962, folder: Jamaica 1961–62—A, Box 123, NSCF: Countries, JFKP, JFKL.

66. Document Attached to Brief, State Department for Kennedy, 26 June 1962, folder: Jamaica 1961–62—B, Box 123, NSCF: Countries, JFKP, JFKL; U.S. Embassy-London to Secretary of State, 31 July 1962, folder: Jamaica 1961–62—B; Rusk to U.S. Consulate-Kingston and U.S. Embassy-London, 3 August 1962, folder: Jamaica (August 1962–May 1963)—A, Box 123, NSC Files: Countries, JFKP, JFKL.

67. Scope Paper, "Jamaican Independence Celebrations," attached to Memorandum, Rewinkel to Burdett, 31 July 1962, Box 2, RG 59 Lot Files: Caribbean Dependencies, NA; U.S. Embassy-London to Secretary of State, 6 July 1962, folder: Jamaica 1961–62—B, Box 123, NSC Files: Countries, JFKP, JFKL.

68. Munroe, *Decolonization*, 164.

69. Nettleford, "Mission to Africa: The Rastafari and the Nation," in *Manley*, Nettleford, ed., lxviii, 277–278.

70. Underlining the political costs of the referendum not only to the federation but also to Jamaica's prospects once the result forced Manley out, a friend wrote him to lament racialism's rise: "For Jamaica? With the Bustas and the Millard Johnsons? One can only pray." Elkins to Manley, 19 September 1961, folder: 4/60/2B/25, Manley Papers, JA.

71. Intelligence Report, "Situation and Prospects in the West Indies Federation," 30 January 1961, folder: West Indies Federation, Box 149, RG 59: PPS 1957–61, NA. The leader was the son of the Rev. Claudius Henry, who had bilked thousands of Jamaicans via the sale of fraudulent "return tickets" to Africa. Nettleford, *Manley*, 278; *NYT*, 4 April, 16 September 1961; 17 August, 16 September, 1 November 1960.

72. "Jamaican Minister Speaks at Howard," 8 February 1960; "Jamaican Leaders Talk to Students," 8 March 1962, *The Hilltop*, Microfilm M07—Mi4932, Reading Room, MSRC.

73. See Mary C. Waters, *Black Identities: West Indian Immigrant Dreams and American Realities* (Cambridge, 2001), 34–43.

74. Draft of NSC-6002, 25 January 1960, folder: West Indies, US Policy Toward, 1958–60, Box 19, WHO, OSANSA, NSC Series—Briefing Subseries, DDEL. Referring to discrimination experienced by African diplomats in Washington, one JBC commentator noted that "America's race relations has [*sic*] now become a key issue of Foreign Relations, and in the Cold War this is crucial." Commentary, JBC, 7 July 1961, folder: #159, Semi-Public Records 3/9/1 (JBC), JA.

75. Report, "Situation and Prospects in the W.I.F.," 30 January 1961.

76. *Daily Gleaner*, 18 September 1961.

77. Wilkins to Bustamante, 3 August 1962, folder: Staff—Roy Wilkins—Jamaica Trip 1962, Box A316, General Office Files Part III, NAACP Papers, LOC.

78. Commissioner to Under-Secretary of State, 21 April 1962.

79. Brubeck to O'Donnell, 21 June 1962, folder: June 10–21, 1962, Box 3, White House Staff Files: Bundy File, State Department Memoranda, JFKP, JFKL. Kennedy agreed, but as late as 30 July still had not settled on a speaker. O'Donnell to Brubeck, 30 July 1962, folder: July 30–August 9, 1962, Box 3, White House Staff Files: Bundy File, State Department Memoranda, JFKP, JFKL.

80. *Daily Gleaner*, 31 July 1962. Most of the U.S. delegation was able to attend both ceremonies.

81. See, for example, "Trinidad Become [*sic*] Nation with Dr. Williams its Firm Leader," *Chicago Defender (National Edition)*, 1–7 September 1962; and "'Square' Ceremony," *Pittsburgh Courier*, 8 September 1962.

82. Moore wrote that "Though conscious of deep fraternal feelings toward our fellow Caribbeans in Jamaica and Trinidad-Tobago, we could not take part joyously in these independence celebrations because...almost as many people in the [other colonies] yet remained colonial subjects of Britain, still denied the basic human right of self-determination...The national liberation movement of the Caribbean people has not been accomplished, since all these people are not yet free and independent nor united." Richard B. Moore, "Independent Caribbean Nationhood—Has it Been Achieved or Set Back?" in Turner and Turner, *Moore*, 291, 301.

83. *Daily Gleaner*, 3 September 1969, quoted in *Manley*, ed. Nettleford, 293; Diary entry, 9 August 1962, Manley Diary, cited in *Manley*, ed. Nettleford, 311.

84. "To Plough the Land and Gather the Fruit," Speech Delivered at Opening of 1st Parliament, Norman Manley, 6 August 1962, in *Manley*, ed. Nettleford, 312.

85. Manley managed to be both, as did the *New York Times* in welcoming his new country and saluting his rival: "Life is not going to be easy for Jamaica [but Bustamante's] zest and optimism will be helpful ingredients to usher a new nation into a troubled world." *NYT*, 6 August 1962; Commentary, JBC, 7 August 1962, folder: #497, Semi-Public Records 3/9/1 (JBC), JA.

86. U.S. Consulate-Port of Spain to State Department, 6 August 1962, folder: Political Affairs—Trinidad 1962, Box 6, Classified General Records 1953–63, RG 84: Port of Spain, NA.

87. *Time*, 7 September 1962, in fiche #005,307–5, SC Clipping File.

88. *Trinidad Guardian*, 30 August 1962; "Independence Address," Rudranath Capildeo, 31 August 1962, in Capildeo, *Lotus and the Dagger: The Capildeo Speeches, 1957–1994* (Port of Spain, 1994), 108.

89. "Independence Youth Rally," Eric Williams, 30 August 1962, in *Forged*, ed. Sutton, 328; "Independence Day Address," Eric Williams, 31 August 1962, in Cudjoe, *Speaks*, 266.

90. *Time*, 7 September 1962.

91. Memorandum of Conversation, Williams, Hastie, Hamilton, et al., 2 September 1962, Box 1, RG 59 Lot Files: Trinidad & Tobago, NA; Hastie to Rusk and Kennedy, 13 September 1962, folder: Trinidad, General 1961–63 (#2), Box 165a, NSCF: Countries, JFKP, JFKL.

92. For an analysis of the WIF collapse, see Wallace, *Caribbean*, 214–227. On the impact of the Jamaican referendum, see Noel Brown, "Jamaica and the West Indies Federation: A Case Study on the Problems of Political Integration," Ph.D. diss. (Yale University, 1963), 354–417.

93. James to Adams, 3 April 1961, folder: #105, Box 5, James Collection, UWISA.

94. Nkrumah to Manley et al., 8 June 1962, folder: 4/60/2B/27, Manley Papers, JA.

95. Quoted in *NYT*, 8 August 1962.

Conclusion

1. 1966 was also the year British Guiana achieved independence, although that colony had of course not been part of the WIF.

2. For a chilling account of the overlap of violent crime, postcolonial politics, and the mainland connection for an independent Jamaica, see Laurie Gunst, *Born Fi' Dead: A Journey Through the Jamaican Posse Underworld* (New York, 1996).

3. W. E. B. DuBois describes "double consciousness" in the chapter "Of Our Spiritual Strivings" in DuBois, *The Souls of Black Folk* (Chicago, 1903). On the "multi-layered" identities of West Indians abroad, see Waters, *Black Identities*, 47–49.

4. Shalini Puri, *The Caribbean Postcolonial: Social Equality, Post-nationalism, and Cultural Hybridity* (New York, 2004). See also Aisha Khan, *Callaloo Nation: Metaphors of Race and Religious Identity among South Asians in Trinidad* (Durham, 2004).

5. Amy Chua, *World on Fire: How Exporting Free Market Democracy Breeds Ethnic Hatred and Global Instability* (New York, 2004).

6. Connelly, "Taking off the Cold War Lens."

Bibliography

Manuscript and Archival Collections

National Archives (II), College Park, Maryland
    Record Group 38, Records of the Department of the Navy
    Record Group 40, Records of the Department of Commerce
    Record Group 59, Records of the Department of State
    Record Group 84, Records of Foreign Service Posts of the Department of State
    Record Group 218, Records of the Joint Chiefs of Staff
    Record Group 273, Records of the National Security Council
    Record Group 306, Records of the United States Information Agency
    Record Group 319, Records of the Army Chief of Staff
    Record Group 338, Records of Army Commands
    Record Group 353, Records of Interdepartmental/Intradepartmental Committees
    Record Group 469, Records of U.S. Foreign Assistance Agencies
Library of Congress, Washington, D.C.
    Benjamin Gerig Papers
    Averell Harriman Papers
    Rayford Logan Papers
    NAACP Papers
Moorland-Spingarn Research Center, Howard University, Washington, D.C.
    E. Franklin Frazier Papers
    Alain Locke Papers
    Rayford Logan Papers
    Dabu Gizenga Collection on Kwame Nkrumah
Bethune Museum and Archives, Washington, D.C.
    National Council of Negro Women Papers

Schomburg Center for Research in Black Culture, New York, New York
    Phelps-Stokes Collection
    W. Alphaeus Hunton Papers
    Ralph J. Bunche Papers
    St. Clair Drake Papers
    George Padmore Letters
Franklin D. Roosevelt Library, Hyde Park, New York
    Franklin D. Roosevelt Papers as President
    Stephen Early Papers
    Henry Field Papers
    Leon Henderson Papers
    Harry Hopkins Papers
    Charles W. Taussig Papers
    Rexford Tugwell Papers
    Sumner Welles Papers
    John Winant Papers
Harry S. Truman Library, Independence, Missouri
    Harry S. Truman Papers as President
    Dean Acheson Memoranda of Conversation
    Oral History Files
    Wilson Beale Papers
    Wallace Campbell Papers
    Oscar Chapman Papers
    Clark Clifford Papers
    Robert L. Dennison Papers
    James Earley Papers
    George Elsey Papers
    Kenneth Hechler Papers
    David Lloyd Papers
    Edward G. Miller. Jr., Papers
    Philleo Nash Papers
    Charles G. Ross Papers
    Stephen Spingarn Papers
Dwight D. Eisenhower Library, Abilene, Kansas
    Dwight D. Eisenhower Records as President
    Dwight D. Eisenhower Papers as President
    White House Office Files
    Sherman Adams Papers
    Evan P. Aurand Papers
    Leonard Burchman Papers
    John F. Dulles Papers
    Dennis A. Fitzgerald Papers
    James C. Hagerty Papers
    John W. Hanes Jr., Papers
    Bryce Harlow Papers
    Christian Herter Papers
    C. D. Jackson Papers and Records
John F. Kennedy Library, Boston, Massachusetts
    John F. Kennedy Papers as President
    Oral History Files
    Arthur Schlesinger Papers

Seeley G. Mudd Library, Princeton University
 Hamilton Fish Armstrong Papers
 Allen W. Dulles Papers
 John F. Dulles Papers
 Edward Mead Earle Papers
 Ferdinand Eberstadt Papers
 George F. Kennan Papers
 David E. Lilienthal Papers
 H. Alexander Smith Papers
Charles E. Young Library, University of California-Los Angeles
 Ralph J. Bunche Papers
 Brian Urquhart Papers
Smathers Library, University of Florida
 George Smathers Papers
United Kingdom National Archives (formerly Public Record Office), Kew, England
 Foreign Office Files
 Colonial Office Files
 Office of the Prime Minister Files
 Cabinet Files
 War Office Files
Institute of Commonwealth Studies, London, England
 C. L. R. James Papers
 Richard Hart Papers
National Archives, Ottawa, Canada
 RG 25, Records of the Department of External Affairs
Ministère des Affaires Étrangères, Paris, France
 Archives de Ministère des Affaires Étrangères
Barbados Department of Archives, Bridgetown, Barbados
 Grantley Adams Papers
University of the West Indies, Cave Hill, Barbados
 Main Library - West Indies & Special Collections
 Federal Archives Centre
Main Library, University of the West Indies, St. Augustine, Trinidad
 West Indiana—Special Collections
 Fitzroy Baptiste Collection
 C. L. R. James Collection
 Eric E. Williams Memorial Collection
Main Library, University of the West Indies, Mona, Jamaica
 Institute of Social and Economic Studies (ISES) Documentation Center
  Richard Hart Papers
  Arthur Creech-Jones Papers (copies)
 West Indies & Special Collections
  Microfilm Collections
National Library of Jamaica, Kingston, Jamaica
 MS 126a, People's National Party Pamphlets
 MS 234, Jamaica Progressive League
 MS 353, W. Adolphe Roberts Papers
 MS 1639, Sangster Memorial Collection
 MS 1893, Walter McFarlane Papers
 MS 2035, Norman Manley Autobiography and Diaries
 MS 2107, May Farquharson Collection

Jamaica Archives, Spanish Town, Jamaica
Semi-Public Records, Jamaica Broadcasting Corporation
Norman Manley Papers

Published Government Documents and Documentary Collections

British Documents on the End of Empire: The West Indies, eds. S. R. Ashton and David Killingray (London: Institute of Commonwealth Studies, 1999).

————. *Imperial Policy and Colonial Practice*, ed. S. R. Ashton (London: HMSO Books, 1996).

————. *The Labour Government and the End of Empire, 1945–1951*, 3 vols., ed. Ronald Hyam (London: HMSO Books, 1992).

————. *Conservative Government and the End of Empire, 1957–1964*, eds. Ronald Hyam and William Roger Louis (London: Stationery Office Books, 2000).

Constitutional Development of the West Indies, 1922–1968: A Selection from the Major Documents, ed. Ann Spackman (St. Lawrence: Caribbean Universities Press, 1975).

Papers of the National Association for the Advancement of Colored People (microfilm).

Report, *British Caribbean Federal Capital Commission*, Mudie Commission, 1956 (microfilm).

Report, *Conference on West Indian Federation*, London, 1953 (microfilm).

Report, *Conference on Closer Association of the British West Indian Colonies*, Montego Bay, September 11–19, 1947 (microfilm).

Report, *West India Royal Commission Report*, Moyne Commission, 1945 (microfilm).

Schomburg Center in Black Culture, New York Public Library. Clipping File (microfilm).

U.S. Department of State. *Foreign Relations of the United States*, 1947–1962.

————. *Second Meeting of the Ministers of Foreign Affairs of the American Republics*, Havana, July 21–30, 1940.

Books

Acheson, Dean. *Present at the Creation: My Years in the State Department*. New York: Norton, 1969.

Alexander, Robert J., ed. *Presidents, Prime Ministers, and Governors of the English-Speaking Caribbean and Puerto Rico: Conversations and Correspondence*. Westport: Greenwood Publishing Group, 1997.

Anderson, Carol. *Eyes off the Prize: The United Nations and the African American Struggle for Human Rights, 1944–1955*. New York: Cambridge University Press, 2003.

Anderson, Terry. *The United States, Great Britain, and the Cold War, 1944–1947*. Columbia: University of Missouri Press, 1981.

Ansprenger, Franz. *The Dissolution of Colonial Empires*. New York: Routledge, 1989.

Atkins, G. Pope. *Latin America and the Caribbean in the International System*. 4th ed. Boulder: Westview Press, 1999.

Ayearst, Morley. *The British West Indies: The Search for Self-government*. New York: New York University Press, 1960.

Baptiste, Fitzroy. *The United States and West Indian Unrest, 1918–1939*. Mona: University of the West Indies Press, 1978.

————. *War, Conflict, and Cooperation: The European Possessions in the Caribbean, 1939–1945*. Westport: Greenwood Press, 1988.

Baylis, John. *Anglo-American Defence Relations, 1939–1980: The Special Relationship.* New York: St. Martin's Press, 1981.

Bell, Wendell, ed. *The Democratic Revolution in the West Indies: Studies in Nationalism, Leadership, and the Belief in Progress.* Cambridge: Schenkman Publishing, 1967.

Bell, Wendell. *Jamaican Leaders: Political Attitudes in a New Nation.* Berkeley: University of California Press, 1964.

Bell, Wendell, and Oxaar, Ival. *Decisions of Nationhood: Political and Social Development in the British Caribbean.* Denver: University of Denver, 1964.

Benjamin, Jules R. *The United States and the Origins of the Cuban Revolution: An Empire of Liberty in an Age of National Liberation.* Princeton: Princeton University Press, 1990.

Benn, Dennis. *The Caribbean: An Intellectual History 1774–2003.* Kingston: Ian Randle, 2004.

Bernstein, Barton J., ed. *Politics and Policies of the Truman Administration.* Chicago: Quadrangle Books, 1970.

Blanshard, Paul. *Democracy and Empire in the Caribbean: A Contemporary Review.* New York: Macmillan, 1947.

Bolland, O. Nigel. *Colonialism and Resistance in Belize: Essays in Historical Sociology.* Mona: University of the West Indies Press, 2004.

———. *On the March: Labour Rebellions in the British Caribbean, 1934–1939.* Kingston: Ian Randle Publishers, 1995.

———. *The Politics of Labour in the British Caribbean: The Social Origins of Authoritarianism and Democracy in the Labour Movement.* Kingston: Ian Randle, 2001.

Borgwardt, Elizabeth. *A New Deal for the World: America's Vision for Human Rights.* Cambridge, Mass.: Harvard University Press, 2006.

Borstelmann, Thomas. *The Cold War and the Color Line: Race Relations and American Foreign Policy Since 1945.* Cambridge, Mass.: Harvard University Press, 2001.

Boxill, Ian. *Ideology and Caribbean Integration.* Mona: University of West Indies Press, 1997.

Brands, H. W. *The Specter of Neutralism: The United States and the Emergence of the Third World, 1947–1960.* New York: Columbia University Press, 1989.

Brereton, Bridget. *A History of Modern Trinidad, 1783–1962.* Kingston: Heineman, 1981.

Brewer, Susan. *To Win the Peace: British Propaganda in the United States during World War II.* Ithaca: Cornell University Press, 1997.

Bryce-Laporte, Roy, and Mortimer, Delores. *Caribbean Immigration to the United States.* Washington: Smithsonian Institution, 1983.

Buhle, Paul. *Tim Hector: A Caribbean Radical's Story.* Jackson: University Press of Mississippi, 2006.

Burk, Robert F. *The Eisenhower Administration and Black Civil Rights.* Knoxville: University of Tennessee Press, 1984.

Campbell, David R. *Writing Security: United States Foreign Policy and the Politics of Identity.* 2nd ed. Minneapolis: University of Minnesota Press, 1998.

Cannadine, David. *Ornamentalism: How the British Saw Their Empire.* New York: Oxford University Press, 2002.

Carnegie, Charles V. *Postnationalism Prefigured: Caribbean Borderlands.* New Brunswick: Rutgers University Press, 2003.

Carr, Raymond. *Puerto Rico: A Colonial Experiment.* New York: Random House, 1984.

Chevannes, Barry. *Rastafari: Roots and Ideology.* Syracuse: Syracuse University Press, 1995.

Chua, Amy. *World on Fire: How Exporting Free Market Democracy Breeds Ethnic Hatred and Global Instability.* New York: Anchor, 2004.

Cobley, Alan, ed. *Crossroads of Empire: The European-Caribbean Connection, 1492–1992.* Cave Hill: University of the West Indies Press, 1994.

Cooper, Frederick, and Stoler, Ann Laura, eds. *Tensions of Empire: Colonial Cultures in a Bourgeois World.* Berkeley: University of California Press, 1997.

Cooper, Frederick. *Decolonization and African Society: The Labor Question in French and British Africa.* New York: Cambridge University Press, 1996.

Corkran, Herbert. *Patterns of International Cooperation in the Caribbean, 1942–1969.* Dallas: Southern Methodist University Press, 1970.

Costain, Anne, and McFarland, Andrew, eds. *Social Movements and American Political Institutions.* Lanham: Roman and Littlefield, 1988.

Crassweller, Robert. *The Caribbean Community: Changing Societies and U.S. Policy.* New York: Praeger Publishers, 1972.

Cudjoe, Selwyn, ed. *Eric E. Williams Speaks: Essays on Colonialism and Independence.* Wellesley: Calaloux Publications, 1993.

Cullather, Nick. *Secret History: The CIA's Classified Account of its Operations in Guatemala, 1952–1954.* Stanford: Stanford University Press, 1999.

Dabydeen, David, and Brinsley, Samaroo, eds. *India in the Caribbean.* London: Hansib Publishing, 1987.

Dallek, Robert. *Franklin D. Roosevelt and American Foreign Policy, 1932–1945.* New York: Oxford University Press, 1979.

DeConde, Alexander. *Ethnicity, Race, and American Foreign Policy: A History.* Boston: Northeastern University Press, 1992.

Deosaran, Ramesh. *Eric Williams: The Man, His Ideas, and His Politics (A Study of Political Power).* Port of Spain: Signum Publishing, 1981.

Dietz, James L. *Puerto Rico: Negotiating Development and Change.* New York: Rienner, 2003.

Dilks, David, ed. *The Diaries of Sir Alexander Cadogan, 1938–1945.* New York: Putnam, 1972.

———. *Retreat from Power: Studies in Britain's Foreign Policy of the 20th Century.* London: Macmillan, 1981.

Divine, Robert. *The Reluctant Belligerent: American Entry into World War II,* 2nd ed. New York: McGraw-Hill, 1979.

Dobson, Alan P. *Anglo-American Relations in the Twentieth Century: Of Friendship, Conflict and the Rise and Decline of Superpowers.* New York: Routledge, 1995.

———. *Peaceful Air Warfare: The United States, Britain, and the Politics of International Aviation.* Oxford: Clarendon Press, 1991.

Dominguez, Jorge. *To Make a World Safe for Revolution: Cuba's Foreign Policy.* Cambridge, Mass.: Harvard University Press, 1989.

Dudziak, Mary L. *Cold War Civil Rights: Race and the Image of American Democracy.* Princeton: Princeton University Press, 2000.

Eaton, George. *Alexander Bustamante and Modern Jamaica.* Kingston: LMH Publishing, 1975.

Eckes, Alfred. *The United States and the Global Struggle for Minerals.* Austin: University of Texas Press, 1979.

Eden, Anthony. *The Reckoning: The Memoirs of Anthony Eden, Earl of Avon.* Boston: Houghton Mifflin, 1965.

Edmonds, Robin. *Setting the Mould: The United States and Britain, 1945–1950.* New York: Oxford University Press, 1986.

Eisenhower, Dwight D. *The White House Years: Mandate for Change, 1953–1956.* Garden City: Doubleday, 1963.

———. *The White House Years: Waging Peace, 1956–1961.* Garden City: Doubleday, 1965.

Emerson, Rupert. *Africa and United States Policy.* Englewood Cliffs: Prentice-Hall, 1967.

————. *From Empire to Nation: The Rise to Self-Assertion of Asian and African Peoples.* Cambridge, Mass.: Harvard University Press, 1962.

Engel, Jeffrey A. *Cold War at 30,000 Feet: The Anglo-American Fight for Aviation Supremacy.* Cambridge, Mass: Harvard University Press, 2007.

Escobar, Arturo. *Encountering Development: The Making and Unmaking of the Third World.* Princeton: Princeton University Press, 1995.

Feinberg, Richard E. *The Intemperate Zone: The Third World Challenge to United States Foreign Policy.* New York: Norton, 1983.

Fernandez, Ronald. *The Disenchanted Island: Puerto Rico and the United States in the Twentieth Century.* 2nd ed. Westport: Praeger, 1996.

Ferrell, Robert, ed. *Off the Record: The Private Papers of Harry S. Truman.* New York: Harper & Row, 1980.

Fox, Annette Baker. *Freedom and Welfare in the Caribbean: A Colonial Dilemma.* New York: Harcourt, Brace, 1949.

Fraser, Cary. *Ambivalent Anti-Colonialism: The United States and the Genesis of West Indian Independence, 1940–64.* Westport: Greenwood Press, 1994.

Friedman, Max P. *Nazis and Good Neighbors: The United States Campaign against the Germans of Latin America in World War II.* New York: Cambridge University Press, 2003.

Furedi, Frank. *The New Ideology of Imperialism: Renewing the Moral Imperative.* London: Pluto Press, 1994.

Gaddis, John Lewis. *The Cold War: A New History.* New York: Penguin Press, 2005.

————. *The Long Peace: Inquiries into the History of the Cold War.* New York: Oxford University Press, 1987.

————. *Strategies of Containment: A Critical Appraisal of Postwar American National Security Policy.* New York: Oxford University Press, 1982.

————. *We Now Know: Rethinking Cold War History.* New York: Oxford University Press, 1997.

Gardner, Lloyd. *Economic Aspects of New Deal Diplomacy.* Madison: University of Wisconsin Press, 1964.

Gleijeses, Piero. *Shattered Hope: The Guatemalan Revolution and the United States, 1944–1954.* Princeton: Princeton University Press, 1992.

Gomez, Michael. *Reversing Sail: A History of the African Diaspora.* New York: Cambridge University Press, 2004.

Gooding, Earl. *The West Indies at the Crossroads.* Cambridge: Schenkman Publishing, 1981.

Graham, Ronald. *The Aluminum Industry and the Third World: Multinational Corporations and Underdevelopment.* London: Zed Press, 1982.

Green, David. *The Containment of Latin America: A History of the Myths and Realities of the Good Neighbor Policy.* Chicago: Quadrangle Books, 1971.

Grimal, Henri. *Decolonization: The British, French, Dutch, and Belgian Empires, 1919–1963.* Translated by Stephan De Vos. Boulder: Westview Press, 1978.

Gunst, Laurie. *Born Fi' Dead: A Journey through the Jamaican Posse Underworld.* Reprint ed. New York: Owl Books, 1996.

Haglund, David G. *Latin America and the Transformation of U.S. Strategic Thought.* Albuquerque: University of New Mexico Press, 1984.

Hahamovitch, Cindy. *The Fruits of Their Labor: Atlantic Coast Farmworkers and the Making of Migrant Poverty, 1870–1945.* Chapel Hill: University of North Carolina Press, 1997.

Hahn, Peter, and Heiss, Mary Ann. *Empire and Revolution: The United States and the Third World Since 1945.* Columbus: Ohio State University, 2001.

Hannaford, Ivan. *Race: The History of an Idea in the West.* Baltimore: Johns Hopkins University Press, 1996.

Harbutt, Fraser. *The Iron Curtain: Churchill, America, and the Origins of the Cold War*. New York: Oxford University Press, 1986.

Harney, Stefano. *Nationalism and Identity: Culture and Imagination in a Caribbean Diaspora*. London: Zed Books, 1996.

Harris, Joseph. *African-American Reactions to War in Ethiopia, 1936–1941*. Baton Rouge: Louisiana State University Press, 1994.

Harris, Joseph, ed. *Global Dimensions of the African Diaspora*. 2nd ed. Washington: Howard University Press, 1993.

Hart, Richard. *Forward to Freedom*. Kingston: People's Educational Organization, 1952.

———. *The Origin and Development of the People of Jamaica*. Kingston: People's Educational Organization, 1952.

———. *Rise and Organize: The Birth of the Workers and National Movement in Jamaica, 1936–1939*. London: Karia Press, 1989.

———. *Towards Decolonisation: Political, Labour and Economic Developments in Jamaica 1938–1945*. Bridgetown: Canoe Press, University of the West Indies, 1999.

Hathaway, Robert. *Ambiguous Partnership: Britain and America, 1944–1947*. New York: Columbia University Press, 1981.

Henke, Holger, and Reno, Fred, eds. *Modern Political Culture in the Caribbean*. Mona: University of the West Indies Press, 2003.

Henry, Charles P., ed. *Ralph J. Bunche: Selected Speeches and Writings*. Ann Arbor: University of Michigan Press, 1995.

Henry, Charles P. *Ralph Bunche: Model Negro or American Other?* New York: New York University Press, 1999.

Hess, Gary R. *America Encounters India, 1941–1947*. Baltimore: Johns Hopkins University Press, 1971.

Higman, B. W. *Writing West Indian Histories*. London: Macmillan Education, 1999.

Hine, Darlene Clark, and McLeod, Jacqueline, eds. *Crossing Boundaries: Comparative History of Black People in Diaspora*. Bloomington: Indiana University Press, 2001.

Hixson, Walter. *Parting the Curtain: Propaganda, Culture, and the Cold War, 1945–1961*. New York: St. Martin's Press, 1997.

Hogan, Michael. *A Cross of Iron: Harry S. Truman and the Origins of the National Security State, 1945–1951*. New York: Cambridge University Press, 1998.

———. *The Marshall Plan: American, Britain, and the Reconstruction of Western Europe, 1947–1952*. New York: Cambridge University Press, 1987.

Holloway, Jonathan Scott. *Confronting the Veil: Abram Harris Jr., E. Franklin Frazier, and Ralph Bunche, 1919–1941*. Chapel Hill: University of North Carolina Press, 2001.

Holt, Thomas C. *The Problem of Freedom: Race, Labor, and Politics in Jamaica and Britain, 1832–1938*. Baltimore: Johns Hopkins University Press, 1992.

Horne, Gerald. *Black and Red: W. E. B. DuBois and the Afro-American Response to the Cold War*. Albany: SUNY Press, 1986.

———. *Cold War in a Hot Zone: The United States Confronts Labor and Independence Struggles in the British West Indies*. Philadelphia: Temple University Press, 2007.

———. *Red Seas: Ferdinand Smith and Radical Black Sailors in the United States and Jamaica*. New York: New York University Press, 2005.

Howe, Glenford. *Race, War, and Nationalism: A Social History of West Indians in the First World War*. Kingston: Ian Randle Publishers, 2002.

Hull, Cordell. *The Memoirs of Cordell Hull*, 2 vols. New York: Macmillan, 1948.

Hunt, Michael. *Ideology and U.S. Foreign Policy*. New Haven: Yale University Press, 1987.

Immerman, Richard. *The CIA in Guatemala: The Foreign Policy of Intervention*. Austin: University of Texas Press, 1982.

Jacobs, Virginia Lee. *Roots of Rastafari*. San Diego: Avant Books, 1985.

James, C. L. R. *A Convention Appraisal: Dr. Eric Williams ... A Biographical Sketch*. Port-of-Spain: P. N. M. Publishing, 1960.

James, Winston. *Holding Aloft the Banner of Ethiopia: Caribbean Radicalism in America*. New York: Verso Press, 1996.

James, Winston, and Harris, Clive. *Inside Babylon: The Caribbean Diaspora in Britain*. New York: Verso Press, 1993.

Janken, Kenneth Robert. *Rayford W. Logan and the Dilemma of the African American Intellectual*. Amherst: University of Massachusetts Press, 1993.

Kahler, Miles. *Decolonization in Britain and France: The Domestic Consequences of International Relations*. Princeton: Princeton University Press, 1984.

Karabell, Zachary. *Architects of Intervention: The United States, the Third World, and the Cold War, 1946–1962*. Baton Rouge: Louisiana State University Press, 1999.

Kaufman, Burton I. *Trade and Aid: Eisenhower's Foreign Economic Policy, 1953–1961*. Baltimore: Johns Hopkins University Press, 1982.

Keppel, Ben. *The Work of Democracy: Ralph Bunche, Kenneth B. Clark, Lorraine Hansberry, and the Cultural Politics of Race*. Cambridge, Mass.: Harvard University Press, 1995.

Khan, Aisha. *Callaloo Nation: Metaphors of Race and Religious Identity among South Asians in Trinidad*. Durham: Duke University Press, 2004.

King, Stephen, Bays, Barry, and Foster, P. Renee. *Reggae, Rastafari, and the Rhetoric of Social Control*. Jackson: University Press of Mississippi, 2002.

Knight, Franklin W., and Palmer, Colin, eds. *The Modern Caribbean*. Chapel Hill: University of North Carolina Press, 1989.

Knight, Franklin W. *The Caribbean: The Genesis of a Fragmented Nationalism*. New York: Oxford University Press, 1978.

Kolko, Gabriel. *Confronting the Third World: United States Foreign Policy, 1945–1980*. New York: Pantheon Books, 1988.

Krenn, Michael. *Black Diplomacy: African Americans and the State Department*. Armonk: M. E. Sharpe, 1999.

———. *The Chains of Interdependence: U.S. Policy toward Central America, 1945–1954*. Armonk: M. E. Sharpe, 1996.

———. *Race and U.S. Foreign Policy from the Colonial Period to the Present*, 5 vols. New York: Garland, 1998.

Kryder, Daniel. *Divided Arsenal: Race and the American State during World War II*. New York: Cambridge University Press, 2001.

LaFeber, Walter. *Inevitable Revolutions: The United States in Central America*. New York: Norton, 1983.

———. *The New Empire: An Interpretation of American Expansion, 1860–1898*. 35th Anniversary ed. Ithaca: Cornell University Press, 1998.

———. *The Panama Canal: The Crisis in Historical Perspective*. New York: Oxford University Press, 1979.

La Guerre, John Gaffar. *The Politics of Communalism: The Ordeal of the Left in Trinidad and Tobago, 1930–1955*. St. Augustine: Pan Caribbean, 1979.

———. *The Social and Political Thought of the Colonial Intelligentsia*. Mona: University of the West Indies Press, 1982.

Langley, Lester. *America and the Americas: The United States in the Western Hemisphere*. Athens: University of Georgia Press, 1989.

———. *The Americas in the Age of Revolution*. New Haven: Yale University Press, 1998.

———. *The Americas in the Modern Age*. New Haven: Yale University Press, 2003.

———. *The United States and the Caribbean in the Twentieth Century*. 4th ed. Athens: University of Georgia Press, 1989.

Lauren, Paul Gordon. *Power and Prejudice: The Politics and Diplomacy of Racial Discrimination*. Boulder: Westview Press, 1988.

Layton, Azza Salama. *International Politics and Civil Rights Policies in the United States, 1941–1960*. New York: Cambridge University Press, 2000.

Leffler, Melvyn. *A Preponderance of Power: National Security, the Truman Administration, and the Cold War*. Stanford: Stanford University Press, 1992.

Leutze, James R. *Bargaining for Supremacy: Anglo-American Naval Collaboration, 1937–1941*. Chapel Hill: University of North Carolina Press, 1977.

Lewinson, Edwin. *Black Politics in New York City*. New York: Twayne Publishers, 1974.

Lewis, Gordon. *Puerto Rico: Freedom and Power in the Caribbean*. New York: Monthly Review Press, 1974.

Lewis, Rupert. *Garvey: Africa, Europe, the Americas*. Lawrenceville: Africa World Press, 1994.

Louis, William Roger, ed. *Imperialism: The Robinson and Gallagher Controversy*. New York: Franklin Watts, 1976.

Louis, William Roger, and Bull, Hedley, eds. *The "Special Relationship": Anglo-American Relations Since 1945*. Oxford: Clarendon Press, 1986.

Louis, William Roger, and Brown, Judith M., eds. *The Oxford History of the British Empire: Volume IV: The Twentieth Century*. New York: Oxford University Press, 2001.

Louis, William Roger. *Ends of British Imperialism: The Scramble for Empire, Suez, and Decolonization: Collected Essays*. New York: I. B. Tauris, 2006.

———. *Imperialism at Bay: The United States and the Decolonization of the British Empire, 1941–1945*. New York: Oxford University Press, 1978.

Love, Eric T. L. *Race over Empire: Racism and U.S. Imperialism, 1865–1900*. Chapel Hill: University of North Carolina Press, 2004.

Lowenthal, David. *The West Indies Federation: Perspectives on a New Nation*. New York: Columbia University Press, 1961.

Macdonald, Douglas. *Adventures in Chaos: American Intervention for Reform in the Third World*. Cambridge, Mass.: Harvard University Press, 1992.

Macmillan, Harold. *At the End of the Day, 1961–1963*. New York: Harper & Row, 1973.

———. *Riding the Storm, 1956–1959*. New York: Harper & Row, 1971.

Macmillan, William M. *Warning from the West Indies: A Tract for Africa and the Empire*. London: Faber and Faber, 1936.

Mahoney, Richard. *JFK: Ordeal in Africa*. New York: Oxford University Press, 1983.

Maingot, Anthony P. *The United States and the Caribbean: Challenges of an Asymmetrical Relationship*. Boulder: Westview Press, 1994.

Malik, Kenan. *The Meaning of Race: Race, History, and Culture in Western Society*. New York: New York University Press, 1996.

Mars, Perry. *Ideology and Change: The Transformation of the Caribbean Left*. Detroit: Wayne State University Press, 1998.

McCormick, Thomas J. *America's Half-Century: United States Foreign Policy in the Cold War*. Baltimore: Johns Hopkins University Press, 1989.

McCoy, Donald, and Ruetten, Richard. *Quest and Response: Minority Rights and the Truman Administration*. Lawrence: University Press of Kansas, 1973.

McFerson, Hazel. *The Racial Dimension of American Overseas Colonial Policy*. Westport: Greenwood Press, 1997.

McMahon, Robert J. *The Cold War on the Periphery: The United States, India, and Pakistan.* New York: Columbia University Press, 1994.

———. *Colonialism and Cold War: The United States and the Struggle for Indonesian Independence, 1945–1949.* Ithaca: Cornell University Press, 1981.

McPherson, Alan. *Yankee No! Anti-Americanism in U.S.–Latin American Relations.* Cambridge, Mass.: Harvard University Press, 2003.

Meeks, Brian. *Narratives of Resistance: Jamaica, Trinidad, the Caribbean.* Mona: University of the West Indies Press, 2000.

Meighoo, Kirk Peter. *Politics in a Half Made Society: Trinidad and Tobago, 1925–2001.* Kingston: Ian Randle Press, 2003.

Meriwether, James. *Proudly We Can Be Africans: Black Americans and African, 1935–1961.* Chapel Hill: University of North Carolina Press, 2002.

Monge, Jose Trias. *Puerto Rico: The Trials of the Oldest Colony in the World.* New Haven: Yale University Press, 1999.

Mordecai, John. *The West Indies: The Federal Negotiations.* London: Allen and Unwin, 1968.

Morgan, D. J. *The Official History of Colonial Development,* 5 vols. Atlantic Highlands: Humanities Press, 1980.

———. *Aid to the West Indies.* London, Overseas Development Institute, 1964.

Morgan, Kenneth O. *Labour in Power, 1945–1951.* Oxford: Clarendon Press, 1984.

Munasinghe, Viranjini. *Callaloo or Tossed Salad? East Indians and the Cultural Politics of Identity in Trinidad.* Ithaca: Cornell University Press, 2002.

Munroe, Trevor. *The Cold War and the Jamaican Left, 1950–1955: Reopening the Files.* Kingston: Kingston Publishers Limited, 1992.

———. *Jamaican Politics: A Marxist Perspective in Transition.* Kingston: Heinemann Publishers, 1990.

———. *The Politics of Constitutional Decolonization: Jamaica 1944–62.* Mona/ISER: University of the West Indies, 1972.

Naipaul, V.S. *The Middle Passage: The Caribbean Revisited.* New York: Macmillan, 1963.

Neptune, Harvey. *Caliban and the Yankees: Trinidad and the United States Occupation.* Chapel Hill: University of North Carolina Press, 2007.

Nettleford, Rex, ed. *Norman Washington Manley and the New Jamaica: Selected Speeches and Writings 1938–68.* New York: Africana Publishing Corporation, 1971.

Nettleford, Rex. *Mirror Mirror: Identity, Race, and Protest in Jamaica.* Kingston: Collins & Sangster, 1970.

Noer, Thomas. *Cold War and Black Liberation: The United States and White Rule in Africa, 1948–1968.* Columbia: University of Missouri Press, 1988.

O'Sullivan, Christopher D. *Sumner Welles, Postwar Planning, and the Quest for a New World Order, 1937–1943.* New York: Columbia University Press, 2007.

Offner, Arnold. *Another Such Victory: President Truman and the Cold War, 1945–1953.* Stanford: Stanford University Press, 2002.

Orde, Anne. *The Eclipse of Great Britain: The United States and British Imperial Decline, 1895–1956.* New York: St. Martin's Press, 1996.

Osgood, Kenneth. *Total Cold War: Eisenhower's Secret Propaganda Battle at Home and Abroad.* Lawrence: University Press of Kansas, 2006.

Osterhammel, Jurgen. *Colonialism: A Theoretical Overview.* Translated by Shelley L. Frisch. Princeton: Markus Wiener Publishers, 1997.

Ovendale, Ritchie, ed. *The Foreign Policy of British Labour Governments, 1945–1951.* Leicester: Leicester University Press, 1984.

Pach, Chester. *Arming the Free World: The Origins of the United States Military Assistance Program, 1945–1950.* Chapel Hill: University of North Carolina Press, 1991.

Palmer, Colin. *Eric Williams and the Making of the Modern Caribbean*. Chapel Hill: University of North Carolina Press, 2006.

Paterson, Thomas, ed., *Cold War Critics: Alternatives to American Foreign Policy in the Truman Years*. Chicago: Quadrangle Books, 1971.

———. *Kennedy's Quest for Victory: American Foreign Policy, 1961–63*. New York: Oxford University Press, 1989.

Paterson, Thomas. *Contesting Castro: The United States and the Triumph of the Cuban Revolution*. New York: Oxford University Press, 1994.

Paul, Kathleen. *Whitewashing Britain: Race and Citizenship in the Postwar Era*. Ithaca: Cornell University Press, 1997.

Pearce, Jenny. *Under the Eagle: U. S. Intervention in Central America and the Caribbean*. London: South End Press, 1983.

Perkins, Whitney. *Constraint of Empire: The United States and Caribbean Interventions*. Westport: Greenwood Press, 1981.

Pierpaoli, Paul G. *Truman and Korea: The Political Culture of the Early Cold War*. Columbia: University of Missouri Press, 1999.

Pike, Frederick. *FDR's Good Neighbor Policy: Sixty Years of Generally Gentle Chaos*. Austin: University of Texas Press, 1995.

Pilkington, Edward. *Beyond the Mother Country: West Indians and the Notting Hill White Riots*. London: Tauris Press, 1988.

Plummer, Brenda Gayle, ed. *Window on Freedom: Race, Civil Rights, and Foreign Affairs, 1945–1988*. Chapel Hill: University of North Carolina Press, 2003.

Plummer, Brenda Gayle. *Rising Wind: Black Americans and U.S. Foreign Affairs, 1935–1960*. Chapel Hill: University of North Carolina Press, 1996.

Poole, Bernard L. *The Caribbean Commission: Background of Cooperation in the West Indies*. Columbia: University of South Carolina Press, 1951.

Porter, A. N., and Stockwell, A. J. *British Imperial Policy and Decolonization, 1938–1964*. 2 vols. New York: St. Martin's Press, 1987.

Post, Ken. *Arise Ye Starvelings: The Jamaican Labour Rebellion of 1938 and its Aftermath*. The Hague: Martinus Nijhoff, 1978.

———. *Strike the Iron: A Colony at War: Jamaica, 1939–1945*, 2 vols. Atlantic Highlands: Humanities Press, 1981.

Proudfoot, Mary. *Britain and the United States in the Caribbean: A Comparative Study in Methods of Development*. New York: Praeger, 1953.

Puri, Shalini. *The Caribbean Postcolonial: Social Equality, Post-nationalism, and Cultural Hybridity*. New York: Palgrave Macmillan, 2004.

Rabe, Stephen. *Eisenhower and Latin America: The Foreign Policy of Anticommunism*. Chapel Hill: University of North Carolina Press, 1988.

———. *The Most Dangerous Area in the World: John F. Kennedy Confronts Communist Revolution in Latin America*. Chapel Hill: University of North Carolina Press, 1999.

———. *U.S. Intervention in British Guiana: A Cold War Story*. Chapel Hill: University of North Carolina Press, 2006.

Randall, Stephen J., and Mount, Graeme. *The Caribbean Basin: An International History*. New York: Routledge, 1998.

Reed, Adolph L., Jr. *W. E. B. DuBois and American Political Thought: Fabianism and the Color Line*. New York: Oxford University Press, 1997.

Regis, Louis. *The Political Calypso: True Opposition in Trinidad and Tobago*. Gainesville: University Press of Florida, 1999.

Reynolds, David. *The Creation of the Anglo-American Alliance, 1937–1941: A Study in Competitive Co-operation.* Chapel Hill: University of North Carolina Press, 1982.

Robinson, A. N. R. *The Mechanics of Independence: Patterns of Political and Economic Transformation in Trinidad and Tobago.* Mona: University of West Indies Press, 2001.

Robinson, Armstead L., and Sullivan, Patricia, eds. *New Directions in Civil Rights Studies.* Charlottesville: University Press of Virginia, 1991.

Rohlehr, Gordon. *Calypso and Society in Pre-independence Trinidad.* Port of Spain: G. Rohlehr, 1990.

Roorda, Eric P. *The Dictator Next Door: The Good Neighbor Policy and the Trujillo Regime in the Dominican Republic, 1930–1945.* Durham: Duke University Press, 1998.

Rosenberg, Jonathan. *How Far the Promised Land? World Affairs and the American Civil Rights Movement from World War I to Vietnam.* Princeton: Princeton University Press, 2005.

Ross, Steven T. *U.S. War Plans, 1939–1945.* Malabar: Krieger Pub. Co., 2000.

Rothwell, Victor. *Britain and the Cold War, 1941–1947.* London: Cape, 1982.

Rusk, Dean. *As I Saw It.* New York: Norton, 1990.

Ryan, David, and Pungong, Victor, eds. *The United States and Decolonization: Power and Freedom.* New York: Palgrave Macmillan, 2000.

Ryan, Henry. *The Vision of Anglo-America: The US–UK Alliance and the Emerging Cold War, 1943–1946.* New York: Cambridge University Press, 1987.

Ryan, Selwyn. *The Politics of Succession: A Study of Parties and Politics in Trinidad and Tobago.* St. Augustine: University of the West Indies Press, 1978.

———. *Race and Nationalism in Trinidad and Tobago: A Study of Decolonization in Multiracial Society.* Toronto: University of Toronto Press, 1972.

Said, Abdul Aziz. *Ethnicity and U.S. Foreign Policy.* New York: Praeger, 1977.

Schlesinger, Arthur M., Jr. *A Thousand Days: John F. Kennedy in the White House.* Boston: Houghton Mifflin, 1965.

Schlesinger, Stephen, and Kinzer, Stephen. *Bitter Fruit: The Story of the American Coup in Guatemala,* 2nd ed. Cambridge, Mass.: Harvard University Press, 1999.

Schoultz, Lars. *Beneath the United States: A History of U.S. Policy toward Latin America.* Cambridge, Mass.: Harvard University Press, 1998.

Schwartzberg, Steven. *Democracy and U.S. Policy in Latin America during the Truman Years.* Gainesville: University Press of Florida, 2003.

Scott, William R. *The Sons of Sheba's Race: African-Americans and the Italo-Ethiopian War, 1935–1941.* Bloomington: Indiana University Press, 1993.

Seal, Anil, ed. *The Decline, Revival, and Fall of the British Empire: The Ford Lectures and Other Essays by John Gallagher.* New York: Cambridge University Press, 1982.

Shepherd, George, ed. *Race Among Nations: A Conceptual Approach.* Lexington: Heath Lexington Books, 1970.

———. *Racial Influences on American Foreign Policy.* New York: Basic Books, 1970.

Siewah, Samaroo, ed. *The Lotus and the Dagger: The Capildeo Speeches, 1957–1994.* Tunapuna: Chakra Publishing House, 1994.

Singh, Kelvin. *Race and Class Struggles in a Colonial State: Trinidad 1917–1945.* Calgary: University of Calgary Press, 1994.

Singh, Nikhil Pal. *Black is a Country: Race and the Unfinished Struggle for Democracy.* Cambridge, Mass.: Harvard University Press, 2004.

Smith, Gaddis. *The Last Years of the Monroe Doctrine, 1945–1993.* New York: Hill and Wang, 1994.

Smith, George David. *From Monopoly to Competition: The Transformations of Alcoa, 1888–1986*. New York: Cambridge University Press, 1988.

Smith, Peter H. *Talons of the Eagle: Dynamics of U.S –Latin American Relations*, 2nd ed. New York: Oxford University Press, 2000.

Smith, Robert Freeman. *The Caribbean World and the United States: Mixing Rum and Coca-Cola*. New York: Twayne/Maxwell Macmillan International, 1994.

Smith, Tony. *America's Mission: The United States and the Worldwide Struggle for Democracy in the Twentieth Century*. Princeton: Princeton University Press, 1994.

———. *Foreign Attachments: The Power of Ethnic Groups in the Making of American Foreign Policy*. Cambridge, Mass.: Harvard University Press, 2000.

———. *The Pattern of Imperialism: The United States, Great Britain, and the Late-industrializing World Since 1815*. New York: Cambridge University Press, 1981.

Spinner, Thomas J. *A Political and Social History of Guyana, 1945–1983*. Boulder: Westview Press, 1984.

Springhall, John. *Decolonization Since 1945: The Collapse of European Overseas Empires*. New York: Palgrave, 2001.

Statler, Kathryn, and Johns, Andrew, eds. *The Eisenhower Administration, the Third World, and the Globalization of the Cold War*. New York: Rowman & Littlefield, 2006.

Stephenson, Yvonne. *A Bibliography on the West Indian Federation*. Georgetown: University of Guyana Library, 1972.

Stoler, Mark A. *Allies and Adversaries: The Joint Chiefs of Staff, the Grand Alliance, and U.S. Strategy in World War II*. Chapel Hill: University of North Carolina Press, 2000.

Stueck, William. *The Korean War: An International History*. Princeton: Princeton University Press, 1995.

Sullivan, Patricia. *Days of Hope: Race and Democracy in the New Deal Era*. Chapel Hill: University of North Carolina Press, 1996.

Sutton, Paul K., ed. *Forged from the Love of Liberty: Selected Speeches of Dr. Eric Williams*. Port of Spain: Longman Caribbean, 1981.

Szulc, Tad, ed. *The United States and the Caribbean*. Englewood Cliffs: Prentice-Hall, 1971.

Thomas, Deborah. *Modern Blackness: Nationalism, Globalization, and the Politics of Culture in Jamaica*. Durham: Duke University Press, 2004.

Thomas, Roy, ed. *Trinidad Labour Riots of 1937: Fifty Years Later*. St. Augustine: University of the West Indies Press, 1987.

Thomas-Hope, Elizabeth. *Caribbean Migration*. Mona: University of West Indies Press, 2002.

Thorne, Christopher. *Allies of a Kind: The United States, Britain, and the War Against Japan, 1941–1945*. London: Hamish Hamilton, 1978.

Truman, Harry S. *Memoirs: Years of Trial and Hope*. 2 vols. Garden City: Doubleday, 1955–1956.

Tugwell, Rexford. *Changing the Colonial Climate*. New York: Arno Press, 1970.

———. *The Stricken Land: The Story of Puerto Rico*. Garden City: Doubleday, 1947.

Turner, W. Burghardt, and Turner, Joyce Moore, eds. *Richard B. Moore: Caribbean Militant in Harlem*. Bloomington: Indiana University Press, 1988.

Turner, Joyce Moore. *Caribbean Crusaders and the Harlem Renaissance*. Urbana: University of Illinois Press, 2005.

Urquhart, Brian. *Ralph Bunche: An American Life*. New York: W. W. Norton, 1993.

Vickerman, Milton. *Crosscurrents: West Indian Immigrants and Race*. New York: Oxford University Press, 1998.

Von Albertini, Rudolf. *European Colonial Rule, 1860–1940: The Impact of the West on India, Southeast Asia, and Africa*. Westport: Greenwood Press, 1982.

Von Eschen, Penny. *Race Against Empire: Black Americans and Anticolonialism, 1937–1957*. Ithaca: Cornell University Press, 1997.

Wallace, Elizabeth. *The British Caribbean: From the Decline of Colonialism to the End of Federation*. Toronto: University of Toronto Press, 1977.

Walters, Ronald W. *Pan-Africanism in the African Diaspora: An Analysis of Modern Afrocentric Political Movements*. Detroit: Wayne State University Press, 1997.

Ware, Gilbert. *William Hastie: Grace under Pressure*. New York: Oxford University Press, 1985.

Waters, Mary C. *Black Identities: West Indian Immigrant Dreams and American Realities*. Cambridge, Mass.: Harvard University Press, 2001.

Watkins-Owens, Irma. *Blood Relations: Caribbean Immigrants and the Harlem Community, 1900–1930*. Bloomington: Indiana University Press, 1996.

Watt, D. Cameron. *Succeeding John Bull: America in Britain's Place, 1900–1975*. Cambridge: Cambridge University Press, 1984.

Watts, R. L. *New Federations: Experiments in the Commonwealth*. Oxford: Clarendon, 1966.

Weiss, Nancy. *Farewell to the Party of Lincoln: Black Politics in the Age of FDR*. Princeton: Princeton University Press, 1983.

Welch, Richard E., Jr. *Response to Revolution: The United States and the Cuban Revolution, 1959–1961*. Chapel Hill: University of North Carolina Press, 1985.

Welles, Sumner. *The Time for Decision*. New York: Harper, 1944.

———. *Where Are We Heading?* New York: Harper, 1946.

———. *World of the Four Freedoms*. New York: Columbia University Press, 1943.

Westad, Odd Arne. *The Global Cold War: Third World Interventions and the Making of Our Times*. New York: Cambridge University Press, 2005.

Weston, Rubin. *Racism in U.S. Imperialism: The Influence of Racial Assumptions on American Foreign Policy, 1893–1946*. Columbia: University of South Carolina Press, 1972.

White, Walter. *A Man Called White: The Autobiography of Walter White*. New York: Viking Press, 1948.

———. *Rising Wind*. New York: Doubleday-Doran, 1945.

Whitham, Charlie. *Bitter Rehearsal: British and American Planning for a Post-War West Indies*. Westport: Praeger Publishers, 2002.

Wilgus, A. Curtis, ed. *The Caribbean at Mid-century*. Gainesville: University of Florida Press, 1951.

———. *The Caribbean: British, Dutch, French, United States*. Gainesville: University of Florida Press, 1958.

———. *The Caribbean: Current United States Relations*. Gainesville: University of Florida Press, 1966.

———. *The Caribbean: Political Problems*. Gainesville: University of Florida Press, 1956.

Williams, William A. *Empire as a Way of Life*. New York: Oxford University Press, 1980.

———. *The Tragedy of American Diplomacy*. 4th ed. New York: Norton, 1988.

———. *The United States, Cuba, and Castro: An Essay on the Dynamics of Revolution and the Dissolution of Empire*. New York: Monthly Review Press, 1962.

Wilson, Henry S. *African Decolonization*. London: Edward Arnold, 1994.

Wood, Bryce. *The Dismantling of the Good Neighbor Policy*. Austin: University of Texas Press, 1985.

———. *The Making of the Good Neighbor Policy*. New York: Columbia University Press, 1961.

Woods, Randall B. *A Changing of the Guard: Anglo-American Relations, 1941–1946*. Chapel Hill: University of North Carolina Press, 1990.

Woods, Randall B., and Jones, Howard. *Dawning of the Cold War: The United States' Quest for Order*. Athens: University of Georgia Press, 1991.

Yergin, Daniel. *The Prize: The Epic Quest for Oil, Money, and Power.* New York: Simon & Schuster, 1991.

———. *Shattered Peace: The Origins of the Cold War and the National Security State.* Boston: Houghton Mifflin, 1977.

Yerxa, Donald A. *Admirals and Empire: The United States Navy and the Caribbean, 1898–1945.* Columbia: University of South Carolina Press, 1991.

Articles and Dissertations

Adamthwaite, Anthony. "Britain and the World, 1945–1949: The View from the Foreign Office." *International Affairs* 61/2 (Summer 1985): 223–236.

———. "Overstretched and Overstrung: Eden, the Foreign Office, and the Making of Policy, 1951–1955." *International Affairs* 64 (1988): 241–259.

Anderson, Carol. "From Hope to Disillusion: African Americans, the U.N., and the Struggle for Human Rights, 1944–47," *Diplomatic History* 20/4 (Fall 1996): 531–564.

Anstey, Caroline. "The Projection of British Socialism: Foreign Office Publicity and American Opinion, 1945–1950." *Journal of Contemporary History* 19 (1984): 417–451.

Baptiste, Fitzroy. "The British Grant of Air and Naval Facilities to the United States in Trinidad, St. Lucia, and Bermuda in 1939 (June–December)." *Caribbean Studies* 16 (1976): 5–43.

Basdeo, Sahadeo. "Walter Citrine and the British Caribbean Workers Movement during the Moyne Commission Hearing, 1938–9." *Journal of Caribbean History* 18/2 (1983): 43–59.

Bell, Christopher. "Thinking the Unthinkable: British and American Naval Strategies for an Anglo-American War, 1918–1931." *International History Review* 19/4 (November 1997): 789–808.

Belmonte, Laura. "Defending a Way of Life: American Propaganda and the Cold War, 1945–1959." Ph.D. Diss., University of Virginia, 1996.

Brown, Noel Joseph. "Jamaica and the West Indies Federation: A Case Study on the Problems of Political Integration." Ph.D. Diss., Yale University, 1963.

Brown, Tammy L. "Re-visioning Blackness: West Indian Intellectuals and the Discourse of Identity, New York City, 1920–1980." Ph.D. Diss., Princeton University, 2007.

Burn, North. "United States Base Rights in the British West Indies, 1940–1962." Ph.D. Diss., Tufts University, 1964.

Child, John. "From 'Color' to the 'Rainbow': U.S. Strategic Planning for Latin America, 1919–1945." *Journal of International Studies* 21/2 (Summer 1979): 233–259.

Clarke, Colin. "Colonialism and its Social and Cultural Consequences in the Caribbean." *Journal of Latin American Studies* 15/2 (1983): 491–503.

———. "The Quest for Independence in the Caribbean." *Journal of Latin American Studies* 9/2 (1977): 337–345.

Colby, Jason Michael. "'Banana Growing and Negro Management': Race, Labor, and Jim Crow Colonialism in Guatemala, 1884–1930." *Diplomatic History* 30/4 (September 2006): 595–622.

———. "Jim Crow Empire: Race and United States Colonialism in the Caribbean Basin, 1865–1930." Ph.D. Diss., Cornell University, 2005.

Connelly, Matthew. "Taking off the Cold War Lens: Visions of North–South Conflict during the Algerian War for Independence." *American Historical Review* 105/3 (June 2000): 739–769.

Cox-Alomar, Rafael. "Britain's Withdrawal from the Eastern Caribbean 1965–67: A Reappraisal." *Journal of Imperial and Commonwealth History* 31/3 (September 2003): 74–106.

Darwin, John. "British Decolonization Since 1945: A Pattern or a Puzzle," *Journal of Imperial and Commonwealth History* 12/2 (1984): 187–209.

Dudziak, Mary L. "Desegregation as a Cold War Imperative." *Stanford Law Review* 41 (1988): 61–120.

———. "Josephine Baker, Racial Protest, and the Cold War." *Journal of American History* 81/3 (September 1994): 543–570.

Duke, Eric. "Seeing Race, Seeing Nation: Conceptualizing a 'United West Indies' in the British Caribbean and Diaspora." Ph.D. Diss., Michigan State University, 2007.

"Federation" (special issue). *Social and Economic Studies* 48/4 (1999): 1–286.

Fraser, Cary. "Crossing the Color Line in Little Rock: The Eisenhower Administration and the Dilemma of Race for U.S. Foreign Policy." *Diplomatic History* 24/2 (Spring 2000): 233–264.

———. "The New Frontier of Empire in the Caribbean: The Transfer of Power in British Guiana, 1961–1964." *International History Review* 22/3 (September 2000): 583–611.

———. "The Twilight of Colonial Rule in the British West Indies." *Journal of Caribbean History* 30/1–2 (June 1996): 1–27.

Green, William A. "The Creolization of Caribbean History." *Journal of Imperial and Commonwealth History* 14/3 (1986): 39–68.

Haglund, David G. "George C. Marshall and the Question of Military Aid to England, May–June 1940." *Journal of Contemporary History* 15 (October 1980): 745–760.

Haines, Gerald K. "Under the Eagle's Wing: The Franklin Roosevelt Administration Forges an American Hemisphere." *Diplomatic History* 1/4 (December 1977): 373–388.

Hanson, Gail. "Ordered Liberty: Sumner Welles and the Crowder–Welles Connection in the Caribbean." *Diplomatic History* 18/3 (Summer 1994): 311–333.

Harbutt, Fraser. "Churchill, Hopkins, and the 'Other' Americans: An Alternative Perspective on Anglo-American Relations." *International History Review* 8/2 (1986): 236–262.

Harris, Richard. "Making Leeway in the Leewards, 1929–1951: The Negotiation of Colonial Development." *Journal of Imperial and Commonwealth History* 33/3 (September 2005): 393–418.

Harrison, Richard. "Testing the Water: A Secret Probe towards Anglo-American Military Co-operation in 1936." *International History Review* 7/2 (May 1985): 214–234.

Henry, Keith S. "The Black Political Tradition in New York: A Conjunction of Political Cultures." *Journal of Black Studies* 7/4 (1977): 455–484.

Herring, George C. "The Truman Administration and the Restoration of French Sovereignty in Indo-China." *Diplomatic History* 1/2 (June 1977): 97–117.

Hess, Gary R. "Accommodation Amid Discord: The United States, India, and the Third World." *Diplomatic History* 16/2 (June 1992): 1–22.

High, Steven. "The Racial Politics of Criminal Jurisdiction in the Aftermath of the Anglo-American 'Destroyers-for-Bases' Deal, 1940–50." *Journal of Imperial and Commonwealth History* 32/3 (September 2004): 77–105.

Hinds, Allister E. "Sterling and Imperial Policy, 1945–1951." *Journal of Imperial and Commonwealth History* 15/2 (1987): 148–169.

Holland, R. F. "The Imperial Factor in British Strategies from Attlee to Macmillan, 1945–1963." *Journal of Imperial and Commonwealth History* 12/2 (1984): 187–208.

Horne, Gerald. "Race from Power: U.S. Foreign Policy and the General Crisis of 'White Supremacy.'" *Diplomatic History* 23/3 (September 1999): 437–462.

———. "Who Lost the Cold War? Africans and African Americans." *Diplomatic History* 20/4 (Fall 1996): 613–626.

Immerman, Richard. "Confessions of an Eisenhower Revisionist." *Diplomatic History* 14 (1990): 11–24.

Jackson, Shona N. "Between Myth and Nation: Rethinking Caribbean History, Politics, Literature, and Aesthetics." Ph.D. Diss., Stanford University, 2005.

Johnson, Howard. "The Anglo-American Caribbean Commission and the Extension of American Influence in the British Caribbean, 1942–1945." *Journal of Commonwealth and Comparative Politics* 22/2 (1984): 180–203.

———. "The United States and the Establishment of the Anglo-American Caribbean Commission." *Journal of Caribbean History* 19/1 (1984): 26–47.

Kelley, Robin D. G. "'But a Local Phase of a World Problem': Black History's Global Vision, 1883–1950." *Journal of American History* 86 (December 1999): 1045–1078.

Kelley, Robin D. G., and Patterson, Tiffany Ruby. "Unfinished Migrations: Reflections on the African Diaspora and the Making of the Modern World." *African Studies Review* 43/1 (April 2000): 11–46.

Kent, John. "United States Reactions to Empire, Colonialism, and Cold War in Black Africa, 1949–1957." *Journal of Imperial and Commonwealth History* 33/2 (May 2005): 195–220.

Krakau, Knud. "American Foreign Relations: A National Style." *Diplomatic History* 7/4 (December 1984): 253–272.

Krenn, Michael. "'Unfinished Business': Segregation and U.S. Diplomacy at the 1958 World's Fair." *Diplomatic History* 20/4 (Fall 1996): 591–612.

LaFeber, Walter. "The 'Lion in the Path': The U.S. Emergence as a World Power." *Political Science Quarterly* 101/5 (1986): 705–718.

———. "Roosevelt, Churchill, and Indochina: 1942–1945." *American Historical Review* 80/5 (December 1975): 1277–1295.

Laville, Helen, and Lucas, Scott. "The American Way: Edith Sampson, the NAACP, and African American Identity in the Cold War." *Diplomatic History* 20/4 (Fall 1996): 565–590.

Layton, Azza Salama. "International Pressure and the U.S. Government's Response to Little Rock." *Arkansas Historical Quarterly* 56 (Fall 1997): 257–272.

Louis, William Roger. "American Anti-colonialism and the Dissolution of the British Empire." *International Affairs* 61/3 (1985): 395–420.

Louis, William Roger, and Robinson, Ronald. "The Imperialism of Decolonisation." *Journal of Imperial and Commonwealth History* 22/3 (1994): 462–511.

McMahon, Robert J. "Eisenhower and Third World Nationalism: A Critique of the Revisionists." *Political Science Quarterly* 101/3 (Summer 1986): 456–457.

Palmer, Annette. "Black American Soldiers in Trinidad, 1942–44: Wartime Politics in a Colonial Society." *Journal of Imperial and Commonwealth History* 14/3 (1986): 203–218.

Parker, Jason. "'Capital of the Caribbean': The African American–West Indian Harlem Nexus and the Transnational Drive for Black Freedom." *Journal of African American History* 89/2 (Spring 2004): 98–117.

———. "Cold War II? The Eisenhower Administration, the Bandung Conference, and the Re-periodization of the Postwar Era." *Diplomatic History* 30/5 (November 2006): 867–892.

———. "Remapping the Cold War in the Tropics: Race, Communism, and National Security in the West Indies." *International History Review* 24/2 (June 2002): 318–347.

Perry, Kennetta Hammond. "Black Migrants, Citizenship, and the Transnational Politics of Race in Postwar Britain." Ph.D. Diss., Michigan State University, 2007.

Plummer, Brenda Gayle. "'Below the Level of Men': African Americans, Race, and the History of U.S. Foreign Relations." *Diplomatic History* 20/4 (Fall 1996): 639–650.

Priest, Tyler. "Banking on Development: Brazil in the United States's Search for Strategic Minerals, 1945–1953." *International History Review* 21/2 (June 1999): 297–330.

Reynolds, David. "A 'Special Relationship'? America, Britain, and the International Order Since 1945." *International Affairs* 62/1 (1985–86): 1–20.

Romano, Renee. "No Diplomatic Immunity: African Diplomats, the State Department, and Civil Rights, 1961–1964." *Journal of American History* 87/2 (September 2000): 546–580.

Rotter, Andrew. "The Triangular Route to Vietnam: The United States, Great Britain, and Southeast Asia, 1945–1950." *International History Review* 6/3 (August 1984): 404–423.

Rush, Anne Spry. "The Bonds of Empire: West Indians and Britishness, 1900–1970." Ph.D. Diss., American University, 2004.

Sbrega, John J. "The Anticolonial Policies of Franklin D. Roosevelt: A Reappraisal." *Political Science Quarterly* 100/1 (1985): 97–116.

Smith, Tony. "New Bottles for New Wine: A Pericentric Framework for the Study of the Cold War." *Diplomatic History* 24/4 (Fall 2000): 567–592.

Steele, Richard W. "The Pulse of the People: Franklin D. Roosevelt and the Gauging of American Public Opinion." *Journal of Contemporary History* 9/4 (1974): 195–216.

Tarling, Nicholas. "'Ah-Ah': Britain and the Bandung Conference of 1955." *Journal of Southeast Asian Studies* 23/1 (March 1992): 74–112.

Trask, Roger. "The Impact of the Cold War on United States–Latin American Relations, 1945–1949." *Diplomatic History* 1/2 (Summer 1977): 283–311.

Von Eschen, Penny. "Challenging Cold War Habits: African Americans, Race, and Foreign Policy." *Diplomatic History* 20/4 (Fall 1996): 627–638.

Waters, Robert, and Daniels, Gordon. "The World's Longest General Strike: The AFL-CIO, the CIA, and British Guiana." *Diplomatic History* 29/2 (April 2005): 279–307.

Index